AF477898

Rethinking European Order

Also by William Wallace

THE DYNAMICS OF EUROPEAN INTEGRATION (*co-editor*)

FOREIGN POLICY AND THE POLITICAL PROCESS

FOREIGN POLICY-MAKING IN WESTERN EUROPE (*with W. E. Paterson and others*)

THE FOREIGN POLICY PROCESS IN BRITAIN

OPTIONS FOR BRITISH FOREIGN POLICY IN THE 1990s (*with Christopher Tugendhat*)

POLICY-MAKING IN THE EUROPEAN UNION (*with Helen Wallace and others*)

REGIONAL INTEGRATION IN WESTERN EUROPE

THE TRANSFORMATION OF WESTERN EUROPE

Rethinking European Order

West European Responses, 1989–97

Edited by

Robin Niblett
Vice President for Strategic Planning and Senior Fellow
Europe Program
Center for Strategic and International Studies (CSIS)
Washington, DC

and

William Wallace
Professor of International Relations
London School of Economics and Political Science

First published 2001 by
PALGRAVE
Houndmills, Basingstoke, Hampshire RG21 6XS and
175 Fifth Avenue, New York, N. Y. 10010
Companies and representatives throughout the world

PALGRAVE is the new global academic imprint of
St. Martin's Press LLC Scholarly and Reference Division and
Palgrave Publishers Ltd (formerly Macmillan Press Ltd).

ISBN 0–333–91571–2

This book is printed on paper suitable for recycling and
made from fully managed and sustained forest sources.

A catalogue record for this book is available
from the British Library.

Library of Congress Cataloging-in-Publication Data
Rethinking European order : West European responses, 1989–97 / edited by
Robin Niblett and William Wallace.
       p. cm.
    Includes bibliographical references and index.
    ISBN 0–333–91571–2
    1. Europe, Western—Foreign relations—1989– 2. Europe—Politics and
    government—1989– I. Niblett, Robin, 1961– II. Wallace, William, 1941–
    D1058 .R44 2000
    327'.094—dc21
                                                         00–041515

10   9   8   7   6   5   4   3   2   1
10   09   08   07   06   05   04   03   02   01

Printed in Great Britain by Antony Rowe Ltd, Chippenham, Wiltshire

Contents

Preface

This volume emerged out of a number of discussions in Oxford in 1993–95, on the apparent drift and indirection of policy within West European governments on the strategic choices which they faced over the future of European international politics after the cold war. Students of international relations are taught to think of governments as rational actors pursuing deliberate strategies. Yet here were governments of large and small West European states, adopting apparently contradictory positions, adapting incrementally to external change, shifting uncomfortably in response to external pressures and reluctantly given commitments. Mitterrand's proposals for a European confederation, NATO's development of Partnership for Peace (PfP), the EU's successive offers to the former socialist states of 'Europe Association' agreements, structured dialogues and 'pre-accession strategies', all carried the marks of ambiguous compromise: intended to convey half-promises of future membership in some distant future, from governments which wished to postpone structural change within the European region as long as possible.

The relationship between the academic discipline of international relations and the policy world of government was also a matter of active debate in the early 1990s. American academics agonized over their failure, as a policy science, to predict the end of the cold war. Francis Fukuyama, Samuel Huntington and others sketched out broad visions of the potential shape of the post-cold war world. But few within the American profession addressed themselves to such policy relevant issues as the integration of Russia and other former socialist states into the institutions and practices of the 'Western' world, or the implications of the transformation of the European region for the key strategic and economic transatlantic relationship. In Britain, questions of the 'relevance' of academic international relations and the costs and benefits of contacts with government were hotly debated at successive annual conferences of the British International Studies Association. *Two Worlds of International Relations: Academics, Practitioners and the Trade in Ideas*, edited by Christopher Hill and Pamela Beshoff, provided some of the background for this British debate; while *Theory and Practice in Foreign Policy-Making*, which emerged from workshops within the European Consortium for Political Research in 1991 and 1992, extended its survey of policymaker/academic relations across Western Europe.[1]

The transformation of Europe's international order which followed the disintegration of socialist regimes across central and eastern Europe, between 1989 and 1992 is the first major alteration in the structure and assumptions of European international relations since the establishment of an academic international relations profession, scattered among European universities and policy institutes. A subsidiary issue for investigation in this volume, therefore, has been how far redefinition of the concepts of European order and national foreign policy since 1989 has been led by governments, by political leaders and officials, how far it has expanded beyond the traditional network of policy elites to bring in this recently established resource of outside expertise.

European students of international relations have found it difficult to get out from under the dominant influence of the American profession: following each new transatlantic intellectual debate, responding to (or reacting against) American theories and conceptual models. Similarly, West European governments throughout much of the cold war followed the intellectual and policy lead of their dominant American ally – the British more often responding loyally, the French reacting against. The most striking exception to this general rule was the German government's development of *Ostpolitik* in the late 1960s, formulating a long-term strategy for east–west relations which did much to shape the outcome of the Conference on Security and Cooperation in Europe (CSCE, 1972–74, with successive review conferences in later years) and to differentiate global superpower relations from European détente. President de Gaulle's earlier concept of a Europe 'from the Atlantic to the Urals' had, it is true, challenged American political and intellectual hegemony; but it had neither led to any coherent strategy towards the transformation of Europe nor attracted much support from other West European governments.

A further underlying question for this study was therefore to investigate how far the established pattern of American strategic leadership and West European followership was disrupted by the end of the cold war. 'European Political Cooperation' (EPC) among the member governments of the European Community had, after all, been under way for twenty years when the Berlin Wall came down. One immediate response to the prospect of German reunification was to reshape EPC into a 'Common Foreign and Security Policy', agreed to by the twelve EU members at Maastricht in December 1991. There was therefore an established collective framework within which West European governments could concert their responses to this massive shift in their international environment; posing for us the question how far this made for a convergence of national responses, how far divergent national traditions and domestic political constraints nevertheless made for distinctive patterns of adjustment.

The process of transition from one relatively stable pattern of European international relations, embedded in the confrontation between 'East' and 'West' and in the opposing alliances, political and economic institutions, and structures of ideas and assumptions which each group developed, towards an alternative (hopefully stable) pan-European pattern, is still under way. The series of decisions taken in the spring and early summer of 1997, however – admitting three new members to NATO, revising the EU treaty to strengthen (*inter alia*) the common foreign and security policy, and setting out the agenda for EU eastern enlargement – marks a sufficiently clear end-point for our study.

This was, in effect, the conclusion of the first stage of transition. It had been established that post-cold war European order would be built upon the eastward enlargement of Western institutions, not (as some had dared to hope in 1990–91) on the creation of pan-European institutions through the transformation of the CSCE into an effective and influential Organization for Security and Cooperation in Europe. The process of enlargement, so hesitantly begun, had now been set in train. There was no consensus, either among or within European states, as to how far or how fast that process should move; nor on the status and role of the USA within this slowly-emerging regional system; nor about that of Russia, or of other former Soviet states; or of Turkey; nor of the states of Europe's dependent southern periphery, around the Mediterranean. But the overall pattern, we argue, had been set, though more through the gradual accumulation of partial decisions than through deliberate and strategic overall design.

With two exceptions, the editors and contributors to this volume were together in St Antony's College, Oxford, in the early 1990s, giving us the opportunity to compare ideas and discuss these developments as they evolved. We invited Christopher Hill and Filippo Andreatta to join us, to widen our coverage to include the Italian experience. The contributors come from five of the seven countries studied, enabling us to draw on domestic debates in different languages across Western Europe as well as to assess the degree of linkage between these debates. We are grateful to the (British) Economic and Social Research Council for the financial support which enabled Robin Niblett to research the French and Spanish chapters, and to act as convenor for our collective discussions and editorial drafts. We have benefited enormously from the development of email, enabling us to exchange queries and comments as the volume has taken shape. And we owe an immense debt to the skills and the patience of Jennifer Chapa, who has hammered the final version of the manuscript (and occasionally the contributors and editors) into shape.

Robin Niblett
William Wallace

Note

1. Christopher Hill and Pamela Beshoff (eds), *Two Worlds of International Relations: Academics, Practitioners and the Trade in Ideas* (London: Routledge, 1994); Michel Girard, Wolf-Dieter Eberwein and Keith Webb (eds), *Theory and Practice in Foreign Policy-making: National Perspectives on Academics and Practitioners in International Relations* (London: Pinter, 1994). See also William Wallace, 'Truth and Power, Monks and Technocrats: theory and practice in international relations', *Review of International Studies* 22 (1996) pp. 301–21.

List of Abbreviations

AFSOUTH	Allied Forces South (NATO's southern command)
AN	Alleanza Nazionale
ARRC	Alliance Rapid Reaction Corps
CEECs	Central and East European Countries (the former socialist states between Germany and the CIS, accepted in the early 1990s as applicants to EU)
CERI	Centro Espanol de Relaciones Internacionales
CFE	Conventional Forces in Europe treaty
CFSP	Common Foreign and Security Policy
CIS	Commonwealth of Independent States
CiU	Convergencia i Union
CJTF	Combined Joint Task Forces
CSCE	Conference on Security and Cooperation in Europe
CSCM	Conference on Security and Cooperation in the Mediterranean (proposed)
DC	Democratico Cristiano
EBRD	European Bank for Reconstruction and Development
EC	European Community (until 1992, the institutional structures established by the Treaties of Paris and Rome; after 1992, the first pillar of the EU)
ECB	European Central Bank
EEA	European Economic Area
EFTA	European Free Trade Area
EMS	European Monetary System
EMU	Economic and Monetary Union
EPC	European Political Cooperation (the intergovernmental framework for foreign policy co-operation among EC member states, established in 1970; replaced by CFSP from 1992)
ERM	Exchange Rate Mechanism (of the EMS)
ESDI	European Security and Defence Identity
ETA	(Basque revolutionary organization)
EU	European Union (the three-pillar structure established under the Maastricht Treaty of European Union, 1992)
IAI	Istituto Affari Internazionale (Rome)
IFOR	Implementation Force (follow-on force to SFOR in Bosnia)
IGC	Intergovernmental Conference (of the EU)
ISPI	Istituto Studi Politici Internazionale (Milan)
MEP	Member of the European Parliament
NACC	North Atlantic Cooperation Council

NATO	North Atlantic Treaty Organization
NGO	Non-governmental organization
OEEC	Organization for European Economic Cooperation
OECD	Organization for Economic Cooperation and Development (the reshaped and expanded OEEC from 1961 onwards, with the USA, Canada, Japan, Australia and New Zealand as additional extra-European members)
OSCE	Organization for Security and Cooperation in Europe
PCI	Partito Communista Italiano
PDS	Partito Democratico della Sinistra
PfP	Partnership for Peace
PJC	Permanent Joint Council (of NATO and Russia)
PNV	Partido Nacional Vasco (Basque National Party)
PP	Partido Popular
PSOE	Partido Socialista Obrero Español
QMV	Qualified Majority Voting
RC	Rifondazione Communista
SDI	Strategic Defence Initiative
SEA	Single European Act (1986)
SFOR	Stabilization Force (the NATO-led force in Bosnia which succeeded UNPROFOR)
TEU	Treaty on European Union (Treaty of Maastricht, 1992)
WEAG	West European Armaments Group
WEU	Western European Union
UNPROFOR	UN Protection Force (in Bosnia)

Notes on the Contributors

Lisbeth Aggestam is a research fellow at the Department of Political Science, University of Stockholm. She is currently completing a doctoral thesis at the University of Stockholm on foreign policy role conceptions in the EU. Her most recent publication is as co-editor of *Security and Identity in Europe: exploring the research agenda* (London: Macmillan, 2000).

Filippo Andreatta teaches International Relations at the University of Bologna at Forli.

Steven Everts is a research fellow with the Centre for European Reform in London. He holds an MA in international relations from Leiden University, and completed his Oxford D.Phil. on West European reactions to German unification in 2000.

Anthony Forster is a lecturer in politics at Nottingham University. His study of *Britain and the Maastricht Negotiations* (London: Macmillan) was published in 1999; he has also written a number of articles on European defence cooperation and British foreign policy.

Christopher Hill is Montague Burton Professor of International Relations at the London School of Economics. His most recent book was *The Actors in Europe's Foreign Policy* (with others, London: Routledge 1996).

Hartmut Mayer is lecturer in political studies at St Peter's College, Oxford, and is completing his D.Phil. thesis on German foreign policy and European political cooperation.

Robin Niblett is Director of Strategic Planning and fellow in European studies at the Center for Strategic and International Studies, Washington DC. He completed an Oxford D.Phil. in 1995 on the European Union's management of negotiations with the former socialist states after 1989.

William Wallace is professor of international relations at the London School of Economics. From 1990–1995 he was Walter F. Hallstein Fellow at St Antony's College, Oxford, and from 1978–1990 Director of Studies at the Royal Institute of International Affairs. His most recent book (with Helen Wallace and others) is *Policy-making in the European Union* (4th edition, Oxford: Oxford University Press, 2000).

Cold War Pre 1989
NATO Members
Warsaw Pact
Iron Curtain
ICELAND
NORWAY
SWEDEN
FINLAND
Atlantic Ocean
N IRELAND
GREAT BRITAIN
IRELAND
DENMARK
NETHERLANDS
Baltic Sea
U S S R
BELGIUM
EAST GERMANY
POLAND
LUX
WEST GERMANY
CZECHOSLOVAKIA
FRANCE
SWITZ.
AUSTRIA
HUNGARY
ROMANIA
ITALY
YUGOSLAVIA
Black Sea
PORTUGAL
SPAIN
CORSICA
BULGARIA
ALBANIA
SARDINIA
Mediterranean Sea
GREECE
TURKEY
SICILY
MALTA
CRETE
CYPRUS
0 miles 500
0 kms 500

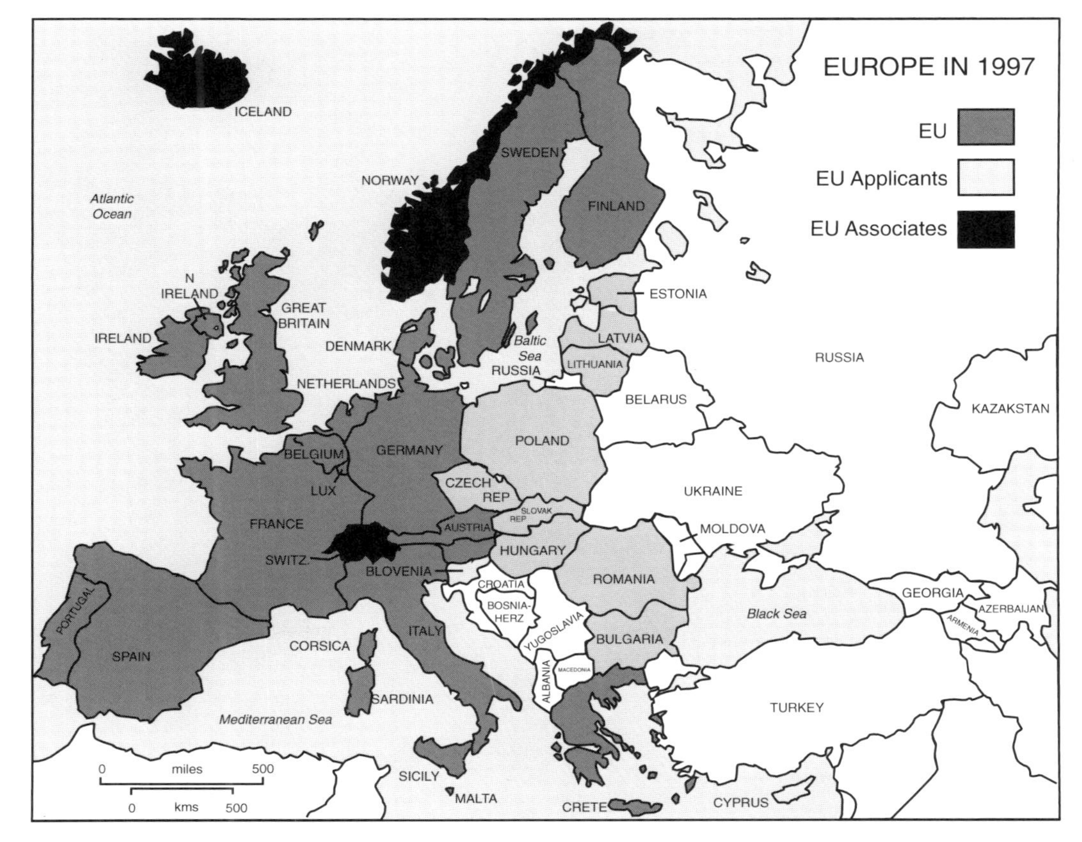

EUROPE IN 1997
EU
EU Applicants
EU Associates
ICELAND
NORWAY
SWEDEN
FINLAND
ESTONIA
LATVIA
LITHUANIA
RUSSIA
BELARUS
RUSSIA
KAZAKSTAN
Atlantic Ocean
N IRELAND
IRELAND
GREAT BRITAIN
DENMARK
NETHERLANDS
Baltic Sea
BELGIUM
LUX
GERMANY
POLAND
CZECH REP
SLOVAK REP
UKRAINE
MOLDOVA
FRANCE
AUSTRIA
HUNGARY
SWITZ.
BLOVENIA
CROATIA
BOSNIA-HERZ
YUGOSLAVIA
ROMANIA
BULGARIA
GEORGIA
AZERBAIJAN
ARMENIA
Black Sea
PORTUGAL
SPAIN
CORSICA
ITALY
SARDINIA
ALBANIA
MACEDONIA
Mediterranean Sea
SICILY
MALTA
CRETE
CYPRUS
TURKEY
0   miles   500
0   kms   500

1
Rethinking European Order: West European Responses, 1989–97 – Introduction

William Wallace

For forty years from 1949 to 1989, Europe was divided between two international orders. The line of the 'iron curtain' marked a sharp divide between two military alliances, two sets of international institutions, two patterns of economic development and interdependence. The gradual evolution of European détente since the early 1970s had eased tensions, allowed for modest increases in east–west trade, for the growth of Western tourism in eastern Europe, and for a multilateral dialogue between the two orders through the Conference on Security and Cooperation in Europe (CSCE). But there remained a sharp boundary between political, economic and social systems across the centre of Europe until the summer of 1989, when governments in Poland and Hungary moved away from the socialist model and the Hungarian foreign minister himself helped to tear down the fence which separated his country from 'Western' Austria.

Eight years later, with the decision of the NATO Council in June 1997 to enlarge eastwards, and the publication by the European Commission the following month of the multi-volume *Agenda 2000* with its blueprint for EU enlargement, the outlines of the emerging post-cold war European order were clear – though its geographical reach and boundaries remained uncertain. Two Western institutions, the North Atlantic Treaty Organization and the European Union, were to provide its central focus: embodying explicit assumptions about values and principles of domestic and regional order, establishing hierarchies of access and influence, defining and enforcing rules across a wide range of political, social and economic interactions, maintaining multilateral frameworks within which member governments might bargain, with third countries and private actors pressing to exert influence over their agendas. The CSCE, transmuted into the Organization for Security and Cooperation in Europe in the aftermath of the transformation of 1989–90, had been pushed to one side (and the successor states to the Soviet Union, as full OSCE members, with it). The former socialist states thus remained outside the central institutions of Europe's emerging institutional order, pressing to be allowed in: applicants for entry, rather than full participants in defining the rules and boundaries of post-cold war Europe.

The aim of this study is to examine how West European governments moved from the cold war consensus of the 1980s to the acceptance of a limited and multi-stage enlargement of the institutions which the 'West' had developed – under American protection and leadership – during the cold war. Its focus is primarily on the domestic debate within different West European democracies: the process through which both governments and élites outside governments adjusted their ideas and assumptions about Europe's international system and their place within it. Chapter 2 examines the multilateral international frameworks within which Western governments interacted, through which they developed successive common positions (and compromises) as they responded to the challenges post-socialist governments presented. It also discusses the crucial American role, through NATO, in reshaping Europe after 1989, in spite of the withdrawal of the majority of US troops from central Europe and the determination of successive US administrations to ensure that their European allies carried the main financial burden. Chapters 3–9 explore the evolving policy debate within the major West European countries between 1989 and 1997. Chapter 10 draws a number of conclusions from this gradual transformation of European order for our understanding of the balance between domestic factors and external constraints in international politics, as well as of the role of ideas and intellectuals in the shaping of international order.

International order is itself a contested term. We use the term throughout this volume to describe a relatively stable pattern of shared assumptions, rules and institutions which together constitute what Hedley Bull defined as not only a 'state system', but more broadly also a 'society of states'.[1] European international relations, as Fred Halliday and others have argued, have alternated over the past 500 years between periods of 'international revolution', during which the rules of international and domestic order were themselves at issue, and periods of order in which the rules of international interaction and the qualifications for recognition as an international actor were broadly accepted.[2] The European region at the outset of the cold war was the focus for a revolutionary confrontation, between the (predominantly) democratic, market-based, American-led Western order and the authoritarian Soviet-led state–socialist order. What began in the 1940s as a conflict in which both sides were supporting internal subversion of each other's domestic orders as well as developing opposing alliances had stabilised in the 1970s and 1980s. Behind the massively armed stand-off in central Europe, neither alliance directly challenged the legitimacy of each other's order: the USSR was preoccupied with maintaining its domestic and international position within the CMEA/Warsaw Pact, while Western governments were promoting gradual reform through dialogue with state–socialist regimes.

International order as a society of states rests upon shared values about political legitimacy, economic organization and social hierarchy. The two international orders of the cold war were intrinsically linked to conflicting ideas – or, ideologies – of domestic political, economic and social order. The USA and the USSR, alliance leaders and political hegemons, both assumed that a shift in the domestic order within one of their allies towards the opposing model would lead to defection from their state system. Loss of self-confidence within the Soviet leadership about the superiority of their model of domestic order was reflected in their demand to be accepted as a 'European' state in the 1980s, reluctantly accepting through the CSCE process that this gave Western governments a structural advantage in assessing how far short of 'European' – or, Western – standards their domestic orders fell.[3]

Well before the Berlin Wall came down, it was therefore apparent that acceptance as a full member of a post-cold war European order would be conditional on provision of basic political and civil rights within post-socialist regimes. Beyond this, however, dissidents, socialist reformers and some within the West shared a range of ideas about democratic socialism and social democracy, about the attractions of 'the Swedish model' to states emerging from state socialism. From the opening of negotiations on the 'Europe Agreements' in December 1990, through successive European Council declarations to the *Agenda 2000* paper of 1997, West European governments developed in increasing detail the economic, political and administrative conditions for membership of the European Union: the goal to which the applicant states pressed as the defining criterion for full participation in the post-cold war regional international order.

The boundaries of an international order are set both by the conditions attached to membership and by the geographical limits which the major players consider appropriate. Europe's competing cold war orders defined each other's boundary. The iron curtain divided 'East' from 'West': eastern Europe (including the Eurasian USSR) from Western Europe (together with North America's Canada and USA, and with east-Mediterranean Greece and Turkey). The West was labelled, in cold war terminology, 'the first world', the East 'the second world': the third world to the south became the main arena for competition between their competing models of political and economic development. Earlier European international orders had much less well-defined boundaries. Core regions exerted loose control over their peripheries; influence and emigration, flowed east and south across the steppes, the Black Sea and the Mediterranean, to retreat again as extra-European powers surged forward.[4]

The boundaries and constituent states of a redesigned European order after 1989 were neither natural nor self-evident. The first post-socialist governments, in Poland and Hungary, aimed above all to join the West and leave the East behind; while Soviet reformers were determined to hold to their vision of a wider 'common European home'. The place within such a regional order of the United States, of Turkey, of the former socialist states of south-east Europe, the eastern Baltic and the Black Sea, were all open to question: to be included or excluded according to the mental maps which policymakers sought to impose on the geography of political and economic change.

'International orders are often the result of conscious strategy. Wars are often ended by treaties whose purpose is that of designing forms of international order.'[5] How rational that design, how well-informed the assumptions on which it is based, is a matter for later historians to assess. Some theorists of international relations posit rational choice and full information for policymakers, pursuing defined national interests. Most students of international relations look for underlying trends, evidence of strategic objectives or even of grand designs in the actions of policymakers.

One of the most striking features of the transition from the cold war order, however, is how loosely desired end-points were defined, how incrementally the rules and institutions in place by 1997 took shape over the intervening years. In the immediate aftermath of the collapse of the socialist system, American officials conjured up visions of a 'new world order', while they and a minority within European governments sketched the broad outlines of a 'new European architecture' and a 'second Marshall Plan'. The setbacks and crises of 1991–92 however silenced such voices. From then on Western policies developed incrementally, through a succession of small initiatives, compromises among governments, and immediate responses to external pressures and events. The strongest theme which runs through the chapters which follow is of the reluctance of West European governments to redefine assumptions and objectives, the difficulties they faced in shaking off the conventional wisdom – embedded in myths of national history and identity – which had guided them through the cold war. Received ideas shaped perceptions of national interest in a rapidly changing international context, making for incremental adjustment much more than strategic reorientation. West European governments shuffled forward, international crises and multilateral diplomacy pushing them on, domestic politics holding them back, in an incremental drift from one decision to another which took them gradually towards an interim agreement on the institutions, members, rules and boundaries of a wider European order. As Chapter 10 makes clear, however, the package of decisions which were reached in the early summer of 1997 were themselves only a staging point in the reconstruction of a stable regional system, a European society of states for the 21st century.

Reformulating order in Europe: the intellectual context

Stable patterns of regional or global order appear to rest upon both real and ideal foundations. For E.H. Carr, '"international order" and "international solidarity" will always be slogans of those who feel strong enough to impose them on others'.[6] For Kenneth Waltz, international order emerges, tortuously, from the competition between states operating in an anarchic international system: balances of power, though temporary, constitute the only basis for international order.[7] Robert Gilpin and Paul Kennedy describe how international orders inevitably decay in the wake of fundamental shifts in the military and economic capabilities of Great Powers.[8] Thus, for Realist writers, the structure of an international order is determined by the distribution of power among its major constituent states. Since the relative distribution of power among major actors shifts over time, order is always transitory. The end of the cold war challenged the prevailing distribution of power among Western states; the new 'power inequalities' were likely to lead to a dangerous period of instability before another stable balance could be established.[9]

On the other hand, how those actors mobilize their resources and interpret their interests also depends upon their prevailing assumptions: about the appropriate structure of relations among the units of such an international order which they are prepared to recognize as legitimate, and about the appropriate role which they should play themselves within that order.[10] Hedley Bull argued that all states have a vested interest in upholding a loose system of international order, even if it is based on no firmer a base of shared interests and values than the common quest for self-preservation.[11] Beyond that, the bonds of economic interdependence between modern, industrialized states make the maintenance of international order a matter of rational common interest.[12] Further than that, the inertia of established patterns of relations, the utility to all recognised actors of shared rules and institutions in facilitating mutual transactions, holds systems of states together. 'International orders are broad framework arrangements governing the activities of all (or almost all) the members of international society over a wide range of specific issues'.[13] From this perspective, governments and other European actors would strive to sustain existing institutional arrangements even after the structural conditions which gave rise to them had passed away.[14]

Strongest of all in holding international order in place are the shared political and cultural values which constitute – in Bull's terms – a society of states. Each stable international order which Europe has experienced has rested upon a loose consensus of governing ideas as well as upon a loose balance of power among its major units. Concepts of 'Christendom', of 'Europe', of the rights and duties of states and of their rulers, of the principles which should shape and guide relations among them, have played an important part in underpinning order in Europe throughout the centuries.[15]

In this book we examine how far political élites within Western Europe, both within and outside governments, reconsidered their prevailing assumptions in the light of the radical shifts in the distribution of power between west and east that took place in 1989–92. The study does not focus primarily on changes in the distribution of power in Europe after the cold war. It examines how self-consciously governments in Western Europe, and their surrounding policy élites, attempted to reconsider the intellectual foundations of their foreign policies after 1989, their understandings of the structure and dynamics of the international environment in which they operated and of the opportunities it offered and the constraints which it imposed in light of the changed international context. Each country chapter asks to what extent West European policymakers and their advisers attempted to reformulate their ideas and concepts, or conversely to retain established ideas and concepts despite the experience of external transformation.

It is important to remember that the transformation of European order since 1989 took place within an intellectual environment enriched since 1945 by the development of a network of institutes of international affairs and security studies, by the flowering in West European universities of the academic discipline of international relations, by the establishment of substantial planning staffs in West European foreign ministries (and of a network of regular bilateral and multilateral exchanges among planning staffs), and by the strengthening of parliamentary committees and parliamentary and party advisory work on foreign affairs. The foreign policy debate within Western Europe in the 1970s and 1980s had become accustomed to the regular succession of 'Declarations' and strategy papers which flowed from multilateral intergovernmental meetings, the publication of joint reports and the deliberate floating of new concepts and critiques by think tanks and unofficial groups.[16]

Within this, however, there remained a degree of separation between those who dealt with politico-military issues, largely within an Atlantic framework, and those who focused on politico-economic issues, who were often inclined to treat West European integration as a largely autonomous process abstracted from the broader security context which contained it. The concept of Europe as a 'civilian power', which acquired wide currency during the 1970s, represented and symbolized this separation from economic from security issues.[17] There also existed in Western Europe a very real separation between the academic and policymaking communities, caused, in part, by the different horizons to which each community looked in their deliberations. Academics most often approached the study of international relations either from a historical or a theoretical standpoint, concerned less with the practicability of their conclusions than with their intellectual rigour. Policymakers, on the other hand, sought practical advice on how to cope with near-term crises within multilateral negotiations. In part, the separation between the two communities in Western Europe reflected the continuing lack of mobility between the two career paths throughout the 1970s and 1980s.[18]

Continuing American security and intellectual hegemony gave both official and unofficial American ideas pre-eminence within this evolving debate. It was not, however, an entirely one-way street; West European assumptions and conceptualizations also flowed across the Atlantic in this multilateral dialogue. West German promotion of *Ostpolitik*, contained within the new pan-European framework of the CSCE, provided a vehicle for reimagining the shape and the values of European order: a political strategy and a set of concepts which often aroused suspicions across the Atlantic but which evoked sympathetic echoes across the east–west divide.[19]

In the early 1980s, élite opinion within Britain and France was often moving in different directions from within Germany, in reinterpreting developments within the Soviet Union and the possibilities for systemic change. One could trace the slow and hesitant evolution of potential alternative orders in the revival of the WEU, the intermittent search for a more distinctive West European foreign policy, and the response of governments and outside bodies to Mikhail Gorbachev's active challenge to the Western conventional wisdom on pan-European relations. But it should be noted that Western governments in these years were often responding to reformulations from the east – to dissident insistence on the relevance of central Europe, to Gorbachev's rhetorical invocation of 'our common European home' – rather than promoting initiatives of their own. Western governments and the outside intellectual community were slow to grasp the potential significance of the changes within the USSR and east-central Europe from 1985–86 on. In contrast to the development of *Ostpolitik* (at a time when the USA was distracted from leadership in Europe by the traumas of Vietnam), no West European government had anticipated or planned for these radical changes; nor had many outside government dared to imagine so rapid a transformation or its implications.

Our focus in this book is thus on the reformulation of ideas of European order within Western Europe in the period of transition from the Western order after the cold war era. We seek to examine the conceptual language used by West European policymakers during the sudden transition from the cold war to post-cold war periods to explain change – and continuity – in their foreign policies, to build and maintain domestic support for policies, and, similarly, to build and maintain preferred patterns of relations with other states. Each chapter asks, wherever possible, from where these ideas were drawn, whether from within the government, from outside sources within the country, from specially-commissioned enquiries or independent publications, or from foreign or multilateral sources. Given the intensity of multilateral consultations, the high institutionalization of West European co-operation on foreign policy through the EC, EPC, WEU and NATO, it is particularly interesting to discover how far one could discern a transnational (or transgovernmental) debate – as against a series of distinctive national debates each based upon different state traditions, national memories and myths, geographical positions and perceived interests.

We are also concerned, therefore, with the shifting consensus of ideas within broader political and intellectual communities outside government, from party-based study groups to policy institutes, from commentators in the quality press to the academic world, asking how far they sought to reinterpret the conventional wisdom and how closely they interacted with policymakers.

We are looking for the implicit and explicit assumptions about the dynamics of international order within which national foreign policies were formulated; including assumptions about the shifting boundaries between relevant regional bases for order – European, Eurasian, Atlantic, Mediterranean – and about the appropriate balance between regional and sub-regional groupings and the wider global order.[20] Necessarily, therefore, we must also touch on assumptions about the centrality – or declining centrality – of the state as an actor in the post-cold war European order.

It is not our primary purpose to tie an explanation of the West European policy debate to competing (largely American) theoretical approaches to the understanding of international relations, such as neo-realism, idealism, and liberal institutionalism. Our opening assumption is that the complexities of international and transnational relations in the European region in the early 1990s could not be reduced to fit within such simple frameworks without gross distortion of description and analysis. The continuing importance of military power and its projection – one pillar of the realist approach – is evident; the withdrawal of Soviet troops, the disintegration of the Warsaw Pact, the subsequent withdrawal of two thirds of American forces from Western Europe, were all crucial in altering the underlying structure of European order. Whether, however, the states of western or central Europe, as they emerged from under the superpower domination of the past 40 years, were still primarily motivated by territorial rivalry and military insecurity – the second pillar of the realist approach – is open to question. In this respect, the international politics of western Europe often appeared 'postmodern', pursuing a different agenda of 'transparency, mutual openness, interdependence and mutual vulnerability'.[21]

The central importance of institutions and rules in the established Western order, and the appeal of accession to those institutions for the ex-socialist states of central Europe, is clear. But the normality of transgovernmental coalitions within those institutions, the difficulties which all governments faced in defining or holding together national strategies except for brief moments in European Councils and NATO summits, must throw considerable doubt on the rational-choice models of liberal institutionalism, in which coherent governments are imagined to be bargaining on the basis of good information and clear objectives.[22] As later chapters argue, any attempt to explain the reactions of Britain or France, for example, to the unification of Germany, the transformation of central and eastern Europe and the partial disengagement of the USA between 1990 and 1995 in terms of the pursuit of rational state interests alone, would miss most of the twists and turns their uncomfortable governments made.

Our preoccupation with the ideas and images of international order challenges any reduction of international relations to a rational calculus of defined national interests. Ideas and concepts in international relations gain acceptance – or lose credibility – according to their plausibility in explaining observed political, military, economic and social phenomena. But they are not simple reflections of such phenomena. More than one plausible intellectual framework is often available, particularly during relatively fluid periods of international relations. Realist, Idealist, or Institutionalist approaches are relevant, therefore, to the extent that they help characterize the competing conceptual frameworks and mental maps with which European policymakers and commentators grappled as they became aware of the gradual erosion of the structure of cold war international order in Europe. Acceptance of an alternative conceptual framework or mental map – of the idea of common security instead of collective security, for example, of Poland and Germany as neighbours within central Europe rather than antagonists across the east–west divide – can change the context within which information is interpreted and policies are made.

The history of the last seven years, however, confirms that the intellectual framework within which foreign policies are formulated is not easily rebuilt, not infinitely malleable in the minds of policymakers and their advisers. States in their foreign policies rest upon national identity and its components – myths and memories, traditions of national purpose, of national friends and national enemies – which are only open to gradual reinterpretation, by leaders prepared to invest much time and political credit in the process of reinterpretation. The nation state is held together by ideological as well as legal, political and economic ties. Foreign policy, the action of governments which derive their legitimacy from their claim to represent their nation states, cannot therefore be an entirely rational process.[23]

Patterns of transition between European orders

Structures of international order have emerged most often in European history out of the chaos of prolonged or revolutionary wars. The Westphalian Settlement concluded the slaughter and destruction of the Thirty Years' War, registering the end of the Hapsburg attempt to achieve European hegemony and negotiating rules for a European society of states. The Treaty of Utrecht brought to a close the wars of the Spanish succession (and the attempt of Louis XIV's France to replace the Hapsburgs as the dominant power in Western Europe), strengthening those rules to underpin an international order which lasted until the revolutionary challenge of 1789. The Congress of Vienna marked the final defeat of revolutionary, then Napoleonic, France, ushering in one hundred years during which European international relations evolved without a general war.[24]

In the 20th century, the Versailles Settlement followed from the surrender of Germany and the disintegration of the Hapsburg, Ottoman and Tsarist empires in 1918. It attempted to design a new European order of nation states to replace the half-national, half-imperial order which had collapsed into war and revolution between 1914 and 1919. In the margins of the Versailles conference, idealists and power-politicians jostled in the corridors, pursuing their contradictory principles to achieve an unstable compromise. Young attachés watched with alarm as their political leaders imposed harsh conditions on defeated Germany, uncoordinated with the institutionalized League of Nations which the American delegation wanted to sponsor or with the principles of national self-determination and minority rights which were supposed to guide the redrawing of national boundaries.[25] 'Decisions were taken not as the result of systematised study and discussion but only when some individual topic reached a condition of crisis. Through out there was no considered order of priority, no thought out plan of descending from the general to the particular.'[26] The Versailles Settlement left Europe disordered, to drift within twenty years into another general war.

Learning from this, allied governments in the midst of the Second World War pulled together teams of advisers and planning groups in London and Washington to imagine and design their preferred postwar order. The rhetoric and language of the Western international order had begun to take shape far in advance of 1945, in the Atlantic Charter, in the declaratory statements of wartime summits. Drawing on their perceptions of the strengths and weaknesses of the inter-war international order and its 'long nineteenth century' predecessor, they formulated preferred political and economic values, drafted declarations on human rights and democratic self-government, and drew up the rules and designed the constitutions for the international institutions which they believed would be essential to the establishment and maintenance of a stable post-war order: formally a global order, but one within which the reshaping of Europe was assumed to be the centre.[27]

Self-evident American hegemony among the 'western' allies gave American preferences pre-eminence in this evolving debate. The Soviet Union and nationalist China, wartime allies like Britain dependent on American supplies, stood back or offered lip service support. The Soviet Union, however, was never a willing party to these plans; and wartime conference diplomacy had agreed only on the outlines of post-war European order before the German surrender. The peace conference which wartime planners had anticipated never took place. The United States and the Soviet Union instead imposed their preferred version of a post-war settlement on those parts of a devastated European continent which they had occupied in 1944–45. American plans for an institutionalised global order were thus translated into plans for Western order, into which the Western zones of divided Germany were to be integrated.[28]

The Second World War ended with devastation across the whole of Europe, and with atomic bombs dropped on Japan. The cold war ended with a whimper, with the demolition of the Berlin Wall and the disintegration of the German Democratic Republic. From a Western perspective, the revolution took place only in the central and eastern part of Europe – historically Europe's periphery, which had lagged behind and followed over centuries the economic and social development of Europe's western core.[29] The hopes of dissidents in central and eastern Europe during the 1980s had been for a 'return to Europe', a reincorporation into the West from which they had – as they saw it – been forcibly separated by subjugation to the East, represented by the Soviet Union. An underlying paradox of the period after 1989 was that post-communist governments in central and eastern Europe, from Poland and Slovenia to Ukraine, wanted the *West* European order to remain as it was – while welcoming their countries in. Emerging out of a revolution within their own country and region, they asked in effect to accede to the established order of the cold war West. They demanded to join every West European organization they could, most importantly the European Community/ European Union and NATO.[30]

In contrast, there was no revolution in Europe's Western states: no sense of crisis or immediate awareness of the need for radical changes. Germany alone was directly affected, physically, politically, socially and economically; as Hartmut Mayer explains in Chapter 3, the German public and political élite were therefore necessarily more engaged in debating how to reshape the assumptions of national policy. Even within Germany, in the Rhineland and Baden-Wurtemberg, the impact of unification filtered through gradually rather than immediately, except for those who had had family ties with the Länder behind the iron curtain. New migrants competing for jobs, higher taxes to pay for unification, the West German (and West European) recession deepened by interest rates raised as the German government borrowed to finance transition costs it had underestimated, strains on West Germany's high-wage economy and social compact as cheaper skilled labour became available not far to the east – all these crept into the German public consciousness in the early 1990s, to sharpen public reluctance to contemplate opening their comfortable world to a wider Europe. In France, in Britain, in Italy, above all in distant Spain, the world did not feel utterly changed in the spring of 1990 from the spring before. Domestic concerns and established priorities easily crowded the transformation of central and eastern Europe off the front pages and out of the television news.

West European policymakers perceived no clean break in international relations. There was no *Stunde Null* (as in 1945 Germany) from which victors and vanquished had to reconstruct domestic and regional orders. There was, therefore, no appropriate point at which to stop and redefine the structure of Europe: no Congress, no extraordinary intergovernmental conference along the lines of Vienna, Versailles or Dumbarton Oaks at which the institutions, rules, balance and boundaries of a reshaped regional system might be hammered out among all the interested powers.

In hindsight the breaching of the Berlin Wall in November 1989 stands out as *the* turning point which marked and symbolised the passing of the cold war order, briefly capturing the imagination of Western public opinion. But – as Chapter 2 makes clear – the disintegration of the socialist regime in the

German Democratic Republic was not the first stage in this European transformation. Political transition in Poland and Hungary had moved sufficiently far by the spring of 1989 for Western governments to concert their efforts to support it. Many saw these developments as the escape of central Europe from Soviet domination: the reunification of Germany, with three states with historical links to Germany and the West moving from one camp to another.

Political revolution then, however, spread to Romania and Bulgaria in the winter of 1989–90, and in the course of 1990 to the Baltic and Caucasian republics within the Soviet Union itself. While in the course of 1991 member governments of NATO attempted to negotiate a new alliance strategy, in parallel with negotiations within the European Union's intergovernmental conference on the definition of a 'common foreign and security policy', first Yugoslavia and then the Soviet Union itself disintegrated. There followed in 1992 rebellion in Chechnya, refusal by the government of Tatarstan to sign the new federal treaty, and rumblings from several regional governments of the vast Russian Republic about their future relations with Moscow; it was not clear for some months whether Russia itself would disintegrate into smaller units. Western governments had unsuccessfully used what little influence they had to discourage the disintegration both of Yugoslavia and of the Soviet Union. They were left to struggle with the resulting conflicts in Croatia and Bosnia, while Czechoslovakia in its turn moved towards division, with problems over Macedonia and Albania adding to the confusion.

Even in the immediate aftermath of the collapse of socialist regimes across central Europe it was clear to the most acute observers that the end of the cold war represented as fundamental a shift in the underlying political structure of the European continent as had occurred in 1789–95, 1917–19 and 1945–49.[31] The reunification of Germany itself transformed the foundations of a European order which had been built on its division; the re-emergence of Poland and the withdrawal of Soviet forces from across central Europe were also evidence of radical change. Yet the United States showed little sign of withdrawing from its leading role in European security. The number of US troops in Germany was reduced but the US administration actively maintained a leadership role within NATO. West European governments were preoccupied with completing the EU's 1992 Programme, and with an already-planned Intergovernmental Conference on Economic and Monetary Union. The flow of ethnic Germans and others from the East, as borders opened up, raised fears in Germany and Austria of large-scale migration disrupting domestic social order; but for other states there was only a trickle of arrivals to bring home the significance of east European transformation. They had little reason to call into question the military alliances and economic institutions that had grown out of the cold war confrontation between east and west; the institutions remained in place, the question of relations with the east taking its place on an already-crowded agenda.

The world we have lost

The Western international order which evolved between 1945 and 1960 was built under American political, economic and intellectual hegemony. It was held in place by common recognition of a Soviet threat, and by the United States' provision of security guarantees for Western Europe via NATO. Europe's defeated would-be hegemon, Germany, shrunken to half its pre-war extent by Soviet redrawing of its eastern boundaries and by the division of what remained between east and west, was contained within this carefully constructed order, rebuilt and re-educated under American patronage and pressure into one of its central economic and military components.[32] Following the collapse of the wartime Grand Alliance and the slide towards the ideological hostility of the cold war, the United States diverted its efforts to create a new European order into the Marshall Plan and the OEEC, and reformulated the idea of collective security around the Western Alliance. The United States also promoted West European integration as the solution to European interstate rivalries and a means of binding Germany together with its neighbours. These ideas and US institution-building gave shape to the European order for forty years thereafter. The work of allied planners, interacting with and interpreting international political and economic developments, gave their governments a rationale for policy and a framework within which to operate. As important, it provided a set of ideas and images around which to build and maintain public support for foreign policy and with which to explain and justify the costs imposed and the burdens undertaken.

The values and assumptions round which the Americans constructed this stable system were incorporated into a network of 'global' as well as regional institutions, from the IMF and GATT through the Atlantic Alliance to the OEEC/OECD.[33] Established during the years of unchallenged American power and prestige in the late 1940s and early 1950s, they proved strong enough – and useful enough – to maintain their intellectual hegemony long after the balance of economic (though not of military) strength had tipped away from the USA towards a revived Western Europe. The cold war Western international order was from the outset designed to be more highly institutionalized than any previous interstate order. The density of its institutions, the embedded character of the assumptions which they incorporated, were reinforced over the decades which followed by the intensification of multilateral relations among the component states and by joint responses to economic growth and technological change.[34]

Realists attribute the stability of this Western order to the maintenance of US military supremacy, and the continuing dependence of the West European allies on American nuclear and conventional military guarantees in the face of a Soviet threat. The conventional rearmament of Germany did not fundamentally disturb this balance, since the United States continued to extend crucial military resources to the protection of Western Europe, and to expect in return to receive support from West European states for its regional and global strategy. Even when US economic wealth diminished in relation to its West European allies in the 1960s, the perception of a continued Soviet threat to Western interests encouraged successive US governments to retain their security commitment to Western Europe, while discouraging EC states from attempting to incorporate a security dimension into their process of integration. Realists also argue that the United States underwrote European order by minimizing the destabilizing impact that shifts in the relative economic strength of EC member states posed to the political cohesion of Western Europe.[35] Thus, the US security guarantee, provided through NATO, underwrote the process of political and economic integration that has characterized relations between West European states since the signing of the Treaty of Rome in 1957. International order in Western Europe was sustained by direct US involvement in its security as well as by the glue of the external Soviet threat.

Yet around this dependent power relationship there accumulated a range of institutionalized rules and habits, of implicit and explicit assumptions about appropriate relationships, acceptable and unacceptable behaviour, which amounted to far more than can be accounted for through Realist analysis alone.[36] The Atlantic Alliance, with its integrated command structure and its multilateral foreign policy consultations, institutionalized American international leadership. The structures of West European integration grew up within this Western framework, resting upon the delicate counterpoise of the Franco-German and the American–German relationships. The idea of a 'transatlantic bargain', in which West Europeans had agreed to accept American determination of Western international economic policies in return for American security guarantees, was accepted on both sides of the Atlantic. It was given institutional expression first in the OEEC, then in the revised OECD, spelt out more clearly in President Kennedy's 'grand design' for a two pillar Atlantic Community.

The loss of American monetary dominance, with the end of dollar–gold convertibility, and the hesitant beginnings of West European foreign policy co-operation in 1970–72, led to a vigorously Realist assertion of the 'linkage' between security provision and economic co-operation. This was spelt out with brutal clarity in Henry Kissinger's 'Year of Europe' speech, April 1973.[37] But the compromise struck between the USA and its European allies, within the NATO framework, at Ottawa in June 1974, fell far short of what the Nixon administration had wanted. Multilateral institutions, the rhetoric of shared values within the Atlantic Community, the ambivalent relationship between the goals of Atlantic co-operation and West European integration, divergent assessments of Western policy towards Eastern Europe and the Middle East, all shaped the outcome.

The vigour with which the Nixon administration reasserted this European–Atlantic, security–economic linkage itself underlined the degree to which

West European governments had separated economic relations from security policy. Foreign economic policies were managed first within West European institutions and then within Western; security policy was managed first within NATO and then east–west. Different hierarchies within Western governments dealt with these separate multilateral exchanges; only occasional meetings of heads of government brought the whole range of Western policies together. Even there, Group of Seven conferences from 1974 focused on multilateral economic co-ordination, while the informal Group of Four (without Japan, Canada and Italy) discussed politico-military strategy – until responses to the crises of 1979–80 brought these two overlapping dialogues together.[38] The development of 'European Political Cooperation' (EPC) outside the framework of the European Community did little to narrow this institutional divide in multilateral management of security and economic relations. Political directorates within foreign ministries managed national inputs into EPC, while economic directorates managed inputs to EC policy-making jointly with domestic ministries, leading to disjointed policies.

In politico-military matters, then, the United States led and the West Europeans followed. NATO entrenched American leadership; 350 000 US troops in Europe, the Sixth Fleet in the Mediterranean and several thousand tactical nuclear weapons deployed across NATO Europe, were the visible embodiment of West European dependence on their transatlantic protector. The bitterness left by de Gaulle's challenge to American alliance leadership and France's subsequent withdrawal from the integrated military structures of NATO made other governments more reluctant to question established patterns. For British governments above all, the counterpart of American leadership was West European followership: the acceptance of the role of junior partner together with the modest ambition of influence over policy-making in Washington. The stance adopted by Dutch and German governments was similar – though modified in Bonn by development of a civilian *Ostpolitik* which nevertheless carried long-term security implications. Italian governments were more dependent on American security provision, less active in developing security policies, while actively pursuing economic advantages in east–west trade. The comfortable self-image of Europe as a civilian power, leaving hard security and the projection of power to the Americans while preoccupied with economic integration and external economic relations, was a convenient myth. It allowed European political leaders to spend less on defence, even to some extent to opt out of power politics: to criticize American security leadership without challenging it.

In hindsight, it can be argued that the 1980s witnessed growing tensions in Western Europe's security relationship with the United States. Dissatisfaction with the Carter administration's response to the Polish, Iranian and Afghanistan crises in 1979–80, against the background of a widening divergence between European and American assumptions about east–west relations and the Arab–Israeli conflict, gave added impetus to European

Political Cooperation.[39] US propaganda surrounding the strategic defence initiative (SDI) and Reagan's apparent willingness to countenance nuclear disarmament at his summit with Mikhail Gorbachev in Reykjavik provoked further unease. Yet the Atlantic security relationship had been marked by recurrent differences since the death of Stalin in 1953. So long as the Red Army remained in central Europe in strength, West European governments were reluctant openly to question the direction of American security policy, let alone to offer an alternative strategy; even French determination to demonstrate independence was predicated on the assumption that the American commitment to contain both the USSR and Germany remained strong.

Aside from its overlapping institutional structures, West European order during the cold war also developed its own distinctive vocabulary and imagery: its mental maps of preferred groups of countries, of bridging linkages and boundaries. The concept of 'the West' (as opposed to 'the East'), already well-rooted in German, Catholic and European liberal literature, was redefined as the basis for a 'Western civilization' which Western Europe had developed and transmitted to the New World. The Atlantic thus became the bridge between these two pillars of a common culture – rather than the divide between brash American individualism (and capitalism) and the corporate and socially-integrated European society which proponents of a European 'third force' between the USA and USSR preferred to imagine. The concept of an 'Atlantic Community' was implicit in the Atlantic Charter of 1941. It became explicit in the post-war rhetoric of American Atlanticists and their West European supporters, acquiring such a firm hold on intellectual imagination that – as Louis Halle recalls – even ornithologists began to discover previously unrecognized links between European and North American breeds of birds.[40]

The mental maps of a (Western) Europe intrinsically linked to North America fitted the military realities of cold war confrontation, smothering older images of a Germanic 'central Europe'. Rising generations of affluent West Europeans in the 1970s and 1980s took it for granted that they might travel freely between Finland and Greece, across the oddly-shaped crescent of 'OECD-Europe' which French politicians labelled the 'European Social Space', later defined as the 'European Economic Area'. Contacts with intellectual dissidents in Poland, Czechoslovakia and Hungary from the late 1970s onward, promoted by the pan-European imagery of the CSCE (and reinforced by the growth of West European tourism into east-central and south-eastern Europe, and by the powerful image of a Polish pope as head of the 'Western' Catholic church) brought the idea of central Europe back into weak focus – though it remained overshadowed by the harsh military reality of a heavily-armed frontier across the middle of continental Europe, by continuing limitations on economic interaction and personal travel across that frontier.

Competing images and mental maps also formed part of the ideological battle within Western Europe. American money and military power, its immense prestige within Western Europe, its image as an open and dynamic modernizing society, gave its claim to intellectual leadership additional appeal. This image was conveyed by American troops as they swept across Western Europe in 1944–45 and reinforced by American advisers as they stayed to sponsor West European reconstruction. West European élites reoriented themselves to this transplanted Europe across the Atlantic. For nearly 40 years after the Second World War, larger numbers of students from France, Germany and Britain extended their higher education in American universities than in each other's countries.[41] Vienna and Berlin had been displaced by New Haven and Cambridge, Massachusetts; for West Europeans, New York had become closer than Prague.

In the first post-war years the idea of a 'third force', of Europe between the two semi-European superpowers, was smothered by the intensity of cold war confrontation. Those who did not look west looked east, to a Soviet-led socialist Europe. The death of Stalin and the recovery of Western Europe's economy left space for alternative challenges to American hegemony, most vigorously from President de Gaulle, whose studied ambiguity moved from a French-led Western Europe to a wider Europe 'from the Atlantic to the Urals'.[42] Social Democrats within Germany clung to hopes of reunification through the demilitarization of central Europe, until the Berlin Wall was erected in 1961; painfully reformulating the strategy of *Ostpolitik* in the years which followed as a deliberately gradual path towards long-term transformation.[43]

The hierarchy of states within this Western order was from one perspective clear, while from another deliberately unclear. The United States remained without question the alliance leader – the Western hegemon – until after the unification of Germany in October 1990, as attested by the role of American policymakers in the 'Two Plus Four' negotiations which led to unification, and in the redefinition of Western strategic priorities immediately after the demolition of the Berlin Wall.[44] Britain, France and Germany were America's three key West European partners. Italy – despite its comparable size and its strategic position – remained throughout a less active or engaged player. The Netherlands counted as the most active and constructive of America's smaller partners, providing much more than a proportionate share of conciliators and administrators within Western international institutions. The Nordic countries developed their own concept of a regional sub-system, a 'Nordic balance' in which a neutral but armed Sweden held the central position between neutralized Finland and NATO-member Norway. Spain until after the death of Franco was excluded from much of this intense multilateral network, dependent on a separate bilateral relationship with the USA.

What was left unclear, however, was the relative positions within this group of states of the USA's three principal West European allies: Britain, Federal Germany and France. None of the three were entirely happy at any point with the places assigned them in this American-imagined international community. Successive British governments clung to their claim to a special relationship with the USA within the alliance, spending a higher proportion of their GNP on defence than almost any other European NATO member over several decades in order to maintain that claim. But they resisted repeated American efforts to push them into closer association with France and Germany, from 1949 onwards, both because of continuing domestic confusions about Britain's approach to relations with Germany and because a determined preference for a privileged bilateral relationship over a multilateral US–European partnership.[45] Rearmament and economic recovery raised questions of Germany's status in Western bilateral and multilateral consultations: pressed most explicitly in the politico-military field by Frans-Josef Strauss and others from 1957–66.[46] There remained an underlying ambivalence in Germany's international role, however, until reunification, in which a gradually-increasing American emphasis on Germany's position as Washington's 'preferred partner' in Western Europe was counterbalanced by German acceptance that American leadership provided a desirable alternative to the development of a more active German foreign policy in competition or co-operation with France and Britain.

French governments struggled to assert a privileged position for themselves during the cold war, while acutely conscious of their relative weakness in comparison even with a divided Germany: moving from de Gaulle's 1958 proposal for a three-power *Directoire* to his direct challenge to America's Western leadership and its resolution in the acceptance after 1966 of a semi-detached French role within the Western alliance. This echo of a European 'third force' aroused some sympathy within West Germany, as well as within some governments of Warsaw Pact countries. But it lacked economic and military credibility. The Warsaw Pact's invasion of Czechoslovakia in August 1968 destroyed the already fading attraction of this Gaullist vision.

The rhetoric of Atlantic solidarity, and the institutions (and the military commitments) which held it in place, persisted through the 1970s and 1980s. The 'soft power' of Atlanticist ideas, the mental map of a Western Europe defined by lines drawn in the 1940s, continued to govern day-to-day policy, and to hold a firm grip on the popular imagination.[47] Only the visible removal of the physical barriers between east and west, the surge of human movement across the old boundaries from 1989 on, the reemergence of half-forgotten states from behind the 'iron curtain', made for a confused upsurge of alternative images: of differing definitions of 'Europe', of the Baltic and Black Sea re-emerging as regions which linked together the countries around their waters rather than dividing them, of the Danube basin, the old Hapsburg links from the Alps to the Adriatic. For Western policymakers and commentators who had spent all their professional lives – and made their careers – within the strategic paradigm of the cold war, however, such alternative images were not immediately compelling.

International order and economic and social change

Looking back, the stability – even inertia – of this accumulation of interlinked ideas and images over more than 30 years, from their successful establishment as the conventional wisdom of the Western international order in the early 1950s, to the partial and gradual recognition of underlying changes in the course of the 1980s, is remarkable. For within this stable institutional, security and ideological order Western Europe underwent an extraordinarily rapid and sustained process of economic change. The balance of economic advantage across the Atlantic shifted radically in Europe's favour, from an American structural surplus and an outward flow of US investment to a European trade surplus and a two-way flow of direct investment and short-term funds. The economic balance within Western Europe shifted almost as radically: from Britain as Europe's largest economy in the early-1950s, the focus for north European trade as much as the reviving German economy, to a Germany-centred West European economy in the mid 1980s which had drawn the rapidly-developing economies of southern Europe into its orbit.[48]

As Eric Hobsbawm has reminded us, domestic economic and social change was no less dramatic. 'The past 30 or 40 years have been the most revolutionary era in recorded history. Never before has the world, that is to say the lives of the men and women who live on earth, been so profoundly, dramatically and extraordinarily transformed within such a brief period.'[49] A quarter of the working population in the Western half-continent were still in agriculture in 1950, and a similar proportion in the staple heavy industries of mining, iron and steel, metalworking and engineering which represented (for socialists and for economic planners) 'the commanding heights' of the industrial economy. The steam engine and the horse were slowly giving way to the electric motor and the automobile. Limited life expectancy left only a few elderly to depend on the benefits of the European welfare state. The telephone remained a rarity; the radio was coming to supplement the printed page as a means of mass communication; and once the forced displacements of war had ended the overwhelming majority of Europe's population resumed lives entirely contained within their own national boundaries.

At the end of the 1980s the state-controlled economies and societies of east-central and eastern Europe still displayed some aspects of this transitional agricultural–industrial model. Their regimes were still pursuing the model of mass industrial society towards which Western Europe had been developing thirty years before. Western Europe's society and economy, by contrast, was going through a further social and economic transformation: gradual rather than abrupt, creeping forward year by year, but nevertheless as profound a transformation as the strategic revolution represented by the events of 1989–91. West European society had become far more integrated across national boundaries, far more integrated also in consumer fashions and cultural tastes, far more ethnically diverse – above all, far more affluent in all respects.[50]

American advisers in the 1950s had seen the creation of an affluent society in Western Europe as the surest bulwark of democracy against Communism: replacing the passions of industrial mass society with the permissive consensus born of affluence underpinned by competent government.[51] The student revolts of 1968 demonstrated that this was too simple and self-confident a picture. But the self-absorbed domestic politics which characterized Western Europe in the 1980s displayed many of the characteristics that the 'end of ideology' school had predicted thirty years before: focused on public services, tax burdens and fiscal redistribution, employment and welfare, and largely unconcerned with foreign policy. Western negotiators at Versailles in 1919, Ernest May notes, were acutely conscious of public opinion at home, stirred up by east European exiles and by a nationalist press. Western negotiators in the early 1990s received much less press coverage from media which now 'catered to popular interests instead of creating them'. Those popular interests were private and domestic, not public and international.[52]

After the 'thirty glorious years' of post-war West European growth, the 1970s and early 1980s saw painful industrial restructuring, slower economic growth and an end to full employment. This reflected the scale of the transfer of employment and wealth-creation away from labour intensive manufacturing industries. It also reflected adjustment to the interrelated revolutions in communications, electronics and financial markets, with the development of new industries and services, and the need to reshape patterns of ownership and regulation to take advantage of the opportunities the new technologies offered. West European integration in the 1960s had been driven partly by 'the American challenge' – the fear that national companies supplying separate national markets, with research and development financed by national governments and capital markets, would fall further behind the USA. The resurgence of economic integration in the 1980s was partly driven by fears not only of American but also of East Asian industrial and technological advances, with European industrialists pressing governments to respond.[53]

The West European welfare state – the social democratic compromise embedded in the establishment of industrial democracies across the continent – had contributed a great deal to the region's socio-economic transformation. By the late 1970s, however, it had become the victim of its own success. The increasing costs of providing health care, the strain which rising life expectancy imposed on state pension provision, had helped to raise public expenditure to 45 per cent of West European GDP. Changing patterns of employment, the emancipation of women in the home and at work, had also weakened the foundations of a welfare society built upon provision for a male industrial workforce, and had raised its costs. The staple heavy industries, largely state-owned, which had provided mass employment and underpinned post-war economic growth, were shrinking; state-owned monopolies in transport and in communications were facing international competition and technological change.

West European national governments now found themselves, however, in an increasingly weak position from which to reconstruct a domestic consensus on the balance between the public and private sectors, between market economics and social welfare. The density of cross-border transactions, the development of multinational production and marketing, the disappearance of mutual suspicion about potential military aggression between West European states and the establishment of an apparently firmly-based security community, all contributed to a partial displacement of the role of the nation state in Western Europe. Each national government's autonomy in managing its national economy was constrained by the operations of multinational companies, and by the impact of continuing technical innovation. Monetary and fiscal policies were limited by the integration of financial markets, control of frontiers loosened by the pressure of numbers now crossing them. Competition for government spending, between the provision of welfare, health and education, public investment, support for technological research and development, and agricultural and industrial subsidies constrained their options further. This contradiction between the growth of government spending and the draining away of control over the levers of economic policy led many observers to identify a 'crisis of the nation state' in Western Europe in the 1980s.[54]

Institutional innovation in West European integration in the 1980s, from the Single European Act to the relaunch of Economic and Monetary Union, was in large part a response to these strains and challenges.[55] It was also a response to successive enlargement of institutions created for a Community of six member states with a containable diversity of national tastes, cultures, political and economic needs, which by 1986 had become a much more diverse Community of twelve. The policy agenda of West European multilateral governance, limited in the 1950s and 1960s to a limited number of sectors of economic management and regulation, was gradually expanding into areas which were close to the central functions of the state. Concerns over public disenchantment with the process of European integration had led political leaders to talk about 'European citizenship'; crossborder movement had necessitated crossborder co-operation among police forces and judicial authorities. Fears of crossborder competition driving down standards, which social democratic governments had achieved in worker protection and social benefits, had placed social policy on the Community agenda.

The old European agenda and the new

West European governments were thus deeply preoccupied with an existing agenda for political and economic change when Europe's security order to their east was transformed. The European Commission was attempting to negotiate a closer partnership with its EFTA neighbours which would avoid the threat of further applications for full EC membership.[56] EC member governments were already preparing for another Intergovernmental Conference, to begin only four years after the Single European Act had been signed, to amend the Rome Treaty further to introduce Economic and Monetary Union. Several member states were committed to a further extension of Qualified Majority Voting (QMV), already extended in the SEA; some wished to extend the authority of the European Parliament. Western Europe thus had a full plate of policy concerns in 1989, an established agenda for multilateral diplomacy alongside – and only loosely linked to – the east–west security agenda.

Not least of the difficulties which governments faced in the years after the Wall came down arose from these two competing agendas: the old objective of completing the West European 'project', and the new agenda of creating a wider Europe with inclusive institutions. The debate over 'core Europe', outlined in Chapter 2, was partly a reflection of this continuing commitment to the old agenda, driven by fear of losing the achievements of West European integration in widening European institutions to accommodate neutral and ex-socialist states. American officials and members of Congress pressed for rapid EU enlargement, to provide maximum support for economic and political transition in central and eastern Europe. The applicant states were impatient for entry, rightly seeing integration into the West as a determining priority in foreign and domestic policy. West European governments, nevertheless, had other competing priorities, both domestic and international. The ministers who responded to the transformation of European order struggled to give this strategic issue time and attention alongside more immediate problems, attempting to master this new dossier as they negotiated the difficult details of dossiers they had worried over before the Wall came down.

The paradox which this book explores, of a security order transformed from armed confrontation to peaceful transition, but only reluctantly addressed by the West European governments and élites which benefited from this removal of threat, is easiest to explain in terms of West European preoccupation with the pre-existing complexities of its established agenda. In sharp contrast to most previous changes of Europe's international political order, West European societies remained prosperous throughout the transition – though insecure, suffering from recession, high unemployment and cutbacks in social expenditure, and therefore more self-preoccupied even than democratic states in the upswing of the economic cycle. Revolution in the east thus contended with domestic anxieties in the west. Economic and social changes within Western Europe were, for voters and for political élites, far more immediate than changes within Poland or Russia; changes in former Yugoslavia only became more immediate when refugees reached EU countries, or when requests were made for troops to be sent.

Relations with Germany were still far more important, in 1997, for political leaders in France, the Netherlands, Denmark and Britain, than relations with

Poland or Hungary, however vigorously the leaders of these newly-democratic countries might attempt to persuade them otherwise. In the long run, the reorientation of some 100 million people in a dozen countries from east to west, with the retreat of Russia from central Europe, will be seen to have fundamentally transformed the structure and institutions of European order. But in the long run, as John Maynard Keynes remarked, we are all dead. In the short run most politicians address themselves either to the most familiar issues or to the most unavoidable ones; and most of their advisers, in political parties, in the media, in institutes and in universities, appear to do the same.

Notes

1. Hedley Bull, *The Anarchical Society* (London: Macmillan 1977) p. 13.
2. Fred Halliday, *Rethinking International Relations* (London: Macmillan, 1994), chap. 6; David Armstrong, *Revolution and World Order: the revolutionary state in international society* (Oxford: Blackwell, 1993).
3. Marianne Hanson, *The Conference on Security and Cooperation in Europe: the evolution of a code of conduct in East-West relations* (Oxford University, DPhil, 1992).
4. William Wallace, *The Transformation of Western Europe* (London: Pinter/RIIA, 1990), chap. 2.
5. John Hall, *International Orders* (Cambridge: Polity, 1996), p. 28.
6. E.H. Carr, *The Twenty Years' Crisis* (London: Macmillan, 1946) p. 87.
7. Kenneth Waltz, *Theory of International Politics* (Reading, MA: Addison Wesley, 1979).
8. Robert Gilpin, *War and Change in International Politics* (Cambridge: Cambridge University Press, 1981); Paul Kennedy, *The Rise and Fall of the Great Economic Powers: Economic Change and Military Conflict from 1500 to 2000* (London: Unwin Hyman, 1988).
9. John Mearsheimer, 'Back to the Future: Instability in Europe after the Cold War', *International Security* (Summer 1990) p. 18.
10. Judith Goldstein and Robert O. Keohane (eds), *Ideas and Foreign Policy: beliefs, institutions and political change* (Ithaca, NY: Cornell, 1993).
11. Hedley Bull, *The Anarchical Society*, pp. 16–19.
12. Edward Morse, *Modernization and the Transformation of International Relations* (New York: Free Press, 1976) pp. 10, 20, 84–7; Arthur Stein, 'Coordination and Collaboration: Regimes in an Anarchic World', *International Organization*, 36 (Spring 1982) p. 123.
13. Oran Young, *International Cooperation: building regimes for natural resources and the environment* (Ithaca, NY: Cornell, 1989) p. 13.
14. Robert O. Keohane and Joseph S. Nye, *Power and Interdependence: World Politics in Transition* (Boston: Little Brown, 1977); Robert O. Keohane and Stanley Hoffman, 'Conclusion: structure, strategy, and institutional roles', in Keohane, Nye and Hoffman (eds), *After the Cold War: international institutions and state strategies in Europe, 1989–1991* (Cambridge, MA: Harvard University Press, 1993).
15. John A. Hall, *International Orders* (Cambridge: Polity, 1996).
16. William Wallace, 'Between two worlds: think tanks and foreign policy', in Christopher Hill and Pamela Beshoff (eds), *Two Worlds of International Relations* (London: Routledge, 1994); Diane Stone, Andrew Denham and Mark Garnett (eds), *Think tanks across nations: a comparative approach* (Manchester: Manchester University Press, 1998).

17. François Duchêne, 'The European Community and the Uncertainties of Inter-dependence', in Max Kohnstamm and Wolfgang Hager (eds), *A Nation Writ Large?* (London: Macmillan, 1973); Hedley Bull, 'Civilian Power Europe: a contradiction in terms?', *Journal of Common Market Studies*, 21:1–2 (1982) pp. 149–65.
18. Michel Girard, Wolf-Dieter Eberwein and Keith Webb (eds), *Theory and Practice in International Relations: national perspectives on academics and professionals in International Relations* (London: Pinter, 1994).
19. Timothy Garton Ash, *In Europe's Name: Germany and the Divided Continent* (London: Jonathan Cape, 1993).
20. The concept of 'Eurafrica', now almost entirely forgotten, carried a powerful resonance in French foreign policy for 20 years after the Second World War, when the French empire still spanned the Mediterranean. No similar trans-Mediterranean concept re-emerged among the jumble of geopolitical images which resurfaced in the early 1990s.
21. Robert Cooper, *The Post-Modern State and the World Order* (London: Demos, 1996) p. 26. *The Post-Modern State* was originally written as a planning paper in the British Foreign and Commonwealth Office; its author was at the time head of the FCO Planning Staff.
22. Philip Budden, *The Making of the Single European Act: the United Kingdom and the European Community, 1979–1986* (Oxford University, DPhil, 1994); Anthony Forster, *Britain and the Maastricht Negotiations* (London: Macmillan, 1999).
23. Judith Goldstein and Robert O. Keohane, 'Ideas and foreign policy: an analytical approach', chap. 1 in Goldstein and Keohane (eds), *Ideas and Foreign Policy*; William Wallace, 'Foreign Policy and National Identity in the United Kingdom', *International Affairs* (January 1991) pp. 65–80.
24. Martin Wight's *Power Politics* (London: RIIA, 1998, first published in pamphlet form in 1946) provides a classic interpretation of the interaction between revolution and the construction of international order in Europe in mediaeval and modern Europe. See also John A. Hall, *International Orders* (Cambridge: Polity, 1996).
25. John Maynard Keynes, one of these young attachés, published a denunciation of the Versailles Settlement in *The Economic Consequences of the Peace* (London: Macmillan, 1919). Other British attachés included Arnold Toynbee, Philip Kerr (later Lord Lothian), Harold Nicolson, Lord Robert Cecil, Alfred Zimmern (later the first professor of international relations at Oxford), and Philip Noel-Baker (later the LSE's first professor of international relations); their dissatisfied conversations in the margins of the conference led to the establishment of the Royal Institute of International Affairs to encourage a more informed debate outside government. William Wallace, 'Between two worlds: think tanks and foreign policy', in Christopher Hill and Pamela Beshoff (eds), *Two Worlds of International Relations*.
26. Winston Churchill, *The World Crisis: the aftermath* (London: 1929), p. 142; quoted in David Armstrong, Lorna Lloyd and John Redmond, *From Versailles to Maastricht* (London: Macmillan, 1996), p. 9.
27. Evan Luard, *A History of the United Nations*, Vol.1 (London: Macmillan, 1982). Two more sceptical accounts are given in T.M. Campbell, *Masquerade Peace: America's UN Policy, 1944–5* (Tallahassee: University of Florida Press, 1973), and Mark Mazower, *Dark Continent: Europe's twentieth century* (London: Allen Lane, 1998), chap. 6.
28. Alfred Grosser, *The Western Alliance: European–American relations since 1945* (London: Macmillan, 1980), chaps 1–3.

29. Geographical subdivisions of 'Europe' are unavoidably subjective. 'Central Europe' has been a historically contested term, used by Friedrich Neumann to describe areas under German political, social and economic influence, by Austrian writers to describe the Hapsburg empire. Here it is used in the way in which Polish and Czech dissidents in the 1980s, and post-socialist governments in the early 1990s, defined it: as including those countries which were not part of the Soviet Union but which were excluded from 'Western Europe' from the late 1940s through enforced membership of the CMEA and the Warsaw Pact. 'Eastern Europe', in this definition, refers to countries which were part of the former Soviet Union: Ukraine, Belarus, Moldova, the Baltic states and Russia itself. 'South-eastern Europe' is used to describe those non-Soviet states which had not formed part of the Hapsburg or German empires: Romania, Bulgaria, Albania and Yugoslavia. Yugoslavia was of course a contested territory between Hapsburgs and others, and western Romania was under Hapsburg rule – historical fault lines which are still sadly relevant today. William Wallace, *The transformation of Western Europe* (London: Pinter/RIIA, 1990), chap. 2.
30. The European Community formally became the European Union with the ratification of the Maastricht Treaty on European Union in 1993. Here the convention adopted is to refer to the EC until the end of 1991, and to the EU from the initialling of the Treaty in January 1992. Post-socialist states were anxious to become associated with all three pillars of the EU, not just the EC itself.
31. Michael Howard, 'The Remaking of Europe', *Survival*, 32:2 (March–April 1990) pp. 99–106.
32. Thomas A. Schwartz, *America's Germany: John J. McCloy and the Federal Republic of Germany* (Cambridge, MA: Harvard University Press, 1991).
33. François Duchêne, *Jean Monnet: the first statesman of interdependence* (New York: Norton, 1994), explains how far the construction of West European integration was an American-led enterprise resting on American concepts. See also John Ikenberry, 'Creating yesterday's New World Order: Keynesian "new thinking" and the Anglo-American post-war settlement', in Judith Goldstein and Robert O. Keohane (eds), *Ideas and Foreign Policy* (Cornell University Press, 1993); W. Wallace, *Regional integration: the West European experience* (Washington: Brookings, 1994), chap. 2.
34. John Gerard Ruggie (ed.), *Multilateralism Matters* (New York: Columbia University Press, 1993); Robert O. Keohane, *After Hegemony: cooperation and discord in the world political economy* (Princeton, NJ: Princeton University Press, 1984).
35. Joseph Joffe, 'Europe's American pacifier', *Foreign Policy* (1984) pp. 64–82; John Mearsheimer, 'Back to the Future: Instability in Europe After the Cold War', *International Security*, 15:1 (1990).
36. Robert Keohane, Joseph Nye and Stanley Hoffman (eds), *After the Cold War*, op. cit..
37. Henry Kissinger's 'Year of Europe' initiative, in April 1973, was a reminder to West European allies of American assumptions about this inherent linkage between security and economic ties. William Wallace, 'Atlantic Linkage: the year of Europe', *International Affairs*, 52:2 (1976) pp. 157–86.
38. Robert D. Putnam and Nicholas Bayne, *Hanging Together: the seven-power summits* (London: Heinemann, 1984).
39. Philippe de Schoutheete, *La Coopération Politique Européene* (Brussels: Labor, 2nd edn, 1986); Simon Nuttall, *European Political Cooperation* (Oxford: Clarendon Press, 1992).
40. Louis Halle, *The Cold War as History* (London: Chatto and Windus, 1967).

41. Frederico Romero, 'Cross-border population movements', chap. 10 in William Wallace (ed.), *Dynamics of European Integration* (London: Pinter, 1990).
42. Harold van B. Cleveland, *The Atlantic Idea and its European Rivals* (New York: McGraw-Hill/Council on Foreign Relations, 1966).
43. Grosser, *The Western Alliance*, chaps 7–9; Anton DePorte, *Europe between the Superpowers: the enduring balance* (New Haven, Conn.: Yale University Press, 1986), chaps 9–10.
44. Philip Zelikow and Condoleeza Rice, *Germany unified and Europe Transformed: a study in statecraft* (Cambridge, Mass: Harvard University Press, 1995).
45. 'Great Britain … can hardly be said to have had a comprehensive approach to the German problem' – from 1943 to the 1980s. Anton de Porte, *Europe between the Superpowers* p. 142, op. cit..
46. Grosser, *The Western Alliance*, op. cit..
47. The concept of 'soft power' is taken from Joseph S. Nye, *Bound to Lead: the changing nature of American power* (New York: Basic Books, 1990).
48. Per Wijkman (and Roberto Aliboni), in Wallace (ed.), *Dynamics of European Integration*, op. cit..
49. Eric Hobsbawm, 'The time of my life', *New Statesman*, 21 October 1994, p. 31.
50. Manuel Castells, *End of Millennium*, volume III of the trilogy on *The Information Age* (Oxford: Blackwell, 1998), chaps 1 and 5, provide an excellent account of the contrast between West European transformation and East European stagnation in the 1970s and 1980s.
51. Leon Lindberg, *The Political Dynamics of European Integration*, (Stanford, Ca: Stanford University Press, 1963); Ernst B. Haas, *Beyond the Nation State*, (Stanford, Ca: Stanford University Press, 1964). See also Seymour Martin Lipset, *Political Man: the Social Bases of Politics* (Garden City, NJ: Doubleday, 1960).
52. Ernest R. May, 'Public Opinion', chap. 2 in Samuel F. Wells and Paula Bailey Smith (eds), *New European Orders, 1919 and 1991* (Washington, DC: Woodrow Wilson Center Press, 1996). May also notes the significant contraction in foreign correspondents retained by major Western newspapers between 1919 and 1991, and the parallel decline in foreign content in the press.
53. Albert Bressand and Kalypso Nicolaidis, 'Regional Integration in a Networked World Economy' and Margaret Sharp, 'Technology and the Dynamics of Integration', chaps 2 and 3 in Wallace (ed.), *Dynamics of European Integration*, op. cit..
54. The literature is reviewed in William Wallace, 'Rescue or retreat? The nation state in Western Europe, 1945–1993', *Political Studies* 42: 5, 1994.
55. William Wallace (ed.), *The Dynamics of European Integration* (London: Pinter, 1990).
56. Helen Wallace (ed.), *The Wider Western Europe: reshaping the EC/EFTA relationship* (London: Pinter, 1991).

2

Concepts of European Order after the Cold War: In with the Old, Out with the New

Anthony Forster and Robin Niblett

From 1989 to 1997, West European governments were engaged in intensive multilateral negotiations with their American counterparts and with the post-socialist governments to their east. Adjustment to the demands and expectations of the states of east-central and eastern Europe, involved both a redefinition of 'Europe' and a reconsideration of the European–Atlantic linkage. However, what eventually emerged from this process was a partial agreement to preserve the existing transatlantic order, by incrementally enlarging existing institutions but without fundamentally re-examining the foundations upon which it was built.

The aim of this chapter is to examine the nature of this multilateral process of adjustment. It examines both the discourse and substance of this multilateral debate: the emergence of the idea of 'European Security and Defence Identity' (ESDI) as a central concept for a new Europe; the evolution of thinking within NATO, WEU and the EU as to how their respective institutions should adapt and how they might relate to each other. This chapter underlines the importance of the debate among the West European countries, their inability to face up to difficult choices, and the guiding hand of the United States in reshaping European order through direct intervention within NATO and indirect pressure on the European Union. The first section looks at the search for new security arrangements, focusing on the institutional tensions which emerged as governments considered how to respond to the changes they faced. The second explores the debates concerned with the adaptation of the European Community into a European Union, with the development of a single currency and a common foreign and security policy (CFSP). The third section analyzes the process of integrating the East into Western political and security institutions, and the struggle to bring the two tracks together.

Only in the first flush of enthusiasm in 1989–90, we note, did the debate within the West primarily focus on the architecture of pan-European order. As more and more socialist regimes collapsed, as first Yugoslavia and then the

USSR itself disintegrated, West European governments became more self-preoccupied. The transformation of Europe presented itself to core member states of the EU as a threat to what they had established over the previous forty years, more than as a promise of a wider peaceful order. The long-running dispute between France and its neighbours over the structure of the transatlantic relationship continued, with the European members of NATO continuing also to look westward to the United States to provide security leadership. Successive US Administrations, in turn, were determined to ensure both that the economic and financial burdens of assisting political and economic transition were shouldered by Western Europe and that strategic and security leadership was retained by Washington, through NATO. Intermittent attention from Washington policymakers, combined with underlying disagreements among West European governments, made for a hesitant and disjointed response to demands from post-socialist governments to 'rejoin the West'.

The search for new security arrangements

It was the Bush administration which moved most rapidly to set the terms of debate on the transformation of Europe, and to ensure that the unification of Germany and the reorientation of east-central Europe towards the West safeguarded its interests. James Baker, in the first post-Wall declaration on the security structure of post-cold war Europe, spelt out in his Berlin speech of December 1989 the continuing importance of NATO. Chapters 3–5 note the close American–German partnership in negotiating German unification, while French and British leaders struggled to adjust. Within Western Europe, two strategic visions of Europe's post-cold war security emerged in the immediate aftermath of the events of 1989. The first and most radical, promoted by Hans-Dietrich Genscher and the German foreign ministry, questioned the logic of strengthening a distinct 'West' European security organization – whether inside the EC or NATO. This radical vision foresaw the construction of a pan-European institutional structure which would draw all European states together into a new system of collective security. During 1989 and early 1990, Genscher argued consistently that a stable post-cold war European order had to include at its heart the Soviet Union as an equal partner in the management of European security. Supporters of this vision suggested that the Conference on Security and Cooperation in Europe (CSCE), which included all members of both the Warsaw Pact and NATO, was the most likely institution to be acceptable to both of the old alliances.

The credibility of the CSCE peaked in the autumn of 1989, with NATO and Warsaw Pact members signing the long-awaited Conventional Forces in Europe (CFE) arms reduction agreement. This created a Conflict Prevention Centre in Prague, and contained a commitment to hold annual summit meetings in Vienna. Despite this remodelling of CSCE, German support did not extend far beyond the Auswärtiges Amt. Once West Germany had secured Soviet approval for rapid unification, with the former East Germany to be incorporated into the Atlantic Alliance, official German support faded. Moscow's support for the idea that the CSCE should absorb both cold war alliances also carried far less weight after the implosion of the Soviet Union undermined Russia's ability to negotiate terms for the post-cold war security order. The admission of the new states of the CIS to the CSCE raised its membership from thirty-five to over fifty, and extended its concerns to security problems in Central Asia and the Caucasus, making it far less obvious a vehicle to take on an effective role in preventing or policing crises within Europe. From the end of 1991 onwards, despite Russia's repeated admonishments, the CSCE evolved along a different path, leading to its reincarnation as the OSCE: a functional, specialist second order organization, responsible for early crisis prevention (primarily fact-finding missions) and election-monitoring, rather than a successor organization to NATO and the Warsaw Pact.

The second vision, advanced most forcefully by the French government, with partial support of other 'Europeanist' governments (notably the Belgians and Spanish) and the Commission, recognized that NATO should remain in place to provide the strategic transatlantic linkage between the United States and Europe, and to serve as an insurance policy against some form of Soviet revanchism. This group, however, also argued that a window of opportunity had opened to allow primary responsibility for Western European security to devolve to the West Europeans themselves, through the development of a defence dimension to the European integration project. This was, as remarked above, not an entirely novel idea. It echoed French Gaullist concepts of the 1960s, with a similar ambivalence about the transatlantic relationship and the place of the USSR in European order.

As part of the broader Franco-German bargain on German unification, President Mitterrand and Chancellor Kohl issued a joint proposal in April 1990 that a second intergovernmental conference (IGC) on 'Political Union' should run in parallel with the IGC on Economic and Monetary Union (EMU) already agreed at the Strasbourg European Council in December 1989.[1] The aim of this plan for Political Union was the elevation of European Political Cooperation (EPC), into a more grandly named and more ambitious 'common foreign and security policy' (CFSP). The function of the initiative in policy terms, however, turned out to be primarily inspirational, 'more of a guiding star than a road map', since it was not clear exactly what CFSP was, nor how it should be achieved.[2] Indeed, there was little agreement on the details between the French and Germans themselves. Other Europeanist member states which supported the principles behind the idea of a CFSP therefore felt unable actively to press their case.[3] Instead, a majority of member states refused from early 1991 onwards to advance the debate on defence in the IGC without first securing agreement from the Americans over the relationship between the Alliance and the European Union.[4]

In the absence of leadership from others, it was left to Commission President Jacques Delors to attempt to address what he saw were the fundamental questions: what was the destiny of Europe and what were its ambitions? His answers set out an ambitious proposal for a common foreign and defence policy, including shared foreign policy analysis and a reciprocal commitment to come to the defence of member states. In institutional terms, the WEU would be progressively absorbed into the European Union, with the Union incorporating WEU's collective defence guarantee.[5] The perceived audacity of the Commission even among its traditional supporters, and the uncompromising language of Delors, led many to distance themselves from the Commission President, and to fear an insatiable appetite for an ever-expanding set of responsibilities. However, the most serious consequence of Delors' initiative was to provoke Washington (with British encouragement) to intervene actively in the twelve's IGC negotiations.

US policymakers balked at the fundamental questions which Delors posed, especially his suggestions that politicians should not seek refuge in compromises 'in an attempt to escape the basic issue of what we intend to do together'.[6] For the US the fundamentals centred on three points: that there should be no European caucus inside NATO; no marginalization of non-EC members of NATO; and no alternative European military organization.[7] In setting out what were in essence preconditions for continued US involvement in Europe, the US intervention very quickly turned European arguments for an independent defence organization into something much weaker, a European Security and Defence Identity (ESDI), thus shifting the debate from questions of European autonomy to various options for the Europeanization of NATO. The intervention by the Bush administration therefore proved decisive in setting the parameters, if not the final outcome, of the debate over 'European security architecture' – the phrase implying the need for redesign rather than for a new European construction. To this end, US policymakers and officials used the legitimizing discourse of creating a European pillar of NATO to justify the primacy of the transatlantic alliance. Underpinning this reaction was the determination of the Bush administration to use NATO as a platform for continued US influence over the reintegration of the CEECs into the West, over developments in Russia and the Former Soviet Union (FSU), and over regional emergencies outside Europe, particularly in the Middle East.[8]

In the spring and early summer of 1991, the debate on European security architecture crystallized around two aspects of how defence and foreign policy might be associated with the European integration project. The first issue was whether WEU should be directly subordinated to the European Council, or whether it should retain institutional autonomy. The principle at stake was whether the WEU should form a permanent 'bridge' linking the European Union and NATO, as the British and Dutch governments argued, or should it serve, as France (supported by Italy, Belgium and Spain) argued, as a 'ferry' gradually transporting its defence functions from WEU to the European

Union.[9] The second issue was whether the WEU would acquire an operational capability, with the right to operate within as well as outside the NATO area, or merely remain an institutional forum for discussions among European defence and foreign ministers. Behind this issue lay the question of whether WEU should develop into an alternative defence organization to NATO. For pro-integration, 'maximalist' EU member states, the Europeanization of NATO was a necessary, but not a sufficient condition for the creation of a European security and defence identity.

Partial resolution of these issues came when American and British officials successfully pressed for an early decision on reshaping NATO's force structure, in advance of the Alliance's Strategic Review to be announced in autumn 1991.[10] Publicly they argued that speed was of the essence, since NATO's integrated military command – the backbone of the organization – was under enormous pressure as governments scrambled to deliver a peace dividend. In private they hoped that an early decision on Europeanization of NATO would pre-empt Franco-German moves to create an independent European defence structure, and refocus debate on creating a ESDI inside NATO.[11] Accordingly, in May 1991, defence ministers announced that NATO had agreed to reshape its organization away from the deployment of national corps along the inner German border to a new, multinational and more flexible structure. Its centrepiece was to be a new multinational Alliance Rapid Reaction Corps (ARRC), capable of deployment outside the NATO area, commanded by the British with the Germans in command of the air component.[12]

In an effort to regain the initiative, Mitterrand and Kohl announced in October their personal decision to expand the Franco-German Brigade to create a 'Euro' Corps – an embryonic army that would be placed at the disposal of the European Union.[13] However, believing that it had secured the primacy of Alliance structures in the realm of European defence, the British government now joined with the Italian government to announce that it was prepared to accept that the European Union should have as a long-term objective the creation of a common defence policy on matters concerned with general threats to Western Europe, and a common security policy on matters concerned with confidence building measures, proliferation, and export of arms technology. The British continued to insist, however, that the European Union should not consider defence matters – issues concerned with command structures and the deployment of military forces – that might challenge the role of NATO.[14]

This theological debate between two essentially contradictory positions was quickly overshadowed by events taking place outside the IGC. The invasion of Kuwait in August 1990 and the Gulf war which followed demonstrated that, irrespective of member states' aspirations, the WEU and its members lacked the political coherence and the military capabilities to act in most operations outside the NATO area without the United States.[15] On the other hand, American insistence that management of the developing conflict within

Yugoslavia, in spring and summer 1991, was a West European responsibility demonstrated that West European governments could no longer rely upon US political leadership as a matter of course.

In the face of these external pressures, a degree of convergence began to emerge between the major European protagonists about the need for West Europeans to do more for their own defence, but falling short of an autonomous European defence organization separate from NATO. In June 1991, EU foreign ministers quickly moved beyond the traditional instruments of EPC and deployed peace monitors in former Yugoslavia – compelled by the necessity for rapid decisionmaking to combine EPC and Community competences into a single decision. Following heated discussion at the NATO Rome Summit on 7–8 November 1991, moreover, there was finally agreement on the new NATO Strategic Concept, which approved the development of European multilateral forces within NATO but pledged that NATO would remain Europe's primary defence organization.[16]

It was against the backdrop of the Rome NATO declaration that the argument on CFSP was resumed at the IGC. What resulted was an ambiguous package-deal solution which satisfied every government a little, but no one government completely.[17] In a rhetorical flourish to satisfy the Europeanists, the signatories claimed in the opening clauses of the Treaty that the EU 'hereby establishes a common foreign and security policy' (Article J.1). In fact, no such policy existed. The detailed text and implementing articles were acceptable to the British government and its allies precisely because the national veto was untouched and because the negotiations left the most difficult decisions to be addressed in a future Intergovernmental Conference, to be convened in 1996. For the maximalists, the Maastricht Treaty transformed EPC into CFSP; it allowed the Union to move beyond 'common positions' to the possibility of undertaking 'joint actions' in the foreign policy sphere (Article J.3), but established complicated procedural mechanisms to carry these out and left open how they might be funded.

In the defence field, the treaty was equally ambiguous, suggesting that member states would move from the formulation of common foreign and security policy to 'the eventual framing of a common defence policy, which might in time lead to a common defence' (Article J.4.1). Although a revitalized WEU was to become the defence arm of the European Union and the European pillar of NATO, foreign ministers meeting in the forum of the Council of Ministers were only permitted to request, rather than instruct, WEU to carry out defence actions (Article J.4.2). A 'Declaration' on WEU attached to the treaty created an operational planning cell and moved the civilian secretariat to Brussels, to be nearer NATO, the Commission and Council Secretariat. There was, however, no mention of what forces might come under WEU command, or where they might operate. The final element of the reactivation of WEU was to offer 'full' or 'observer' membership to all EU member states and 'associated' status to European members of NATO who were not in the EC. In one sense, a reactivated WEU became an institutional 'half-way house', the defence arm of the European Union and the European pillar of NATO. In reality, this compromise did little more than to codify existing practices, including some new practices which had been forced on governments by external events during the year-long negotiations.[18] However it satisfied the more maximalist states, in so far as they placed greater value on establishing a political commitment to the idea of a European defence organization and an EU common foreign and security policy than on particular procedural methods to achieve them.

During 1992–96, West European governments and the United States attempted both to implement and to build upon the arrangements that they had hastily mapped out in 1991. The continuing disintegration of Yugoslavia soon exposed the weak foundations of the compromises so painstakingly crafted during 1991. The confrontation between Germany and its EU partners over EU recognition of Croatia, between December 1991 and January 1992, immediately highlighted the fragility of CFSP procedures when confronted with deeply-held national positions. The EU's grudging support in January 1992 for the German position in favour of rapid recognition was followed by German support for a French and British-led proposal to impose an arms embargo on the sovereign governments in Zagreb and Sarajevo, which were battling to establish their newly-recognized independence. Thus, aside from dispatching an EU police force to Mostar, the new CFSP concentrated, after 1991, on preventing disunity among EU members towards the crisis in Bosnia, but failed to develop proactive common policies to try to resolve the situation. Throughout the Bosnian crisis, EU governments revealed that they lacked the commonality of views, the shared sense of purpose and the necessary military capabilities to manage this complex crisis collectively. Not only did they appear to miss America's ability to mediate and to lead, it also became clear that attempting to manage such a crisis independently of the United States carried risks of exposing dangerous transatlantic rifts. But for the Americans, too, there were lessons to be learned, and the conclusion drawn was that leadership and influence could not be exerted from the sidelines. The US administration and Congress recognized the consequences of this lesson when they grudgingly agreed to include US forces in the UN intervention force despatched to implement the Dayton accords.

In the months which followed the conclusion of the Maastricht Treaty, NATO, WEU, and national officials laboured out of the limelight to define an effective post-cold war relationship between the two organizations, aware that there were only four years before the whole issue would be reopened at the 1996 IGC. In Brussels, the delay in ratifying the Treaty on European Union was one factor leading the WEU to develop stronger links with NATO than with the EU; another was the good personal relationship between the two secretaries-general, Manfred Wörner (NATO) and Wim van Eekelen (WEU).[19] From early 1994 onwards, an acceptable division of responsibilities between a revamped NATO and a revived WEU gradually emerged.[20] Compromises were assisted by the economic recession of 1992–95 and the drive to meet the tough economic criteria for monetary union, which forced France and its Europeanist supporters to reassess the viability of building a more self-sufficient European military force structure. On the other hand, Bill Clinton's arrival in the White House led to a relaxation in US resistance to an enhanced European defence effort. His administration's aim was to enable West European governments to take on greater responsibility for confronting crises around Europe's periphery, while trying to ensure that this greater activism was channelled through NATO, thus permitting the United States to continue to influence the course of events.

The compromise between Atlanticists and those who advocated a stronger ESDI centred on the concept of the Combined Joint Task Force (CJTF), launched by the Americans at the NATO Brussels Summit in January 1994 and approved two years later in June 1996 at the Berlin Summit. CJTFs would allow West European governments to form 'coalitions of the willing', using national forces assigned to NATO, but also with the right to request the use of NATO's headquarters, command facilities, communications systems, and logistical support for non-NATO WEU missions. Acceptance of the CJTF concept represented a significant scaling back of Europeanist ambitions for some form of autonomous defence organization, not least because most European countries were unwilling to make the necessary financial commitment to realize this aim. At the same time it marked a concerted push by the Americans after the Bosnia debacle to introduce a military structure that better reflected their own desire to combine a reduced military involvement in West European security with a continued close participation in the military planning and political consultation associated with future European military operations.

In summary, the package agreed at the 1996 Berlin summit was, like the Rome NATO declaration and new strategic concept of 1991, a compromise between the French and American positions, with the German and British governments mediating between the two. It anchored the ESDI within NATO, in return for accepting a more sharply-defined European pillar within the alliance. On this basis the French government would rejoin the integrated military structure, from which President de Gaulle had withdrawn thirty years before. There was also to be a further restructuring of NATO's commands, to enhance the European role. With British and German officers serving in senior posts in NATO's northern and central commands, the French hoped that they might claim NATO's southern command, in Naples, which covered the central and eastern Mediterranean, and included the US Sixth Fleet and substantial American air forces. While delicate negotiations were still under way about a potential shared command, President Chirac made this a formal and public demand; and the Americans, for whom the eastern Mediterranean and the Middle East had become strategically the most important area since the end of the cold war, refused to concede. This public dispute, in which both status and substance were at stake, blocked French re-entry into the NATO integrated military structure.

Partly because of this, French hopes of promoting their preferred definition of ESDI during the 1996 IGC came to naught.[21] Despite a widespread feeling that CFSP procedures had failed to facilitate an effective EU response to international crises, both in Bosnia and subsequently in Albania, and despite pressure from the Commission and European Parliament, the Amsterdam Treaty of June 1997 offered only institutional tinkering, without changing the fundamentals of the existing decisionmaking structure, or ending the formal separation of the WEU and EU.[22]

Thus the debate over Europe's new security architecture had shrunk back to a continuation of the long-running Franco-American dispute over the restructuring of the Atlantic alliance. Pan-European structures, to bring Russia as well as the lands in between Germany and Russia into a common institutional framework, had faded from intergovernmental discussions. The attractions of the 'peace dividend' to governments struggling to maintain welfare states and to balance budgets were stronger than any ambitions to play a larger security role. A majority of West European governments preferred to maintain the established institutional arrangements, with the underlying bargain that West European states accepted American security leadership through NATO in return for a continuing US military commitment to the European region. This attachment to the institutional status quo was strengthened by the divergent national views of the key protagonists as to the benefits and losses associated with change. The result was that references to the need to build a 'European defence' dissipated into an acceptance of incremental change that would neither upset the existing institutional structure nor force clear defeats on governments with very different approaches.

The process of European integration

The debate over Europe's future security architecture was not the only one to expose significantly different approaches among West European governments over post-cold war institutional reform. Nor was it the only one to result in largely incremental rather than revolutionary change. In the early part of 1990, most EC member governments came to the conclusion that the end of the cold war, far from demanding a radical overhaul of the European Community, made it imperative that EC member states focus first on accelerating the pre-existing agenda of political, economic and institutional integration. In essence, this meant that the intergovernmental negotiations in 1990–91 leading up to the Maastricht Treaty were concerned primarily with securing a continuation of the old West European order, rather than with an attempt to build a new European order that would bridge the divide between the West and eastern halves of Europe.[23] The British, even more incremental in their approach, resisted this conclusion without proposing any alternative strategy.

Agreement among other governments on the general strategy did not mean, however, that West European leaders found it easy to reach consensus on the best ways to deepen West European integration. President Mitterrand placed greatest emphasis on incorporating a watertight timetable for the launch of economic and monetary union (EMU) into the Maastricht Treaty, seeing in EMU an effective constraint on future German economic power. A proposal which had initially been promoted as the logical completion of the single market, now took on an additional strategic dimension. Chancellor Kohl saw the acceptance of the French timetable for monetary union as part of a package of measures to reassure Germany's partners that Bonn wanted a 'European Germany and not a German Europe'.[24] In return, however, Bonn hoped that the parallel IGC on Political Union would strengthen the popular legitimacy of the EU, by enhancing the role of the European Parliament and by extending the use of majority voting in the Council of Ministers.[25] To the Belgian, Dutch and Spanish governments, as well as to the Germans, the IGC negotiations also presented an opportunity to integrate a number of informal existing practices and sub-systems of the EC (European Political Cooperation and the Trevi Group) into one institutional framework.[26] These more 'integrationist' member states, in common with the Commission and the European Parliament, argued for the creation of a single institutional structure: a 'tree' in which the common institutions – Council, Commission, Court, and Parliament – formed the trunk, with foreign and security policy and justice and home affairs (JHA), as added branches.

President Mitterrand defined 'political union' rather differently, focusing primarily on establishing intergovernmental management of a common foreign and security policy.[27] British ministers, while sharing many of the French concerns about rapid German unification, were opposed to any significant steps towards Political Union. However, they were fearful of the consequences of exclusion, and, for this reason, joined the French government in offering an alternative metaphor of the European Union as a more intergovernmental 'temple'. The 'temple' proposal, far from being a revolutionary alternative, derived from the Gaullist Fouchet plans of the early 1960s.[28] EU discussion of CFSP and justice and home affairs would take place under separate intergovernmental 'pillars' alongside the established European Community, from which the Court would be excluded and where the Commission and Parliament would have only limited influence.

To reconcile these approaches, the Luxembourg presidency presented a draft treaty in June 1991, under which existing EC competencies would form the first pillar of the new European Union; this would include greater use of majority voting, with enhanced co-decision powers for the EP, as sought by the German government and other pro-integrationists. The second (CFSP) and third (JHA) pillars would use essentially intergovernmental procedural mechanisms, as sought by the French and British.[29] After a concerted Dutch effort to reverse this structure was rebuffed in September, the European Council endorsed the temple structure at the Maastricht summit in December. Reflecting the awkward nature of the compromise, EU heads of government included an undertaking to review the Treaty in 1996, with a view to *'communautarizing'* the two intergovernmental pillars.[30]

The most significant achievement of the Maastricht summit was the agreement on a fixed timetable for the establishment of economic and monetary union. In the Treaty on European Union all EU members, save the British and (subsequently) the Danish, pledged to form a monetary union at the latest by 1 January 1999 among those member states who were deemed by the Commission to have met a set of five economic criteria by mid 1998.[31] The European Central Bank (ECB), a new supranational institution, would be responsible for managing the single currency and for establishing monetary policy for EMU members, including setting interest rates and the exchange rate of the new currency. The Maastricht Treaty also established a new 'Cohesion Fund', to provide additional financial assistance to those poorer EU members states who would have to make the greatest structural efforts to meet the Maastricht EMU criteria.

The unification of Germany had provided the political context for the 1991 IGC: reinforcing the determination of Germany's neighbours to lock the German economy irrevocably into a monetary union and extending the ambitions of West European integration in foreign policy and defence. Further than that, the implications of the revolutions of 1989–91 were left off the agenda. The policy and institutional implications of further enlargement were deliberately excluded. In the context of 1990–91, enlargement in the first instance did not mean looking ahead to the long-term prospect of Polish or Hungarian membership, even though representatives of their post-socialist regimes were pressing their claims as they travelled around from capital to capital, but accepting the candidacies of those West European EFTA member states (Austria, Finland, Sweden and potentially Norway and Switzerland) which were moving from negotiating closer association to pressing for full membership. The orientation and aims of the Maastricht Treaty on European Union (TEU) focused on the existing members, striking a new package deal among the EU's core member states.

There was however a substantial gap between the ambitions and rhetoric of the Treaty and its reality. Even as the Treaty was ratified, the economic recession deepened, with German government borrowing to finance the costs of unification driving up interest rates across Europe. As levels of unemployment and government debt began to climb across the EU, many of the bargains agreed at Maastricht appeared to be on the verge of unravelling. At the Edinburgh summit in December 1992, net contributors to the EU budget resisted the rise in the EU budgetary ceiling necessary to accommodate the EU's new Cohesion Fund. In August 1993, the ERM collapsed as international financial institutions challenged the commitment of the French government to maintain its high parity with the Deutschmark in the lead up to monetary union, while suffering from growing unemployment and low levels of economic growth. Following close on the ejection of Italy and the United Kingdom from the ERM in October 1992, the subsequent agreement to rescue the ERM by widening the acceptable level of fluctuation between European currencies appeared to call into question the ability of EU member states to meet the stringent conditions set at Maastricht for monetary union.[32]

The increasingly precarious position of the Conservative government in London added a further dimension to post-Maastricht instability. Not only did the British government become more sceptical about deeper European integration, but it also became more inclined to rock the boat, allowing underlying tensions among other EU member states to come to the fore.[33] Blocking tactics began to extend beyond the British to other states, especially following the election victory in France of Jacques Chirac in May 1995. Indeed, Chirac's decision to suspend the Schengen Convention in a dispute with Holland over its drug laws, combined with Spanish concerns about obstacles to intra-EU extradition, to undermine the likelihood of the EU's third pillar being subsumed into the first, irrespective of British reservations.

Difficulties and delays caused by domestic politics in the United Kingdom and Denmark (and also in Greece) led many within the original six member states to question the compatibility of maintaining the *acquis* of West European integration even within the existing 12-member EU, let alone within a wider and more diverse community. Similar difficulties and delays within France, however, threatened the core of the community and of the *acquis*: the close relationship between France and Germany round which West European integration had been constructed. As the prospect of a wider, transformed Europe opened up, West European élites, therefore, became preoccupied with maintaining and reinforcing a narrower Europe: a tightly-integrated core, round which a wider group of peripheral states might be more loosely gathered. The Schäuble-Lamers paper of September 1994, discussed in more detail in Chapter 3, emphasized the dangers of France and Germany drifting apart, as northern states with close ties to Germany joined the EU, while problems in the Mediterranean preoccupied the French. The paper looked to a tighter core group – with the relegation of other current members to an outer circle – as the way forward. The deviant behaviour of the British, the Danes and the Greeks within the existing EU would thus be contained, by allowing them to opt out of closer co-operation while an inner group moved on to monetary union and from there, perhaps, towards a European federation.

In this 'core Europe' discourse, any further enlargement represented a threat, not only to hopes of closer integration but even to what had been achieved so far. Hardly surprisingly, preparations for further enlargement did not attract much attention in these introverted discussions on the EU's future direction. Nevertheless, the dynamic of negotiations carried three of the five EFTA candidates (Austria, Finland and Sweden) into the EU in January 1995, while in successive European Councils EU heads of government were giving ground to the demands of post-socialist regimes to be offered a road map towards eventual membership. It was with some reluctance and confusion of purpose, therefore, that member governments in the second half of 1995 embarked on preparations for a further IGC, to which they were committed under the terms of the TEU.

After several months of negotiation, a 'Reflection Group' of senior national officials laid out in December 1995 the parameters for the 1996 IGC, combining a range of proposals that had been circulating in national capitals since the last IGC. These included extending the scope of majority voting, simplifying the decisionmaking procedures between the Council and the European Parliament, cutting the size of the Commission, recalibrating the voting weight in the Council of Ministers more closely to national population levels, doing away with the system of rotating six-month Council presidencies, and improving decisionmaking under the CFSP.[34]

All of these proposals were presented as improvements in the EU's institutions and procedures in themselves. But they would also ease the EU's adjustment to further enlargement. The British and other governments had accepted an extension of majority voting in the 1986 Single European Act as a necessary corollary to enlargement of the EC from 10 to 12; effective decisionmaking in an EU of 18–20 would require further concessions.

'Maastricht Two', as this follow-on IGC was often labelled, was formally convened by the Turin European Council in March 1996.[35] The Irish government, which succeeded the Italians in the presidency, was mandated to present a draft treaty for the Dublin European Council of December 1996, with an open deadline for completion of the final treaty.[36] Worsening relations between the British Conservative government and its partners, however, led to displacement of the Reflection Group's proposals by negotiations on 'flexibility' and 'closer co-operation': pursuing the concept of a core group which would move ahead, sidelining uncooperative member states and preventing new members from slowing down the intended pace of further integration.[37] The concept of flexibility initially drew wide support. It appeared to endorse the selective approach to integration which had enabled the British government to opt out of the Maastricht provisions for EMU and the then eleven to opt in to the Social Chapter. It therefore promised to solve the British problem both for the British and their more pro-European partners.[38] At the same time, flexibility would permit the French and Germans to negate the inevitable pressures for dilution that would accompany future EU enlargements and to continue their search for a more politically integrated relationship within the EU.

As the negotiation proceeded, however, two fundamental obstacles emerged to undermine the concept of 'flexibility'. First, Article N of the TEU stated that groups of countries could only deepen their integration within the EU's institutional framework providing this received the unanimous support of all EU members, irrespective of their interest in participating. In a clear challenge to this principle, Kohl and Chirac argued that the IGC should amend the Treaty of Rome to remove this right of veto. Fearful of the idea of an exclusive Franco-German liaison at the heart of Europe, however, a number of states, with the British and the Spanish in the lead, challenged the Franco-German position. Secondly, EU members and the Commission could not explain how they would overcome the procedural complexity of having a single institutional framework oversee relationships between states involved in increasingly different levels of legal and political integration. A number of commentators foresaw a European Union riven by a new series of economic and political divisions.[39]

By the close of 1996, the dilemma facing the EU was clear. EU members had to decide whether to proceed as the Commission and a number of EU member states advocated and implement radical and wide-ranging reform of the EU in 1997, so that the EU would be prepared institutionally for future enlargements. Alternatively, the IGC could be relegated into a more modest affair, offering 'flexibility' as a way to bypass temporarily the need for far-reaching EU institutional reform and leaving key structural and decisionmaking reforms to be decided either at the time of, or shortly after, the next EU enlargement, whenever that might be. Just as the 1991 IGC had ended by postponing a number of difficult issues until a later conference, so the 1996–97 IGC was drifting towards a further postponement of strategic decisions.

Towards the close of 1996, the latter approach gained growing support. This was not simply the product of institutional inertia. In 1996, as in 1991, the debate over EU political reform was shadowed by a parallel and increasingly heated negotiation over the future of monetary union. As the French, German and other EU governments sought to come to final agreement on the mechanics of launching and living with EMU, the fear grew that a simultaneous effort to force through large-scale institutional reform in the IGC might overload the EU agenda and hamper the crucial preparations for the launch of EMU.

This eclipse of the 1996 IGC reflected an emerging awareness that EMU represented the sort of core EU bargain that had been lacking at Maastricht; a bargain that offered a truly revolutionary step forward for the EU integration process. It had the advantage that it was based upon an economic consensus that predated the end of the cold war and German unification. EMU also appeared to constitute a bold collective response (as had the Single European Act) to an external threat: the EU's continuing loss of global economic competitiveness during the late 1980s and early 1990s. On the one hand, meeting the EMU criteria would force EU governments to start cutting excessive government spending and tackle the non-wage costs of labour. On the other hand, the formation of an EU monetary core could also offer the

French, German and other continental EU governments a co-operative political framework within which they could work to sustain the important social bargains that were the source of their domestic political legitimacy. Finally, for many pro-integrationists, it was clear that EMU, not further negotiations on EU institutional reform, offered the best prospect for leading to a European Political Union among the core West European states.[40]

As was the case with EU institutional reform, however, the preparations for EMU revealed a fundamental difference in approach between France and Germany, the two countries who had struck the initial bargain over monetary union. For Chancellor Kohl, with his eye on the 1998 election campaign, it was imperative that the Deutschmark be replaced by a currency that would not erode German savings or draw the German economy into a weakly-managed and inflation-prone currency zone. In order to avoid such an eventuality, Theo Waigel proposed, in spring 1996, that all prospective EU members sign up to a 'Stability Pact' that would commit governments to sustain the fiscal prudence of the Maastricht criteria into the foreseeable future. For Chirac and the French government, on the other hand, it was imperative that EU governments be given the means to serve as a political counterweight to the new EU Central Bank. In the long-term, this would enable the French government to exercise joint leadership over Europe's economic management. In the near-term, the government could try to prevent the new ECB from continuing the Bundesbank's tight monetary policy which French officials believed was partly responsible for France's and the EU's high unemployment levels. Waigel's proposed Stability Pact threatened to limit seriously the government's room for manoeuvre in the fiscal realm while leaving the Bundesbank with complete authority over monetary policy.

The Franco-German dispute over the future management of the single currency came to a head at the Dublin European Council in December 1996. The compromise solution offered by the Irish presidency enshrined the fiscal targets sought by the German government and backed these with a schedule of financial penalties for delinquent governments, but that ensured that these penalties, far from being automatic, would require a majority vote by member states and would be waived if an EMU member entered into an economic recession. This compromise was further refined after the victory of the socialist government in the French parliamentary elections of June 1997, when Lionel Jospin insisted on rechristening the pact as the 'Stability and Growth Pact' and accepted a special EU summit on job creation later in the year.

With the terms of economic and monetary union dominating the attention of senior EU leaders during this period, it was hardly surprising that the Amsterdam Treaty fell far short of the original ambitions of the Reflection Group report. As noted above, EU leaders made only cosmetic changes to the functioning of the EU's CFSP. In addition, aside from a modest extension of qualified majority voting, EU leaders chose to adopt none of the proposed institutional reforms. In the place of hard choices, EU governments appended a protocol to the Amsterdam Treaty which pledged that at least one year before the membership of the EU exceeded twenty states, EU members would convene another IGC to adopt those institutional reforms that had been neglected in Amsterdam.

Redrawing the boundaries of European order

In June 1997, when the Commission submitted its 'Opinions' on the applications for EU membership from the CEECs, it appeared that the EU's commitment to an eastern enlargement would challenge many of the internal bargains upon which the European Union was based. From the outset, however, the fact that West European governments chose not to alter fundamentally the existing institutional division between European security and economic affairs meant that their response also progressed down separate, if parallel, institutional tracks. The EU took on the role of economic leadership, while the United States, through NATO, became the principal protagonist in extending the West's security umbrella over these countries. Unfortunately, this division of labour caused increasing tension between the United States and Europe as time progressed.

Integrating the East into the European Union

Between 1945 and 1988, West European governments had maintained only the most superficial ties with their east European neighbours.[41] Only in June 1988, in the wake of the reform process inspired by Gorbachev's policies of 'glasnost' and 'perestroika', did the European Community and Comecon sign a Declaration of Mutual Recognition. As Communist governments dramatically fell from power during the popular revolutions of 1989, the EC was in the process of completing a series of limited Trade and Cooperation Agreements with Comecon members that would formalize the stunted economic relationship that had grown up under cold war conditions. Suddenly, West European governments and the Community had to rethink completely their approach towards central and eastern Europe.

At the G-7 summit in Paris in July 1989, the United States and its European allies agreed to establish the 'Phare' programme of grant assistance for Poland and Hungary.[42] Under US and German pressure, the G-7 handed responsibility for co-ordinating the emergency grants from G-24 countries to the European Commission, in a clear sign of the lead role that the Community, and not Germany alone or the United States, should play in reintegrating the two halves of Europe.[43] But developing a more strategic West European response beyond emergency assistance proved a far more complex process. On 18 November 1989, a little over a week after the fall of the Berlin Wall, President Mitterrand, then holder of the EU presidency, hurriedly invited EC heads of government to a dinner at the Elysée to discuss developments in central and eastern Europe. They agreed upon two proposals: to create a European Bank to help with reconstruction and development in the east (later named the European Bank for Reconstruction and Development, the EBRD) and to task the Commission with preparations for the negotiation of EC association agreements with the most eligible of the new democracies.[44]

As West European governments and the Commission struggled to put flesh on the bones of these proposals in the winter of 1989–90, differences in approach among West European leaders quickly became apparent. Fearful lest the continuing process of West European integration would block speedy unification between east and west Germany, Chancellor Kohl and his Foreign Minister Dietrich Genscher made vocal appeals for the rapid enlargement of the European Community towards the east.[45] They were supported by the British and Dutch governments.[46] Mitterrand, however, took a diametrically opposed view, arguing that enlarging the EC should only be tackled once the Community had looked inwards and prepared itself for the post-cold war environment through deepening the process of West European integration.[47]

The differences between the French and German governments were narrowed when in spring 1990, Mitterrand agreed to French support for rapid German unification in return for German support, in principle, for monetary union. With EU leaders now becoming increasingly preoccupied with the political and procedural complexities of the IGCs on Political and on Monetary Union, it was the External Affairs Directorate of the Commission (DGI) which took the lead, submitting a bold EC Action Plan to the Dublin European Council in April 1990. This envisaged the speedy negotiation of a series of far-reaching Association Agreements (later renamed 'Europe' agreements) with the new European democracies which would propel these countries to the top of the EC's trading 'pyramid of privilege'.[48] It also foresaw the creation of a genuine free trade area between western and eastern Europe, spanning not only trade in goods, but also in services and capital. The Action Plan explicitly made clear, however, that the question of enlargement would be postponed to a later date.

EU Foreign Ministers endorsed the Commission's Action Plan in September 1990. At that point Hungary, Poland and Czechoslovakia were the only three countries that had clearly established transitional regimes and were, therefore, ready to enter into immediate negotiations with the EU. It quickly became apparent, however, that DGI's vision of a broad-based free trade agreement with these countries threatened to impose potentially serious financial costs on some specific EU sectors, countries and long-established economic regimes. Under pressure from national officials and representatives of sectoral Commission DGs, the EU's negotiating mandate was reduced,[49] and by summer 1991, the negotiations between the EU and the prospective Associate countries had reached an impasse. This stalemate was only broken when the failed Soviet putsch of 19 August 1991 highlighted the fragility of the reform process in the former Soviet bloc. EC foreign ministers now agreed at an emergency meeting on 20 August to improve their negotiating position towards the three central European countries (CE3), granting CE3 producers gradual access to EC markets in their 'sensitive' sectors.

It soon became apparent that the value of the agreements lay less in their economic detail than in the framework they established to manage the political and economic integration of the western and eastern halves of Europe. Once the agreements had been initialled on 17 December 1991, recalcitrant EU member governments found it harder to resist the steady external pressure for the EU as a whole to take concrete steps to open its markets and to make clear commitments to bring its eastern neighbours within a reasonable timescale into full membership.[50] At the Copenhagen European Council in June 1993, EU leaders decided to resurrect the concept first proposed by Commissioner Frans Andriessen of encouraging a multilateral political dialogue between the EU and the associated CEECs, including enlarged meetings of the European Council and of EU foreign ministers meeting under the auspices of the CFSP provisions.[51] This approach, christened the 'structured relationship', was formally approved and put into practice at the European Council in Essen in December 1994.[52]

The preamble to the Europe Agreements had stated that 'the final objective' of the associated countries was to become members of the Community, and indeed that 'this association, in the view of the Parties, will help to achieve this objective'.[53] This statement provided the legal platform for declarations in the European Council summits of Lisbon (June 1992) and Edinburgh (December 1992) that made gradually more explicit the EU's commitment to enlargement. The position was formalized at the Copenhagen Council with the statement that 'the associated countries in Central and Eastern Europe that so desire shall become members of the European Union'.[54]

This softening of the EU's initially reluctant attitude towards enlargement had several causes, not least of which was the personal crusade by Chancellor Kohl, supported most openly by the British and Italian governments and the Commission, to set the process of EU enlargement to the east firmly on track after 1992. As later chapters discuss, this was an initiative which other governments, including the French, chose not to resist. The ability of national officials from domestic ministries, protecting the interests of their client groups, to slow the momentum towards enlargement was also limited by the comprehensive scope of the Europe Agreements. The Commission's unprecedented inclusion of 'third pillar' issues such as co-ordination on anti-narcotics policy and border controls meant that the Commission was able to present the European Council at Essen in December 1994 with a 'pre-accession' strategy that deviated little from the structure of the existing Europe Agreements and, therefore, only required minimal internal debate.[55] The question of EU enlargement, far from being an 'up or down' decision, had become a gradual and self-reinforcing process – progressing from the Europe Agreements, to pledges of membership, to pre-accession strategies.

On the other hand, precisely because EU enlargement had become a multi-tiered process, there was a growing frustration both in central and east European capitals and in Washington that accession, although guaranteed in principle, would remain out of reach for many years. This concern was exacerbated by the conditions for accession imposed by the Copenhagen European Council, which included the economic requirement of a 'functioning market economy as well as the capacity to cope with the competitive pressures and market forces within the Union'. This appeared unduly harsh given the supposedly political rationale for the EU's decision to enlarge eastwards and that such demands had not been made of Spain, Portugal and Greece in the mid 1980s.[56] Rather than helping the applicants adapt to some of the more exacting challenges of EU membership from inside the Union, the EU expected and required the CEECs to adapt first, albeit with technical assistance from an expanded Phare programme.[57]

Finally, the concerns of CEEC governments were heightened further by the explicit linkage established first in Copenhagen and then at the Madrid European Council in December 1995 between enlargement and EU internal reform.[58] The Madrid conclusions, while asking the Commission to 'expedite preparation of its Opinions', made it clear that the Opinions should only be delivered 'after the conclusion of the Intergovernmental Conference'. In addition, the Madrid conclusions requested that the Commission produce an evaluation of the impact of enlargement on Community policies, especially the CAP and structural policies, and on the future 'financial framework of the Union'. These conclusions, while understandable from an EU planning perspective, threatened to shackle the pace of enlargement to the ability of EU governments to arrive first at difficult compromises on internal EU institutional reform and second on a revision of the EU's highly contentious agricultural and financial assistance policies.

Enlarging NATO

Despite the growing US frustration with the pace of the EU's enlargement process, the debate over whether and how to integrate the CEECs into western Europe's primary security institution – NATO – followed a surprisingly similar path between 1990–95. For the majority of CEECs, accession to the EU, although fundamental to their future economic prosperity and political stability, was insufficient to exorcise the fear of a revanchist Russia. NATO was the only organization that appeared to offer an effective guarantee against any future Russian aggression.

Accession to NATO, however, was fraught with political difficulty. The Bush administration was anxious to move quickly after the fall of the Berlin Wall to help stabilize Eastern Europe and to minimize the institutional isolation of the CEECs. US policymakers saw NATO as a useful adjunct to the EU in this respect, but did not foresee NATO enlargement as a viable option in the near-term, especially after the difficult process of persuading Russian leaders to accept united Germany's entry into NATO. Instead, under US instigation, NATO leaders meeting in Rome in December 1991 decided to establish the North Atlantic Cooperation Council (NACC), which provided a forum under NATO's aegis for former members of the Warsaw Pact to discuss military matters and security concerns with NATO members. Although this was well received, it still fell far short of the aspirations of CEEC governments.

The United States found itself caught in a growing domestic dilemma on this issue after the arrival of the Clinton administration in the White House in January 1993. On the one hand, President Clinton and his policy advisers highlighted the spread and consolidation of democracy world-wide as the central plank of US post-cold war foreign policy.[59] On the other hand, the US State Department, with the new Deputy Secretary of State Strobe Talbott taking the lead, placed the consolidation of democracy in Russia at the centre of this world view. Talbott shared the concerns of a majority of West European governments that any discussion of NATO enlargement before Russia stabilized its reform process could be highly counterproductive.[60]

Under increasing external and domestic pressure, especially after Republicans seized both Houses of the US Congress in November 1994, US officials struggled to come up with a solution that would satisfy these conflicting interests. After intensive negotiations between US Supreme Allied Commander in Europe General John Shalikashvilli and Pentagon officials, the US government presented to the Brussels NATO summit of January 1994 a proposal for a series of 'Partnership for Peace' agreements (PfPs) with NATO's former Warsaw Pact enemies. This was an artful compromise. On the one hand, PfPs further postponed the issue of NATO enlargement, on the other hand they provided a formal framework for greater military co-ordination and exercises between NATO and non-NATO European countries. They therefore gave hope that those east European countries that signed the agreements, and worked to put into practice their stipulations for military interoperability with NATO and for civilian control of the military, would be in a position to join NATO as soon as the political will to take this step coalesced in the West. The PfP agreements served a parallel purpose to the EU's Europe Agreements, therefore, being interpreted both as an alternative to and as a first step towards NATO membership.

Influential US commentators such as Brzezinski and Kissinger were unimpressed by this apparent fudge on the NATO enlargement question, while Republicans in the US Congress and Senate ushered through a series of declaratory acts placing on the record their support for NATO enlargement.[61] In western Europe, however, there was greater support for the proposals, since West European governments were ambivalent about an eastward extension of NATO's security guarantees. The French government for instance feared that NATO's initiatives would serve as a platform to extend US political influence into eastern Europe. Even traditional Atlanticist governments, such as the British, worried that an extension of NATO's security umbrella eastwards would undermine the military credibility and effectiveness of NATO.[62] However, ministers in the German government, most of all Defence Minister Volker Rühe, argued in favour of a rapid NATO enlargement. This activism coincided with a shift of approach within the Clinton administration, which moved (like its predecessor, the Bush administration) to regard Germany as its leading partner in managing post-cold war Europe. A Germany that felt more secure as a result of NATO enlargement could also be expected to shrug off some of its cold war reticence about proactive involvement in European security, and shoulder with the United States an important portion of the burdens not only of Russian stabilization but also of Europe's post-cold war defence.

In an effort to resolve these pressures for and against a more active NATO response to the CEECs, NATO members agreed at their summit in December 1994 to launch a study on NATO enlargement. This study, released in September 1995, discussed a number of issues to be resolved in the enlargement process, but essentially signalled the Alliance's agreement that enlargement would now proceed.[63] As with the EU's Copenhagen declaration, however, conditions were set out for accession, including an undertaking for new members to 'preserve the Alliance's political and military capability to perform its core functions of common defence', and settle any ethnic, territorial, or international disputes. Above all, however, it was made clear that Russia needed to be accommodated and on this point the study was stronger on rhetoric than the mechanics of accession.

The struggle to bring the two tracks together, 1995–97

Between 1995 and 1997, the two processes of EU and NATO enlargement moved forward significantly, but by no means in the co-ordinated manner that some had argued for.[64] Progress towards NATO enlargement was dramatic, but this owed more to a shift in the domestic debate in the United States than to any new Western strategic perspective. Following Boris Yeltsin's victory in the 1996 Russian presidential elections, competition for the votes of citizens of Polish and other East European ancestry became a key aspect of the US presidential election campaign of November the same year. This resulted in public and explicit pledges to enlarge NATO eastwards by the end of the century, which the re-elected Clinton administration quickly sought to honour in time for the NATO summit in Madrid in July 1997.

First, however, US officials had to enter into an intense negotiation with their Russian counterparts on a framework for future NATO–Russia relations in the context of an enlarged NATO. European governments were left largely on the sidelines of this negotiation, with US Defence Secretary Bill Perry at one point suggesting Russia's possible inclusion in all NATO structures save those associated with Article 5 provisions and the military structure.[65] After further US negotiation with the Russians, and consultation with the European NATO governments, the NATO–Russia Founding Act was signed in Paris on 27 May 1997. It created a new European security institution: the Permanent Joint Council (PJC). The PJC would meet monthly, to allow NATO members and the Russian government to consult, co-ordinate and where possible take joint actions on 'issues of common interest related to security and stability in the Euro-Atlantic area', including peacekeeping, arms control and proliferation.[66]

With the Founding Act signed, the Clinton administration turned its attention to the debates surrounding the issue of enlargement. A major source of disagreement was the issue of cost, not only to the applicants, but also to existing members who would have to adapt their force deployments as well as NATO's command, communications and logistical infrastructure to cover an expanded NATO area. US concerns over the costs were fanned by the widely differing estimates offered by the Congressional Budget Office and experts from the US RAND Corporation (commissioned by the US State Department).[67] In contrast to the earlier widespread congressional support for the idea of enlargement, the approach of the actual decision to enlarge NATO united a disparate set of opponents, ranging from 'cold warriors' who feared a loss of NATO's military effectiveness to 'liberals' who opposed the drawing of a new line of division through the heart of Europe and feared its impact on Russia's political evolution. Nevertheless, the Clinton government consistently argued the case for enlargement and prepared to formalize that commitment in Madrid.[68]

US officials took an equally tough stance in their meetings with their NATO Europe allies. They refused to compromise on their insistence that NATO's first enlargement should be limited to the three leading candidates, Poland, Hungary and the Czech Republic, arguing that these countries were the best prepared, while also pointing to the political reality that the US Congress would not ratify a larger number. US officials were not reticent either about promoting US policy as NATO policy. After the Bergen meeting of NATO defence ministers in September 1996, for example, Secretary Perry took it upon himself to inform representatives of the Baltic states that they were 'not yet ready' for NATO.[69]

The Madrid summit thus endorsed what was, to all intents and purposes, a non-negotiable US position, and NATO members formally invited Poland, Hungary and the Czech Republic to begin accession negotiations. In response to the failed French and Italian demands that Slovenia and Romania also be included in NATO's first enlargement wave, which had attracted the support of the majority of European NATO governments, the Madrid Communiqué recognized their specific progress towards democracy and the rule of law, and pledged to review their applications in 1999.[70] Most importantly, however, NATO leaders stated that their goal was to sign the Protocol of Accession by December 1997 and 'to see the ratification process completed in time for membership to become effective by the 50th Anniversary of the Washington Treaty in April 1999'. Thus, by mid 1997, NATO had taken the first definitive step towards extending its institutional boundary eastwards, marking an important stage in the evolution of a new European security order.

On the surface, the European Union appeared to make similar progress on the question of enlargement between 1995 and 1997. By the end of 1995, the list of potential EU entrants from the former socialist bloc had swelled to ten, to include the three Baltic states and all the CEECs, while excluding the countries west of the Urals but east of Poland (Ukraine, Moldova, Belarus and most importantly, Russia). Following the mandate it received from the Madrid European Council of December 1995, the Commission began to prepare its 'Opinions' on the applicants' requests to join the EU.[71] These Opinions were finally submitted to EU governments in July 1997, just nine days after the NATO Madrid summit decision on NATO enlargement, and to the surprise of many observers, proposed that the EU open negotiations not only with Poland, Hungary and the Czech Republic, but also with Estonia and Slovenia. The Commission judged that both the latter would meet both the political and the economic conditions established at Copenhagen within the 2002 timeframe for accession that it had unofficially been adopted.

The NATO and EU decisions in the summer of 1997 to enlarge and to identify their first wave of new entrants closed the first chapter in the West's efforts to expand its security and economic institutions to its eastern neighbours. The near-simultaneous timing of these two decisions, however, was largely fortuitous. The decisions were taken within separate institutional frameworks, under distinct sets of pressures. The NATO Secretariat and the European Commission and Council Secretariat were both in Brussels, three kilometres apart; but they might as well have been in different countries. Each had their separate permanent national representations, co-ordinating extensive networks of working groups and consultative committees. These, however, linked into separate domestic ministries in national capitals, co-ordinated respectively by political and economic directorates with national foreign ministries, with little overall direction below prime ministerial offices. Relations with the USA dominated the debate within NATO; multilateral consultations among West European governments shaped the EU response. As a result these two parallel but only half-co-ordinated decisions left a number of worrying questions unresolved.

First, NATO's so-called 'Open Door' policy was somewhat misleading. It remained highly doubtful whether the door would be open to the Baltic states, while even a more modest second enlargement in central Europe could only be achieved after consultation with Russia in the PJC, as well as another US congressional inquisition. At the same time, the EU's commitment to enlarge eastwards, and to embrace one of the Baltic states in the medium-term as well as the other Baltic and east European states in the longer-term, raised the possibility that WEU security guarantees (acquired through EU membership) would be extended by WEU members to non-NATO members.

Second, the submission of the Commission's Opinions was only the first step in what promised to be a tortuous process of enlargement for the EU. In contrast to NATO's pledge of a date to complete not only the negotiations, but also the ratification process, the EU had no formal timetable for enlargement. This was a reflection of the complexity of the upcoming negotiations with the applicants and the challenges they would face in adopting the EU's extensive *acquis*. But it also reflected the fact that EU enlargement negotiations, like all EU external negotiations, would require an extensive process of internal, intra-EU negotiation, with no clear hegemon to take the lead. Moreover, EU enlargement negotiations are far more complex than EU trade negotiations, since the Council must approve all related EU 'common positions' by unanimity.[72] During 1996–97, the Commission had prepared its Opinions largely in secret. Now, with the enlargement process officially launched, individual EU governments and national sectoral ministries were in a position to influence every detail of the EU's negotiating position.

The fundamental problem was that enlargement to the east threatened to undermine some of the key intergovernmental bargains upon which the cohesion of the Union had rested since its inception. It would further increase the political leverage of Germany in an EU whose orientation, at least after the first round of eastern enlargement, would be towards the Baltics and north-eastern Europe; it would create an imbalance in the relative weight of large and small EU member states; it would raise questions about the feasibility of greater European political integration, from foreign to social policy; and it would overturn the long-established costs and benefits linked to the EU's major redistributive policies, the CAP and the Structural and Cohesion Funds.[73] It was inevitable, therefore, that EU governments would proceed with great caution.

The determination of EU governments not to allow enlargement to undermine these bargains was reflected in their decision, following the failure of the 1996–97 IGC to agree on a package of institutional reforms, that an enlargement of the EU beyond 20 states would require prior reforms in this area. The same defensiveness underpinned the Madrid European Council's request that the Commission submit an evaluation of the effects of enlargement on Community policies and financing at the same time it submitted its Opinions on the applications. The Commission's response was to present its analysis and recommendations in a single comprehensive document, *Agenda 2000: for a Stronger and Wider Union*. The Commission thus hoped to force EU governments to deal with the enlargement question and the issues surrounding it as part of a single package, thereby preventing individual ministers or interest groups from blocking specific elements of the enlarge-ment programme and, instead, encourage heads of government to strike reciprocal bargains.[74] The danger, of course, was that the size and importance of this package could make it unwieldy and that striking cross-cutting bargains would prove very time-consuming, especially given the demands already being made on ministers' time by the issue of monetary union. This meant that the long-standing frustration of US policymakers throughout the post-cold war period on the slow pace of EU enlargement would continue to grow. EU leaders, on the other hand, would continue to resent American insensitivity to the complexity of incorporating the CEECs into the European Union, an institution whose legal framework, unlike NATO's, imposed constraints and costs at every level of the daily life of its member states.

Conclusion

If the rhetoric of western leaders at the end of the cold war was to be believed, their priority was to break down the divisions between the two halves of Europe. It is all the more remarkable, therefore, that the eight years between 1989 and 1997 should have witnessed not an overhaul, but rather a deepening of the two principal pillars of the cold war order: NATO and the European Union. Moreover, although both institutions reached out to their eastern neighbours during this period, it was only in 1997 that decisions were taken actually to draw them into the West's common institutional frameworks. During the preceding eight years, the priority for the majority of West European political leaders had been to deepen existing Western institutions irrespective of the effects of this process on the countries to their east.

It can be argued that, in historical terms, eight years is not such a long period for instituting a shift from one European order to the next.[75] However, this chapter has shown that, while the dramatic changes to the established order during 1989–92 seemed to offer the opportunity to implement a bold new vision for Europe, even more powerful forces pushed policymakers in the direction of preserving the institutional status quo and permitting only incremental adjustments. Some forces were largely outside the control of West European leaders. In the aftermath of the Maastricht Treaty, for example, economic recession retarded the prospects of a rapid eastern enlargement of the EU, eroded public support for the process of European integration, and undermined the more evolutionary proposal of an autonomous European defence identity. Just as important, however, were those forces that operated within Western Europe's existing institutional framework.

First, Western policymakers were not presented with a clean slate in 1989–90 on which they could redraw the political, economic and security structures of Europe. West European institutions had won the cold war. The collapse of communism not only served as apparently incontrovertible confirmation of the correctness of West European values, but also strengthened Western institutions. As a result, West European responses to the challenges of the end of the cold war remained trapped within the artificial compartmentalization between NATO for security matters and the EU for economic issues.

Second, each institution had embedded both bargains and procedures over the span of the previous forty years. In NATO, the United States and

United Kingdom were unwilling to accept reforms that would challenge their leadership positions. Whereas the United States had threatened in 1945–46 to disengage from Europe completely, it was not prepared to do this after 1989. This lent an air of unreality to post-1989 calls for Europe finally to take charge of its own security. As a result, the compromise eventually fashioned in NATO was not built on a grand new concept, but was simply an uneasy compromise.

In the EU, the interconnected political and economic bargains which underpinned existing West European integration satisfied all members of the existing club to a greater or lesser extent. Ministers and bureaucrats resisted radical internal reform or rapid enlargement partly to protect existing political and material benefits, but also out of a fear of the impact of rapid change on the future stability of Europe. Concerns about the potentially overbearing influence of Germany at the heart of an undivided continent and within a weakened EU, encouraged West European policymakers to continue thinking of post-cold war European order in terms of containment and balance of power – although the instruments to sustain that balance would be functional (new EU pillars), economic (EMU) and bureaucratic (QMV, co-decision) rather than military. It is, therefore, perhaps not surprising that many of the concepts that guided and justified the choices made between 1991–96 in both institutional tracks were old concepts that had first been crafted in the very different circumstances of a divided Europe.

Third, the attachment of Western leaders to their existing institutional arrangements ensured outcomes that reflected not only the defensive instincts of their member governments, but also the different institutional dynamics at work in NATO and in the European Union. Both institutions rely on unanimity for major institutional change. However, the West European willingness to accept and the US desire to exercise leadership in NATO generated concrete progress on the security front by July 1997. It also prevented the forging of linkages between internal reform and external initiatives. The Franco-US dispute over NATO command, for example, was not allowed to block the decision on enlargement in Madrid.

Fourth, in contrast to 1945–50, West European governments lost the unifying external stimulus of American leadership on European integration. American interventions in the period 1989–96 in the EU's development were sporadic and uneven, in contrast to its active role in the security debate and on NATO enlargement. Lacking an external driver on the EU side, West European leaders had to fabricate deadlines for completing the IGCs on Political and Economic Union in December 1991, in order to force through major common initiatives. The existence of a Franco-German motor that encompassed two fundamentally divergent visions of European integration complicated the task of taking major strategic decisions and instituted a bias for temporary compromises and the postponement of difficult decisions, whether on EU institutional reform or on a specific timetable for enlargement.

Last and most significantly, divergent national concepts not only between France and Germany, but also among all EU member states about the preferred shape of the new European order, further impeded the prospects for wholesale change. In the absence of a dominant player in the negotiations, there appeared to be no shared conceptual vision among West European governments on security, on enlargement, or on institutional evolution. Faced with these constraints, West European governments found it easier to settle for incrementalism over strategic change, for the deferral of difficult decisions and for the piecemeal change of existing institutional structures. The following chapters of this book reflect in more detail on the ways in which specific national perspectives about the future of European order interacted to produce the resulting incremental West European response to the challenges of the post-cold war world.

Notes

1. For the Mitterrand and Kohl proposal see *Agence Europe* 5238, 20 April 1990. In fact, this had been preceded by a Belgian initiative on 21 March 1990. For a discussion of the importance of this see Philippe de Schoutheete, 'The Treaty of Maastricht and its Significance for Third Countries', *Österreichische Zeitschrift Fur Politikwissenschaft*, 1992/3, pp. 247–60.
2. Isabel Hilton, *Independent*, 27 April 1990.
3. De Schoutheete, 'The Treaty of Maastricht', p. 260, op. cit..
4. For the link between the NATO and EC debates see Anand Menon, Anthony Forster and William Wallace, 'A Common European Defence?', *Survival*, 34:3, Autumn, 1992, pp. 98–118. Anthony Forster, 'The European Community and Western European Union', in A. Moens and C. Anstis (eds), *Disconcerted Europe: The Search for a New Security Architecture*, (Boulder: Westview, 1994) p. 58.
5. George Ross, *Jacques Delors and European Integration*, (Cambridge: Polity Press, 1995); for the speech see Jacques Delors, 'European Integration and security', *Survival*, March–April 1991 (32:2, 1991), pp. 99–109.
6. Ross, *Jacques Delors*, op. cit., p. 97.
7. For press reports of this intervention see David Usborne, 'US warns EC not to disrupt role of NATO', *Independent*, 6 March 1991, Sarah Lambert, 'Washington's alarm at EC Defence Plan', *Independent*, 9 March 1991.
8. See Paul Gebhard, *The United States and European Security*, Adelphi Paper No. 286 (London: IISS, February 1994). American officials did not see their efforts to reduce the costs of the US commitment to NATO (primarily in terms of reducing troops levels in Europe from their cold war levels of 325 000 to a still significant 100 000) as a precursor to a dilution of US political influence within the Alliance.
9. For a further discussion of this see Anthony Forster, 'The European Community and Western European Union' in Charles Anstis and Alexander Moens (eds), *Disconcerted Europe: The Search for a New Security Architecture* (Boulder, Westview Press, 1994).
10. Defence Policy Planning Committee, M-DPC-1 (1991), 38, NATO Press Service.
11. A study sponsored by the British Royal United Services Institute suggested that a European defence force would require an additional 1.5 per cent of GDP on top of current levels of expenditure for ten years. Quoted in 'The Defence of Europe', *The Economist*, 25 February 1995, p. 25.

12. See Michael Evans 'British troops to spearhead new NATO force', *The Times*, 25 May 1991, and Joseph Fitchett 'The new NATO: A Mobile Force for Post-Cold War Era', *International Herald Tribune*, 27 May 1991.

13. The Franco-German Initiative is reproduced in *Atlantic Documents*, 1738, 18 October 1991.

14. The Anglo-Italian Declaration is reproduced in *Europe Documents*, 1735, 5 October 1991.

15. For a review of the different West European contributions to the Gulf war see Nicole Gnesotto and John Roper (eds), *Western Europe and the Gulf* (Paris: Institute for Security Studies, WEU, 1992).

16. *The Transformation of the Alliance*, (NATO: Office of Information and Press, 1991).

17. *Agence Europe*, 11 October 1991; Finn Laursen and Sophie Vanhoonacker (eds), *The Intergovernmental Conference on Political Union*, (Maastricht: European Institute of Public Administration, 1992) p. 244.

18. Forster and Wallace, 'Common Foreign and Security Policy' in Helen Wallace and William Wallace (eds), *Policy-Making in the European Union*, (Oxford: Oxford University Press, 1996). For an excellent discussion of the resulting 'capability/ expectations' gap see Christopher Hill, 'The Capability–Expectations Gap, or Conceptualising Europe's International Role', *Journal of Common Market Studies*, 31:3 (September 1993), pp. 305–28.

19. The reactivation of WEU is considered in Anne Deighton (ed.), *European Security, Defence and Integration: Western European Union 1954–96*, (Oxford: Oxford University Press, 1997).

20. Important initial milestones in this process were the WEU Petersberg Declaration, June 1992, (Identification of WEU missions) and the Edinburgh European Council Summit, December 1993, (elaboration of Treaty on European Union provisions).

21. The genesis of the security agenda for the 1996 IGC can be found in the loose ends left by the Maastricht agreement (Article J.4 and J.10) and the WEU treaty provision that member states can withdraw from WEU by giving one years notice in 1998. For a discussion of the importance of this date see Aguilar, 'The Future of European Security and the Preparation of Maastricht II: Reply to the Fortieth Annual Report of the Council', Document 1458, Explanatory Memorandum (Brussels: Assembly of the Western European Union, 1995).

22. See, for example, 'Memorandum on the United Kingdom Government's Approach to the Treatment of European Defence Issues at the 1996 Intergovernmental Conference', deposited in both Houses of Parliament on 1 March 1995.

23. Helen Wallace, 'European Governance in Turbulent Times', *Journal of Common Market Studies*, 31:3 (1993), pp. 293–303.

24. Timothy Garton Ash, *In Europe's Name: Germany and the divided continent* (London: Jonathan Cape, 1993) p. 386.

25. Richard Corbett, 'The Intergovernmental Conference on Political Union', *Journal of Common Market Studies*, 30:3 (September 1992), pp. 271–98. For one view that economic union necessitated political union see the evidence of Karl-Otto Pöhl to the House of Lords Select Committee on the European Communities, *Economic and Monetary Union and Political Union*, (Vol. II, session 1989–90), House of Lords Paper 88-II, Evidence, col. 374, p. 73.

26. For a description of the various sub-systems see Philippe de Schoutheete, 'The European Community and its sub-systems', in William Wallace (ed.) *The Dynamics of European Integration* (London RRIA/Pinter, 1990) pp. 106–24.

27. For a discussion of French motives see Robert Tiersky, 'France in the New Europe', *Foreign Affairs* (Spring 1992) p. 132; and Jolyon Howorth, 'France since the Berlin Wall: defence and diplomacy', *The World Today*, 47:4 (1990), p. 129.
28. The temple idea is thought to come from Philippe de Boissieu, a senior French Foreign Office official who in turn was resurrecting a number of ideas taken from the Fouchet plans. See 'The Union Makers', *Economist*, 9 November 1991, p. 30.
29. For the text see 'Draft Treaty Articles with a view to achieving a Political Union', *Europe Documents*, no. 1709/10, 3 May 1991.
30. See *Financial Times* leader, 'A Vision of Europe', 20 June 1991; see also *Agence Europe*, 10 July 1991.
31. A stable relationship within the ERM for two years; long term interest rates below 2 per cent of the average of the three member states with the lowest inflation; and inflation not more than 1.5 per cent above their average; budgets should not exceed 3 per cent of GDP and public debt ratio should not exceed 60 per cent of GDP unless excesses are exceptional. See Articles 2, 3, 4 102–109 and attached protocols.
32. See Andrew Duff, 'The Main Reforms', in Andrew Duff, John Pinder and Roy Pryce (eds), *Maastricht and Beyond* (London: Routledge, 1994), p. 22.
33. A further example of Britain's increasing disinclination to toe the line was John Major's veto of the appointment of the Franco-German candidate, Jean-Luc Dehaene, Prime Minister of Belgium, as the new President of the European Commission. The compromise solution of former Luxembourg Prime Minister Jacques Santer to succeed Jacques Delors reflected the widespread preference for a less interventionist leader of the EU's executive branch.
34. This included the formation of an EU planning cell and the principle of 'constructive abstention' to prevent individual states from blocking the actions of the majority; *Reflection Group's Report* (Brussels: EU Council Secretariat, 5 December 1995).
35. Presidency Conclusions of the Madrid European Council, *Europe Documents*, no. 6629, 17 December 1995.
36. Presidency Conclusion of the Florence European Council, *European Documents*, no. 6755, 23 June 1996.
37. This categorization was offered by Peter Ludlow and Niels Ersboll, *Preparing for 1996 and a Larger European Union*, Special Report no. 6 (Brussels: Center for European Policy Studies, 1995), p. 55.
38. In a speech at the University of Leiden in reply to the Lamers and Balladur proposals, John Major had also called for a more 'flexible' European Union, with the same provision that no member be excluded from an area of policy in which it wants to participate, and is qualified to participate. See John Major, 'Europe: A Future that Works', speech given at the University of Leiden, Netherlands, 7 September 1994.
39. Frank Vibert, *Structured Flexibility in the European Union* (London: European Policy Forum, 1996).
40. As Jacques Delors had concluded, the largely rhetorical debates about establishing Political Union through institutional reform were likely to be counterproductive. See remarks by Jacques Delors to the Institutional Committee of the European Parliament, January 1994.
41. Economic relations and diplomatic contacts evolved bilaterally into limited forms of barter trade and some cultural exchanges, with Germany the only EC member state to pursue an active *Ostpolitik* from 1969 onwards. EC leaders made little effort

to establish a formal relationship with Comecon, believing that such a relationship would legitimize Soviet economic hegemony over central and eastern Europe and knowing that the command economy system of Comecon members obstructed a more open trading relationship between the two blocs. For a good overview see John Pinder, *The European Community and Eastern Europe* (London: Pinter/RIIA, 1991) pp. 8–36.

42. G-7 Declaration, 16 July 1989 in *EPC Documentation Bulletin*, 2:194 (1989), p. 26.

43. Peter Riddell, *Financial Times*, 17 July 1989, described in detail 'the delicate footwork over the week-end by the United States and Germany'.

44. See *Bulletin of the EC* (11/89) p. 56. It was Margaret Thatcher who first mooted the idea of extending Association agreements to the new democracies, *Agence Europe*, no. 5177, 22–23 January 1990, p. 4.

45. See *Agence Europe*, no. 5096, 23 September 1989, p. 4 and no. 5106, 7 October 1989, p. 4.

46. See the speech by Margaret Thatcher to the Aspen Institute in Colorado on 5 August 1990, reported in *The Federal News Service*, 5 August 1990, p. 6. Thatcher's reasoning had more to do with wanting to promote an alternative EU response to German unification than with deeper West European integration.

47. See Chapter 4 for a more detailed discussion of the French approach, including Mitterrand's proposal for a European Confederation.

48. *COM (90) 398 Final*.

49. Robin Niblett, *The European Community and the Central European Three, 1989–92*, op. cit., pp. 167–87.

50. Thus, the inclusion of sensitive sectors in the agreements served as a 'wedge' to accelerate the trade concessions already on offer to the CEECs. The first effort to accelerate the EU's programme of trade concessions surfaced at the European Council in Copenhagen in June 1993; see Rollo, 'The EC and Central Europe', pp. 19–20.

51. *Bulletin of the EC*, (6/93) p. 13.

52. *Bulletin of the EC*, (12/94) p. 21.

53. For the change in EU negotiating mandates see *Agence Europe*, no. 5549, 21 August 1991, pp. 2–3. For a text of the final agreement, see *OJ L 347*, 31 December 1993 for the text of the agreement with Poland.

54. *Bulletin of the EC*, (6/93) p. 13; also see Rollo, 'The EC and Central Europe', p. 19; and the European Council declarations from Lisbon (26–27 June 1992), and Edinburgh (11–12 December 1992).

55. *Bulletin of the EC* (12/94) pp. 20–6.

56. Eurostat estimated Ireland's GDP in 1970 based on current purchasing power parities at 59.5 per cent of the EC average; Greece in 1980 at 58.2 per cent; and, in 1985, Portugal at 52.5 per cent and Spain at 71.7 per cent; quoted in Loukas Tsoukalis, *The New European Economy* (Oxford: Oxford University Press, 1991). The Center for Economic Policy Research estimated per capita income on accession as 50 per cent of the EC average for Ireland, 41 per cent for Greece, 49 per cent for Spain, and 23 per cent for Portugal; *Is Bigger Better? The Economics of Enlargement* (CEPR: London, 1992).

57. From 1995–99 the Phare budget was set at ECU6.7 billion, spread over the ten CEEC applicant countries

58. The Copenhagen conclusions stated that, 'the Union's capacity to absorb new members, while maintaining the momentum of European integration, is also an important consideration in the general interest of both the Union and the candidate countries'.

59. National Security Strategy, 1994 (Washington, DC: US GPO).

60. For a detailed description of the evolution of the US position including details of the internal US negotiations, see Gerald B. Solomon, *The NATO Enlargement Debate 1990–97: Blessings of Liberty* (Washington, DC: Praeger, CSIS, 1998), pp. 26–36.

61. On 27 January 1994, the Senate passed a 'sense of the Senate' resolution to this effect, and on 14 April and 5 May 1994, respectively, the House passed the 'NATO Expansion Act of 1994' and the 'NATO Revitalization Act', in the former case pushing for NATO enlargement for Poland, Hungary, the Czech Republic and Slovakia by 1999.

62. Sir David Gillmore, 'Representing Britain Overseas: Post Cold War Challenges', *RUSI Journal* (December 1993).

63. NATO, *Study on Enlargement* (Brussels: NATO Secretariat, September 1995).

64. See, for example, William Wallace, *Opening the Door: The Enlargement of NATO and the European Union* (London: Center for European Reform, 1996).

65. 'NATO and Russians Edging Closer', *International Herald Tribune*, 27 September 1996.

66. *The Founding Act on Mutual Relations, Cooperation, and Security Between NATO and the Russian Federation,* (Brussels: NATO Secretariat, May 1997).

67. Ronald D. Asmus, Richard L. Kugler and F. Stephen Larrabee, 'What Will NATO Enlargement Cost', *Survival*, 38:3 (1996); also see their earlier piece, 'NATO Expansion: The Next Steps', *Survival*, 37:1 (1995); *The Costs of Expanding the NATO Alliance* (Washington, DC: Congressional Budget Office, March 1996).

68. For the full range of arguments made by US administration officials as well as former government officials and other policy experts in favour of and against NATO enlargement, see US Senate hearings.

69. 'Perry Tells the Baltics: You're Not Ready', *International Herald Tribune*, 28 September 1996.

70. Madrid Declaration on Euro-Atlantic Security and Cooperation, 8 July 1997.

71. For a detailed analysis of this process, see Graham Avery and Fraser Cameron, *The Enlargement of the European Union* (Sheffield: Sheffield Academic Press, 1998) pp. 37–92.

72. As one of the Commission negotiators observed, EU enlargement negotiations are, in essence, 'a kind of intergovernmental conference between the Member States and the applicant country'. In EU trade negotiations, the Commission plays a central role, chairing all negotiating meetings and with the right to resort to qualified majority voting to break internal EU deadlocks; Avery and Cameron, *The Enlargement of the EU*, p. 28.

73. There was considerable disagreement over what the potential financial costs to existing EU members of enlargement would be. There were wide disparities in the figures that governments, academics and organisations attached to the extension of the EU's CAP and Structural Funds to new members under the enlargement process, irrespective of the restraining impact that 'derogations' would have on CEEC exports. See, for example, Richard Baldwin, *Towards an Integrated Europe* (London: CEPR, 1994); Commission CAP reports ... Moreover, there was the countervailing argument that these costs should be set against the positive dynamic economic impact of further market opening in Europe.

74. Avery and Cameron, *The Enlargement of the EU*, pp. 101–2, op. cit..

75. Simon Serfaty makes this point in 'America and Europe, Beyond Bosnia', *Washington Quarterly*, 19:3 (Summer 1996).

3

Central Power, Central Debate? The German Foreign Policy Community and the Rethinking of European Order

Hartmut Mayer

A fundamental debate on the structure of post-cold war Europe was inescapable in Germany. The spray-painted rubble of the Berlin wall symbolized the demolition of the previous foundations of Germany's domestic as well as foreign policies. Lifting the iron curtain affected Germany far more directly than any other West European country. It certainly benefited most, making it for a very short time 'the happiest people of the world'.[1] But such euphoria faded rapidly in light of the tremendous economic and political burdens which 1989 imposed on Germany and on Europe as a whole.

As in other countries, the German debate focused first and foremost on Germany's needs and on its own role in the future Europe. Fully thought-out concepts of a pan-European order were relatively rare, although such broader thinking has often been implicit in what has been said about Germany's position and interests in a new Europe. Furthermore, the focus of the German debate significantly changed over time. Between 1989 and 1991 Germany was preoccupied with stabilizing the situation and immediately binding the unified country into pre-existing West European structures. Policies reflected knee-jerk reactions which closed an old chapter in Germany's history rather than beginning a new one. With the conclusion of the Maastricht treaty and the collapse of the Soviet Union at the end of 1991, a more fundamental debate on German roles, goals and priorities broke out. Between 1992 and 1994 there was a lively debate on policy preferences and choices, with different schools of thought emerging.

While this free intellectual reflection seemed to spawn many new (and some old) options for Germany, practical and increasingly pressing political demands increasingly narrowed the range of perceived options. As a result, the German debate between 1994 and 1996 focused on concepts for a more flexible institutional order which would reflect the enormous political and economic differences of eastern and western European countries, while providing a stable security structure for all of them. Political leaders were more and more torn between the different imperatives of *Westpolitik* and *Ostpolitik*, and between domestic and international priorities. From 1996 onwards, it became the government's priority to bring a 'flexible' but integrated order into existence and to ensure that it would be strong enough to withstand future uncertainties.

In contrast to many other West European states, the German political system contains a network of experts and institutions which collectively constitutes a solid and well-respected international affairs community. A public debate on European order between 1989 and 1997 took place among academics, political analysts, politicians and journalists: exchanging ideas and arguments in various political party circles, in planning staffs, in universities, think tanks and the quality media. As in other European countries, however, it is difficult to evaluate the exact influence of expert debate on the actual policymaking process.[2]

There was certainly an active and institutionalized exchange between academic thinking and practical policymaking. There were some regular study groups in which senior academics shared expertise on particular foreign policy aspects with serving politicians. Personal assistants and advisers to politicians mostly had long-established contacts with the academic community, ensuring a steady flow of ideas. Compared to Washington, with its open competition among institutes, lobbies and political consultants in advising both the Administration and Congress, the direct influence of the German international affairs community was limited. The community itself has been stronger in developing broad concepts than in providing quick, policy-oriented advice on concrete and pressing issues. Moreover the influence of this expert community on the general public has remained limited. The quality newspapers, which convey their arguments to a wider informed public, are losing ground in a changing media environment with a growing emphasis on entertainment. The circulation of some of the quality media, for example *Die Zeit*, is going down. Compared to previous decades, the overall influence of quality newspapers in the public debate is declining, despite the sustained excellence of publications such as the *Frankfurter Allgemeine, Süddeutsche Zeitung* and *Die Zeit*. Nevertheless some of the ideas expressed and developed in the German expert community do shine through the dark and dense filters of party politics to illuminate the wider public debate.

The German response to the end of the cold war also differed from the domestic debate in other European countries in the closeness of its intellectual and political links to parallel debates elsewhere: most importantly within its major partners, the USA and France. The expert community were habitually attentive to intellectual trends within the United States, Germany's political sponsor and security provider since 1945. Political leaders were similarly habitually attentive to perceptions in Paris, their key European partner. But the German political and intellectual élite were also aware that their words carried echoes in Warsaw and in Moscow, and that they had to respond to the fears and expectations of their eastern neighbours. Unification – as Hans-Peter

Schwarz argued – had made Germany once again the central power in Europe, however uncomfortable its leaders and its citizens felt in that position. Self-preoccupation was as strong a temptation for Germans as for British and French; but it was harder to ignore the dangers of that temptation.

German reactions 1989 to 1991: change through continuity

The German debate on the shaping of a post-cold war order naturally had a head-start on its western neighbours. While other Western European countries had felt quite comfortable with the divided European order, leaders of the Federal Republic since 1949 had developed long-term concepts and strategies for an alternative architecture which would allow peaceful unification in harmony and agreement with all neighbours. This goal was even written into West Germany's provisional constitution.[3]

In the early years of the Federal Republic two basic ideas had emerged on how to create an order in which German unification would be possible: *Germany as bridge* (between Eastern and Western Europe) or, alternatively, *Germany as a magnet* (as part of a superior and attractive West). One of the most ardent advocates of Germany as a mediator between east and west was Jakob Kaiser, a CDU politician in Berlin, who argued that 'Germany had to be bridge and mediator between East and West, in the interest of Germany and of Europe'[4] and rejected Germany's membership of the cold-war blocks. The Social Democrats in the late 1940s and 1950s promoted similar ideas.

Adenauer as chancellor however successfully imposed his preferred foreign policy strategy over these competing concepts. Adenauer's strategy of western integration was based on at least three principles: first, that Germany had to choose partners, that neutrality was not an option; second, that western integration was the only feasible way to end allied occupation and regain sovereignty; third, that West Germany as part of a strong and united West would both contain eastern expansion and become a magnet for change within the East.[5] Bringing West Germany into the western camp, therefore, had priority over early German unification. There was also a cultural foundation for Adenauer's western orientation. Western integration reflected, this Rhineland Catholic wrote, 'our way of life which was developed over centuries based on Christian and humanistic values'. Germany should be bound in with those countries and peoples which shared 'the same beliefs about the state, the individual, freedom and property'.[6]

Politics of strength, such as the Hallstein doctrine of breaking diplomatic relations with every nation which recognized the GDR, seemed to be appropriate in the 1950s. After the Berlin Wall had stabilized the division of Germany, however, and superpower détente began to evolve, a reconceptualization of the 'provisional' basis of the Bonn Republic was necessary.[7] CDU-led governments under and after Adenauer as well as the Grand Coalition under Kurt Georg Kiesinger struggled to overcome the stale confrontation between the two German states.[8] But it was the Brandt/Scheel government which developed a new *Gesamtkonzept*: Brandt's new *Ostpolitik*.

Egon Bahr, head of the foreign ministry's planning staff from 1966 to 1969 and chief negotiator of *Ostpolitik* after 1969, saw *Ostpolitik* as part of a 'grand design', leading to a reunified Germany contained in a Europe freed from the antagonistic military blocs of the cold war.[9] It was based on the assumption that only if regimes in the east were reassured about the post-war territorial *status quo* would they be confident about liberalization, peaceful co-operation and détente. This in the long term would create the conditions for a gradual fusion of the two Europes and thus of divided Germany. Brandt's *Ostpolitik* did not displace Adenauer's western integration, as charged by the CDU at the time. The eastern treaties were, as Egon Bahr stated, 'the consequence of the treaties with the West'; *Ostpolitik* rested on the foundations of *Westpolitik*.[10]

While the original post-war debates on Germany's role in Europe had been centred around the basic choice between 'either east or west' or 'neither east nor west', the foreign policy consensus which emerged after the late 1960s was a western bound '*sowohl als auch*', 'west as well as east'. This simultaneous commitment to Adenauer's western integration and Brandt's *Ostpolitik* remained the essential guideline for German policies towards a new post-cold war European order.[11] While the post-cold war situation theoretically provided room for a revival of concepts such as neutrality, mediation between east and west, or pan-European collective security, it was the widely shared consensus on the combined legacies of Adenauer and Brandt, deeply rooted in German political culture, which pre-determined the parameters of domestic discussion on a new European order. Kohl and Genscher – a Chancellor who regarded himself as the inheritor of Adenauer's political legacy, a foreign minister who had entered his office as Brandt resigned – symbolized this continuity.

With the demolition of the Berlin wall, German unification and the recovery of full sovereignty, many questions were raised as to whether Germany would continue its multilateral foreign policy orientation or whether it would shift towards a more unilateral or nationalistic path. In a widely read article of October 1990, Stanley Hoffmann predicted a major German turnaround towards selfishly pursuing 'just enough integration' to fulfil the needs of German farmers, industry and service sectors, 'just enough diplomatic coordination to keep receiving a European stamp of approval', but foremost 'enough freedom for diplomatic manoeuvres to prevent unwanted restrictions as far as foreign policy and defence are concerned'.[12] On the contrary, however, the Kohl government, throughout the period 1989 to 1997 and despite growing dissatisfaction in political and business circles, continued to be the most enthusiastic proponent for binding the country into an ever closer European Union and, thereby, even surrendering some of the sovereignty the unified nation had just regained. Germany opted to continue with the strategy of co-operative self-binding which had made the old Federal Republic a successful international player in the cold war era.[13] Multilateralism as the method of foreign policymaking was never seriously questioned between 1989 and 1997. As Wolfgang Ischinger, head of the planning staff at the foreign ministry, said: 'German foreign policy does not need to be reinvented'.[14] Germany's post-cold war strategy, however, was not a linear continuation of the old one, but a modified version of *Weiter So*.

German reactions 1989–1991

Chancellor Helmut Kohl saw the events of 1989 as 'a very short window of opportunity', a phase where action rather than conceptualization was required. In order to succeed, Germany had to stick to established cold war concepts and convictions, promising to integrate a united Germany into the existing western institutions. The initial stage of German approaches to post-cold war Europe, lasting from the collapse of the Berlin Wall to the conclusion of the Maastricht treaty in December 1991, marked, therefore, a final period of old thinking rather than a new and fresh beginning.[15] On 8 November 1989, the day before the opening of the Berlin Wall, Chancellor Helmut Kohl revived Adenauer's dictum that 'reunification and westintegration, Germany – and Europe – policies are the two sides of the same coin'. The commitment to the western community, he reaffirmed, was 'irrevocable': 'We are not wanderers between East and West, and we have learned from the history of this century.'[16]

Unlike in 1949, opposition politicians stood alongside the CDU. While emphasizing that a future European Union should open itself for co-operation with Eastern European countries, Hans-Jochen Vogel (SPD) warned Germany not to slow down the process of European integration.[17] Willy Brandt himself, one week later, called for an 'active *Ostpolitik* of the European Community',[18] a goal which, in the debate of 16 November 1989, was also emphasized by Hans-Dietrich Genscher.[19] Overall, the West German foreign policy establishment was united in its view that Germany had to remain firmly bound into the international community. Otherwise, even a benign Germany would always cause anxiety among its neighbours and set in motion the traditional cycle of distrust, fear and hostility.

Willy Brandt's dictum of 10 November 1989 that 'the unnatural division will not last' and that 'we are now in the situation where what belongs together will grow together' clearly placed unification on the agenda.[20] The general principles of the post-Berlin Wall German debate, however, were set in Chancellor Kohl's Ten Point Plan, which he set out to the *Bundestag* on 28 November 1989. The Chancellor made clear that 'the future architecture of Germany was to be integrated in the architecture of the whole of Europe' (point six), that the European integration process would remain the 'decisive continuity' of any pan-European development (point seven), and that the CSCE would become the heart of a pan-European order. In the parliamentary debate which followed, both FDP and SPD speakers supported Kohl's approach.[21]

The double principle of 'self-determination' and of 'international embeddedness', therefore, guided German strategy between 1989 and 1991. The German government had to negotiate its path towards unification with its allies, past initial suspicions about the continuing German commitment to West European integration, and past attempts to block or slow down the unification process from Britain and France. At the NATO Brussels summit of December 1989, the American President George Bush took the opportunity to endorse German self-determination 'without prejudice to its outcome', and spelled out American conditions for possible unification: Germany should not only remain in NATO, but should also be part of an 'increasingly integrated European Community'.[22] The conditions for potential unification were therefore set: NATO membership for a united Germany (particularly stressed by the US and the UK), deepening of European integration (in particular demanded by France), an acceleration of the CFE disarmament negotiations and a strengthening of the CSCE as the pan-European umbrella organization.

Anticipating that the Soviets would resist NATO membership for a unified Germany, the alternative of 'either unification or NATO' was publicly discussed during January 1990.[23] In late January Foreign Minister Genscher put forward the compromise proposal that united Germany should remain a NATO member but that its military structures should not be extended to the former DDR: a suggestion which was rejected by his coalition partners in the CDU.[24] Such debates were soon brushed aside by the Kohl government's repeatedly stated commitment to both NATO and the EC; but it remained evident that the Soviet Union would only permit unified Germany's membership of NATO as part of a new pan-European order from which the Soviets would also benefit. After Gorbachev's general green light for unification on 10 February 1990, it was left to the Two Plus Four process to negotiate strategies and details on the international problems of unification. Multilateral diplomacy between February and September 1990, within Two Plus Four and outside, ensured that Germany remained embedded in western institutions while opening up the prospect of a new European security architecture.[25] The results of the Two Plus Four process, and acceptance of German unification, were formalized at the CSCE Paris summit in November 1990.

Kohl's second preoccupation was to assuage French reservations about German unification by stressing Germany's complete commitment to continued West European integration. In a private visit to Mitterrand's country house in Latché on 4 January 1990, Kohl reassured Mitterrand that a unified Germany would be firmly bound into the European Community, and that Franco-German co-operation would remain the engine for further European integration.[26] This mutual acceptance that German unification would require a deepening and an institutional adjustment of the European

Community determined Franco-German policies and initiatives in the years ahead, with a succession of Franco-German initiatives which set the framework for the intergovernmental conference agenda.[27]

These joint initiatives, however, disguised underlying differences between German proposals on the institutional deepening of the EU and French intergovernmental ideas, as well as between the German conception of a European pillar of NATO and the French commitment to a looser Atlantic Alliance. Here, as on the balance between NATO and the CSCE in a post-cold war European order, German political leaders were ambiguous, even contradictory, giving different impressions to different negotiating partners. Bonn's tolerance for ambiguity in foreign policy was deeply rooted in its cold war experience, as a semi-sovereign state manoeuvring between the divergent demands of its allies and occupiers, as well as in the structure of West German coalition politics and in the carefully-guarded competencies of different ministers and ministries.

The initial response to post-cold war Europe was thus marked more by continuity and reassurance than by new departures. The German government, which clearly directed the national debate, remained committed to multilateral institutions and negotiations as the framework for foreign policy. Germany's unilateral recognition of Slovenia and Croatia on 23 December 1991 is often seen as evidence that this multilateralist commitment was breaking down; but this was much more the unfortunate outcome of a series of miscalculations.[28] German policies between 1989 and 1991 were otherwise prudent responses to outside pressures. The challenges resulting from the breakdown of the socialist system fed in to the Maastricht negotiations, but specific East European issues were deliberately excluded from the IGC agenda. It was only after Maastricht and the collapse of the Soviet Union that a more fundamental debate on European order and Germany's role within it began to emerge.

Rethinking Germany's role in Europe 1992–94

Between 1992 and 1994 a lively and often diffuse debate took place among academics, political analysts, politicians and journalists which collectively constitute the German international affairs community. Ideas and arguments were exchanged in various political party circles and foundations, in universities, think tanks (such as the *Stiftung Wissenschaft und Politik*, the Deutsche Gesellschaft für Auswärtige Politik, the *Bertelsmann Foundation, the Centrum für angewandte Politikforschung*) and in quality media (most importantly the *Frankfurter Allgemeine Zeitung, Die Zeit* and *Süddeutsche Zeitung*). It is difficult to evaluate the exact influence of this debate on policymaking, given the institutionalized osmosis of study groups through which senior academics share expertise with serving politicians and the focus on developing broad concepts rather than immediate policy advice.

This German debate was distinctive not only in its variety and diffusion of standpoints, but also in the close linkage between ideas about European order and reflections on a future global order and on Germany's place within it. Since the German expert community were habitually attentive to intellectual trends within the United States, concepts of global order were predominantly borrowed from the American literature. Joseph Nye, for example, identified five potential models: a return to bipolarity; multipolarity; a three- or two-bloc world; unipolar American hegemony; and a multilevel structure.[29] In response, Eckhard Lübkemeier posited three major approaches to world order: 'polar models', neo-realist approaches, and culture and civilization approaches.[30] German politicians often loosely referred to these models. They served as guidelines and points of reference, justifying both policy initiatives and wider conceptual strategies.

Polar stability

One of the most powerful of the 'polar' approaches argued that the former bipolar world would be replaced by a *multipolar* system in which chiefly economic strength rather than military capacities would determine actors' positions in the world. The United States, Japan, the EU, possibly China and Russia, and on a regional level, India and Brazil were usually seen as the poles in this new structure.[31] A widely-received variant of this was the concept of a tripolar regionalism, with competing trading blocs organized around regional hegemons.

Two other polar approaches were of interest to German academics and policymakers. 'Unipolarists' argued that the end of the cold war left the United States as the only economic and military superpower. Only the United States therefore could continue to provide a credible military insurance against emerging threats to the new world order.[32] 'Transpolarists', however, claimed that economic power will be 'de-nationalized', meaning that the role of states will decrease in favour of transnational actors such as multinational firms, interest groups, banks and financial systems. Advocates of this approach believe that the new global structure will favour 'civilian powers' such as Germany and Japan whose policies are grounded in sophisticated forms of domestic and international co-operation.[33] Growing domestic economic problems in Germany after 1991 however cut across this optimistic vision. German economists and the business community echoed fears among the broader electorate about the increasing threat to the 'German model' – Germany's corporatist capitalism, with its life-time social welfare guarantees – from the sharp winds of economic globalization.

Neo-realist instability

While polar models generally assumed a stable future world order, there were those who foresaw the possibility and increased likelihood of war and crises. With the absence of the unifying Soviet threat, hidden antagonisms and old rivalries could break through even in the western camp, making wars in

Western Europe possible.[34] This 'Hobbesian pessimism' was reflected in a mainly historical and self-conscious debate on German identity in the early 1990s, a debate on the dragons and lessons of the past, on newly defined national interests and on classical geo-strategic and geopolitical concerns. The debate was mainly carried out by historians, described by Janning as 'traditionalists who perceive themselves as realists'.[35] In their view, the old German question, that is the potential for German hegemony and the danger of anti-German alliances in the European balance of power, would remain the decisive problem of European order. The new situation after 1989 was completely different from the cold war, but quite similar to the circumstances facing Germany between 1871 and 1945. The country had been brought back to its old '*Mittellage*' as Europe's central power.

Historians such as Hans-Peter Schwarz, Michael Stürmer, Gregor Schöllgen and Arnulf Baring led this debate. Hans-Peter Schwarz, in a succession of books and articles on the centrality of Germany in the emerging new European state system, recommended that Germany should make the best use of its own national resources, should define its national interests and should develop pragmatic policies seeking to achieve nationally defined goals in order to balance Europe from its centre.[36] Their critics replied that these German historians risked misinterpreting the specific demands of the post-cold war context by overemphasizing historical analogies.[37]

Despite such counterarguments as that liberal, market-oriented and prosperous democracies do not fight each other, and that mutual interdependence in Western Europe rules out the possibility of war, neo-realist assumptions played an important role in the German debate on post-cold war order.[38] Chancellor Kohl persistently portrayed the necessity of an irreversible political integration of Europe as *the* decisive question of peace or war in Europe in the 21st century. Such a view, which in Kohl's case seemed to be a genuine belief rather than exaggerated rhetoric, stemmed from realist assumptions and fears.

Cultural friction

Questions of culture and identity also played an important part in the German debate on the future of Europe. Samuel Huntington's widely discussed hypothesis of a 'clash of civilizations' made explicit other underlying German assumptions about the foundations of a post-cold war order: that differences between western and non-western cultures would draw new dividing lines, replacing the ideological and political boundaries of the bipolar world.[39] Wolfgang Schäuble, for example, the leader of the CDU faction in the Bundestag and Helmut Kohl's potential successor, argued in a lecture on the 'Christian identity of Europe':

> Huntington's thesis of a war between cultures might be, in its con-
> sequences, exaggerated, but there is no doubt that these global cultural

conflicts and challenges exist, and that we Europeans have to give an answer to them. For me it is unquestionable that the answer can only be a common European answer. The same is true for all other dangers and risks which Europe is facing today. We will only be able to master them as a close community. However, we can only become a real community if we manage to discover our common roots. One of the most decisive foundations is doubtlessly our common historical and cultural heritage ... The peoples and nations of Europe are united in a common identity, in a community of common values with roots reaching back to the medieval Christian and to the archaic ages.[40]

Schäuble saw European integration and the German form of a social market economy as being a reflection of Christian values. He argued that 'our Christian heritage even contains a concrete instruction on how to organize the future of Europe. It provides us with guidelines which we have to follow when designing the architecture of Europe. One, for example, concerns the economic integration of Europe.'[41]

However important the construction of a common European identity might be, a simplistic equation of Christianity with Europe reveals a deep-seated provincialism in parts of the German political élite. Knowledge of and even interest in non-western cultures, former chancellor Helmut Schmidt has claimed, is 'almost null' and represents a 'dangerous deficit'.[42] The same beliefs were again revealed in spring 1997 when Kohl, at a meeting of Europe's Christian Democratic leaders, implied that Turkey's unacceptability in the EU was partly due to its being a Muslim country.[43]

Europe as a 'Schicksalsgemeinschaft'

Despite the differences between these theoretical approaches to European and global order, German politicians were able to derive from them an apparently coherent set of policy prescriptions after the upheaval of German unification and the Maastricht IGC. These revolved around what chancellor Kohl persistently called '*Europa als Schicksalsgemeinschaft*', Europe as a 'community of a common destiny'. Whatever the future global order might look like, Europe would secure its position only as a united and autonomous entity – and not as the sum of its traditionally antagonistic parts.

Thus, the neo-realist emphasis on the potential for war *within* Europe required a politically unified Europe and the extension of the positive experience of western integration to the new danger zones in the east. Second, assuming a multipolar world order predominantly determined by economic factors, Europe could only maintain its influence from the foundation of a strong internal market with an outward looking political arm (CFSP) and coherent external trade policies. The prospect of a global order organized around two or three regional blocs was seen as a strong argument for economic and monetary union. If the strength and competitiveness of the American economy flowed largely from its vast internal market and from the position of the dollar as the global monetary anchor, Europe could only compete by possessing matching structures. Third, preservation of common culture required European political unity. All arguments for further European unification in the domestic German debate were based on one or more of these world views.

However, the German debate did not fully address the delicate issues deriving from the transpolar, globalization, world view. There was instead a hopeful consensus that European integration could create a safeguard against the negative effects of globalization and to protect social and cultural standards (against 'social dumping'). The negotiation of the Social Chapter of the Maastricht treaty clearly reflected these concerns, stemming from a deeply rooted resistance to the Anglo-Saxon model of market liberalization and a determination to maintain Germany's social market economy as far as possible.

The intellectual debate on European order: options and schools of thought

These world scenarios all appeared to argue in favour of European unification, but naturally they could not define the resulting interests for Germany within a transformed Europe. The German foreign policy community debated a number of possible priorities: deepened *core Europe*, strengthening instead a *wider West*, giving priority to *Mitteleuropa*, pursuing a *Moscow-first strategy* or developing *global ambitions*. For academic clarity these options were discussed as alternative strategies, although any sensible European order would have to provide a combination of them.[44] The imperatives of a deepened European Union and of a strengthened transatlantic alliance were widely shared inside and outside Germany; the three last options were largely accepted within Germany as unrealistic as single strategies, though attracting much attention from non-German commentators who wished to portray European integration as a mere cover for German hegemonic aspirations. In order to clarify the diffuse debate, Gunther Hellmann has identified five different 'schools of thought': *normalization-nationalists, internationalists, Europeanists, Eurosceptics* and *pragmatic multilateralists*.[45] His rigorous categorizations are certainly disputable, since boundaries often overlap, but they nevertheless provide the best systematic overview on the German debate.

Thankfully the least influential school of thought consisted of the 'new right', small nationalistic circles within the CDU, CSU and the FDP, who emphasized that a reunited Germany should give priority to rebuilding itself as a proud nation state.[46] These so-called '*normalization-nationalists*' stressed the predominantly positive virtues of German history and culture and were sceptical towards western values which, in their view, undermined a distinct German identity.[47] Hence, they gave priority to the nation state over international institutions and agendas. They did not have a vision on European order except for a blunt rejection of supranationality.

At the other end of the spectrum, German 'internationalists', represented on the left wings of the SPD, the Greens and the SED's successor PDS, were rooted in the traditions of idealism and pacifism. They saw global challenges such as environmental survival, world poverty and sustainable development as top priorities. Committed to 'global governance', internationalists stressed the necessity for greater German leadership towards this modern agenda.[48] Priority should be given to organizations with wide or 'universal' membership; NATO should be replaced by a collective security structure.[49] Nevertheless, they supported closer European integration, with an emphasis on civil, social and environmental issues, in order to make the union a role model for other industrialized regions.[50]

In the centre of Germany's political spectrum, as Hellmann calls them, *Europeanists, Eurosceptics* and *pragmatic multilateralists* shared similar modified realist views, but disagreed over what a realist perspective implied for German policy. The vast majority of foreign policy experts in the CDU, CSU, FDP and SPD could be labelled as *Europeanists* or *pragmatic multilateralists*.

As in other countries, there were however a growing number of conservative Eurosceptics who (unlike the British) appreciated the achievements of post-war integration but believed that integration had gone far enough. They rejected the idea of a federal Europe which supersedes the nations. Instead, they foresaw an unavoidable return to Great Power politics, with Germany resuming its 'natural role' as the 'central power in Europe'.[51] Gregor Schöllgen, one of the prominent, moderate Eurosceptics argued that:

> Today it seems that, despite all resolutions, announcement and pleas, political union in the original and real sense is unlikely to become a reality in the foreseeable future. The prospect that the failure of political union could permanently set back the process of European integration also in those areas which most require progress – economic policy, security policy, refugee policy and environmental policy – is serious. Above all, we cannot exclude the possibility that the failure of European integration in these areas might lead to a resurgence of nationalism in Western Europe ... [An] ... explosive combination ... cannot in principle be excluded ... Europe, including the western part of the continent, is balanced on a knife-edge.[52]

Germany should therefore 'define its national interests clearly and plainly, both for itself and for others'.[53]

Such views were mainly advanced by the conservative historians who provided the jump-start for the overall German debate. Politically their most pressing point was not to sacrifice the D-Mark, a message with wider appeal in the German electorate. Since Eurosceptics anticipated increasing rivalries within Western Europe, in particular with Britain and France, they strongly supported the continued presence of the Americans as Europe's stabilizer. 'The new shape of Europe', Arnulf Baring proposed, 'should consist of a more modest, less ambitious European Union, a continuation of NATO which means a strong US–British–German alliance: and an increased German international responsibility'.[54]

In the end, 'the Federal Republic will have to play a part which matches its importance, by no means for selfish reasons only. Europe needs Germany, and a Germany in the heart of Europe which is too weak is ... no less worrisome than one which is too strong'.[55] As a 'reborn nation-state' Germany should therefore 'define its national interests clearly and plainly, both for itself and for others'. Since 'power is a factor in the lives of individuals, peoples and states' the Germans 'are called upon to make their power available' and to use it in the 'service of life-saving, peace-keeping and civilized purposes'.[56]

Pragmatic multilateralists, on the other hand, shared the deeply ingrained conviction that Germany's interests could only be realized if they corresponded to those of its allies. More than other intellectual schools they stressed the continuities of pre- and post-1989 German foreign policy. Their approach to European institutional order remained flexible so long as it was debatable which of the institutions would acquire what role and how they could compliment each other. Once it became widely accepted that Germany depended on a condensed network of all of these institutions, with NATO and the EU as anchors, they supported an incremental adjustment of western institutions, a gradual expansion of NATO and the EU and an active concern for Russian interests. These multilateralists recognized that Germany more than any other member state had to respond to eastern pressures for access to western institutions. They saw Germany as navigating a careful course between being the advocate of Central and Eastern Europe, the motor of western European integration and the decisive link in the transatlantic alliance.

Finally, the vast majority within the government itself were *Europeanists*. They advocated the creation of a fully united and federal Europe. Europeanists promoted a 'Maastricht First' policy, since enlargement (in their view) would weaken existing achievements, with the development of a core group to deepen European integration.[57] Other European countries could then be grouped around this European core, which would become the continent's engine, its anchor of stability and the focus for a future federal structure. Europeanist thinking, at least in Germany, was progressive and conservative at the same time: progressive in overcoming the old nation state and in its commitment to supranational solidarity; conservative in seeking to replace nation states with a wider entity, Europe, based on similar notions of cultural uniqueness, of power and interest policies in competition with other nations or regions. 'Europeanism' therefore appealed to many audiences for a variety of sometimes incompatible reasons. What made *Europeanists* distinct was their wholehearted optimism that the union will succeed. As will be shown below,

Europeanists also supported the wider western framework of transatlantic co-operation as an indispensable element in building a secure and united Europe.[58]

Developing German foreign policy interests, 1992–94

Even if academics and commentators were unable to reach a consensus on the ranking of priorities and the compatibility of goals, the political élite within the CDU/FDP coalition government gradually developed a clear sense of the principal challenges facing Germany after the cold war. During this period, the Social Democrats were left on the sidelines of debates on Europe, either agreeing with government lines or being unable to present consistent counterproposals, having apparently lost their conceptual bearings.[59] In addition, after the victory of the 'realists' against the 'fundamentalists' in the Green party, the Greens began to adopt a less utopian perspective – thus broadening the foreign policy consensus even further.[60] Overall, as two astute British analysts of German foreign policy concluded, 'there is little to suggest that the federal government's European diplomacy will be restricted in the immediate future by party political constraints', given the 'persistence of consensus among the established parties'.[61]

It is hard to evaluate the direct impact of the German academic community upon German policymaking in this period. There was certainly an ongoing osmosis, but it seems that the German government's decisions between 1992 and 1994 were more driven by day-to-day pressures and political needs than by any elaborate concept of European order. It was not until 1994 that any new *Gesamtkonzept* appeared on the German foreign policy agenda.

The government in practice followed the Europeanist rationale. Foreign Minister Klaus Kinkel summarized Germany's basic objectives in a key speech in April 1994, stating that:

> In Europe we are faced with three essential questions determining our destiny: How can we secure peace? How can we ensure economic prosperity for our peoples? How can we preserve our place in the global context? For Germany the answer is unequivocal: only with and within the European Union and together with our partners in the western alliance can we master these challenges. This fundamental decision governs German foreign policy in an increasingly complicated world in which, despite all the problems, Europe will gradually unite.[62]

As Kinkel's formulation made clear, Germany's principal foreign policy interests and priorities remained focused on Europe, hesitantly accompanied by some 'global debuts'.[63] Some American observers described German foreign policy in this period as a 'holy trinity', consisting of 'European integration', 'transatlantic relations' and 'world trade'.[64] A closer look however suggests a more narrow and clearly hierarchical list of interests.

Germany's first and most pressing concern remained the full implementation of the Maastricht agenda, completing what *The Economist* called, the 'new Emurope'.[65] The project of Economic and Monetary Union with its tight economic convergence criteria and a European Central Bank located in Frankfurt was very much based on German ideas and concepts. If EMU were indeed to be realized, it seemed it would be largely on German terms, despite the reservations expressed by certain SPD politicians in 1992 about the wisdom of the automatic transition from the second to the third phase of Monetary Union.[66] Such criticism, however, was not fundamental at the time. It was not until 1995 that the entire EMU project became the subject of increasingly critical discussion. The 1993 Supreme Court ruling on Maastricht and EMU had insisted that the European Council was not allowed to distance itself from the convergence criteria when deciding on the first member countries. Until 1995 most German analysts foresaw only a few countries being able to fulfil the criteria. Therefore, it seemed obvious that only participants with very similar economic features would enter the initial EMU core in 1999. Hence, plausible negative effects of EMU as a result of hardly compatible national economies and job markets were not seriously discussed at the time.

Second, Germany sought to foster stability in central and eastern Europe by supplying generous financial assistance to the region and by supporting the gradual entry of these countries into western institutions. More than any other Western European country, Germany was exposed to potential instabilities in the eastern and south-eastern part of the continent. In order to stabilize the new democracies the country therefore provided more bilateral financial aid than any other state. Germany alone, in absolute terms, paid about two thirds (66 per cent) of all western aid to the CIS and eastern European states.[67] In 1993, it gave about DM90 billion (about £40 billion) to the CIS states as well as an additional DM37 billion to the eastern European countries.[68]

In addition, Germany was also the main advocate of closer links between former socialist countries and western institutions. Throughout 1990 and 1991 Germany was one of the driving forces behind the first association agreements with the then three transition states – the so called Europe Agreements – as well as the launch and extension of the EC Phare programme. From early 1992 onwards Germany also pushed for association agreements with the Baltic states, against the resistance of France and the EC commission.[69] The question of EU membership for central and eastern European countries turned out to be a greater challenge. Between 1992 and 1994, intergovernmental debates still centred upon the dichotomy between deepening or widening the EU. While the British advocated widening towards the east (aiming for an overall loose and less cohesive Community) and the French pushed for deepening among the twelve (partly to maintain France's balance within the EU *vis-à-vis* Germany) the German position was to avoid making a choice between deepening or widening; Kohl began to emphasize the parallel necessity for both.[70] However, the German government did not put forward any proposal on how to reconcile widening with deepening. Some 'prototypes' of the later concepts for a multi-speed Europe and 'differentiated integration' were discussed within the academic community as early as winter 1991–92, but they did not arouse much public or political response.[71]

Instead, German politicians gradually developed a clear preference for expanding the western security institutions, NATO and WEU, before granting membership to the EU. The SPD opposition, in particular, warned the government not to make 'irresponsible promises of fast EC membership to the central and eastern reform states'.[72] The political and economic costs of unification had made German opinion much more hesitant about any further enlargement, even to Germany's immediate eastern neighbours. Kohl's support at EU summits in 1992–93 for a clear commitment to EU eastern enlargement masked an underlying ambivalence. Leading CDU politicians such as Volker Rühe spoke in similarly ambivalent terms of 'a realistic membership perspective'.[73] The real message was spelled out in a joint article by Helmut Kohl and Edouard Balladur, published in *Le Monde* and the *Frankfurter Allgemeine Zeitung* on 27 May 1994:

> We have to be aware that the way of these countries into the European Union is a difficult and a long one. It is therefore important, to stress to them already today that they are in principle welcome in the European Union.[74]

In contrast, the German government (in particular Defence Minister Volker Rühe) was, with the US Administration, the main driving force behind the policy of an eastern expansion of NATO.[75] Chancellor Kohl made clear that 'this has always been a goal of German foreign policy – and it will remain to be so'.[76] The German government also pushed the WEU to offer 'associate partner status' to the Visegrad and the Baltic states plus Romania and Bulgaria. This allowed these countries to attend biweekly WEU ambassadors' sessions and to contribute troops to WEU missions, although they received no security guarantees in return.[77] The third major German goal was to support and stabilize the reform process in the former Soviet Union. The government constantly stressed that 'if the reforms in Russia fail' and the country returned either to 'communist structures' or to a 'military dictatorship', then 'it will become very expensive for the West and for the Germans'.[78]

Germany's approach to Russia, however, was fundamentally different than towards eastern Europe. The Kohl government established a broad base of bilateral aid, expanded trade and cooperation mechanisms, but did not seek to integrate Russia into western European institutions. Volker Rühe was outspoken in his view that 'it is the most natural thing' that Russia 'can never become a member of either the European Union or NATO'.[79] On a personal level, Chancellor Kohl developed a very close relationship with the Russian leader Boris Yeltsin, and some observers contended that Kohl acquired the role as 'the west's single most effective bridge-builder to Moscow'.[80] Overall, however Germany followed a realpolitik strategy, fostering an ever closer dialogue with Russia without holding out any promises of future inclusion in any of Western Europe's institutions. Germany's close consultation with Russia carefully avoided any echoes of the old and often repeated 'Rapallo complex': of playing off the east against the west.

The fourth key German objective concerned the redefinition of transatlantic relations after the end of the cold war. After President George Bush's invitation to establish a German–American 'partnership in leadership', and Clinton's view that 'America has no better friend than Chancellor Kohl', some German policymakers began to see Germany, rather than the UK, as the senior European partner of the United States.[81] Such joint initiatives as the proposal for the North Atlantic Cooperation Council (NACC) and NATO's 'partnership for peace' programme encouraged this view.[82] Foreign Minister Klaus Kinkel went furthest, in the spring of 1995, in proposing three new institutions: a 'transatlantic political cooperation' (TAPC) based on the EPC-model, a 'Transatlantic Free Trade Zone (TAFTA) and a 'transatlantic learning community' co-ordinating policies and exchange on the 'new domestic policy challenges facing the West'.[83] Kinkel's proposals, however, received at best a lukewarm welcome in Washington. From an American perspective, the quality of German–American partnership largely depended on whether Germany would take on more global responsibilities, or would remain predominantly a European power. Some American analysts liked to see Germany serving as the 'US branch manager' for Europe, a much less appealing image than the partnership which German leaders sought.[84]

While many academic commentators saw the three policy options – 'core Europe', 'wider West' and 'Mitteleuropa' – as incompatible, the Kohl government appeared to advocate pursuing all at once. As the dominant economic power at the heart of Europe, the government saw itself as 'the advocate of the whole of Europe'.[85] The government's fundamental interest, therefore, was to create interlinked layers of stability in Europe. This meant building a fully integrated core Europe, surrounded by a layer of bilateral and multilateral affiliation agreements with eastern Europe, with an outer layer of bilateral and multilateral support for Russia. This European order would in turn be protected through continuing western co-operation, with a deepened German–American 'partnership in leadership' as its central axis. This layer-cake model provided the outline for the more focused post-1994 debate on how to bring such a model into practice.

1994–97: 'flexibility' as the German *'gesamtkonzept'* for a new European order

With eastern countries pressing for access and with the EMU deadline fast approaching, the German debate between 1994 and 1997 refocused on two central ambitions: the creation of EMU and the enlargement of the EU and NATO. These issues overshadowed broader controversies over questions of European order. From 1994 onwards German policymakers and commentators began openly to develop a set of concepts for a new European architecture which would draw together all its various and sometimes conflicting foreign policy aims. Conceptually, the years between 1994 and 1996 were innovative. The search for more 'flexibility' became the chief objective for academics and policymakers, with various suggestions on how to achieve it. The public debate, however, narrowed significantly. With the EMU deadline fast approaching, political and public discussions after 1994 refocused on the European Union itself much more than on the wider Europe.

Concepts of a 'flexible' European order

The June 1994 Corfu European Council recognized that an EU with potentially 27 members, with much greater political and economic diversity, would require major changes in its structure, institutions and policies. Now it was becoming clear that enlargement was rolling forward and that the potential incompatibilities between widening and deepening had to be overcome, the idea of a more flexible Europe attracted increasing attention. The question was whether such adjustment could simply be achieved by an institutional muddling through or whether, in typical German fashion, it required a well thought through *Gesamtkonzept*.

As early as 1974 Willy Brandt had spoken about different speeds in integration. In 1984, law professor Eberhard Grabitz had suggested *'abgestufte Integration'*, a concept of different layers of integration.[86] In 1989, prior to unification, the Chancellor's advisers Michael Mertes and Norbert Prill had promoted the concept of 'concentric circles' around a central core.[87] Partly based on these previous models, from 1994 onwards concepts of a more flexible Europe emerged. Josef Janning has identified two distinct approaches: 'core protagonists' and 'new integrationists'.[88] Some German analysts proposed to return to an exclusive 'core Europe', following the analysis that widening and deepening the EU were both essential for Germany, but that there would never be a sufficient majority of member states sharing both preferences. The landmark document was the famous Schäuble–Lamers paper, drafted primarily by CDU MdB Karl Lamers for the CDU Bundestag *Fraktion* (of which Schäuble was leader) in September 1994. It advocated a 'variable geometry' or 'multispeed' Europe with a limited number of states in a more deeply-integrated 'hard core', which would give 'the Union a strong centre to counteract the centrifugal forces generated by constant enlargement'.[89] Its heart would be limited to participants in EMU, most likely the original six members minus Italy. The Schäuble–Lamers paper saw such a core Europe as the ultimate resort if other attempts failed.

Closely echoing the CDU paper, the Ebenhausen think tank researcher Christian Deubner published in 1995 the first conceptual book on a core

Europe in the German debate, spelling out the advantages of narrowing core Europe down to the original EEC founders minus Italy.[90] Germany, France and Benelux as a group could not only achieve monetary union but also defence union. In the EU's third pillar, Deubner also saw the Schengen Agreement as the basis for joint decisions among the five. To achieve this, the five could build on the institutional structures of the Benelux Union and the established co-operation provisions of the Franco-German treaty.[91]

Fearful lest an exclusive European core could once again split the continent, but acknowledging the benefits of variable geometry, 'new integrationists' advocated instead a more 'differentiated integration'. This refined concept for a Europe of 27 nations was developed by Josef Janning and Werner Weidenfeld of the Munich-based think tank, the *Centrum für angewandte Politikforschung*.[92] In January 1996, 'differentiated integration' became the basis for an international forum sponsored by the Bertelsmann Foundation.[93] 'Differentiated integration' aimed to deepen integration to varying degrees in different policy areas. With no fixed timetable, the optimal number of countries would 'opt-in' to overlapping core circles whenever willing and ready to meet their specific requirements. First priority should be given to establishing EMU. The concept also envisaged a differentiated pattern of leadership in the European Union. The current and alternating six-month presidency which prepares and represents all Union affairs would be replaced by elected one-year presidencies within the different circles. Thus the CFSP presidency could be different from the EMU presidency. Last but not least, the concept implied major restructuring of the European Union budget and its various funds.[94]

It is difficult to measure the direct impact of this concept on the government's position in EU negotiations. It is worth noting that ideas of 'differentiated integration' or 'partial membership' were later advocated by the CDU foreign policy expert, Rudolf Seiters, and others.[95] The Munich group around Werner Weidenfeld was certainly influential in promoting ideas and advising policymakers in the CDU, including Chancellor Kohl, as well as active in promoting German ideas for the future organization of Europe through publications and international symposia. Professor Weidenfeld was in effect a classic example of a 'policy entrepreneur', with his own research group (backed by the extensive resources of the Bertelsmann Foundation), excellent contacts both in Europe and the USA and direct access to the Chancellor. These ideas became part of the currency of German political debate; though how far they directly influenced German decisions is hard to measure. As Bulmer and Paterson have argued, Chancellor Kohl tended to distance himself from such 'kite-flying' exercises as the Schäuble–Lamers paper and the Bertelsmann group's proposals, in order to retain the flexibility to make strategic adjustments in European policy and to be able to play the role of consensus-builder in EU negotiations.[96]

Pushing Europe ahead: the german government's policies 1994–97

Despite this vigorous intellectual debate, the German government itself had not by the summer of 1997 spelt out any detailed concept of how to integrate and associate the European periphery with a strengthened core. The German political élite nevertheless converged around the image of a structured, multilevel but integrated pan-European order. The German President Roman Herzog represented this emerging consensus in stating that while he rejected the idea of Europe as an advanced free trade area, he also rejected a 'core Europe' if this were a final goal in itself.[97] German concepts and interests necessarily encompassed more than a narrow EMUrope.

Lacking a clearly articulated *Gesamtkonzept*, however, did not mean adopting a more flexible Europe as a guide to policy. On EMU, for example, Chancellor Kohl frequently argued that 'the slowest vessel cannot delay the entire convoy'.[98] The government remained publicly committed to all five sets of interests described above, and in particular to NATO enlargement, but its most pressing priority was the completion of the unfinished Maastricht project.[99] Apart from such rhetorical declarations as Kohl's characterization of EMU as 'the decisive question for war and peace in the 21st century', structural changes in German decision making also indicated the growing importance of shaping policy on EU affairs.

The Foreign Office in 1993 created for the first time a separate European division in order to play a greater role in the formulation of European policy. In December 1994 the German parliament set up a specialized and potentially very powerful Committee for European Union affairs. However, the most important development was that Chancellor Kohl asserted his constitutional power to determine the guidelines of policy (*Richtlinenkompetenz*) over the field of European integration.[100] The Chancellor's Office, as during the process of German unification, again became the central body where major German EU strategies were formulated. Once again, Kohl seemed to follow a pattern which he devised whenever dealing with great issues: concentrate on vision rather than on details. As *The Economist* put it, the principle is to 'establish a point of no return, march past it, never mind about popularity and let the details take care of themselves'.[101] Kohl applied this formula in his early years as chancellor, brushing aside public opposition when he assured Germany's commitment to the western policy of strength. He used the same method in pushing through German unification and was now trying to do the same with EMU.[102]

For a long time any kind of challenge either to Maastricht or to EMU had remained taboo within the German political élite. After 1994 though, some anti-European sentiment gradually surfaced among German political leaders. Some regional leaders, most prominently Edmund Stoiber, the CSU Bavarian prime minister, and Gerhard Schröder, SPD minister-president of Lower Saxony, started to criticize the economic aspects of integration, including monetary union, arguing that their 'country is being taken for a financial ride by the European Union'.[103] From autumn 1995 onwards, some Social Democrats in regional elections in southern Germany raised doubts over the timetable of EMU, trying to turn the growing public resistance against the project into a political trump card for the SPD.

This populist approach brought out the latent scepticism about EMU, opening up during 1996 a more public debate, with increasingly harsh tones in both camps.[104] Opinion polls showed that two-thirds of ordinary Germans were opposed to the euro, but that they were equally convinced it would come regardless. In January 1997 only 13 per cent of Germans believed that EU membership was beneficial for the country, 43 per cent thought that advantages and disadvantages would balance each other, while 40 per cent saw predominantly negative effects.[105] The same opinion poll showed Gerhard Schröder, one of the possible SPD candidates for chancellor in 1998, for the first time beating Helmut Kohl in a head-on contest for the chancellorship. Schröder positioned himself as a moderate critic, primarily questioning the rigorous timetable for EMU. He called for a strict interpretation of the convergence criteria and suggested deferral if European economies were not ready. In addition, he demanded that popular scepticism not be suppressed by élite consensus and called for a serious public debate.[106] President Roman Herzog in reply warned the nation against making EMU an election issue.[107]

The strength of the élite consensus – or of the taboo over questioning this political priority – was reflected in the reluctance of leading German economists to promote a more open debate on the costs and benefits to Germany. With the exception of some Bundesbank economists, most famously Hans Tietmeyer, who insisted on a very strict interpretation of the convergence criteria, German business people abstained from public discussion for a long time. While private bankers were enthusiastic about the prospects of EMU, many medium-size company entrepreneurs were rather hesitant. However, their reservations did not significantly influence the German public debate on EMU, which generally remained removed from ordinary people. The Maastricht ratification process had already uncovered a wide gulf between the German mass public and the country's political and intellectual élites.[108] With regard to Maastricht the élites held together; on EMU the leadership of the SPD now divided over whether to capitalize on the electorate's reservations. Unlike Schröder, SPD party leader Oskar Lafontaine was a strong supporter of monetary union.[109] Former Social Democratic chancellor Helmut Schmidt had become one of the strongest and most respected proponents of EMU. As an important voice in the public debates on the future of Europe, he not only attacked Bundesbank president Hans Tietmeyer as 'the most prominent Eurosceptic' because of his strictly monetarist interpretation of the Maastricht treaty, he also publicly ridiculed Gerhard Schröder as a 'strategic pygmy'.[110] In similar terms to those of Kohl,

Schmidt argued that whoever asked for a deferral of EMU 'endangers our future'.[111]

The reshaping of Europe through enlargement, about which much of the German public appeared equally sceptical and much of the political élite ambivalent, remained a secondary issue half-hidden behind the preoccupation with monetary union and the completion of this pre-1989 Franco-German project. The Franco-German accord, central throughout post-war history and decisive for the completion of the Maastricht agenda, has become increasingly strained after unification and, in particular, since Jacques Chirac's accession to the presidency in 1995. The post-1989 environment, with the disappearance of the Soviet threat as a binding external force, has certainly magnified existing areas of divergence between France and Germany. There are a number of long-established differences of opinion. Regarding EU institutions, France favoured intergovernmentalism with a strong role for the Council, whereas Germany has been federalist. Bonn favoured free trade and global competition for the Union, while Paris still believed in political, occasionally protectionist management of international trade. As a far as a common foreign and security policy was concerned, France wanted to see member states maintaining independent positions while Germany advocated consensus. France's interests focused on the south, Germany's on the east. France promoted an active role and autonomy for Europe in international security policy. Germany felt comfortable under an American umbrella, was reluctant to participate in military manoeuvres and remained fully committed to NATO.[112] Most importantly, with regard to EMU, the Germans were determined to see EMU controlled by an absolutely independent European Central Bank with automatic stability rules, to prevent European governments from undermining its fiscal and monetary orthodoxy, while France continued to fight for political control over the currency. It pleaded for a kind of 'economic government' among the participants in the common currency which would be able to co-ordinate policies for economic stimulation if needed.

The ongoing battles over the nomination for the president of the European Central Bank reflected these divergencies. Those disagreements existed for a long time, but they have become more open in recent years. They will become even more decisive as the creation of a single currency will indeed lead to some form of inner core in Europe. It will require deeper institutionalization of policy co-operation, particularly in the areas of economic, fiscal and possibly foreign policies. It remains to be seen whether to what extent co-ordination in the EMU group will function and whether Paris and Bonn will be capable of acting jointly for the advancement of the whole Union. The key question will be whether the German concept of an integrated EMU core as a catalyst of a federal Europe will crumble as German leaders find it more and more difficult to work with the French; whether the Franco-German partnership will manage to overcome the existing conceptual gaps or whether they will settle for an alternative approach and, in the end, for a different European order replacing

Germany's central focus on a politically integrated Europe. Both governments are fully aware of the special need to co-operate closer then ever in order to ensure the continued compatibility of their European strategies. The Kohl government has been remarkably committed to bridging whatever gaps between Bonn and Paris have arisen or are likely to arise. In 1995 the CDU/CSU parliamentary group has founded a new working group to 'intensify' Franco-German relations.[113] Since Chirac's presidency, Bonn and Paris have stepped up their bilateral summit meetings to one every six weeks. Also the two foreign ministers have multiplied their meetings. Nevertheless, as some observers have argued, the continued scarcity of real common concepts for further integration in spite of such intensification of co-operation makes the prospects for the Franco-German accord all the more discouraging.[114]

Even further, in the aftermath of the disappointing Amsterdam summit in June 1997 which failed to achieve necessary reform of the EU's institutions, voices in the German government and the *Auswärtiges Amt* were suggesting a rethink of the old vision of ever closer political union had become more influential.[115] No doubt, Helmut Kohl and many of his generation remained committed to EMU as the key step for further political integration of Europe. However, his successors might, whether happily or not, accept a fuzzier European order likely to emerge from the currently still contrasting and incompatible national concepts and strategies: a wider Europe, neither consisting of loosely linked nation states nor of a political union with a federal government and army, but rather of a curious mixture of integration and *ad hoc* intergovernmental co-operation.

Conclusion

The German discourse on European order since 1989 has been central to reflections on the future shape of the continent. 'Early at the beach' in characteristic fashion, German political and intellectual leaders between 1989 and 1991 dampened the fears of their allies by sticking to their commitment to multilateral diplomacy and international integration. Having thus reassured their neighbours, Germany's academic community between 1992 and 1994 then developed many intellectual sandcastles, in a vibrant beach olympics. Meanwhile the government, preoccupied with practical problems, developed an outline image of future European order: layers of associated stability zones with EMU as its heart and transatlantic ties as a security guarantee. While the academic community after 1994 dug deeper in developing refined concepts of a flexible European order, the government, lacking a clear vision on a full European order, was focused on bringing EMU into existence.

Monetary union, however, in German eyes was not an end itself, but a means towards the construction of a wider and safer European neighbourhood. How far that neighbourhood should extend, and what should be the architecture for its rebuilding, remained unclear. German policymakers, based on traditional political interests, on historical notions of the German *hinterland* as well as on cultural explanations, paid most attention to Poland, the Czech Republic and Hungary. Chancellor Kohl's repeated declaration that 'the frontiers of Europe should not stop at the frontiers of Germany' gave some other EU governments the impression that the aim was only to move the boundaries of the EU and NATO one country to the east. German policy-makers and commentators were also preoccupied with Russia, Turkey and Ukraine, but were much less clear about their place in a wider institutionalized Europe, or about the destiny of the smaller countries of central and eastern Europe. Germany seemed to be most confused about how to accommodate Turkey in the European house. In addition to insensitive comments about Turkey and Islam, the German government was one of the strongest opponents of explicitly accepting Turkey, alongside the former socialist states of central and south-eastern Europe, as a candidate for EU membership. Mostly for domestic reasons, fearing that membership would lead to mass migration of Turks into Germany, but also due to the CDU's peculiar understanding of Europe as a Christian club, Bonn blocked a more reasonable dialogue with Turkey.

More decisive for the future of the continent was the extent to which German conceptual thinking was shared, approved, rejected or accepted by Germany's partners and neighbours. For the first time in history Germany found itself, as is often quoted, 'surrounded by nothing but friends'. But it was difficult for the German élite to carry their neighbours with them, given those neighbours' continuing uneasiness about potential German hegemony. 'Germany has to lead', the conservative CDU politician Karl Lamers has said, 'but without anybody realizing it'.[116] Indeed it remains one of the compelling questions: whether Germany will turn friends into partners in building European order; whether Germany will become the 'gentle giant or the emerging leader'.[117] The history of European integration has shown that progress needs ideas and initiatives, but that it also needs time and diplomacy. Stability of order is hard to create, but even harder to impose.

There can, however, be no doubt that German conceptual thinking on core Europe was a catalyst for the overall European debate in the mid 1990s. The notion of a 'multi-speed' or 'variable-geometry' Europe, highly contested in 1994, became a more widely accepted approach in the preparations for the 1996–97 IGC; flexibility was one of the main themes of the IGC negotiations. Furthermore, despite unfavourable circumstances and growing unemploy-ment, economic policies throughout Western Europe were driven by the desire to meet the criteria for the EMU. At the same time, most ordinary citizens across Europe seem to have remained either ignorant or hostile towards the promised merits of a single currency.[118] Despite all existing criticism, it seemed in mid 1997 that EMU would go ahead on time on the German rather than the French model, still resting on the twin pillars of fiscal rectitude and price stability.[119]

Behind this drive to complete the pre-1989 agenda, the German government and its partners were drifting towards enlargement negotiations with the Europe Agreement states without any coherent image of how far enlargement might go, or how fast a process it should become. American insistence in the first six months of 1997 on restricting NATO enlargement to only three applicants – Poland, the Czech Republic and Hungary – was very much to German tastes, rather than to French or Italian; Romania and Slovenia did not loom large in German foreign policy priorities. But American negotiations on this, and on the association of Russia with NATO, were conducted almost as much over German heads as over those of the other allies. The final stages of the IGC negotiations, in summer 1997, exposed confusion within the German government, with disagreements among ministries and between the federal government and the Länder. Policymaking in Bonn remained fragmented, with different ministers pursuing their own priorities.

Nevertheless, the German debate was more fundamental and conceptually more rigorous than most others. On the political level, the German government was more outspoken and more assertive in defining and promoting its interests and concepts. It remained however to be seen whether German concepts would turn out to be dikes or sandcastles when the next floods, possibly the full consequences of economic globalization, reached the beaches of the old continent. Even the most confident German political strategists leave room for the surprises of history and, hence, for the limits of all political and conceptual planning. Reflecting on the uncertainties of European order, Wolfgang Schäuble, the CDU's main conceptual thinker on foreign affairs, has recalled one of Otto von Bismarck's pronouncements. 'The statesman', Schäuble quoted, 'is very much like the wanderer in the forest who knows the general direction of his route, but never the exact point where he will eventually leave the wood.'[120]

Notes

1. The mayor of Berlin, Walter Momper, in a public speech on 10 November 1989, a day after the opening of the Berlin Wall. For details see Horst Teltschik, *329 Tage. Innenansichten der Einigung* (Berlin: Siedler 1991) p. 19 (henceforth cited as Teltschik, *329 Tage*).
2. Whether the community's discourse indeed, as Ole Waever suggests, sets the parameters for foreign policy scenarios and choices remains to be debated. See Ole Waever, 'Resisting the Temptation of Post Foreign Policy Analysis', in Walter Carlsnaes and Steve Smith, *European Foreign Policy: The EC and Changing Perspectives in Europe* (London: Sage Publications 1994) pp. 238–73. See also discussion of Weaver's suggestions in Gunther Hellmann, 'Goodbye Bismarck? The Foreign Policy of Contemporary Germany', *Mershon International Studies Review*, no. 40 (1996) pp. 1–39 (henceforth cited as Hellmann, 'Goodbye Bismarck?').
3. The preamble of the German Basic Law expresses the wish of the German people to 'serve global peace as an equal member of a Unified Europe'.

4. Jakob Kaiser, *Deutschland und die Union. Die Berliner Tagung 1946. Reden und Aussprache*, Berlin 1946, p. 17.

5. These points leave aside the often mentioned criticism of Adenauer's severe anti-Prussian sentiment and his general mistrust of what he called the 'asiatic steppe', i.e. the eastern parts of Germany.

6. Konrad Adenauer, *Erinnerungen, Band 1 1945–53* (Frankfurt a.M.: Fischer, 1969) p. 97.

7. For many years, the western partners blamed Bonn for constraining east–west détente through insisting on Germany's 'private conflict'. According to President Nixon, it became time for Germany 'to join the crowd' and play an important part in seeking overall détente. Nixon, cited in Roger Morgan, *West Germany's Foreign Policy Agenda* (Beverly Hills: Sage, 1978) p. 21.

8. For a detailed analysis of the policies prior to Brandt's chancellorship see, among many others, Wolfram Hanrieder, *Germany, America, Europe: Forty Years of German Foreign Policy* (New Haven: Yale University Press, 1989) chap. 6, pp. 170–94 (hereafter cited as Hanrieder, *Germany, America, Europe*). For a good short summary of these years see Avril Pittmann, *From Ostpolitik To Reunification: West German-Soviet Political Relations Since 1974* (Cambridge: Cambridge University Press, 1992) pp. 5–12.

9. For details on Egon Bahr's so called 'grand design' see Walter F. Hahn, 'West Germany's Ostpolitik: the grand design of Egon Bahr', *Orbis*, 16:4 (1973) pp. 859–80 (henceforth Hahn, 'Ostpolitik').

10. Hahn, 'Ostpolitik', p. 878.

11. To ensure the continuation of this consensus, Chancellor Kohl, for example in the Bundestag debate on the 1990 CSCE Paris summit, admitted once again that the CDU's traditional 'scepticism' towards the CSCE and collective détente 'luckily had no grounding'. He explicitly expressed his 'particular respect' for the policies and decisions taken by 'Chancellor Helmut Schmidt and Foreign Minister Hans-Dietrich Genscher', as well as by 'the colleagues Willy Brandt and Walter Scheel'. *Deutscher Bundestag*, Stenographische Berichte, Sitzung 11/236, 22 November 1990, p. 18864 (henceforth: DB, 11/236, 22 Nov 1990).

12. Stanley Hoffmann, 'Abschied von der Vergangenheit: Politik und Sicherheit im Europa der neunziger Jahre', *Europa-Archiv*, Vol. 45, 25 October 1990, p. 604.

13. Gunther Hellmann, ' "Einbindungspolitik": United Germany and the Promise of Foreign Policy Continuity', paper presented at the 36th Annual Convention of the International Studies Association (ISA) in Chicago, 21–25 February 1995, p. 4 (henceforth cited as Hellmann, 'Einbindungspolitik'). I am grateful to Gunther Hellmann, of the Technical University Darmstadt, for allowing me access to his comprehensive private collection of material relevant to this chapter.

14. Ischinger quoted in 'Germany And Its Interests: Hearing secret harmonies', *The Economist*, 20 November 1993, p. 20.

15. The debate on whether Maastricht marked an end or a new beginning in the thinking on European policy is a controversial one. See for example Hans Arnold, ' "Maastricht" – Anfang oder Ende einer Entwicklung?', *Aussenpolitik*, III (1993), pp. 271–80.

16. *DB*, 11/173, 8 November 1989, p. 13018.

17. *DB*, 11/173, 8 November 1989, p. 13023.

18. *DB*, 11/176, 16 November 1989, p. 13336.

19. *DB*, 11/176, 16 November 1989, p. 13365.

20. Quote in Teltschik, *329 Tage*, p. 19.

21. *DB*, 11/177, 28 November 1989, pp. 13510–14. For a discussion of Kohls's plan, see Peter R. Weilemann, 'Der deutsche Beitrag zur Überwindung der europäischen Teilung – Die zehn Punkte von Bundeskanzler Helmut Kohl', *Außenpolitik*, 1 (1990) pp. 15–23.

22. Teltschik, *329 Tage*, p. 65. Also Margaret Thatcher, *The Downing Street Years* (London: HarperCollins, 1993) pp. 759–62, 795.

23. Hans-Dietrich Genscher, *Erinnerungen* (Berlin: Siedler, 1995) p. 710.

24. Teltschik, *329 Tage*, p. 117.

25. On the diplomacy of German unification see among others Teltschik, *329 Tage*; Karl Kaiser, *Deutschlands Vereinigung. Die internationalen Aspekte* (Bergisch-Gladbach: Bastei-Lübbe, 1991); Ulrich Albrecht, *Die Abwicklung der DDR. Die 'Zwei-plus-Vier'-Verhandlungen. Ein Insider-Bericht* (Opladen: Westdeutscher Verlag, 1992); Richard Kiessler and Frank Elbe, *Ein runder Tisch mit scharfen Ecken. Der diplomatische Weg zur deutschen Einheit* (Baden-Baden: Nomos, 1993); Stephen F. Szabo, *The Diplomacy of German Unification* (New York: St. Martin's Press, 1992); Michael R. Beschloss and Strobe Talbott, *At the Highest Level: The Inside Story of the End of the Cold War* (Boston: Little, Brown and Company, 1993); Elizabeth Pond, *Beyond the Wall: Germany's Road to Unification* (Washington, DC: The Brookings Institution, 1993); Philip Zelikow and Condoleeza Rice, *Germany Unified and Europe Transformed* (Cambridge, MA: Harvard University Press, 1995).

26. Teltschik, *329 Tage*, pp. 97–100.

27. 'Gemeinsame Erklärung von Kohl und Mitterand', Presse-und Informationsamt der Bundesregierung (ed.), *Stichworte zur Sicherheitspolitik*, 3 (1991), pp. 16–20. On the Dublin summit see Josef Janning and Melanie Piepenschneider, *Deutschland in Europa. Eine Bilanz europäischer Einigungspolitik* (Melle: Knoth, 1993) pp. 44–5.

28. Beverly Crawford, 'Explaining Defection from International Cooperation. Germany's Unilateral Recognition of Croatia', *World Politics*, 48 (July 1996) pp. 482–521.

29. Joseph S. Nye, 'New Roles in the Post-Cold War Order' in Helga Haftendorn and Christian Tuschhoff, *America and Europe In An Era Of Change* (Boulder, CO: Westview Press, 1993) pp. 87–104.

30. Eckard Lübkemeier, 'The United Germany in the Post-Bipolar World', *International Politik und Gesellschaft*, 2 (1994), pp. 145–61 (henceforth cited as Lübkemeier, 'Germany in Post-Bipolar World').

31. Lübkemeier, 'Germany in Post-Bipolar World', p. 146. American theorists argue that shifting alliances between these roughly equally powerful centres will be the source of and principle for stability in the twenty-first century. See Nye, 'New Roles', p. 97.

32. Charles Krauthammer, 'The Unipolar Moment', *Foreign Affairs*, 70:1 (1990–91) pp. 23–33.

33. Hanns W. Maull, 'Germany and Japan: The New Civilian Powers', *Foreign Affairs*, 69:5, (Winter 1990–91) pp. 91–106. Also Lübkemeier, 'Germany in Post-Bipolar World', p. 147.

34. In particular the widely debated article by John J. Mearsheimer, 'Back to the Future: Instability in Europe After the Cold War', Sean M. Lynn-Jones (ed.), *The Cold War and After* (Cambridge: MIT Press, 1991) pp. 141–92.

35. Josef Janning, 'A German Europe – a European Germany? On the debate over Germany's foreign policy', *International Affairs*, 72:1 (1994) p. 34.

36. Most important among others Hans-Peter Schwarz, *Die Zentralmacht Europas. Deutschlands Rückkehr auf die Weltbühne* (Berlin: Siedler, 1994). See also summary of Schwarz in Janning, 'A German Europe – a European Germany?', pp. 34–5.

37. The Harvard historian Charles S. Maier replied to a self-conscious German colleague at a conference on 'Unified Germany in a Unified Europe' that although being in the 'memory business' himself, he would be fed up with remembering, if this made Germany incapable of acting in accordance with the obvious needs and circumstances of today. Quote in Verena Lueken, 'Für eine Weile ein bißchen weniger Ordnung. Amerikas Elite sieht optimistisch auf "Das vereinigte Deutschland in einem Vereinigten Europa" – Eine Tagung in Harvard', *Frankfurter Allgemeine Zeitung*, 3 November 1995, p. 41.

38. For a discussion on these basic convictions: Michael Doyle, 'Liberalism and World Politics', *American Political Science Review*, 80:4 (December 1986) pp. 1151–69.

39. Huntington sees a severe anti-Western bias in many of the world's cultures, potentially threatening Western interests, values and powers – even with the use of military force. As a consequence, he recommends a revitalization and self-protection of a 'fortress West' based on economic and military strength. Samuel P. Huntington, 'The Clash of Civilizations?' *Foreign Affairs*, 72:3 (Summer 1993) pp. 22–49.

40. Wolfgang Schäuble, 'Die christliche Identität Europas – Erbe und Auftrag', speech delivered on 6 May 1994 at the meeting of the study group of Protestant and Catholic entrepreneurs in Germany (author's translation).

41. *Ibid.*

42. Helmut Schmidt, 'Europa und die Deutschen in einer sich ändernden Welt', *Internationale Politik und Gesellschaft*, no. 1 (1995) p. 13.

43. Quoted in 'Germany and Islam: Eastern reproaches', *The Economist*, 19 April 1997, pp. 42–3.

44. Timothy Garton Ash, 'Germany's Choice', *Foreign Affairs*, 73:4 (July–August 1994) pp. 65–81.

45. Gunther Hellmann, 'Goodbye Bismarck?', op. cit..

46. For an overview see a collection of essays in Heimo Schwilk and Ulrich Schacht (eds), *Die selbstbewußte Nation*, 3rd edn (Berlin: Ullstein, 1995).

47. The term 'normalization-nationalists' ('Normalisierungsnationalisten') was introduced by the SPD intellectual Peter Glotz, editor of the *Frankfurter Hefte*; also Hellmann, 'Goodbye Bismarck?', p. 17.

48. Hellmann, 'Goodbye Bismarck?', p. 14, citing and referring to Albert Statz, 'Das Recht auf Selbstbestimmung muß einhergehen mit der Pflicht zur Selbstbeschränkung: Zur politischen Strategie einer grün-alternativen Außenpolitik', in Katrin Fuchs, Peter von Oertzen and Ludger Volmer (eds), *Zieht die Linke in den Krieg? Beiträge zur Debatte um Kampfeinsätze aus rot-grüner Sicht*, (Cologne: spw-Verlag, 1993) p. 184.

49. For more details see Dieter S. Lutz, *Deutschland und die kollektive Sicherheit: Politische, rechtliche und programmatische Aspekte* (Opladen: Leske und Budrich, 1993).

50. Hellmann, 'Goodbye Bismarck?', pp. 15–16.

51. Most important among others: Hans-Peter Schwarz, *Die Zentralmacht Europas*.

52. Gregor Schöllgen, 'National Interests and International Responsibility: Germany's Role in World Affairs', in Arnulf Baring (ed.), *Germany's New Position in Europe: Problems and Perspectives* (Oxford: Berg, 1994) p. 43.

53. *Ibid.*

54. Arnulf Baring, 'Germany, what now?', in Baring, *Germany's New Position*, pp. 16–17.

55. Schöllgen, *National Interest and International Responsibility*, p. 45.

56. *Ibid.*

57. Konrad Seitz, 'Deutschland und Europa in der Weltwirtschaft von morgen: Partner in der Triad oder Kolonie?', *Merkur*, Vol. 448 (September–October 1994) pp. 828–49.

58. Hellmann, 'Goodbye Bismarck?', pp. 5–9.

59. See, as one example, the decision on the Bundeswehr participation in the IFOR troops in Bosnia. After opposing such participation on moral grounds in 1995, a year later the Social Democrats endorsed the renewal of the Bundeswehr mandate without even requesting a parliamentary debate.

60. Joschka Fischer, *Risiko Deutschland. Krise und Zukunft der deutschen Politik* (Cologne: Kiepenheuer & Witsch, 1994).

61. Simon Bulmer and William E. Paterson, 'Germany in the European Union: gentle giant or emergent leader', *International Affairs*, 72:1 (1996) pp. 24–5.

62. Speech by Klaus Kinkel in Sigmaringen on 29 April 1994, *Bulletin der Bundesregierung*, no. 40, 5 May 1994, pp. 350–1 (author's translation).

63. The expression 'global debuts' is borrowed from Karen Donfried, 'German Foreign Policy: Regional Priorities and Global Debuts', *CRS Report for Congress*, 25 October 1995, (Washington: Congressional Research Service, 1995).

64. Jonathan P.G. Bach, 'The Conceptual Underpinnings of German Foreign Policy: A Thematic Treatment', paper presented at the International Studies Association Annual Conference, Chicago, February 1995.

65. For example Helmut Schlesinger, 'Money is just the start', *The Economist*, 21 September 1996, pp. 25–7.

66. Lionel Barber, 'Bonn sets agenda for monetary union', *Financial Times*, 2 October 1995, p. 2; speech by Hans-Ulrich Klose in *DB*, 12/97, 17 June 1992, p. 7965. 'Rigid stability criteria', the SPD claimed, 'are more important than abstract timetables.' See *DB*, 12/108, 25 September 1992, p. 9223.

67. Speech by Klaus Kinkel on 24 August 1994 in Bonn, reprinted in *Bulletin der Bundesregierung*, no. 76 (1994) p. 714.

68. Speech by Chancellor Kohl in Bonn on 27 May 1994, *Bulletin der Bundesregierung*, no. 41, 31 May 1994, p. 479. To illustrate Germany's financial efforts even better, a Canadian government report compared the per capita spending of the G7 nations to the former Soviet Union and Eastern Europe between 1989 and 1994: Germany $341, Canada $67, France $34, Italy $31, United States $30, Japan $5 and Great Britain $1 (cited in 'Speech by Klaus Kinkel in Sigmaringen on 29 April 1994', *Bulletin der Bundesregierung*, no. 40, 5 May 1994, p. 350).

69. Reinhard Stuth, 'Deutschlands neue Rolle im sich wandelnden Europa', *Aussenpolitik*, no. 1 (1992) p. 28.

70. Reinhard Meier-Walser, 'Deutschland, Frankreich und Großbritannien an der Schwelle zu einem neuen Europa', *Aussenpolitik*, no. 4 (1992) p. 339; Gregory F. Treverton, 'The New Europe', *Foreign Affairs*, 71:1 (1991–92) p. 97.

71. For such early models Heinz Kramer, 'Die EG und die Stabilisierung Osteuropas', *Aussenpolitik*, no. 1 (1992) p. 19.

72. Parliamentary speech by Björn Engholm in *DB*, 12/108, 25 September 1992, p. 9223.

73. For example, speech by Volker Rühe at St Antony's College, Oxford University, 19 May 1994, reprinted in *Bulletin der Bundesregierung*, no. 47 (1994), 24 May 1994, p. 421.

74. Joint article of 27 May 1994 in *Bulletin der Bundesregierung*, no. 51 (1994), 31 May 1994, p. 481 (author's translation).

75. For example, speech by Defence Minister Volker Rühe in Berlin on 21 March 1994 in *Bulletin der Bundesregierung*, no. 28 (1994), 28 March 1994, p. 253.

76. See speech of Helmut Kohl in Bonn, Bundestag, of 13 January 1994, printed in *Bulletin der Bundesregierung*, no. 3 (1994), 17 January 1994, p. 17.
77. Donfried, 'Regional Priorities and Global Debuts', p. 6.
78. Speech by Helmut Kohl in Bonn, 27 May 1994, in *Bulletin der Bundesregierung*, no. 41, 31 May 1994, p. 480.
79. Hellmann, *Einbindungspolitik*, p. 26, citing Robert von Rimscha, 'Rühe: Rußland kann niemals in die NATO', *Tagesspiegel*, 6 July 1994, p. 2.
80. 'Kohl in Russia', *Financial Times*, 4 September 1995, p. 15.
81. Press Conference of the President and Chancellor Helmut Kohl, The White House, 9 February 1995 cited in Donfried, 'Regional Priorities and Global Debuts', p. 23.
82. Pre-history of NACC in Stephen J. Flanagan, 'NATO and Central and Eastern Europe: From Liasion to Security Partnership', *Washington Quarterly* (Spring 1992) pp. 141–51.
83. Speech by Klaus Kinkel at the Council on Foreign Relations, Chicago, 19 April 1995, *Bulletin der Bundesregierung*, no. 32 (1995), 24 April 1995, p. 267.
84. Donfried, 'Regional Priorities and Global Debuts', pp. 23–4.
85. Speech of Foreign Minister Klaus Kinkel in Bonn, 29 June 1994, *Bulletin der Bundesregierung*, no. 63, 30 June 1994, p. 594.
86. Eberhard Grabitz (ed.), *Abgestufte Integration. Eine Alternative zum herkömmlichen Integrationskonzept?* (Kehl am Rhein: Engel Verlag, 1984).
87. Michael Mertes and Norbert Prill, 'Der verhängnisvolle Irrtum eines Entweder-Oder. Eine Vision für Europa', *Frankfurter Allgemeine Zeitung*, 19 June 1989.
88. Josef Janning, 'A German Europe – a European Germany? On the debate over Germany's foreign policy', *International Affairs*, 72:1 (1996), p. 40.
89. Reflections on European Policy, Paper by the CDU/CSU-Fraktion des Deutschen Bundestages, 1 September 1994, Bonn 1994, p. 7. Multi-speed means a shared commitment to common policies but differing timing of implementation. Variable geometry does allow the possibility for countries to opt out of some policies and policy areas. For a further discussion see Helen Wallace and William Wallace, *Flying Together in a Larger and More Diverse European Union* (Netherlands Scientific Council, The Hague: Working Document W 87, 1995).
90. Christian Deubner, *Deutsche Europapolitik. Von Maastricht nach Kerneuropa?* (Baden-Baden: Nomos, 1995).
91. Janning, 'Germany's foreign policy', pp. 40–1.
92. This think tank was directed by Werner Weidenfeld, who held several influential positions at the same time. Apart from being a professor at Munich University he was a senior director in the Bertelsmann Foundation, the government's coordinator for German–American relations and occasionally a political consultant to Helmut Kohl.
93. Werner Weidenfeld and Josef Janning, 'Fortschritt oder Zerfall. Ein Konzept für Europa im Jahr der Entscheidung', *Frankfurter Allgemeine Zeitung*, 22 January 1996. Among the around 50 prominent participants were the German President Roman Herzog, Jacques Santer, Paavo Lipponen, Vaclav Klaus, Vladimir Meciar, Klaus Kinkel, Henry A. Kissinger, Grigorij Jawlinskij, Ruud Lubbers, Richard C. Holbrooke, Carl Bildt and Wolfgang Schäuble.
94. *Ibid.*
95. Christoph Bertram, 'Europas Jahr der Entscheidungen', *Die Zeit*, 31 January 1997, p. 3.
96. Simon Bulmer and William E. Paterson, 'Germany in the European Union: gentle giant or emergent leader?', *International Affairs*, 72:1 (January 1996) p. 24.

97. Rainer Nahrendorf, 'Europa braucht strategischen Impuls', *Handelsblatt*, 22 January 1996.
98. Quote in *Frankfurter Allgemeine Zeitung*, 6 September 1994, p. 1.
99. For example Klaus Kinkel, 'Die NATO-Erweiterung – ein Beitrag zur gesamteuropäischen Sicherheit', *Internationale Politik*, 50:4 (April 1995) pp. 22–5.
100. Bulmer and Paterson, 'Germany in the European Union', p. 20.
101. 'Is Kohl in control?', *The Economist*, 15 February 1997, p. 16.
102. *Ibid.*
103. 'Helmut Kohl's one-man band', *The Economist*, 7 September 1996, p. 33.
104. Andreas Oldag, 'Schrille Töne um den Euro', *Süddeutsche Zeitung*, 20 February 1997, p. 4.
105. 'Die Deutschen–sehr skeptische Europäer', *Süddeutsche Zeitung*, 18 January 1997, p. 8.
106. 'Ein Euro-Zweifler zieht durchs Land', *Frankfurter Allgemeine Zeitung*, 18 January 1997, p. 12.
107. 'German fears about EMU', *The Economist*, 25 January 1997, pp. 35–6.
108. Karl-Heinz Reif, 'Ein Ende des "permissive consensus"? Zum Wandel europapolitischer Einstellungen in der öffentlichen Meinung der EG-Mitgliedsstaaten', in Rudolf Hrbek (ed.), *Der Vertrag von Maastricht in der wissenschaftlichen Kontroverse* (Baden-Baden: Nomos 1993) pp. 23–40.
109. For an analysis of the SPD's struggle for the 1998 nomination see for example Christoph Schwennicke, 'Es kann nur einen geben', *Süddeutsche Zeitung*, 20 February 1997, p. 3.
110. Helmut Schmidt, 'Der zweite Anlauf, die letzte Chance', *Zeitpunkte*, no. 4 (1996) p. 57.
111. *Ibid.*, p. 58.
112. For a more detailed discussion see Dominique Bocquet, 'France And Germany: A Second Wind', in *The Future Of The Franco-German Relationship: Three Views*, Royal Institute of International Affairs Discussion Paper 71 (London: RIIA, 1997) pp. 6–7.
113. Background paper by Karl Lamers and Andreas Schockenhoff, 'Gründung des Arbeitskreises Frankreich der CDU/CSU-Bundestagsfraktion zur Intensivierung der deutsch-französischen Beziehungen. Schwerpunkte der Zusammenarbeit und des Dialogs', 9 October 1995.
114. Christian Deubner, '"The Franco-German Relationship": From Europe To Bilateralism?', in *The Future of Franco-German Relationship*, Bocquet op. cit. p. 18.
115. In particular the AA planning staff began rethinking some of the previous paradigms of German policies towards Europe. Background information by a German diplomat. See also 'Goodbye, federal Europe?', *The Economist*, 15 November 1997, pp. 47–8.
116. Nina Grunenberg, 'Wir werden gebraucht. Aber wozu ?', *Die Zeit*, 12 May 1995.
117. Simon Bulmer and William E. Paterson, 'Germany in the European Union: gentle giant or emergent leader?', *International Affairs*, 72:1 (1996) pp. 9–32.
118. 'Ways towards EMU', *The Economist*, 21 September 1996, p. 19.
119. Lionel Barber, 'Support for pact to ensure EMU stability', *Financial Times*, 23 September 1996, p. 1.
120. Wolfgang Schäuble and Rudolf Seiters, 'Deutsche Außenpolitik im 21. Jahrhundert', Schäuble and Seiters, *Außenpolitik im 21* (Jahrhundert, Bonn: Bouvier, 1996).

4

France and Europe at the end of the Cold War: Resisting Change

*Robin Niblett**

Introduction

It can be argued that France was one of the main beneficiaries, alongside the United States, of the geopolitical freeze that accompanied the cold war.[1] Protected by the unique balance of power which accompanied the bipolar stand-off between the US-led and Soviet-led blocs in Europe, successive French governments were able to build a 'special relationship' with West Germany that overcame their history of acute military antagonism. Germany's division after 1945 and the constraints placed upon the Federal Republic in Western Europe's political–military order quelled French fears that Germany's post-Second World War economic renaissance would once again herald a return to political destabilization in Europe. At the same time, French ministers could indulge in the luxury of an autonomous if seemingly contradictory foreign and defence policy, decrying the injustice of the Yalta division of Europe and rejecting the US strategy of Soviet containment, while relying on the Atlantic alliance to check potential Soviet expansionism and to police Germany's continued division. Even when the European Community failed to live up to French ambitions as a third pole in the bipolar world order, French leaders could still revel in the spectacular diplomatic gesture and 'the keynote speech as a substitute for policy'.[2]

It is easy to see why the end of the cold war proved particularly wrenching for France. German reunification re-evoked a succession of French nightmares, each of which appeared to presage a reassertion of Germany's past hegemonic ambitions and a return to European instability. Not only might a united Germany reinforce its economic predominance within Europe, but also, without the straitjacket of east–west confrontation, it could translate its economic might into additional political leverage at the heart of an undivided

* I would like to thank Simon Serfaty and William Wallace for their very helpful comments on previous drafts and Emilie Delpit for her extensive background research.

European continent. Under these circumstances, German leaders might succumb to a renewed 'Drang Nach Osten' and seek to reassert a sphere of influence over the central and east European countries which escaped the Yalta structure in 1989 only to enter into a geopolitical vacuum.[3] With the disappearance of the Soviet threat, France's status as a nuclear power could no longer serve as a political counterweight to Germany's growing economic strength in Europe. The 'fragile balance of imbalances' sustained during the cold war between West German economic might and France's relative strength in political and military terms was bound to decay.[4] Nor could America be relied upon to continue keeping the Germans down through an open-ended military commitment to European security. On the contrary, from the French perspective, the cold war had caused a hiatus in an instinctive US isolationism, and France could no longer afford to 'free ride' on an alliance that might break down at any time.

French concerns crystallized not simply around the twin fears of German resurgence and US withdrawal, but also around the impact that policies to deal with these two challenges might have upon carefully-nurtured French conceptions of national sovereignty. After the defeat and humiliations of 1939–45, French governments from de Gaulle onwards had placed at the centre of their foreign policy the goal of sustaining France's 'non-dependent' status within the bipolar international order.[5] During the cold war, the division of Germany and the political cohesion of the Atlantic alliance had allowed France to play the role of a self-sufficient 'middle-ranking' world power, while France's neighbours followed the American diplomatic lead in the east–west stand-off. French diplomatic room for manoeuvre was constrained neither by adherence to NATO's integrated military command, from which it withdrew in 1966, nor by EC decision making, which remained limited to regulating economic transactions among EC members.

After 1989, however, confronted with German unification and the danger of US withdrawal, a new generation of French leaders was suddenly confronted with the same double conundrum of European order that de Gaulle had faced in 1945. How could they balance, contain, or blunt the power of Germany on the European continent while ensuring that the new order that contained Germany would still allow France the maximum flexibility to pursue its own national interests? This chapter describes how policymakers from across the French political spectrum struggled after 1989 to deal with the raft of contradictions that emanated from the simultaneous pursuit of these two objectives; contradictions that underlay both the supposedly 'visionary' initiatives of the Mitterrand presidency and socialist government from 1989–93 and the 'pragmatic' European policies of the Balladur and Juppé governments and the Chirac presidency. The chapter describes how French adherence to these twin objectives entangled successive post-cold war French governments in contradictory positions towards Germany, towards EU integration, towards European security, and towards the role of the United

States in underwriting European stability. Given the depth of these contradictions, the chapter illustrates how French leaders favoured rhetorical ambiguity over conceptual clarity when debating Europe's future. It also reveals that, rather than rethinking their conceptions of European order after the cold war, French policymakers ended up dusting off, repackaging and relaunching what were essentially postwar and cold war era initiatives. French leaders remained frozen within their historical conceptual paradigms, even as the problem of dealing with Germany gradually came to be superseded by the pressures of economic globalization and a new era of apparent American global hegemony.

The Mitterrand vision

The end of the cold war cast a particularly bright spotlight on President François Mitterrand, one year into his second presidential term. His actions came to symbolize the French reaction to the tumult that accompanied the rapid collapse of communist regimes in eastern Europe and then in the Soviet Union. The French constitution made this focus inevitable. Although there is some ambiguity under the Fifth Republic's constitution as to whether the president can claim full authority over French foreign and security policy, the fact is that, if the presidency and the government are composed of members of the same political party, then the president is in a position to monopolize the management of the country's external relations and its policy towards Europe.

The President's small personal staff in the Elysée palace – Jacques Attali and Hubert Védrine were his key advisers in 1989–92 – operated independently of the official policymaking procedures of the French Foreign Ministry, the Quai d'Orsay. From 1989 until the Socialists' loss of their parliamentary majority in 1993, the Prime Minister (Pierre Bérégovoy), the Foreign Minister (Roland Dumas) and the minister of European affairs (Elizabeth Guigou) were all Mitterrand appointees and loyalists. Legislative oversight of foreign and European policies is even weaker than in other West European states; the inability of the National Assembly to serve as an effective counterbalance to the French executive under the Fifth Republic is well documented.[6]

The cohesion of the French intellectual and policy élite – the Parisian élite, educated in the grandes écoles and moving from there into government, business and politics – also made for a concentration of power and influence at the centre, without independent structures within which to question the conventional wisdom. French universities ranked lower than the grandes écoles in intellectual prestige; 'the political and social distance' that separates practitioners of foreign policy from academic experts on international relations explains 'why there has been relatively little interaction between the two worlds'.[7] Jacques Attali in this period was at once adviser to the President and one of Paris's most widely-read intellectual authors. A small number of semi-autonomous institutes, such as the Institut Français des

Relations Internationales (IFRI), acted as fora for the discussion of international issues, but their closeness to ministerial influence, and guidance, did not encourage dissent.

Paradoxically, the persistence of wide divergences within both of France's main political coalitions over the approach which France should adopt to European and foreign policy also enhanced presidential freedom of action. As in Britain, political leaders found it inadvisable to spell out party policy in too much detail, let alone to mount an explicit challenge to the governing assumptions of French foreign policy, for fear of provoking damaging splits. As a result the élite debate which was conducted in the opinion pages of *Le Monde, Le Figaro* and a number of influential weeklies, rarely moved beyond arguments over tactics to pose fundamental questions about French European strategy after the cold war. French foreign policy after 1989, as before, was thus conducted from the Elysée, dealing in the first instance directly with the German chancellery.

Hubert Védrine has argued that the socialists' failure to promote a nationalist 'autre politique' in 1981–83 had already convinced Mitterrand that France's economic and political interests would only be secured through the building of a 'European pole of power' in collaboration with Germany. In this sense, Mitterrand's conceptual approach to post-cold war European construction had been forged six years prior to the fall of the Berlin Wall, and he followed 'une même politique' throughout the period 1984–92.[8]

German unification

On the other hand, as Védrine also observed, Mitterrand was the 'very incarnation of political realism', and a man for whom 'only a balance of power can constitute a genuine guarantee of security'.[9] The same historical sense which drove him to try to transcend France's historical antagonism towards Germany also made him acutely aware of the potentially destabilizing effect that rapid German unification could have on international order in Europe. His first instinct, therefore, was to try to stall or delay the unexpectedly rapid rush towards German unification which followed the fall of the Berlin Wall. Most notably, Mitterrand chose to go through with a scheduled visit to East Berlin on 20–21 December 1989, giving rise to reports that he was opposed to unification and that, at the very least, he wished to see the East German state persist as long as was feasible. And yet, Mitterrand's manoeuvrings, which had included a visit with Gorbachev in Kiev earlier in December, appeared to reflect an obsession less with the dangers to France of German unification *per se* and more with the dangers to France and to European stability of allowing unification to go ahead when no new European order had either yet been articulated or set in motion.[10]

This ambiguity towards German unification helps explain the rapid shift in approach which Mitterrand was able to demonstrate once it became apparent in early 1990 that unification by the end of the year was unstoppable.

Underlining his preoccupation with the broader ramifications rather than the simple fact of German unification, French diplomacy focused almost exclusively on drawing from Helmut Kohl a clear commitment to the inviolability of existing borders, most importantly the Oder-Neisse line.[11] Despite the severe tension that this caused for the Mitterrand–Kohl relationship, within two months they and their closest advisers had prepared what would be the pivotal proposal in Western Europe's ensuing efforts rapidly to lay the foundations for a post-cold war European order. Their joint letter to the European Community's Irish presidency in April 1990 called on other EC governments to accept the idea of a second, one-year intergovernmental conference (IGC) that would be launched in January 1991 in parallel with the previously planned IGC on Economic and Monetary Union (EMU), but which would focus on the creation of a Political Union with a new European Security and Defence Identity at its core.

Both at the time and in his memoirs, Mitterrand argued that this proposal represented a conscious rejection of a return to the European balance of power manoeuvring that had characterized France's foreign policy and which, in Mitterrand's opinion, Margaret Thatcher appeared to favour.[12] And yet, when forced to make a choice *vis-à-vis* Germany in 1990 similar to the one de Gaulle and subsequent French governments faced in 1948–54, Mitterrand revealed a similarly Gaullist approach to the institutional deepening of the EC, an approach in which the French national interest and quest for influence and non-dependence repeatedly conflicted with the rhetoric of a new European order based upon the EU. The greatest paradox was that Mitterrand and Kohl and their political followers, although forming the so-called 'locomotive' for Europe's post-cold war restructuring, approached a number of its most important elements from diametrically opposed positions.

The European confederation

The immediate challenge for Mitterrand was to capture the rhetorical high ground and be the first to articulate an overarching conceptual framework for a post cold war European order. Mitterrand wasted little time, announcing during his presidential New Year's eve televised message on 1 January 1990 his plan for a 'European confederation' that would encompass all of the nations of Europe. The confederation proposal illustrated Mitterrand's reliance upon Gaullist conceptions of European order. He spoke of a Europe that would 'return to its history and its geography'; a Europe 'from the Atlantic to the Urals' that would free itself from its dependence on the two superpowers.[13] The proposal was also meant to lessen the danger that the new Europe could revert to the unstable Europe of 1919. Mitterrand's European confederation would help defuse potential recurrences of historical antagonisms in central and eastern Europe by providing a new forum for pan-European dialogue and fostering new economic interdependencies between east and west.[14] The proposal had the added benefit of raising the French diplomatic profile in central and eastern Europe at a time when Mitterrand sought to counter-balance a return to Germany's dominant influence in the region.

That the proposal failed and that it damaged France's reputation among the new central and east European democracies was due to the widespread perception that it was simply a delaying tactic designed to exclude these countries from the European Union. In the latter half of 1989 and early 1990, German politicians such as Hans-Dietrich Genscher raised the ambitious possibility of rapidly enlarging the EC to the east.[15] For Mitterrand, however, talk of EC enlargement was a distraction from his central objective, which was to integrate a united Germany into an institutionally deepened EU, as outlined in the April 1990 Franco-German *démarche*.[16] Enlargement at this stage risked weakening the very institution upon which a stable new European order depended, potentially turning it into an 'Anglo-Saxon' free trade area, within which Germany could reassert its past influence over central Europe, while France would see its own influence diluted. Under these circumstances, the EC, instead of offering an institutional mechanism to curb German power and elevate French interests, would have precisely the reverse effect.[17]

Whether the confederation proposal was indeed simply a delaying tactic or, as Mitterrand argued later in June 1991, an effort to impose an orderly gradualism on a process that risked getting out of hand, his efforts to give substance to the proposal while trying to maintain its separateness from the EC gave a surreal quality to his elliptical statements. The confederation would not, of course, have 'the rigour, constraints, or discipline of the Community', but it would still offer a forum where 'each country will feel that it is the equal of the others'. More damaging was his illuminating statement in an interview with Radio France Internationale that the new democracies should feel comfortable remaining in this ante-room of the Community for 'tens and tens of years'.[18] Mitterrand's apparent ambivalence towards the fate of the countries of central and eastern Europe was confirmed by the French stance in the negotiation of the 'Europe' Agreements with Poland, Hungary and Czechoslovakia, which ran in parallel to the Maastricht intergovernmental conference (IGC). France emerged as one of the EU countries most strongly opposed to granting the applicants improved access to West European markets.[19] Combined with his misjudged decision in August 1991 to appease the Soviet hardliners who attempted to depose Mikhail Gorbachev, Mitterrand's overall attitude towards central and eastern Europe revealed a defensive attachment to the strategic *status quo ante*, and a preference simply to rearrange the parameters of the existing European order, rather than take on directly the challenge of integrating Europe's eastern and western halves.

Maastricht

Mitterrand demonstrated a much firmer grasp of the negotiations to restructure the parameters of Western Europe's own post-cold war order. The government worked assiduously towards its twin objectives of containing the future power of Germany while accepting as few constraints on French room for manoeuvre as possible. In this context, the first priority was to blunt the danger of future German economic monetary hegemony in Europe, by securing under the IGC on EMU (and in tacit exchange for French political support for unification), Kohl's firm agreement to the rapid establishment of a single European currency that would pool Germany's monetary sovereignty with its EC partners. As Védrine observed, Mitterrand was 'perfectly comfortable' about giving up French monetary sovereignty, calculating that France had 'nothing to lose and everything to gain'. France already suffered from a monetary dependence on the Deutschmark and German interest rates, and EMU would permit France to 'reconstitute a part of its sovereignty which had already dissolved'.[20] Anxious to lock in this national gain, Mitterrand proudly boasted of France's role during the Maastricht European Council in securing a tight timetable which committed EU member states to launch EMU by 1 January 1999, even if not all members were ready.[21]

Despite Mitterrand's commitment to monetary union, however, he resisted Kohl's anticipated trade-off: his plans to balance EMU with a broadening of the competence of the Commission and European Parliament in EU internal and external decisionmaking, steps which would have compromised French national influence within the EU. Elizabeth Guigou expressed the government's ambivalence toward a greater political centralization of EU competences when she argued that the government wanted to build 'a Europe with a federal vocation', but only in the sense of wanting to 'evolve toward shared sovereignty by giving a central role to the organ which encapsulates at the highest level both the federal ambition and the role of each state – the European Council'.[22]

Just as Mitterrand was quick to seek integration where French sovereignty had already degraded, he was resistant to delegate power where French national influence still carried weight. The clearest example of this bias was in the field of foreign policy. With the Yugoslav break-up exposing important differences between French and German foreign policy approaches, Mitterrand was sensitive to the fact that a more strictly defined EU common foreign and security policy (CFSP) could serve as an important constraint on Germany's ability to pursue a more assertive foreign policy after unification.[23] On the other hand, while being willing to envisage a limited extension of qualified majority voting (QMV) under CFSP, Mitterrand joined others of his EU colleagues in insisting on maintaining CFSP as a strictly intergovernmental procedure that would permit France to continue operating as freely as it wished.

The European security and defence identity

Whereas the French government appeared to have achieved its objectives in monetary union and in controlling the scope of institutional reform, it failed, however, to use the Maastricht IGC to secure a clear commitment to the creation of a distinct West European Security and Defence Identity (ESDI) under EU auspices. As described in Chapter 2, this was due partly to the intractable opposition of the United States, the United Kingdom, and a small number of other EU member states to a dilution of NATO's role in upholding European security after the cold war. It was also due, however, to Mitterrand's inability to reconcile European security integration with continuing allegiance to the Gaullist ideal of military non-dependence.

Mitterrand saw in the end of the cold war a chance for France to renew its long-standing efforts to reduce Western Europe's security dependence upon the United States, a dependence which Roland Dumas described in 1991 as perpetuating 'l'hégémonie americaine'.[24] French ministers argued that Europe's defence should be provided by Europeans: a favourite refrain of General de Gaulle's which Roland Dumas echoed in October 1991.[25] With the cold war over, the potential decline in NATO's influence offered the government the opportunity to build a parallel European security structure that would give greater weight to its own voice and interests.[26] Mitterrand and his ministers made an immense effort during 1990–91 to build political support for the establishment of a distinct European Security and Defence Identity (ESDI). In fact, French support for the EU's CFSP was based less on its potential to integrate the foreign policy positions of EU members (the objective supported by the German government), as much as it was on the role of CFSP as a precursor to the EU taking responsibility for its own defence.[27] Rejecting a US–UK proposal that the Western European Union (WEU) should become a more effective European pillar within a rejuvenated Atlantic alliance, French ministers promoted instead the vision of an 'organic' relationship between the WEU and the EU as a prelude to the former's eventual integration into the EU.[28]

Mitterrand was galled, therefore, by the way that the US government sought to sustain the primacy of NATO in Europe's post-cold war security order. He believed that a European Defence Identity could only emerge if NATO abdicated some of its responsibilities for Europe's defence. Given the inevitability of a gradual US military withdrawal from Europe, US and British attempts to revitalize NATO during 1990–91 were pilloried by French ministers as misleading, dangerous, and a clear attempt to preserve US political influence over European security for influence's sake.[29] The French government refused to accept the July 1990 NATO summit decision endorsing the principle of creating new multinational forces. French Defence Minister Pierre Joxe was particularly critical of the alliance's decision in May 1991, midway through the IGC process, to begin creating the multinational Rapid Reaction Corps even before the completion of the internal NATO study (in which the French were participating) on a new political rationale and military strategy for the alliance. One French official described the RRC as a 'trompe l'oeil in an American cathedral'.[30] Mitterrand was further infuriated by the creation of the North Atlantic Cooperation Council (NACC) linking NATO with the former Warsaw Pact countries.

Yet Mitterrand's failure to secure wider European support for an alternative vision of European security in 1991, just as his predecessors had failed in the 1960s, was, once again, largely a result of French ambivalence. Any domestic debate about France's role in European security remained hostage to the need to preserve the 'myth of consensus' around an essentially Gaullist paradigm of France's position in the world. Mitterrand, therefore, was trapped in the same conceptual 'immobilisme' that had persisted since de Gaulle's exit from the French political scene. Just as had been the case during the EDC debate, the French government was constrained from supporting its rhetoric with detailed proposals by its conflicting wishes for a post-cold war European security structure. It sought, first, both to lessen US influence while retaining NATO as a hedge against Russian military aggression and, second, both to curtail German room for manoeuvre while leaving France with maximum flexibility to define and manage its own security interests.[31]

The result was an unwillingness or inability by French leaders, from Mitterrand on down, to put any flesh on the bones of their visionary rhetoric in favour of an ESDI. The Mitterrand–Kohl proposal in October 1991 to create a Franco-German corps was more a political gesture to counter Anglo-Saxon manoeuvring in NATO than a clearly thought-out military proposal. Mitterrand's call for an exclusive, four-power conference on nuclear policy in Europe during the closing stages of the Maastricht IGC was hastily followed by his suggestion shortly after the summit that France might consider the 'Europeanization' of its nuclear forces.[32] The two initiatives merely cast a spotlight on the contradiction between French rhetoric in favour of a common European defence and the fact of France's independent nuclear deterrent. The vagueness about how an ESDI might function in operational terms, in contrast to the display of US political and military leadership in the Gulf War in 1990–91, the French government's view of defence as an exclusively national prerogative, and its conflictual approach towards NATO, all raised doubts among France's EU partners about whether a French-led European defence organization could be an effective complement or alternative to NATO's explicitly integrated military command.[33] It was hardly surprising, therefore, that there was little enthusiasm among even France's closest European allies for exchanging the proven integrated structures of the alliance for the ambiguous European security entity that Mitterrand appeared to be offering.

The Maastricht ratification debate

As a number of French commentators have observed, the ratification of the Maastricht treaty in France during spring and summer 1992 became, to a certain extent, a campaign against Mitterrand and an opportunity for electors to vent their frustration with the Socialist government's handling of the economy during the growing European recession after mid 1991.[34] However, the Maastricht ratification also served to take the debate over Europe's future out of the confines of the Elysée. In so doing, it gave politicians from the right and the left the opportunity to express their personal reservations over Mitterrand's post-cold war European policy. It quickly became apparent that ambivalence and opposition to the content of the Maastricht treaty were not simply partisan reflexes, but that these responses ranged across the political spectrum and divided French political parties.

Within the RPR, the main right-wing opposition party, Philippe Séguin drew a direct parallel between the Maastricht treaty and the failed EDC, warning that, 'in 1992, just as in 1954, we are witnessing a swerve toward federalism' that was inimical to French national interests.[35] Echoing the more sceptical tone of most RPR members towards Mitterrand's European strategy, the RPR's 'Manifeste pour l'Union des Etats d'Europe', which was released in December 1990, attempted to project a different vision of Europe after the cold war than that being pursued by Mitterrand, even while recognizing, as did Mitterrand, that Europe could not afford to return to the instabilities of the 1930s. In particular, the RPR warned against responding to the end of the cold war by building an increasingly 'bureaucratic Europe', modelled after a federal superstate and founded upon the premature imposition of a single European currency. Characterizing Mitterrand's determination to deepen the EU before widening it as 'un contresens historique' and as propagating 'l'Europe de l'Apartheid', RPR politicians harked back to General de Gaulle's ambition to build 'la Grande Europe' from the Atlantic to the Urals, and now saw the opportunity to fulfil this ambition by advocating a rapid enlargement of the EU.[36]

Yet the RPR's manifesto betrayed as many ambiguities and contradictions as it imputed to President Mitterrand. The call for a 'Grande Europe, plus légitime, plus démocratique, plus ouverte', was as vague both as de Gaulle's vision some thirty years earlier and as Mitterrand's proposal for a European confederation. The list of areas where the RPR manifesto argued that France should retain national control, far from contradicting Mitterrand, mirrored the government's own stance.[37] Despite its title, the manifesto also appeared to support the government in calling airily for a 'more political' Europe that would extend its reach into a 'harmonized' foreign policy and more co-ordinated European defence policy, and that would accept a stronger role for the European Parliament within the EU's decision making structure. The extent to which these ambiguities reflected the RPR's efforts to keep a lid upon its own internal differences of opinion became painfully clear as the Maastricht ratification debate entered into full swing after the spring of 1992.

On the one hand, RPR Eurosceptics led by Séguin and Charles Pasqua united under the banner of the 'Rassemblement Pour le Non Au Referendum' and rejected the Maastricht Treaty outright in July 1992. They drew particular attention to the 'centrifugal' effect of the march towards a single currency, while also objecting to the clauses on European citizenship, which would give limited voting rights to non-French nationals. They also warned that Germany would only renounce more of its sovereignty if it came to dominate EU institutions and that, as a result, France should cultivate stronger relations with the United Kingdom and southern Europe after the cold war rather than focusing all of its energy on Germany. While Séguin and his allies remained wedded to the cult of French exceptionalism, they offered few practical alternatives to the Maastricht blueprint, either on the monetary front (where they simply echoed John Major's call for a parallel European currency) or on the best means to achieve their vision of a 'Grande Europe' (where their call for a European Security Council was more confusing than constructive). This determined stance of 'nostalgic nationalism and defensive patriotism', as Alain Duhamel characterized it, split the French right.[38]

Although most RPR deputies shared a rhetorical attachment to a 'Europe des nations' and opposed any moves towards a more federal European construction, they rejected the conclusions of the 'non' camp for both strategic and domestic political reasons. RPR pragmatists led by Alain Juppé and Edouard Balladur joined their more pro-European colleagues such as Michel Barnier and Jacques Toubon in arguing that, although Maastricht appeared to be a flawed treaty, it met France's post-cold war strategic interests in two important respects. First, it would limit the chances that Germany would adopt more nationalistic and autonomous policies in the near future while maximising France's ability to balance Germany's increasing political influence. Second, as Juppé and Balladur openly admitted, France would indeed gain more monetary sovereignty than it risked losing as a result of EMU.[39] The increasingly acrimonious tone of the debate between the RPR mainstream and the 'non' camp, both in the National Assembly and in the editorial pages of French newspapers, was not only due to their different strategic conceptions. Equally important for Alain Juppé, as president of the RPR, was the risk that Séguin's efforts to nullify the treaty would wreck the RPR's delicate political alliance with the UDF and undermine the right's electoral chances in the parliamentary elections due in March 1993.

Under the overall leadership of former President Giscard d'Estaing, UDF politicians such as François Léotard, honorary chairman of the Republican Party, Alain Madelin, vice president of the UDF, and his colleagues Charles Millon and Alain Lamassoure consistently argued the case for deeper European integration as a response to the end of the cold war, and sought to separate the debate over ratification from criticism of Mitterrand's performance as French president. While recognizing the defensive benefits of the Maastricht treaty in terms of tempering any future German ambivalence towards Europe, the UDF was equally comfortable with the treaty's provisions for European citizenship and for monetary union, seeing in the latter proposal an important financial discipline upon the French government.[40] Giscard d'Estaing described the UDF's ultimate vision for Europe not as a European superstate, but as a 'decentralized European federation'; and saw the Maastricht treaty as an important step in that direction.[41] In contrast to many in the RPR, therefore, he and other UDF politicians were unequivocal about the need for the EU to focus on institutional deepening before initiating any formal opening to the east, considering even Mitterrand's confederation proposal a dangerous distraction from their central objective. Overall, the UDF approach to the Maastricht debate confirmed Bernard Bosson's observation that 'European construction has always been the cement holding the UDF together'.[42] Caught between the UDF's firm support for the Maastricht treaty, the competing visions within the RPR, and a desire not to be seen to back Mitterrand, Jacques Chirac, the person best placed to synthesize an alternative French vision of post-cold war European order, was unable to make a constructive conceptual contribution to the debate over the best course for European integration during the ratification process, nailing his flag unambiguously to the 'yes' camp only two months before the vote.[43]

Divisions over the best approach to European order were not the sole preserve of the French right. Although the bulk of the socialist party in the National Assembly, including Prime Minister Bérégovoy, supported the President's approach in the Maastricht negotiations, there also existed a polarization between those that saw the Maastricht treaty as a further step toward the creation of a 'united states of Europe', such as Julian Dray and Jean-Luc Melenchon and a small, but vocal group led by Jean-Pierre Chevènement that echoed Séguin and Pasqua in asserting that the Maastricht treaty entailed an excessive transfer of sovereignty, especially over monetary issues, to unelected technocrats in Brussels. This fragmentation within the mainstream parties offered a certain credibility to the more extreme opponents of European integration. The French Communist Party's anti-Europeanism, based on its belief that European integration would extend capitalist bureaucratic control over Europe's economies, found some support from Chévènement's 'Mouvement des Citoyens'.[44] And the mixture of anti-Europeanism and anti-globalism of Jean-Marie le Pen's Front National found echoes in the arguments against Maastricht put forward by the 'Majorité pour l'Autre Europe' of the former UDF member, Phillippe de Villiers. Although they were overshadowed by the mainstream supporters and opponents of Maastricht, these groups forced a more vitriolic form of Euroscepticism into the open in French political debate. And the breadth of the spectrum of French anti-Europeanism thus awakened exposed the fragility of the domestic political base upon which French governments would have to conduct their policies toward Europe after 1992.

Transformation and continuity in the French approach to European order: sources of the new pragmatism, 1993–96

The victory of the conservative RPR–UDF alliance in the parliamentary elections in March 1993, six months after the ratification of the Maastricht treaty by the narrowest of popular margins, brought into 'cohabitation' with François Mitterrand a government that had offered only lukewarm support for the President's Europe policy in the wake of the cold war. The conservative government, led by Prime Minister Edouard Balladur, sought to exploit its position to articulate a fresh French approach toward constructing a new European order. It is important to note that, reflecting the majority view on the right, politicians from the centre of the RPR and from the pro-European UDF held the key posts related to the government's policy towards Europe, with Balladur in the Matignon, Juppé heading the Quai d'Orsay, Alain Lamassoure as Minister for Europe, François Léotard as Minister of Defence, and Edmund Alphandery as Economics Minister. All had supported ratification of the Maastricht treaty. Charles Pasqua's nomination as Minister of Interior Affairs appeared designed partly to take him out of the European debate.

It was not surprising, therefore, that the new government appeared to share the same basic conceptual starting-point as had Mitterrand in 1989–90, categorically discarding the idea of returning to some sort of balance of power European order. As Pierre Lellouche, foreign policy adviser to Jacques Chirac, observed in 1993,

> Once again, Europe is characterized by a pivotal and strong Germany, a backward and unstable Russia, and a large number of small, weak states. And again, France and Great Britain are incapable by themselves of balancing German power or of checking Russian instability, let alone restructuring the entire European order around a Franco-British axis.[45]

There was to be no overt renationalization, therefore, of France's Europe policy, despite the conservative rhetoric during the Maastricht ratification debate. As François Léotard argued in the introduction to the new government's 1994 Defence White Paper, France's and Europe's interests lay,

> not in playing one state off against another, but in succeeding to create, for the first time in the tormented history of this ancient continent, a mutualization of power, both to guarantee the defence of Europe and the common security of the states that are engaged in its construction.[46]

This concept of a 'mutualization of power', although vague, remained consistent with Mitterrand's guiding assumption that France could only ensure its long-term security and European stability – in the face of underlying tensions in Europe and a proliferation of new external threats – through greater co-operation, co-ordination and, if necessary, institutionalization of its policies with those of its European partners. In practical terms, as conservative ministers took every opportunity to stress, this meant maintaining a solid Franco-German relationship at the core of post-cold war European order.[47] At no point over the next three years, despite speculative attacks on the French franc and growing public frustration with a continuation of the 'franc fort' policy, did the government question the desirability of achieving economic and monetary union within the Maastricht timetable.

At the same time, however, conservative ministers soon took issue with specific aspects of Mitterrand's strategic vision for Europe after the cold war. They argued that Mitterrand's efforts to repackage and relaunch some of General de Gaulle's universalist concepts for European order (ranging from his European confederation proposal to his grandiose vision of a European superpower emerging from the rubble of the cold war) were profoundly misguided within the new, far more fluid and complex strategic context. The implosion of the Soviet Union in 1991–92, and Russia's subsequent preoccupation with its transition to a market economy, made it impossible for France to engage Russia in a serious dialogue over a pan-European security architecture, as France had done, with varying degrees of success, both at the turn of the century and during the cold war. The violent break-up of Yugoslavia in 1991–92 and the increased strategic uncertainty in eastern Europe that had followed the collapse of the Soviet Union made Mitterrand's plans for a European confederation patently inadequate.

In addition, Mitterrand's reticence to challenge the bases of France's security and national deterrence policy appeared negligent. France now faced no direct military threat near its borders for the first time in its history, while conflicts in the Gulf and in Bosnia exposed the weakness of France's conventional forces, the potential irrelevance of the French nuclear deterrent, and the political limitations on deploying conscripted forces to deal with distant crises.[48] Conservative ministers drew two additional conclusions from Bosnia. First, the EU's failure to forge a united European response to the conflict, the inability of the WEU to co-ordinate an intervention operation early on and the subsequent heavy-handedness of German efforts to recognize Croatian independence, confirmed conservatives' scepticism about the practical value of the CFSP procedures so painstakingly negotiated during the Maastricht IGC. In contrast, Bosnia demonstrated how effectively NATO had begun to adapt its strategy, forces and procedures for these new sorts of conflicts, while French defence ministry officials had been unable to take an active part in this role redefinition as a result of the previous government's 'immobilisme' and suspicious approach toward NATO's post-cold war role. Most importantly, the election of President Clinton in the United States in November 1992 and the apparent willingness of his administration to assist in the establishment of a European defence identity within NATO (which Clinton explicitly recognized at the NATO summit in Brussels in January 1994) convinced conservative ministers that they now had Washington's approval to develop a European defence capability within NATO rather than in competition with it.

Members of the Balladur government concluded that France had entered a 'post-rational' world.[49] From the new government's perspective, the post-Soviet, post-Maastricht Europe promised to be messy and disorderly and not at all amenable to the sort of wholesale architectural restructuring favoured by the president. Instead, as Alain Juppé, the new French Foreign Minister, argued:

> Within such a fluid environment, the great challenge of the coming years will not necessarily be to construct a great, pre-determined security architecture, but first of all – and this may seem a little modest – to prevent global disorder.[50]

Over the next three years, the conservative government sought to promote a more pragmatic approach toward the construction of Europe's post-cold war Europe. In the end, however, conservative ministers found themselves handicapped by many of the same contradictions between their European and their national objectives that had constrained Mitterrand's European policy before them.

Pragmatism in practice

One of the government's first efforts to define a more 'realistic' approach towards Europe centred around the need for policymakers to be more explicit about the continuing centrality of nation states within the process of European integration, even if this meant taking a more overtly contrary position to Chancellor Kohl on matters of institutional integration than had Mitterrand in recent years. Sensing the greater ambivalence within the new French government toward European integration, the ruling CDU/CSU faction in Bonn released in September 1994 a discussion paper on Germany and Europe which explicitly challenged the French to 'make clear and unequivocal decisions' about their commitment to institutional deepening. The so-called 'Lamers paper' recognized that the 'notion of unsurrendable sovereignty of the Etat Nation still carries weight', but stated that 'this sovereignty has long since become an empty shell'. It articulated Germany's vision of a more federal post-cold war European Union, including the need to enhance the role of the European Parliament to turn it into a law-making body with the same rights as the EU's Council of Ministers; to convert the Council into a form of second legislative chamber; and to enable the Commission to 'take on the features of a European government'.[51]

Balladur and his ministers reacted quickly to the German challenge, issuing a series of statements over the following months that revealed their very different conceptual starting point. Balladur stated that, from his perspective, one of the significant developments of the post-cold war years was, 'the return to realism on the international stage . . . to what General de Gaulle has always perceived as essential: the States, their individuality, their capabilities, and their resolve to act'.[52] He went on to argue that, 'for my part, I do not believe in the role of institutions unless they are based on a deeper reality, that of the will-power of states'. Reflecting their desire to emphasize the role of states as well as of institutions in Europe's new order, Balladur and his ministers sought to set some rhetorical and conceptual boundaries to the sort of Europe that would emerge in the coming years. They stressed, in particular, the need for clarification on two important subjects: Europe's security order and Europe's new institutional architecture.

Building a new European security order

Conservatives shared with Mitterrand and the majority of the French political class a belief in the importance of Europe developing a distinct European security identity and capability.[53] They criticized, however, the contradiction inherent in Mitterrand's obsession with preserving the 'Gaullist consensus' on French security policy while at the same time advocating new levels of European security integration. Alain Juppé went so far as to acknowledge that France's recent grand concepts in the security arena had tended to provoke disquiet and scepticism among France's European partners, precisely because of this contradiction between the president's European security rhetoric and his unwillingness to redefine France's national defence 'consensus'. The Balladur government was determined to move beyond Mitterrand's rhetorical approach and, as one RPR report suggested, develop some 'concrete and pragmatic' steps that would break the existing French conceptual 'immobilisme' on security issues.[54]

In particular, Conservatives also criticised Mitterrand's refusal to accept the need for closer French co-ordination with NATO, especially given the proliferation of new threats to French security interests in the former USSR and in Islamic North Africa and given France's limited national military capabilities. Léotard and Juppé were incensed that Mitterrand's stance was marginalizing France from NATO's important discussions on how to adapt the alliance into a non-Article V organization capable of 'out-of-area' and UN peacekeeping operations.[55] Conservatives believed that the embryonic Eurocorps was of only symbolic rather than operational value in the near to medium-term.[56] They recognized that NATO would remain the dominant security organization in Europe for the foreseeable future and that an ESDI would have to be built within it.[57] They also hoped, however, that a more conciliatory and constructive French approach towards NATO would encourage the United States and France's European partners to take French suggestions for an ESDI more seriously. As Juppé admitted, France's European allies remained suspicious of French defence initiatives, not only because of their ambiguity, but also because of France's history of trying to diminish the US role in European security. As he stated, 'France can no longer separate its policy in favour of a Defence Europe from a positive Atlantic policy.'[58]

While Mitterrand had started to take a more conciliatory line towards NATO after Maastricht, the conservative parliamentary victory led to a genuine increase in the tempo of the French rapprochement to NATO.[59] In April 1993, France discreetly re-joined NATO's Military Committee with full voting rights and, over the following year, French officials established new military missions within the NATO military commands.[60] In the lead-up to the January 1994 NATO summit in Brussels, French officials were closely involved in drawing up the concept of NATO's Combined Joint Task Forces. The new government began to perceive the genesis of a new Franco-US bargain, under which the French would accept a US role in enabling certain European defence actions in return for US/NATO political and material support for the emergence of a genuine European defence identity through the WEU.

While he remained president, however, Mitterrand prevented this modest rapprochement from evolving into the more formal 'normalization' of French relations with NATO sought by his conservative opponents.[61] It was not until Mitterrand's defeat at the hands of Jacques Chirac in the presidential elections of May 1995 that France finally began to shake itself free from the conceptual 'immobilisme' that had left it frozen in a cold war security posture. In September 1995, the first NATO exercise was held in France since 1965. On 5 December 1995, Chirac's Foreign Minister, Hervé de Charette, informed the North Atlantic Council that France would take its place within the various bodies that come under the jurisdiction of NATO's Military Committee.[62] The government's approach appeared to be vindicated when, after six months of intense negotiation, the NATO summit in Berlin in June 1996 formally endorsed the Combined Joint Task Force (CJTF) concept as the embryo of a genuine ESDI at the heart of NATO.

In parallel with its NATO rapprochement, the conservative government sought to encourage the emergence of an ESDI through a series of modest steps. Conscious of the continuing importance of NATO, political indecision among its European partners and budgetary realities, French government officials began to speak of the benefits of alliances based on 'des arrières pensées' (ulterior motives) and of a policy of 'ambiguité constructive' and of 'petits faits accomplis' in the European security arena. Their preference was to build up a range of seemingly *ad hoc* security structures, including not only the Eurocorps (which was being extended to incorporate units from Spain, Belgium and Luxembourg), but also a more far-reaching bilateral defence partnership with the United Kingdom (built around a newly-formed Anglo-French air defence command and the secretive Anglo-French Joint Commission on Nuclear Policy and Doctrine) and rapid reaction air and naval forces with the Spanish and Italians for the Mediterranean.[63] Rather than pressing persistently the need for a formally co-ordinated European defence policy, French officials hoped that co-operation in these separate spheres would gradually encourage the various participating nations to create effective, centralized planning and command facilities.

In a further effort to break the 'immobilisme' of France's defence debate, Chirac immediately instituted a thorough review of France's national security policy and force structure, challenging many of the compromises which, under the constraints of cohabitation, were contained in the 'Livre Blanc de la

Défense'.[64] Chirac first called into question the role of the French nuclear 'force de frappe' as the bulwark of France's national defence (the Livre Blanc had assigned 25 per cent of the procurement budget to nuclear modernization). Despite the highly controversial nature of his decision to break Mitterrand's moratorium and launch a series of nuclear tests in the South Pacific in June 1995, this served as the precursor both to an end to French nuclear testing and to an announcement on 23 February 1996 of a fundamental regrouping of French nuclear forces around only sea and air-based capabilities. On the same day, Chirac announced his plans to end military conscription and create armed forces that could flexibly be deployed to conflicts around the world in the future.[65] In a further effort to lay a firmer base for intra-European security co-operation, Chirac and his ministers also finally began to make some of the hard choices to restructure French defence industry and to prepare it for consolidation along cross-border lines, setting in train (almost four years behind Britain and Germany) the privatization of French defence industry.[66]

The new European institutional architecture

The search for 'pragmatism' among French conservative ministers towards European security issues was mirrored in their approach towards designing Europe's post-cold war institutional architecture. As the debate about NATO enlargement began in early 1994, conservative ministers argued, as had Mitterrand in 1990–91, that NATO expansion would undermine European order by leaving Russia isolated and resentful. Unlike Mitterrand, however, conservative ministers recognized that the new democracies of central and eastern Europe required a real, rather than merely rhetorical anchor to existing Western institutions. Echoing the arguments they had made while in opposition in 1990–92, Balladur and Juppé were explicit in their recognition of the inevitability and, ultimately, the desirability of an enlargement of the Union.[67] In a *Le Monde* article in November 1994 entitled 'Rethinking Europe', Juppé rejected the argument that the Union should remain 'à douze', stating that the *status quo* presented the greatest of dangers. First, long-term equilibrium on the European continent was inconceivable with a rich and powerful Western Europe on one side and new democracies in central and eastern Europe prey to underdevelopment and insecurity on the other. Second, French intransigence on the enlargement question would, at a minimum, undermine French influence within the EU and, at worst, it would tear the Union apart by splitting the Franco-German partnership.[68]

The challenge for the conservative government was not whether to enlarge the EU, but how to enlarge it while at the same time safeguarding its internal cohesion, including a balanced and firm Franco-German relationship. As Balladur argued in September 1994, France's twin ambitions for the next ten years were 'to expand Europe by diversifying it, but safeguarding an effective central core'.[69] From mid 1994 onwards, Balladur and Juppé began to present publicly their view of the institutional parameters of a new European order, a

Europe of 'three circles'. Gone was Mitterrand's ambiguous vision of a European confederation. Instead, conservative ministers sought to set clear geographic and institutional limits for an enlarged European Union. In a series of speeches, they made clear that an enlarged Union would exclude Russia, the Ukraine and the remaining former members of the Soviet Union, since their inclusion would stretch the institutional and political foundations of the European Union beyond breaking point. They argued that Russia should instead be encouraged to build up the Commonwealth of Independent States as a possible second pole of the post-cold war European order, alongside the European Union. In the meantime, the EU would seek to conclude a wide range of trade, financial and political agreements with what French officials referred to as the EU's new 'partner' states, not only those in the former Soviet Union, but also in the Mediterranean. Partner states thus formed the outer of three circles in France's evolving view of the new Europe.[70]

The European Union would form the second circle. Ultimately, it would be composed of a maximum 30 states to include, apart from the current fifteen, the six states of central and eastern Europe, the three Baltic states, Malta and Cyprus, Slovenia and, when practicable, the remaining Balkan states. French officials stressed that the second circle would not simply be a free trade area. All 30 EU members would be subject to the disciplines of the 'community acquis', both in traditional areas such as the single market, competition and social policy, and in the new pillars dedicated to justice and home affairs and to the procedures for developing a common foreign and security policy.

To underline the new government's commitment to forging this second circle around the EU, Balladur presented to the cabinet on 9 June 1993 his plans for a Stability Pact that would help resolve border and ethnic minority disputes among the six central and east European countries (CEECs) and among the Baltic states. The contrast between the concrete goals of Balladur's Stability Pact (primarily to resolve specific regional disputes) and Mitterrand's vague ideas for a European confederation were deliberate.

However, it was towards the central, first circle that the French government paid greatest attention. Ministers concluded that deeper integration could only be realistically pursued by self-selected groups of existing EU members. They defined the first circle, therefore, as being made up of what were variously called 'zones de solidarité particulière' or 'cercles de cooperation renforcée' within the EU. In other words, French policymakers advocated that groups of EU member states should agree among themselves to pursue integration or enhanced co-operation in areas where not all states would be willing or ready to follow.[71] It was envisaged that this reinforced cooperation would always revolve around a Franco-German core – what one RPR position paper described as the 'primordial relationship' for all European integration.[72] The two primary areas suggested by France for enhanced cooperation in 1995 were military co-operation, along the lines described above, and monetary union, precisely the same two areas that Mitterrand had focused on in 1990–92.

Contradictions

Ministers could not be faulted for the neatness of their architectural design for post-cold war European order. However, as the government initiated its preparations for the 1996 IGC, it became apparent that, for all of the 'souplesse' which government officials attributed to it, the government's conceptual framework contained as many contradictions as the Mitterrand vision which it had so heavily criticized. In its position paper ahead of the 1996 IGC, for example, the RPR continued to trumpet de Gaulle's vision of building 'la Grande Europe'; Hervé de Charette stressed that EU enlargement was the number one priority on his agenda and should take place by the year 2000.[73] It was clear, however, that conservative ministers envisaged enlargement for central and east European countries only into the 'second circle'. How the concept of a Europe separated into three circles was meant to square with the government's rhetoric in favour of 'la Grande Europe' was never addressed. In fact, the government's approach dovetailed far more closely than it was willing to admit with Giscard d'Estaing's suggestion in *Le Figaro* in January 1995 that France should downgrade its commitment to the Gaullist vision of 'la Grande Europe' or the 'Europe Espace', as he termed it, and refocus the integrationist drive within a 'Europe-puissance' core.[74]

The government's priority to construct the citadel of the first circle around a Franco-German core, however, was prey to its own set of contradictions. In the field of security and defence, one of the two areas targeted explicitly for reinforced bilateral co-operation, French ministers did little to dispel the impression that one of the main values of a European defence identity and a reinforced CFSP lay in the ability of these two mechanisms to maximize the projection of French national influence.[75] For example, the government's plans for national defence industrial consolidation sought to establish a dominant French industrial pole prior to allowing French companies to engage their European partners in potential crossborder mergers and alliances. Most damaging to Franco-German relations was the way in which Chirac chose not to consult or forewarn France's European allies about many of its most crucial security decisions after 1995, such as the resumption of nuclear testing, plans to end conscription and the cancellation or 'stretching out' of key Franco-German collaborative defence programmes in the 1996.

Equally contradictory was the government's approach to strengthening the EU's CFSP procedures during the 1996 IGC. Ministers wanted to reap the benefits of formal co-operation in foreign and security policy, while paying the minimum price in terms of constraining national flexibility of action.[76] The government continued to push for the incorporation of the WEU into the EU, but refused to countenance any steps towards a NATO-style integration of WEU military forces, arguing that formal European security integration would carry the risk of hindering rather than promoting joint action. Nor would the government accept any extension of EU competence over foreign policy and security matters. As Barnier explained, a common foreign and security policy did not require a 'single' policy. On the contrary, France had to retain the capacity to conduct its own foreign policy initiatives. In fact, Bosnia had confirmed the belief of most conservatives that a common foreign and security policy could never be forged simply through a tightening of institutional procedures.[77] They retained a Gaullist view that only the application of political will and concrete military capabilities by 'great powers', as in the Yugoslavia Contact Group or some future proposed European Security Council, offered any prospects for successful external action. Thus, the French position in the lead-up to the 1996 IGC concentrated on strengthening CFSP as a forum for broad policy consultation (for example, by establishing a new analysis centre in the Council secretariat); on inserting greater flexibility into CFSP (the policy of 'constructive abstention' would allow EU actions even in the absence of unanimous EU support); and on maximizing the political weight of agreed positions (hence the French proposal for a specially-appointed Secretary General for CFSP – 'Mr PESC'), but not on bringing CFSP formally under EU competence.

French ministers were equally ambivalent about the other great French-sponsored European project: EMU. On the one hand, once in power, Chirac quickly reversed the EMU-scepticism he had displayed during his presidential election campaign.[78] For the Chirac administration, as for Mitterrand, the political and strategic consequences of allowing EMU to fail, leaving a united Germany to control the monetary levers of the integrated EU market, were quite simply unacceptable. Conservative ministers, like their socialist predecessors, saw in EMU a mechanism through which France could regain some national control over its monetary policy and through which European politicians could exercise more effective control over economic markets. They also saw EMU as an important defence against America's growing global economic hegemony.[79]

This strategic approach, however, conflicted with German insistence, driven largely by Kohl's need to placate a highly suspicious German electorate, that EMU should be run along strictly monetary lines, with as little political interference as possible. As a result, a Franco-German battle opened in the second half of 1996 over the management of EMU. The argument between Chirac and Kohl over the mechanics of the Stability Pact which was agreed at the Dublin EU summit in December 1996 was among one of the most acrimonious in their post-war bilateral relations.

The simultaneous drive to promote integration but to preserve national flexibility meant that French policymakers also brought an ambivalent approach to the central theme of the 1996 IGC, institutional reform. On the one hand, ministers such as Michel Barnier and advisers such as Pierre Lellouche stressed the need for a 'veritable refounding of European institutions in their entirety' and stated that the government would not accept a lowest common denominator outcome to the IGC in this area.[80] The reasoning for this line of argument was that the EU had to revise its internal working procedures before enlarging to the east, or risk paralysis in EU decisionmaking. At the same time, however, the official French document outlining the French 'orientation' for the IGC stated plainly on its first page that 'realism demands that, one way or another, the distinction between the three principal domains of existing cooperation – what is known as the "pillar architecture" – should be conserved'.[81]

It quickly became apparent that the official French approach towards EU institutional reform, as laid out in the 'Orientation' and the RPR's position paper for the 1996 IGC, retained the minimalist state-centrism put forward by Balladur in 1994 when he argued that,

> the French government is working to give the nations back their place in the European enterprise and, in particular, to ensure the primacy of the political decision-making bodies, those representing the states, over the administrative bodies.[82]

Reflecting this bias, conservative ministers stressed the need for closer monitoring of European legislation by national parliaments as opposed to the European Parliament, proposing the establishment of a parallel 'Haut Conseil Interparliamentaire'. In its 'Orientation', the government also sought to reinforce the role of the Council of Ministers *vis-à-vis* the Commission and to insist that, in the future, the Commission should work within clearly defined national mandates. In the same vein, the government's proactive proposals on institutional reform in the IGC revolved primarily around ensuring that France's national voice not be diluted during the process of future enlargements. Hence, the government's three priorities were, first, to link any extension of QMV to a reweighting of national voting power within the Council in favour of the largest EU states and to a preservation of the national veto; second, to call for a larger EU to be driven by a smaller Commission of some ten Commissioners – including, therefore, at least one French commissioner. The earlier RPR document even mooted weakening the Commission by remodelling and strengthening the European Council along the lines of the UN Security Council, with two-year EU presidencies rotating among the 'five EU permanent members'. Its third priority was to ensure that an avant-garde of EU member states (implicitly French-led) would have the institutional flexibility to establish areas of 'reinforced co-operation'.

Despite the contradictions between the government's rhetoric in favour of wide-ranging institutional reform and its defensive approach toward specific reform proposals, the substance of the French position in the lead-up to the 1996 IGC, which had been developed by a small clique of officials in the Quai d'Orsay and the Elysée, received only scant outside criticism. This did not reflect unanimous domestic approval for the government's stance. Pro-Europeans on the political left criticized the conservative government for seeing no contradiction between its desire for a strong Europe in monetary, security and other fields, and its suspicion toward European institutions and their quest for greater political legitimacy. Elizabeth Guigou, for example, challenged conservatives to admit that France would have to accept a greater degree of genuine political integration if the German government were to lend its support to French plans for bilateral cooperation and for new French initiatives such as an EU Employment Chapter.[83] Guigou and Jean-Louis Bourlanges, both of whom had taken seats in the European Parliament, advocated a bolder French approach to institutional reform in the IGC, with a clearer division of labour between the Council and Commission, but strengthening the executive powers of the latter while streamlining the decisionmaking procedures of the former through greater QMV and increased use of co-decision by the European Parliament.[84]

Laurent Cohen-Tanugi argued that the contradictions in the government position were untenable.[85] In his view, the confederalism of the RPR and its vision of a Europe built around three circles merely described Europe as it already existed, and made no effort to tackle the vexed question of how such a Europe could be improved. He and his colleagues in French academic institutes continued to work with their German counterparts to criticize the intergovernmental compromises of Maastricht and to encourage the government to take a more constructive approach during the IGC.[86] Having relinquished his post as president of the European Commission, Jacques Delors established his own think tank in Paris: Notre Europe. He continued to espouse a functionalist vision of gradually expanding EU competencies, with EMU as the source of the integrationist impulse toward European political union that had not been provided by the Maastricht Treaty. Much like the government and Giscard d'Estaing, Delors shared the view that 'two Europes' were in gestation, the first 'circle' comprised of a more integrationist core and the second including the peripheral states seeking EU membership. Unlike the government, however, Delors called on the government to accept explicitly the division of the EU into 'two Europes', with the first circle developing into a 'federation of nation states', rather than allow enlargement to dilute the institutional cohesion of core EU members.[87]

The influence of these pro-European politicians and academics on French policy was negligible. A fundamental problem for the pro-Europeans was that the UDF and Socialist parties, which had provided the political base for the more pro-European message during the Maastricht negotiations and ratification, both fell into political disarray after 1993. The UDF was distracted by the leadership vacuum which followed the defeat of Balladur as their presidential candidate in May 1995. For its part, the Socialist Party had become divided over the value of the Maastricht legacy – specifically the EMU convergence criteria – as the social consequences of adhering to the EMU timetable became ever more apparent. Former prime minister Laurent Fabius pointed out that EMU, instead of serving as an instrument to defend Europe from the harsh winds of global economic competition, was, in fact, imposing a capitalist free market upon Europe.[88] Other prominent socialists such as Pierre Bérégovoy, Michel Rocard and Henri Nallet argued that France should challenge the German monetarist vision of EMU, and press for some form of counter-balancing European economic government.[89] In adopting this more sceptical tone toward EMU, however, the Socialist Party opened itself to attack from the French right for abandoning the Mitterrand legacy. Articles in *Le Monde* such as Philippe Séguin's 'L'Europe: Voici Pourquoi Laurent Fabius A Raison' merely drew pro-Europeans in the Socialist Party into a defensive and sterile rhetorical debate with the Eurosceptics in the lead-up to the IGC.[90]

La déception

For a brief period during the summer of 1996, France appeared to have found ways to accommodate its twin desires for deeper European integration and continued national autonomy within the new context of a post-cold war Europe. Relations with the United States had improved in the wake of Franco-US co-ordination in Bosnia and of the apparent compromises over the future of European security at the NATO Berlin summit. The initially rocky personal relationship between Chancellor Kohl and President Chirac had softened, as Chirac committed his government wholeheartedly to meeting the EMU convergence criteria. Between autumn 1996 and summer 1997, however, the government began to pay a political price for the inherent contradictions in its approach towards the process of European integration.

One of the most dramatic developments was the collapse of France's *rapprochement* with NATO. The success of the Berlin summit had led to an open discussion of France's return to NATO's integrated military command, and to a sense among French officials that France's return was actively being sought. The French government, however, first sought a gesture of good faith from the Americans, in giving greater weight to its European allies in the distribution of NATO commands. Without the Elysée consulting the ministries, however, Chirac dramatically raised the stakes by proposing, in a letter to President Clinton, that the NATO Southern Regional Command in Naples, a command which also covered the US 6th Fleet in the Mediterranean, should be transferred from American to French leadership. In Washington, where memories of US–European disagreements over Bosnia were still fresh, this was badly received. Moreover, as Gilles Andréani, head of the Policy Planning unit in the Quai d'Orsay, recognized later, European support for the French position was weak, however much support was offered behind closed doors.[91] In the wake of the failure of this public presidential démarche, French officials and ministers came to the firm conclusion that they alone possessed a radically different vision for Europe's post-cold war security order and that their EU partners, along with the United States, preferred an incremental change that preserved as much of the status quo as possible.[92] Franco-US relations declined further as a result of the US insistence on limiting NATO enlargement to three central European states in the lead-up to the Madrid NATO summit of July 1997. Chirac pushed in vain for the inclusion of France's traditional ally, Romania. From the French perspective, this US highhandedness in NATO was symptomatic of a broader and growing US tendency towards hegemonic behaviour, US actions were increasingly perceived in Paris as a direct challenge to French interests and as preying on French weaknesses.

For French officials and politicians, growing signs of US global hegemony made it all the more important for the 1996 IGC to deepen Europe's security, political and economic integration, not only as a positive response to the upcoming enlargement of the EU, but also as a defensive strategy against unchecked US influence.[93] But, here too, concerns among other EU governments about French ambivalence towards EU institutional integration carried a price. As the IGC approached its final stages ahead of the June 1997 EU summit in Amsterdam, the French and German roles discernible in Maastricht in 1991, with the Germans pushing for greater political integration and the French resisting, were reversed. Daniel Vernet, foreign editor of *Le Monde*, described it as an 'irony of history' that Paris now appeared to want to drag its EU partners further down the road to integration than they wished to go, and that France risked finding itself alone not at the rear, but in the *avant-garde*.[94]

France's negotiating position was severely weakened by Chirac's ill-advised and ill-timed decision to hold snap parliamentary elections on 11 June, a month prior to the Amsterdam summit. Chirac's strategy dramatically back-fired, with the conservative government losing to a coalition between Lionel Jospin's socialist party and the communists, leading to a further period of cohabitation and divided foreign policy leadership. At the Amsterdam summit, the new French government was unable to overcome the entrenched positions of both Germany and other EU states in a number of French priority areas. French plans to further ratchet up the relationship between the EU and WEU were blocked. French proposals to reweigh national votes in the Council and to reform the Commission were postponed to a future IGC. Overall, the French government was perceived to have been a 'loser' at Amsterdam, in stark contrast to the positive balance the country had secured at Maastricht.[95]

The Socialists return to government: new bottle, old wine

The Socialist Party had not articulated any clear European policy during the negotiations leading up to the Amsterdam summit. In the immediate run-up to the election, however, socialist deputies and advisers began to air a more confident and explicit line on Europe. Hubert Védrine, who had been Mitterrand's foreign policy advisor, criticized Chirac's rush to find an accommodation with the United States over NATO.[96] Despite agreeing on the need for some political control over European economic and monetary union and on the value of EMU as a bulwark against the pressures of globalization, socialist parliamentarians attacked the government's capitulation to the German campaign for an EMU Stability Pact.[97] Jean-Pierre Chevènement, in his 1996 book *France Allemagne: Parlons Franc*, re-rehearsed the full litany of French fears about the ways in which Germany was using the process of European economic and monetary integration to achieve European dominance.[98] At the centre of the party, Lionel Jospin put forward a list of four demands that he claimed would 'preserve France's own interests'. These included the demand that Italy and Spain join EMU from the outset; that EMU also embrace a pledge to create new jobs; that the European Central Bank be balanced by some form of political mechanism; and that the euro not be over-valued in relation to the US dollar. The demand to extend EMU to other Mediterranean countries reflected not only a desire to protect France from potential currency devaluations by Spain and Italy, it also reflected the deeper-seated fear, raised explicitly by Chevènement and shared by many politicians on the right, of France becoming a lone southern 'outlier' within a German-centred and northern-biased Europe.

Despite these seemingly aggressive demands concerning EMU, the socialist government entered power already trapped in the same conceptual 'impasse' which had dogged French thinking about Europe from 1989 onwards. Hubert Védrine, who became foreign minister in the Jospin government, gave a revealing interview to the journal *Débat*, published a month before the election. Like his conservative predecessors, Védrine rejected the German hypothesis that states had somehow dissolved. He supported, instead, 'the alternative hypothesis, the one that accepts that states continue to exist and that actors have retained their sense of statehood, of their country, of its longevity'.[99] Moreover, within this state-centric world view, Védrine argued that one must still distinguish between 'states' and states that are 'great powers' such as France. Védrine took issue with his socialist and conservative predecessors only in their refusal to recognize openly the fact that France and the EU now lived in a world that is far more competitive, a world that he described as:

> riven by a ferocious economic war, characterized by an evolution that calls into question all of the foundations of France as an entity and of the French state. An American, Anglo-Saxon, ultra-liberal world which biodegrades states everywhere.

Védrine concluded that none of the trends under way in this competitive world is favourable to France, least of all the emergence of the United States as the world's lone superpower. In fact, France risked becoming what he termed 'a diplomatic rentier – a rentier whose economic base is crumbling'. But the response he advocated was Gaullist in tone. France should contribute to the reconstitution of a 'balance of power' on a global scale. A balance of power in which Europe, as a 'puissance européenne', would be a key player.

Védrine, however, acknowledged two fundamental obstacles to the realization of a new global balance of power. In the first place, France was the only core European country that viewed the world through such a realist prism.[100] Second, and most importantly, France was still not ready to step up to the implications of its own conclusion. Védrine expressed the dilemma facing France in the following way:

> What we need is a translation, a transposition of French voluntarism onto a European plane. This is very difficult: we need to 'disappear' in order to be reborn. But we are not reconciled to this. We spend every day in a state of contradiction. We ask ourselves which are the issues upon which it is important to maintain a French approach for as long as possible, in as spectacular a manner as possible, so that, when the time comes, we can integrate in the European black box the maximum amount of French influence.[101]

So long as French thinking was plagued by this fundamental contradiction and so long as France alone possessed the vision of establishing a global balance of power, Védrine conceded that the principal conundrum ('le casse-tête numéro un') for French diplomacy would be to work out how 'we can exercise the maximum amount of French influence in the interior of this emergent European power'. During this period, which Védrine believed could last twenty years, French leaders should act against their instincts and avoid political posturing and strong-arming their EU partners. France should be methodical, patient and tenacious.

It was to prove particularly difficult for the new French administration to put Védrine's preferred approach into practice. Having failed to develop an achievable strategy for Europe after the cold war, France's European policy immediately after Amsterdam returned to the defensive and unpredictable pattern that had been its hallmark during the cold war years. French domestic politics were partly responsible for this apparent drift. The Socialist government, despite the lack of preparation for its unexpected election victory, performed creditably on the economic front. The party's political room for manoeuvre on European policy, however, was hampered by two factors. First, Jospin had to navigate between those on the left who mistrusted EMU and those, primarily in the government, who believed that the 'politique unique' of adherence to the EMU criteria was central both to France's future economic prosperity and to Europe's political stability.[102] Second, Jacques Chirac, using his constitutional purview over French foreign policy, sought to rebuild his personal political reputation as well as project some degree of leadership on the rapidly disintegrating French right partly through taking an activist stance towards Europe.[103] Most damaging to the government was Chirac's Gaullist grandstanding over the presidency of the

European Central Bank after November 1997, which almost derailed the decision at the Brussels summit in May 1998 on which countries would proceed with EMU. Chirac's attitude to the European Central Bank and his flurry of personal foreign policy démarches after Amsterdam – in the Middle East, towards Russia, in South East Asia – gave the impression of France casting about for a role, of seizing tactical targets of opportunity to advance narrow national interests, rather than pursuing any clear strategic vision of a desired goal for Europe.

Conclusion

French conceptions of European order after the cold war remained remarkably consistent, not only from one government to another between 1989 and 1997, but also between these governments and the assumptions that had guided French policymaking during the cold war. First, there was a consensus that Germany's economic power and political influence had to be contained – even if it could not be 'balanced' – if a stable European order was to emerge. France, which had sought to build a European political union in 1952 when West German rearmament was proposed, resurrected the same approach during the Maastricht negotiations of 1990–91 in the face of German unification. Having stepped back at Maastricht from the institutional consequences of its own rhetoric, much as it did in 1952–54, the French government concentrated on building an unbreakable economic bilateral interdependence, much as it had done through the European Coal and Steel Community and then the EEC in 1950–57, this time through a single-minded focus on completing European economic and monetary union. At the same time, however, French concepts of European order after the cold war, just as during the cold war, were intertwined with the desire that France retain and, if possible, strengthen its non-dependent, world power status within any emergent European order.[104] Balladur spoke for much of France's policy élite when he stated that, 'in the first place; Europe is, for France, a supplementary source of power and influence'.[105]

'Europe' was seen as the means to achieve both of these fundamental objectives – the containment of Germany and the projection of France's global and regional interests – as had been the intention from 1945–89. The difference was that, whereas successive French governments were able to juggle these conceptual priorities to France's general strategic benefit during the cold war, the end of the cold war exposed their inherent contradictions. The central contradiction, between the French desire to promote the maximum level of European political and economic integration to contain a united Germany and its determination to resist the impact of integration on French sovereignty, was at the heart of each of the twists and turns in France's Europe policy described in this chapter.

Even the most politically united French administrations after 1989 (Mitterrand–Bérégovoy and Chirac–Juppé) were unable to escape the consequences of this contradiction. Despite his success in setting out a clearly-defined roadmap for monetary union within ten years, Mitterrand made no viable proposals on one of the central strategic challenges to European order: integrating the new democracies of central and eastern Europe into the West. Instead, Mitterrand combined ambiguity about the timing and desirability of EU enlargement with opposition to any eastward expansion of NATO's influence, seeing in the former a threat to French control of Germany and in the latter a further attempt by the United States to extend its political control of European security at France's expense. The self-styled 'pragmatism' of the Balladur government and Chirac–Juppé administration came no closer to overcoming the French contradiction.

The Jospin administration in 1997 began again to edge France back towards NATO, while also pursuing further the bilateral defence dialogue with Britain; but without explaining to its domestic audience the long-term implications of these developments for French sovereignty. Socialist rhetoric in opposition led the new government to hold back the process of economic liberalization on which the Chirac–Juppé administration had embarked. Despite its proclaimed European commitment, French policy looked to European institutions to protect the French socio-economic model from American-led globalization, more than as a framework within which to improve global competitiveness. Ministerial promises to post-socialist regimes of French support for early EU enlargement were balanced by vigorous support for French agricultural interests in resisting reform of the common agricultural policy. French ministers clung to the central importance of the Franco-German partnership, while recognizing that the Berlin republic would wish to pursue interests to Germany's north and east which would threaten French efforts to maintain the established core of Europe.

The wider French public, like its counterparts in other West European states, remained largely disinterested in the details of European integration, leaving the definition of policy and its management to the political élite.[106] The shock of the post-Maastricht referendum had dissuaded political leaders from disturbing the established consensus further; leaving them to adjust policy at the margins without risking an open challenge to existing orthodoxies. The French élite, eight years after the Berlin Wall had come down, were still resisting change and its implications for policy. The cost of that resistance was, however, continuing tolerance of internally-contradictory policies, with the French government held back from redefining European priorities by the tyranny of the conventional wisdom in Paris and beyond.

Notes

1. Pierre Lellouche, 'France in Search of Security', *Foreign Affairs*, 72:2 (Spring 1993).
2. Daniel Vernet, 'The Dilemma of French Foreign Policy', *International Affairs*, 68:4 (1992).
3. In her memoirs Margaret Thatcher recalls a meeting on 29 January 1990 where Mitterrand shared with her his concerns about Germany's 'so-called mission in Central Europe'. *The Downing Street Years* (London: HarperCollins, 1993) p. 798.

4. Dominique Moïsi, 'Insecurities, Old and New, Plague the Paris–Bonn Axis', *The Wall Street Journal, Europe*, 7 February 1995.

5. See, for example, Philip H. Gordon, *A Certain Idea of France: French Security Policy and the Gaullist Legacy* (Princeton: Princeton University Press, 1993). For a description of the French obsession with its 'non-dependence', see Jolyon Howorth, 'France and European Security 1944–94: Re-reading the Gaullist Consensus' in Brian Jenkins and Tony Chafer (eds), *France: From the End of the Cold War to the New World Order* (London: Macmillan, 1996) p. 22.

6. See, for example, Vincent Wright, *The Government and Politics of France*, 3rd edn (New York: Holmes and Meier, 1989).

7. Michel Girard, 'The Uncertainty of Influence: France', in Girard, Eberwein and Webb, eds, *Theory and Practice in Foreign Policy-making: national perspective on academics and professionals in international relations* (London: Pinter, 1994) p. 51.

8. See Hubert Védrine, *La décennie Mitterrand* (Fayard: Paris, 1996) and 'le piano ou le tabouret', in *Le Débat* (1996) p. 170, where Vedrine describes how Mitterrand's policy towards Europe after the Fontainebleau EC summit in 1984 would be, 'avec celle de de Gaulle sur la défense et la disuassion, la plus tenace, la plus volontariste des politiques menées sous la 5ème République'.

9. Védrine, ibid., p. 167.

10. On 4 May 1996, *Le Monde* published the notes taken by an East German official during Mitterrand's one-on-one meetings with East German leaders Hans Modrow and Manfred Gerlach, notes which are held in the federal archives in Potsdam and which were first published by *Der Spiegel* on 29 April 1996. If accounts of Mitterrand's conversations with the East German leadership are to be believed, his final conclusion was that 'what happens to the German people is their own business. But when Europe is at stake then that is also France's business. He who wishes to suppress the existing order should be ready to construct a new one.'

11. See, for example, the joint press conference between Mitterrand and Kohl at the Elysée palace in Paris on 15 February 1992 (French foreign ministry transcript).

12. Mitterrand, *De l'Allemagne, de la France* (Paris: Fayard, 1996) p. 43, and statements at joint press conference with Helmut Kohl at the 58th joint Franco-German summit in Bonn on 15 November 1991 (French foreign ministry transcript); Dominique Moïsi called this threat the return to 'pre-World War I power billiards', in 'Insecurities Old and New', op. cit..

13. See Mitterrand's New Year's address to the French nation on 1 January 1990, reported in *Le Monde* (2 January 1990). Jolyon Howorth described Mitterrand as 'the most complete and subtle artisan of de Gaulle's original European vision', in 'France and European Security 1944–94', op. cit., p. 33.

14. Mitterrand interview with *Radio France Internationale*, 12 June 1991 (French Foreign Ministry transcript).

15. See the comments by Hans-Dietrich Genscher at the 14–15 October 1989 EPC meeting at Esclimont reported in *Financial Times*, 16 October 1989.

16. See Mitterrand's speech to the ecole de Guerre in Paris on 11 April 1991, entitled, 'Quelle sécurité en Europe à l'aube du XXIème siècle' (French Foreign Ministry transcript).

17. Stanley Hoffmann, 'French Dilemmas and Strategies', in Robert Keohane, Joseph Nye and Stanley Hoffmann (eds), *After the Cold War: International Institutions and State Strategies in Europe, 1989–91* (Cambridge, MA: Harvard University Press, 1993) p. 140.

18. *Radio France Internationale*, 12 June 1991 (French Foreign Ministry transcript).

19. From the French perspective, the Europe Agreements exposed the massive advantage that Germany was poised to gain from increased trade and investment with central Europe, in contrast to France's scant economic and political relations with the region.
20. Védrine, 'Le piano ou le tabouret', op. cit., p. 173.
21. See Mitterrand's press conference following the Maastricht summit on 10 December 1991 (French Foreign Ministry transcript); Vedrine explained the Elysée's thinking when he said that, 'if you believe that you still have sovereignty to preserve, you postpone the moment; if you estimate that sovereignty over a particular issue is already illusory, you are then in a hurry', 'Le piano ou le tabouret', op. cit., p. 173.
22. Statement by Elizabeth Guigou to the French National Assembly on 12 December 1990 (French Foreign Ministry transcript).
23. Mitterrand comments in an interview with the *Frankfurter Allgemeine Zeitung* (14 December 1991).
24. Dumas interview with *Libération*, 6 December 1991.
25. Anand Menon, Anthony Forster and William Wallace, 'A Common European Defence?' in *Survival* (Autumn 1992) p. 104.
26. Dumas stated in a speech to the French National Assembly on 27 November 1991 that Maastricht offered the opportunity to 'turn Europe into a leading world power' (French Foreign Ministry document).
27. Roland Dumas stated quite clearly, 'CFSP should open the way towards a common European defence in the wake of a Foreign Ministers' meeting in Brussels to debate the IGC on Political Union on 4 February 1991 (French Foreign Ministry transcript).
28. Roland Dumas, 4 February 1991 (French Foreign Ministry transcript); also see the Kohl–Mitterrand letter to the Italian EU Presidency on 6 February 1990.
29. Roland Dumas interview with *Libération*, 6 December 1991.
30. Quoted in David Yost, 'France and West European Defense Identity', *Survival*, 33:4 (July–August 1991) p. 346.
31. Anand Menon has written extensively on the French 'immobilisme' on security issues – see, for example, 'Continuing Politics By Other Means: Defence Policy under the French Fifth Republic', *West European Politics*, 17:4 (October 1994) p. 80, and 'The Consensus on Defence Policy and the End of the Cold War: Political Parties and the Limits of Adaptation', in Jenkins and Chafer, op. cit., pp. 157–9.
32. *Le Monde*, 12–13 January 1992.
33. Menon, Forster and Wallace, 'A Common European Defence?', op. cit., p. 105. As Dumas recognized at a NATO ministerial meeting in Copenhagen on 6 June 1991, 'the European question (in defence) is above all a political one and a virtual one .... The Atlantic question is different. It is based upon reality'. NATO press conference, 6 June 1991 (French Foreign Ministry transcript).
34. See, for example, Dominique Moïsi, 'The Trouble with France', *Foreign Affairs*, 77:3 (May–June 1998).
35. Philippe Séguin interview in *Le Monde*, 4 July 1992.
36. The manifesto was issued by the RPR's Conseil National on 5 December 1990; Charles Pasqua, 'Union Politique Contre l'Europe de l'Apartheid', in *Le Monde*, 4 January 1990.
37. The manifesto insisted, rather uncontroversially, that the government should retain national control over decisions of war and peace, nuclear deterrence and vital national interests, as well as over monetary policy.

38. Alain Duhamel, 'Les malgré-nous de l'Europe', *Le Monde*, 3 June 1992.

39. See, for example, Edouard Balladur, 'Les dangers du non' in *Le Monde*, 21 August 1992 and Alain Juppé's similar arguments in articles in *Le Monde*, 28 August and 18 September 1992.

40. See the interview with François Léotard in *Le Monde*, 18 April 1992; Charles Millon interview with *Le Monde*, 8 September 1992.

41. Giscard d'Estaing interview on Europe 1–22 April 1992, reported in *Le Monde*, 23 April 1992.

42. *Le Monde*, 15 April 1992.

43. Chirac famously oscillated from elliptical support for the Treaty ('je voterai sans enthousiasme et sans réserve' – *Le Monde*, 26 May 1992) to an unsustainable attempt to rise above the debate ('j'ai decidé to demeurer silencieux sur cette affaire' – *Le Monde*, 15 June 1992) to a very ambiguous 'yes' (*Le Monde* 7 July 1992). In the end, only 58 of the RPR's 126 deputies voted against Maastricht.

44. See, for example, the anti-Maastricht article 'La Logique d'abdication' in *L'Humanité*, 5 December 1991 and the statement by the 'Ligue Communiste Révolutionaire' composed of Chévènement supporters and Trotskyists released on 8 July 1992.

45. Lellouche, 'France in Search of Security', op. cit..

46. *Le Livre Blanc de la Défense* (Paris: Ministry of Defence, 1994) p. 5.

47. In order to underline the continuing centrality of the Franco-German relationship within the French conservative vision of European order, Balladur went so far as to call in November 1994 for a new Elysée treaty to strengthen the existing Franco-German treaty. Balladur recommended strengthened collaboration in areas such as culture and education and increased exchanges between French and German parliamentarians and leaders of regional government, *Le Monde*, 11 November 1994.

48. According to interviews with French foreign ministry officials, Russia's loss of control over Ukraine was fundamental to the French reassessment of the external threat to European security.

49. *Le Livre Blanc de la Défense*, op. cit., p. 2.

50. Alain Juppé, speech to the Quai d'Orsay's Centre d'Analyse et de Prévision on 30 January 1995 (Service de Presse et d'Information, 31 January 1995).

51. CDU/CSU Faktion, 1 September 1994; also see the published debate between Karl Lamers and Jean-Pierre Chevènement in *Géopolitique*, 53 (Spring 1996) pp. 67–77.

52. Edouard Balladur speech to the IHEDN on 21 September 1994 (London, Service de Presse et d'Information).

53. Pierre Lellouche, *L'Europe et sa sécurité* (Assemblée Nationale, Délégation pour les Communautés Européennes, Rapport d'Information no. 1294) pp. 91–2, 102; Jacques Baumel in *Le Monde*, 1 April 1993, 'L'objectif n'est plus de constituer un pilier europeen au sein de l'OTAN, conception dépassée; c'est d'oeuvrer à une véritable autonomie européenne comparable avec l'Alliance'; Baumel was then the Chairman of the Defence Committee of the WEU Parliamentary Assembly and Vice Chairman of the National Assembly's Defence Committee. Also see the speech by François Léotard to the IHEDN on 15 May 1993 (French Foreign Ministry transcript).

54. 'De l'audace et du réalisme: pour des propositions concrètes et pragmatiques', was the title of one of the chapters in Pierre Lellouche's report on *L'Europe et sa Sécurité*, op. cit.. Opponents of the prevailing French consensus came together in loosely organized think tanks such as the 'Forum du Futur', which linked conservative

parliamentarians and senior defence executives (EN). François Fillon and Jacques Baumel were among those conservative politicians who used these channels to charge that the government's loyalty to out-moded Gaullist concepts was preventing France's armed forces from adapting to the new post-cold war security environment, in which France's continuing reliance on its nuclear status masked an inadequate conventional military capability. François Fillon, 'Un nouveau débat', in *Le Monde*, 5 March 1993; Jacques Baumel, *Le Monde*, 1 May 1993.

55. François Léotard's statement on 13 May 1993 (London: Service de Presse at d'Information).

56. See Baumel's article in *Le Monde*, 1 April 1993.

57. Lellouche, *L'Europe et sa sécurité*, op. cit., p. 91.

58. Alain Juppé speech to the Quai' d'Orsay, 30 January 1995 (London: Service de Presse et d'Information).

59. In January 1993, for example, a secret agreement between French and German military commanders and NATO's Supreme Commander of Allied Forces in Europe anticipated the Eurocorps being placed under NATO operational command in the event of a crisis. French officials were also permitted to take a more active role in NATO committees in order to facilitate French participation in coalition operations in Bosnia. See Robert P. Grant, 'France's New Relationship with NATO', *Survival*, 38:1 (Spring 1996) p. 61.

60. France's NATO rapprochement was also spurred by the need to ensure full oversight of French participation in NATO's peacekeeping operations in the former Yugoslavia. See *Le Monde*, 14 May 1993.

61. In one notable instance in April 1994, Mitterrand personally vetoed the participation of Admiral Lanxade, his chief-of-staff, at a meeting of NATO's Military Committee, reported in *Le Monde*, 28 April 1994. The impact of cohabitation on French rethinking of its post-cold war security policy was apparent in the overly exhaustive and incremental approach laid out in the 1994 Defence White Paper.

62. For a review of the French 'rapprochement' with NATO see Grant, 'France's New Relationship with NATO', op. cit., pp. 61–6.

63. In addition, nuclear co-operation with the British was formally initiated at the October 1992 Gleneagles summit and made permanent in July 1993.

64. François Heisborg pointed out that whereas the UK, FRG and US had all cut their armed forces by around 30 per cent between 1988 and 1994, France had only incurred cuts of around 10 per cent, 'La France at sa défense', *Politique Etrangère* (Winter 1995), p. 984.

65. The *Livre Blanc* had described conscription as part of the fabric of the nation, op. cit., p. 127. Reflecting the government's more pragmatic approach, the size of the French rapid reaction forces after this review presupposed that French forces would be designed to form part of a European rapid reaction force, capable of integration into WEU, CJTF, or NATO force packages, depending on the nature of the threat.

66. As Henri Conze, Balladur's head of the Délégation Générale pour l'Armement, explained in February 1995, defence industrial co-operation between France and Germany constituted a logical extension of the political philosophy behind the Schuman plan for a European Coal and Steel Community – it would make war unthinkable between the two countries; speech at the US CREST conference on transatlantic defence co-operation, Paris, February 1995.

67. Balladur speech, 27 June 1994 (London: Agence de Presse et d'Information). In this context, the new government insisted throughout 1994–95 that the EU

should shoulder the main responsibility for post-cold war European stability and that NATO enlargement should follow, not precede, EU enlargement.

68. Alain Juppé, 3 November 1994 (London: Service de Presse et d'Information).
69. Balladur, 1 September 1994 (London: Service de Presse et d'Information).
70. *Ibid.* The metaphor of circles echoed French images of 1960s and 1970s which served to define France's areas of global intervention; see Dominique David, 'The Search for a New Security Strategy in a Shifting Inernational Arena', in Jenkins and Chafer, op. cit., p. 67.
71. See, for example, Juppé's speech of 30 January 1995 and Hervé de Charette's comments on 22 February 1996 (London: Service de Presse et d'Information).
72. Pierre Lellouche, *Vers l'Europe que nous voulons: les enjeux de la CIG de 1996* (RPR, Rapport Preliminaire du Groupe de Travail de l'Europe, January 1996), p. 8.
73. Ibid., p. 4; and also see the speech by Hervé de Charette at the conference on 'L'urgence européenne', hosted in Paris by Jacques Delors on 20 September 1996 (French foreign ministry transcript).
74. Valéry Giscard d'Estaing, 'Manifeste pour une nouvelle Europe fédérative', *Le Figaro*, 11 January 1995.
75. Michel Barnier explained in testimony to the French Senate that without the mechanisms the government was pushing for in the IGC, France's influence would suffer. Michel Barnier statement to the Senate on 22 October 1996 (French foreign ministry transcript).
76. Lellouche, *L'Europe et sa sécurité*, op. cit., pp. 51, 60–1.
77. *Ibid.*, pp. 54, 102.
78. By the time of the Franco-German summit at Baden-Baden on 7 December 1995, Helmut Kohl was able to note at a press conference that it was 'one of the most happy experiences of Franco-German co-operation that we have arrived at a common approach on all of the points associated with economic and monetary policy'. (French Foreign Ministry transcript).
79. Michel Barnier conceded in a debate in the National Assembly that, as constraints 'are imposed on us at a global level, ... Europe can constitute a security, a protection', in any number of areas including the monetary. See his comments during the National Assembly debate on 27 November 1996 ahead of the European Council in Dublin in December (French Foreign Ministry transcript).
80. *L'Europe que nous voulons*, op. cit., p. 7; also see the interview with Michel Barnier in *Liberation* on 5 October 1996.
81. *Les Orientations de la France pour la Conférence Intergouvernementale de 1996* (20 February 1996).
82. Balladur interview with Polish newspaper on 28 June 1994 (French Foreign Ministry transcript); or, as Juppé put it, 'an enlarged Europe will never be a super-state, not even a federal one ... nor could we accept ... an organization in which the Commission was destined to become this super-state's government, with the European Parliament and the Council of Ministers sharing between them the tasks of democratic control'. Alain Juppé, 3 November 1994, (London: Service de Presse et d'Information).
83. Elizabeth Guigou, 'L'illusioniste du Palais-Bourbon', in *Le Monde*, 12 October 1996.
84. 'Pour une réforme ambitieuse du Traité de Maastricht', Mouvement Européen (France), February 1996; interview with Elizabeth Guigou, *Europ* (Hors série no. 3, May 1995) pp. 4–7.
85. Laurent Cohen-Tanugi, 'The French Debate', in *The 1996 IGC – National Debates (1)* (London: RIIA, Discussion Paper no. 66, 1996) p. 23.

86. See, for example, Valérie Guérin-Sendelbach, Ingo Kolbloom, Robert Picht, Hans Stark, and Henrik Unterwedde, 'Questions européennes' in Thierry de Montbrial (IFRI), Karl Kaiser (DGAP), René Lasserre (CIRAC), and Robert Picht (DFI) *Agir pour L'Europe: les relations franco-allemandes dans l'apres-guerre froide*, Travaux et Recherches de l'IFRI (Masson: Paris, 1995) p. 16.

87. Delors interview with *Le Monde*, 25 March 1996.

88. Laurent Fabius, 'Une dernière chance pour sauver l'Europe', *Le Monde*, 7 September 1996.

89. *Le Monde*, 14 October 1996; Henri Nallet, 'Pour une Europe des peuples', *Le Monde*, 3 May 1997.

90. *Le Monde*, 19 September 1996.

91. Gilles Andréani, 'La France et l'OTAN après la Guerre Froide', *Politique Etrangère* (Spring 1998), pp. 77–92.

92. The government's decision to sign a 'secret' new Franco-German security pact, in February 1997, did little to dispel this impression.

93. See, for example, Michel Barnier, 'Pour un concept commun européen de la politique étrangère et de la sécurité', *Le Monde*, 14 February 1997.

94. *Le Monde*, 9 April 1997.

95. *The Economist*, 21 June 1997, p. 37.

96. Interview with Hubert Védrine in *Le Monde*, 30 January 1997.

97. See, for example, the questions posed to government ministers by socialist deputies during the National Assembly debate on 11 November 1996 (French Foreign Ministry transcript).

98. Jean-Pierre Chevènement's, *France Allemagne: Parlons Franc* (Plon: Paris, 1996), contains a pessimistic assessment of the divergent national and cultural priorities of France and Germany and the fruitlessness of attempting to overcome them through European integration.

99. Hubert Védrine, 'Le piano ou le tabouret', op. cit., p. 179. Other quotes are taken from this same article.

100. Védrine's conclusion was that 'no other European country thinks like us ('ne raisonne comme nous').

101. Ibid., pp. 172–3.

102. Delors concluded, *Le Monde*, 25 March 1996, that, once in power, all French governments follow the same prescription. The new socialist government's acquiescence to the 'politique unique' served to open on the left, as on the right, factional and personal splits over France's policy towards Europe.

103. Charles Pasqua's political grouping, 'Demain la France' launched a series of attacks on the euro, on the EMU's Stability Pact, and on the Amsterdam Treaty. Balladur, the defeated presidential candidate, also complained publicly about the important loss of additional French sovereignty entailed in the Stability Pact. See *Le Monde*, 9 December 1997.

104. In his memoirs, Charles de Gaulle criticized those who 'feign surprise over the so-called changes and detours of France's action'. This policy's 'essential goal', he added, was that 'France be and remain an independent nation'. *Discours et Messages*, 5 (1970) p. 97.

105. Balladur stated that, 'En premier lieu, une évidence: l'organisation de l'Europe est, pour la France, un élément supplémentaire de force et d'influence', 30 November 1994 (London: Service de Presse et d'Information).

106. This point is stressed in François Furet, 'L'idée française de la révolution', *Le Débat*, September–October 1997.

5
The British Response: Denial and Confusion?

Anthony Forster and William Wallace

Introduction

The most remarkable aspect of the British foreign policy debate between 1990 and 1997 is how little it appears to have been affected by the transformation of international order. The agonized debate on Britain's European commitment continued to divide the Conservative Party and to fill the Conservative press, with Eurosceptic suspicion of Germany only increased by its re-emergence as Europe's central power. The Labour opposition, which during the early stages of the cold war had flirted with plans for disengagement in central Europe, was largely silent as central Europe was at last transformed. Denial, rather than reconceptualization, has been the predominant British posture at the strategic level; while the 'pragmatic' style of British government has been evident in practical adjustments of defence posture and modest schemes of technical assistance to central and east European countries.

After 1989, as before, the prevailing assumption remained that the United States was Britain's preferred partner; the rhetoric of the Labour government elected in May 1997 echoed that of Mrs Thatcher in this regard. From the intergovernmental conference of 1990–91 to that of 1996–97 the domestic consensus on foreign policy and defence priorities rested on the long-established preference for NATO over the EU. The transformation of the former socialist countries caught prime ministerial attention from time to time, without ever becoming a major political or economic preoccupation. Military involvement in the Gulf in 1990–91 reasserted Britain's position as the USA's most dependable European ally in extra-European crises. In contrast the experience of Bosnia, from the commitment of British troops onwards, exposed transatlantic differences and led to the development of a bilateral defence dialogue with the French. While the characteristic style of French political leaders, however, in responding to external change was to launch grand initiatives – from the Mitterrand plan for a European Confederation to the Balladur proposal for a European Stability Pact – their British counterparts saw themselves as 'pragmatic', providing practical answers to practical problems as they arose.

The absence of public reconsideration of the framework of British foreign policy partly reflects the dominance of prime ministerial style in setting the terms of domestic debate on foreign policy. The collapse of the socialist bloc coincided with the final years of Margaret Thatcher's prime ministership. The Conservative Party was gripped by increasingly bitter ideological divisions, in which attitudes to European integration, transatlantic relations, parliamentary sovereignty, national identity, 'Anglo-Saxon' free market economics and 'continental' corporatism intermingled. Mrs Thatcher's open resistance to the unification of Germany in the winter of 1989–90 was of a piece with the strident tone of her Bruges speech of September 1988 and her growing isolation at successive European Councils in 1989–90. Her determination to resist any 'weakening' in Britain's European policy was a major factor in her loss of office in November 1990.

Her successor inherited a party divided along this ideological fault line; and sought, as a party manager by experience and inclination, to hold his party together by avoiding redefinition of the issues at stake. Foreign policy – above all European policy – thereafter reflected a curious blend of ideological and practical elements. British politicians, and British newspaper columnists, continued to argue over symbolic issues of national sovereignty and status, while useful programmes of technical and military assistance to former socialist states developed almost unremarked in parliament or the media.

The dominance of this Conservative foreign policy consensus through a period of radical external change however requires further explanation. It is not that the country lacked sources for alternative points of view. London was Europe's most important centre for international news reporting and analysis. The city of London was one of the world's three global financial centres, dependent on constant access to information and analysis of global trends. London housed – in the International Institute for Strategic Studies and the Royal Institute of International Affairs – two of the most respected think tanks in Western Europe. Over the previous thirty years the study of International Relations had become firmly established in British universities, far more so than in Germany, France or Italy. The British diplomatic service prided itself on its professional and analytical skills. Nevertheless, neither political debate nor government policy appears to have been markedly affected by inputs from these sources. The rest of this chapter sets out to explore this paradox: that during a period of rapid and radical external change, within a country equipped with better resources for understanding European and global trends than almost any other West European country, the underlying rationale for foreign policy changed so little.

Foreign policy before the Wall came down

British foreign policy in 1989 was a battlefield, in which the Prime Minister herself defined the terms of the conflict. Mrs Thatcher, in her later years as

Prime Minister, saw foreign policy as a 'perpetual struggle against a hostile world' in which the Foreign and Commonwealth Office were 'defeatists, even collaborators'.[1] Her enemies were not only within the European and Commonwealth governments with which she had to deal and on the opposition benches of the House of Commons, but within her own party, government and administration. Her allies were in the Conservative press, the think tanks of the right which she had herself encouraged and across the Atlantic in Washington.

Disagreements within the government over policies towards Europe became increasingly bitter during 1989. Geoffrey Howe was forced out of the Foreign Office in July, reluctantly becoming Leader of the House of Commons; Nigel Lawson resigned as Chancellor of the Exchequer on 26 October. The inexperienced John Major spent a brief four months as foreign secretary before replacing Nigel Lawson at the Treasury, giving way in turn to Douglas Hurd: three foreign secretaries in six months, while the ice of the cold war was cracking. 'The increasingly curious way' in which the Prime Minister made policy, most of all on major questions, had led to a breakdown of Cabinet government.[2] Her foreign policy adviser has since compared 'the activities of Mrs Thatcher's inner circle' to the description in Saint-Simon's memoirs of Louis XIV's court.[3] Senior ministers, responsible for foreign affairs, finance and defence, had less easy access to the Prime Minister and less influence over policy than a small group of trusted advisers.

It had not always been so. Margaret Thatcher in her early years as Prime Minister had displayed not only an instinctive distrust for the professional advice of the Foreign and Commonwealth Office, but also a lively interest in questioning the conventional wisdom of politics and diplomacy. Weekend seminars at Chequers, the Prime Minister's official residence in the country, became a regular part of her workaholic routine. A series of seminars on east–west relations, in 1982–83, at which academics and diplomats were subjected to sharp prime ministerial questioning about the possibilities of change within the USSR, led Mrs Thatcher to anticipate the succession to Andropov and invite Mikhail Gorbachev to visit Britain: developing a relationship which became much closer, and a policy towards the USSR which was more open, than either Britain's American allies or many of her own advisers thought wise.[4]

If the transformation of Europe had come in 1985–86, during the most self-confident period of the Thatcher government, the British response might have been more considered and flexible. By 1989, however, Mrs Thatcher was both tired and beleaguered, and bitterly at odds with senior ministers and with a substantial proportion of her party in the Commons on European policy. Though she had been persuaded to sign the Single European Act, she had resisted increasing pressures from the Chancellor, the Foreign Secretary and the Bank of England to join the Exchange Rate Mechanism of the European Monetary System, from 1985 on: this was the issue over which she dismissed

Geoffrey Howe from the FCO, and over which Nigel Lawson resigned a fortnight before the Berlin Wall came down. Her confident relations with President Reagan had been the cornerstone of her international standing. But President Bush had gone out of his way, on his election in November 1988, to signal that he gave greater priority to partnership with Germany than with Britain, meeting with Chancellor Kohl before Mrs Thatcher. Personal relations between Thatcher and Kohl, never easy, were hardening into mutual disdain; Kohl's effort in April 1989 to rebuild a sense of trust by inviting Thatcher to his home village of Deidesheim was a private and public failure.[5]

Mrs Thatcher operated from a distinctive cluster of assumptions about Britain's historic position in the world. In a speech at Aspen, Colorado in August 1990 she said 'I am unashamedly a believer in the United States and all things American ...'.[6] A devotee of Friedrich von Hayek and others who had escaped from authoritarian governments to the freedom of the Anglo-Saxon world, she saw the European continent as still dominated by corporatist policies and over-mighty states, with the European Community (as she asserted in her 1988 Bruges speech) a vehicle which threatened to impose the same shackles on Britain:

> We have not successfully rolled back the frontiers of the state in Britain only to see them reimposed at a European level, with a European super-state exercising a new dominance from Brussels.

Germany, 'by its very nature a destabilizing rather than a stabilizing force in Europe', would be likely to dominate such a superstate; and should therefore be held in check by a continuing American commitment to Europe, supported by close links between Britain and France. Mrs Thatcher was not afraid to talk about 'the German problem' in 1989–90, and to make it clear that she saw the problem as rooted in 'national character' as well as in geopolitics and economic strength.[7] The structural weakness of her position was that the Bush administration differed sharply in its analysis, and that the British government had made insufficient investment in building a partnership with France to provide a basis for co-operation when the Wall came down.

There was a structural contradiction between Mrs Thatcher's early awareness of the possibilities of change within the USSR, with her warm relationship with Gorbachev, and her continuing (and increasingly isolated) support for the modernization of American short-range nuclear weapons in Germany as regimes in central Europe began to change in 1989. She had spoken in her Bruges speech of Prague, Budapest and Warsaw as 'great European cities', artificially excluded from the institutions which held together 'Europe on both sides of the Atlantic';[8] but this had not led to any consideration of appropriate responses if the Gorbachev reforms went further and the exclusion were to end. As early as November 1988 she was prepared to declare that 'we're not in a cold war now'.[9] But her assumptions about the structure of a post-cold war

Europe were partly realist, seeing the USSR as well as the USA as essential elements in the balance of a Europe of nation states, partly anti-German; in Moscow in September 1989 for consultations with Gorbachev, she assured him that the UK did not consider itself committed by the many NATO declarations it had signed on German reunification.[10] The government which had been first to encourage change within the USSR became in 1990 the most determined to resist change in Europe's political and military order.

Mrs Thatcher's first response in November 1989 was to argue 'that all military matters should continue to be conducted through Nato and the Warsaw Pact ... this arrangement has suited us well and at a time of great change it is necessary to keep this background of security and stability.'[11] Even a year later she was insisting that '... when we talk about a New Security Order our first task is in reality to preserve the essentials of the present order'.[12] The Soviet Union and Poland, it appeared, were to be seen alongside the USA as containing Germany; a unified Germany within a strengthened European Community represented in reality the greater threat to British interests.

The absence of strongly articulated alternative views to those which the Prime Minister so passionately and determinedly expressed requires careful explanation. The United Kingdom is an open, plural society and a working democracy. Mrs Thatcher's particular mixture of warmth towards the United States, deep suspicion of Germany and of the European Community as a whole, and sympathetic support for Mikhail Gorbachev's limited reforms was idiosyncratic; even the political and intellectual right which so strongly supported her pro-American and anti-continental assumptions resisted her openness to Gorbachev and her willingness to envisage evolutionary change in east–west relations. A combination of structural factors in British politics with contingent developments in the late 1980s made for the failure to adjust and above all for the failure to come to terms with the transformation of Germany. The dominance of the executive over Parliament, the low salience of foreign policy in political debate and the willingness of the public to take its cue on most external issues from political leaders, were long-established aspects of the British foreign policymaking process.[13] The particular pattern of debate at the end of the cold war however reflected also the extraordinary atmosphere of bitterness and suspicion within the Conservative Party and government, the capture of the quality press by 'Anglo-Saxon' ideologues, confusion and weakness within both opposition parties, and a degree of demoralization within the universities after a series of cutbacks in resources and of Conservative attacks on 'left-wing intellectuals'.

Parliamentary debate in Britain takes place primarily in the Chamber, between the two frontbenches, far more than 'upstairs' on the committee corridor. The British House of Commons had not established a Foreign Affairs Committee until 1979: eleven MPs, retired ministers and backbenchers selected by party whips, they focused most often on secondary issues, mostly extra-European.[14] The House of Lords, the second chamber, had established a

European Communities Committee in 1974. By the late 1980s this had established a solid reputation for its detailed reports on aspects of EC proposals and policy; it did not however interpret its responsibilities as extending to the foreign policy mechanisms of European Political Cooperation, and entirely lacked the competence to address strategic issues of European international politics. Foreign policy debates on the floor of both chambers suffered from the absence of any regular government statement on foreign policy priorities. The nearest that Parliament came to debating the wider issues of British foreign policy and international development came with the second day of the annual 'Queen's Speech' debate, at the opening of each new parliamentary session and the debate on the annual Defence White Paper.

The most powerful inhibition to open parliamentary debate on European issues, however, came from within the Conservative and Labour parties. Both parties were internally divided on attitudes to Europe in general, and Germany (and, for many, France) in particular; both had changed their official positions, swinging from scepticism to commitment to scepticism, without resolving their internal differences over the previous forty years.[15]

The deepening rift within the Conservative Party in the late 1980s was between the 'Anglo-Saxons', who associated the USA with freedom and free markets and the continent with corporatism, and the 'Europeans' who combined a greater sympathy for economic management and industrial policy with a more relaxed approach to European co-operation. Michael Heseltine had stormed out of the Cabinet in 1986 in a row about whether the Westland helicopter company should pursue a 'strategic' merger with French and German partners or become a junior partner of the American Sikorsky company. Policy towards the European Monetary System had divided Prime Minister from Chancellor and Foreign Secretary from 1986 onwards, a rumbling dispute which eventually brought Mrs Thatcher down. The majority of ministers did not share Mrs Thatcher's increasingly passionate opposition to further European integration, though party conferences cheered her and her supporters enthusiastically. In such a situation it was impossible for the Cabinet to discuss the implications of political change in central Europe, or for the Parliamentary Party to encourage an open debate.[16]

Within the Labour Party since the 1950s attitudes both to the European Community and to NATO and nuclear deterrence had been touchstones of internal divisions between right and left. Its 1983 Election Manifesto had called for withdrawal from the EC; its 1987 manifesto had said less about policy towards Europe, France and Germany than about its attitude to the Cyprus conflict.[17] In the summer of 1989 the Labour Party renounced unilateral nuclear disarmament and endorsed a pro-European stance, returning to its official position of ten years before; but there remained many unreconciled on its parliamentary benches and in its constituency management committees, making for a natural reluctance to challenge the government on European policy or defence.[18] Britain's third political force, the Social

Democrat–Liberal Alliance, had held to a firmly internationalist, Europe-committed, stance. But it had imploded after the 1987 election, with David Owen using nuclear deterrence and a tough stance towards the Soviet Union as symbolic issues on which to resist a merger with the Liberals. The two parties nevertheless merged in March 1988 to form the Liberal Democrats, but the damage to their public image put them in fourth place (behind the Greens) in the 1989 European elections, leaving them without an effective voice in the public debate.[19]

Within the government machine the focus for strategic reappraisal should have been found within the Foreign Office planning staff, the Ministry of Defence policy planners, and the Prime Minister's own policy unit. Mrs Thatcher's suspicion of the Foreign Office had encouraged her to set up an alternative source of advice and expertise on the other side of Downing Street, appointing her own 'Foreign Policy Adviser' and retaining Charles Powell as her foreign policy private secretary; but by 1989 this had become more a devoted group of loyalists than a source of new ideas.[20] The Foreign Office Planning Staff had worked well, and closely, with Geoffrey Howe, who commanded the respect of his staff within an increasingly embattled ministry; but neither Major nor Hurd looked to their officials to provide them with long-term analyses. George Younger and Tom King as ministers of defence were similarly 'safe pairs of hands' who did not look to their officials to sparkle with challenges to the conventional wisdom. The foreign policy machinery of Whitehall continued to operate professionally, responding to international developments and protecting and promoting British interests as it saw them, but without either a domestic consensus to support it or a clear political lead.

The intellectual world beyond Whitehall and Westminster had also become sharply divided. Mrs Thatcher, Keith Joseph and other close advisers in opposition in the 1970s had cultivated sympathetic intellectuals, with the Conservative Philosophy Group, the Institute of Economic Affairs and the new Centre for Policy Studies providing frameworks within which ideas were exchanged.[21] Transfer of ownership of *The Times* and *Sunday Times* to Rupert Murdoch, and of *Daily Telegraph*, *Sunday Telegraph* and weekly *Spectator* to Conrad Black, provided a powerful (and remunerative) platform for this small but committed intellectual counter-establishment.[22] But the bulk of the academic community returned Mrs Thatcher's instinctive mistrust in full measure.

Keith Joseph's appointment as Secretary of State for Education in 1981 had marked a declaration of war on social science, which both he and his prime minister regarded as inherently socialist. A robust defence by Lord Rothschild, asked (as a respected adviser on science and intelligence questions) to report on the utility to government of the Social Science Research Council, saved it from outright abolition. Its budget was nevertheless progressively cut, even more sharply than that for higher education as a whole and its board was restructured to reflect the government's preferred priorities. A specific attempt to close Britain's one Department of Peace Studies, in Bradford, and the withdrawal of research funding from the most Keynesian centre for economic research, in Cambridge, left many university teachers reluctant to engage in public debate along lines critical of the government. The shift in editorial policy in *The Times* also deprived them of the traditional vehicle for élite debate. A group of journalists defecting from *The Times* and *Daily Telegraph* set up the new *Independent* in 1986, complementing the *Guardian* and the weekly *New Statesman* as platforms through which to address the non-Thatcherite audience. But the Labour Party seemed largely uninterested in picking up new arguments – least of all on foreign policy.

The self-conscious attack of the 'new Right' on the conventional wisdom of the Establishment had also shaken the think tanks – as in the USA. Thatcherites saw Chatham House (the Royal Institute of International Affairs) as embedded in the internationalist, Europhile community; and set up or encouraged alternative institutes, mostly small, several closely linked to American counterparts and substantially funded from across the Atlantic. The Adam Smith Institute, the Institute for the Study of Conflict, the Institute for European Defence and Security Studies, the International Freedom Foundation, all received prime ministerial patronage and a sympathetic hearing in the right-wing press. Chatham House meanwhile had been developing a dialogue with Gorbachev's foreign policy institutes and advisers, including Yevgeni Primakov and Yergor Yakovlev, in the face of repeated attacks in *The Times* and elsewhere; its director, Admiral Sir James Eberle, was labelled 'the red admiral' in a number of articles.[23] Government funding for Chatham House, which had approached 10 per cent of its budget in the 1970s, sank back to a modest corporate subscription before recovering (with the sympathetic attention of Geoffrey Howe) to around 5 per cent in the late 1980s. The institute's research staff nevertheless rose during the late 1980s, with funding from companies and from foundations abroad; but it found it easier to persuade corporate supporters to finance studies of Western Europe, the Middle East and East Asia than of eastern Europe and the Soviet Union.[24]

The twilight of the Thatcher government

Immediate responses to the changes in central Europe were refracted through the spectrum of this emotional domestic debate, which was as much about British identity as about Germany or about the future balance of the European continent.[25] Mrs Thatcher and those around her focused on the perceived threat of German unification: caught on the contradictory position that British commitment to closer continental co-operation was not needed as a counterbalance to Germany, but that the prospect of German 'domination' of the continent nevertheless represented a threat to fundamental British interests. 'If there is one instance in which a foreign policy I pursued met with unambiguous failure,' she admits in her memoirs (p. 813), 'it was my policy on German unification.'

She was correct to stress that this was her personal failure, since she no longer carried her party, or her Cabinet, with her; most of her ministers struggled to mitigate the force of her interventions. The bitterness of the argument within the government unavoidably distracted public attention from the broader significance of the changes. The political drama was in London itself, with Franco-German proposals for an intergovernmental conference, multilateral negotiations on the unification of Germany, the redefinition of NATO's tasks and the reorientation of central European regimes westward, providing the backdrop. The intensive round of consultations among heads of government and foreign ministers which marked the winter of 1989–90 meant that political leaders were necessarily the first to redefine priorities. What was however striking in the British case was the absence of any attempt to consult Parliament or to educate the broader public about the importance of the transformation; divisions within the government, and silence from the opposition, left the public to understand that the unification of Germany was another round in Britain's continuing battle with its continental partners.

Mrs Thatcher had first looked to President Mitterrand as an ally in resisting German unification, but was unable to find any broader agreement with the French on strategy. At the Strasbourg European Council on 9 December 1989, where she held two private meetings with Mitterrand, she asserted that the collapse of the Berlin Wall meant the EC should *slow down* European integration. 'It was ironic', she was reported to have said, 'that at a time when countries in the East aspired for more democracy, certain Community partners wanted to remove democratic control of national parliaments over economic and monetary affairs and transfer them to an authority which is undemocratic.'[26] She had also appealed to the Americans for support, spending a whole day at Camp David with President Bush on 24 November, 'lecturing' him while pointing out lines on maps; 'the atmosphere did not improve as a result of our discussions'.[27] At the NATO Summit in December she was isolated; though she continued to pursue a common position with the French throughout January and to warn the Americans against working so closely with Helmut Kohl.

When Mitterrand moved to embrace what he saw as inevitable, adopting a strategy of supporting German unification in return for changes in the agenda of the planned IGC, Mrs Thatcher felt betrayed.[28] But the absence of any alternative strategy to manage German unification, compounded by her trenchant personal style, left Britain isolated as its American and continental allies moved on. At the special European Council in Dublin on 28 April 1990 the British Prime Minister repeatedly attacked her colleagues for launching a parallel intergovernmental conference to create a 'European Union' – something which they could not define. There was, she said afterwards '. . . quite a lot of rhetoric and not enough nitty-gritty.'[29] In the margins of the Summit, and in a contrasting tone, Douglas Hurd as foreign secretary reaffirmed that the British government was not going to leave an empty chair at the negotiations, whatever its reservations on the idea of a second IGC.[30]

Even more damaging was the widely held assumption among Britain's continental partners that extra-EC fora such as the 'Two Plus Four Talks' and NATO were being emphasized in London to subvert the process of unification and to divert attention away from the EC.[31] Relations between Thatcher and Kohl further deteriorated when in July 1990 a Cabinet minister, Nicholas Ridley, expressed vehemently anti-German views in an interview for *The Spectator* – views known to be shared by Mrs Thatcher. The next day press reports (wrongly) reported that a Chequers seminar held several weeks earlier had reached similar conclusions.[32] The abrasive, highly personal style of a Prime Minister convinced that she was right but aware that she was losing the argument was summed up in her remark to the NATO Summit in London in July 1990 'Of course, as colleagues round this table will know, I never had much use for diplomacy anyway, and I've got on very well without it.'[33]

In August 1990 Mrs Thatcher was in Colorado for conversations with President Bush when the Iraqis invaded Kuwait, seizing the opportunity to reassert the Anglo-American special relationship and to offer full British support in defending the principles of the 'new world order'. In September she toured east-central Europe, deepening the suspicion of other EC governments about Britain's resistance to European Union by offering them all early membership. In November she was in Paris for a heads of government meeting of the CSCE, roundly asserting the primacy of NATO, when the results of the ballot in which Michael Heseltine had challenged her for the party leadership were announced – returning to London to learn that her Cabinet was reluctant to give her their full support and to resign.

There had of course been some discussions within the government over these months, as well as a scattering of intelligent comments in Parliament and the Press. Alan Clark, one of Mrs Thatcher's closest ministerial supporters, records in his diary a ministerial meeting at Chequers in January 1990, with papers from the FCO and defence – though the attention he devotes to his hopes of replacing Tom King as minister of defence through his performance there give a flavour of the poisonous atmosphere within the government, with ministers using the Press to plant stories against each other.[34] In February 1990 the Ministry of Defence launched a review of 'Options for Change', which was itself carefully examined by the 11-person man Defence Committee of the House of Commons.[35] Timothy Garton Ash and Lawrence Freedman, from Oxford and London universities, contributed a number of thoughtful articles on the implications of the revolutions in eastern Europe to the *Independent* throughout 1990, as did Norman Stone in the *Sunday Times* – though the 'op-ed' debate in the Murdoch and Black press was more preoccupied with Germany and with the threat of European Union. The *Guardian* published a series of reflective articles on the nature of the new world order in the autumn and winter of 1990.[36] But there was no focus for a national debate; the rival discourses of the progressive establishment and the conservative counter-establishment scarcely touched each other, while Labour and the Conservatives continued to tiptoe round their internal divisions.

The Major government: pragmatic adjustment and ideological inhibitions

It was thus the change in governmental leadership which unlocked the possibilities for change. John Major's election as Conservative Party leader, thus becoming Prime Minister, came after a leadership campaign which had sharply exposed the factional nature of the Conservative Party.[37] His personal style was far more collegial; 'ministers were surprised to be asked to express their opinion and to see it given weight'.[38] He was a party manager, chosen as a man who could hold a divided party together. A generation younger than Margaret Thatcher, John Major had no special emotional commitment to the United States, neither did he 'show any signs of identifying Britain's armed forces with British sovereignty or international status'.[39]

From winter 1990 to the election 1992 the Major government pursued a different European policy, intended to move towards partnership with Germany without provoking direct opposition from the sceptics within its own party. In this it closely resembled the strategy which Harold Macmillan had followed thirty years before, in his attempt to slip Britain into the European Community without admitting to his reluctant MPs and party conference the long-term implications of the move. In spite of the transformation of eastern Europe, this was a Western-oriented strategy, focused on Bonn and Washington; no senior minister visited the countries between Germany and Russia during 1991. The key players were Chris Patten and Douglas Hurd: the first John Major's new party chairman, a Catholic with a sympathetic approach to continental Christian Democracy; the second his foreign secretary, a former professional diplomat and private secretary to Edward Heath, 'a conservative in the classic sense who saw politics as a matter of incremental adjustment to external events'.[40]

At the core of the new approach was the promise of good personal relations between Major and Kohl, building on the goodwill which the German Chancellor had shown towards Britain's new Prime Minister, and recognizing that the German government was now the key player in European negotiations. A carefully orchestrated speech in Bonn in March 1991, in the presence of the German Chancellor and in the headquarters of the CDU, provided the platform for John Major's first prime ministerial speech outside the UK. Deliberately setting out to communicate a change in style and tone from Mrs Thatcher, he reminded his audience that he represented a generation that did not remember the Second World War. He quoted Konrad Adenauer, spoke of the values which Conservatives shared with Christian Democrats, and declared his aim to place Britain 'where we belong – at the very heart of Europe, working with our partners...'[41]

This was mood music, intended to create a better climate for understanding more than to spell out a new foreign policy in detail. Nevertheless, the outlines of a different understanding of the future shape of Europe were there: acceptance of the idea of a European 'defence identity' provided that it 'sustains a long-term American presence', cautious encouragement of further change within the Soviet Union, a more gradual approach to full EC membership for the countries of east-central Europe while assisting them through the necessary political and economic transformation. It had been mainly drafted within the Foreign Office, though it clearly reflected the views of the new Conservative Party leadership. There was little time for ministers to reflect more deeply in spring 1991, with the Gulf War reaching its climax, the IGC well under way, with parallel negotiations within NATO, with worrying developments in the Baltic republics of the USSR and in Yugoslavia.

> Policy in these conditions was shaped less by longer-term aims than by a series of day-to-day decisions taken with little reference to a larger framework ... We felt our way forward and too much of the time lived hand-to-mouth, locked in what Dr Kissinger has called 'the endless battle in which the urgent constantly gains on the important'.[42]

Piece by piece in the course of 1990–91 British policy evolved, balancing between the pressure of external events and the constant murmur of discontent from the Conservative right and the like-minded press, reporting Mrs Thatcher's speeches in the USA attacking federalist tendencies in Europe and calling for a closer transatlantic partnership. Mrs Thatcher had committed the British government to an active role in the Gulf, providing her successors with the standing to argue for closer European defence co-operation within NATO, and to extend alliance planning to 'out of area' as a practical adaptation to the security challenges of the post-cold war world. John Major extended this extra-European involvement by proposing (at a European Council in April 1991) the establishment of 'safe havens' for the Kurdish minority in northern Iraq and contributing British marines to the international force which policed it. When fighting broke out in Croatia in August 1991, with Mrs Thatcher (and the German government) calling for military intervention, the Major government however held back. In the middle of negotiations about the content of the CFSP and the future of NATO, Douglas Hurd nevertheless resisted a military response: British forces were overstretched in the aftermath of the Gulf War and in Northern Ireland, the Americans were not engaged, and the objectives of intervention in a developing civil war seemed unclear.[43]

The IGC and the parallel NATO negotiations were however the main British preoccupations throughout 1991. In both of these ministers took an essentially conservative position: seeking to maintain Britain's leading position within NATO and NATO's leading position in security and defence, while balancing within the IGC between pursuing acceptable compromises and resisting major new commitments which might reopen the fissures within the Conservative Party. The British 'coup' in winning command of the new multinational Alliance Rapid Reaction Corps, in May 1991, cut across Franco-German discussions on European defence integration. It resulted from close working relations with NATO's international secretariat and with the US Department of Defense, as well as with a German defence ministry more oriented towards NATO than the *Auswärtiges Amt.* Within the IGC the British resisted Franco-German proposals for an autonomous common foreign and security policy, preferring a strengthened WEU to remain the European pillar of the Alliance.[44] The government therefore proposed that WEU be given responsibility for military operations in partnership with the United States outside the NATO area.[45] In this way the British effectively used NATO to set their preferred parameters for a European Defence Identity: a leading role for British forces through the ARRC, the Europeanization of NATO as a substitute for an independent ESDI and the continuation of an institutionalized American presence in Western Europe.

In competition with more ambitious Franco-German proposals the British launched a joint proposal with Italy on 4 October 1991, identifying areas of possible compromise before the NATO Rome summit in November and the Maastricht summit the following month.[46] For the first time, the British conceded that the EU should have a role in the gradual formulation of 'common defence policy', though 'common defence' would continue to be integrated within NATO. WEU would have a dual, carefully balanced role as the European pillar of NATO and the defence component of the European Union; it would be required to 'take into account in its activities the decisions of the European Council' as well as those of NATO, but the Alliance would remain the 'essential forum for agreement on policies which refer to the commitments of ... members in matters of security and defence.' It also proposed the creation of a European Rapid Reaction Force under the aegis of the WEU, based on 'double hatted' NATO forces – a concept which re-emerged two years later under American sponsorship as Combined Joint Task Forces (CJTF).

The British did not entirely ignore the eastern part of Europe. Practical assistance was already flowing to Poland, Hungary, Czechoslovakia, Romania and Bulgaria (to be extended over the next year to the Baltic republics and to Russia): the British Knowhow Fund came to be recognized as one of the most effective bilateral programmes of technical assistance, and military training and advice was also extended. In September 1991 the Prime Minister called for the extension of full membership to the states of eastern Europe and the Baltics 'as soon as they are ready politically and economically', and did not explicitly rule out widening this offer to the European republics of the Soviet Union. Their doubtful continental partners suspected the British of using an altruistic stance towards eastern Europe to undermine the goals of European federation, thus 'intensifying controversy over the choice between a wider or deeper community'.[47]

In the endgame of the IGC, culminating in the Maastricht European Council, domestic preoccupations again came to the fore. John Major was most preoccupied during the Maastricht Council with securing an opt-out from the clauses on social policy, phoning Michael Howard (social security minister and a leading Eurosceptic) at several points during the meeting to check that the proposed compromise was acceptable to him. By then the British, in tactical alliance with the French, had succeeded in limiting 'political union' in foreign and security policy to a separate, intergovernmental pillar safeguarded by unanimous voting. As a practical measure to make the WEU more effective, British negotiators had proposed that the WEU secretariat should move its divided secretariat in London and Paris to Brussels. Their main foreign policy and defence interests thus protected, British ministers then allowed the Greek government to insist on acceptance into WEU, further opening up the organization to a mixed group of observers and associates.[48]

John Major returned to London claiming to his party, to Parliament, press and public that the British had won 'game, set and match.' As far as the future organization and shape of European order was concerned, however, the British had colluded with others in postponing awkward choices until later. They had conceded the principle of a common foreign and security policy, but had vigorously questioned whether other governments were ready in practice to commit themselves, and successfully resisted proposals for integrated institutions. They had preserved the centrality of NATO, keeping European defence integration (here in opposition to the French) within the context of the North Atlantic Alliance. They had raised, but not pressed, the question of enlargement to the east. Further progress in West European institutional development, and in progress towards a common foreign and security policy, was put off until a further intergovernmental conference, to be convened in five years' time, well beyond the date of the next British election. Here was a treaty which the Conservative Party should be willing to accept; that was the overriding political imperative.

Domestic constraints on the government's freedom of manoeuvre were compelling. Mrs Thatcher continued to warn against yielding to the threat of a European 'super state'; it was her identification of the social policy proposals as the greatest threat to British interests which had made this the most sensitive dossier in the final negotiation.[49] John Major himself lacked any substantial support in the Conservative press.[50] The *Daily Telegraph*, the most influential newspaper for Conservative constituency parties, took a nationalist, anti-European and pro-American editorial line. The most influential broadsheet newspapers of the News International Group, *The Times* and *Sunday Times*, were 'encouraged' by Rupert Murdoch to adopt a strongly sceptical position on European policy.[51] The *Spectator* nursed resentment at the way in which

Mrs Thatcher had been ousted, disparaging Major's managerial style and intellectual inferiority in comparison with Thatcher. It also mistrusted the corrosive influence of a 'Europeanising' Foreign Office, diplomatically dedicated to the avoidance of conflict.[52] All this fed the suspicions of the right-wing within Parliament and within the government, dedicated to the preservation of Margaret Thatcher's political legacy against the pro-European 'wets' – now again led in the Cabinet by Michael Heseltine, who had returned to office as deputy prime minister.

Outside in the academic and institute world, experts on international relations, on Western and Eastern Europe, were addressing the broader questions raised by the transformation of Europe. The Royal Institute of International Affairs published six Chatham House Papers on related topics between the demolition of the Berlin Wall and the 1992 election, as well as three shorter discussion papers; few attracted much attention in the political press.[53] The Ditchley Foundation sponsored a three-day conference on 'Elements of change in international relations: a foreign policy agenda for the 1990s' in June 1990, which gathered a cross-section of 'policy influentials' from British ministries, think tanks, banks and universities, together with an impressive cross-section of their counterparts from the USA, Germany, France, Canada and Australia.[54] The IISS annual conference in 1991 focused on 'the new security challenges'. The Centre for Economic Policy Research, with support from the European Commission and other sources, began to produce valuable work in east European economies and the challenges of economic transition. Moving at the slower pace characteristic of academic responses, applications began to flow in to the Economic and Social Research Council for research projects on the transformation of central and eastern Europe.

All this activity however lacked a firm connection to the *political* debate in Parliament, the parties and the press. The fracturing of the foreign policy élite by the Thatcherite challenge to the 'Establishment' had divided much of the relevant intellectual community from the government. The Labour opposition, still preoccupied with its own internal tensions, was reluctant to explore new approaches to foreign policy; its foreign affairs team, under Gerald Kaufman, did not cultivate contacts with outside experts or participate actively in think tank seminars and conferences. Its policy statement on the Maastricht IGC, *Labour and Political Union*, was not published until November 1991. It made only brief reference to the revolution in eastern Europe, declared that it would 'implacably oppose' any move towards defence integration within a European rather than an Atlantic framework, referred more warmly to NATO than to the CSCE, and made only a passing comment on the significance of the Yugoslav conflict.[55]

The comment pages of *The Times*, the traditional forum for dialogue among the élite in periods of policy change, were open only to committed supporters of the counter-establishment; the *Guardian*, which attempted during 1991–92 to open its comment pages to a far wider spread of contributors, was unread in the Conservative Party and rarely noticed within the major ministries. The *Financial Times* and *The Economist*, which analyzed European and international developments in more depth, were more widely read within the business community than in politics. The smaller think tanks of the right, which might have commanded the attention of the Conservative government, were themselves disorientated by the fall of Mrs Thatcher. The Centre for Policy Studies had suffered internal divisions over European and foreign policy before the Wall came down. The Institute of Economic Affairs split over attempts to adopt a more nuanced position to cooperation in post-cold war Europe, with its new director and deputy director departing in 1992 to set up the new European Policy Forum.[56]

The characteristics of the defence debate in this period illustrate how compartmentalized was domestic debate on the implications of the changes under way on the European continent. The outcome of the 'Options for Change' review – announced in 1990 and suspended for the duration of the Gulf war – was announced in July 1991.[57] The government was careful to present this major restructuring of its armed forces not as a reorientation of Britain's defence posture, but as a pragmatic adjustment to changed circumstances. The Alliance Rapid Reaction Corps was therefore trailed as tangible evidence of great power status in the aftermath of German unification.[58] Press attention was focused on practical adjustment within NATO and the WEU, without linking these changes to Franco-American bargaining over the definition of NATO's new Strategic Concept or to the esoteric negotiations within the IGC.

Few MPs therefore explored the implications for British foreign and defence policy of these parallel multilateral negotiations under way in Brussels.[59] The government made a virtue of the fact that the defence restructuring dispensed with no major service commitment and maintained one of the highest levels of equipment spending among NATO allies.[60] The issue among the small number of interested backbenchers was 'overstretch' rather than Europeanisation.[61] The majority of the defence debate was not therefore concerned with international status, institutional options, nor even the balance between the three services, but focused on parochial pleas from backbenchers that the army was bearing the brunt of the cuts and that particular regiments be reprieved.[62] Five short references to the negotiations in the IGC in eleven hours of debate reflected how far the presentation of the defence review had been divorced from the negotiations underway in international institutions about the shape of European order after the cold war.[63]

After Maastricht: drift or direction?

Capitalizing on their presentation of Maastricht as a success for Britain, the Conservatives placed foreign policy at the beginning of their manifesto for the general election, declared for April 1992 only weeks after the treaty had been signed. It spoke of the need for 'firm leadership ... a team which can help shape the world for the next century'. 'The Conservatives', it declared in language much more acceptable to Chris Patten and Michael Heseltine than to followers of Margaret Thatcher, 'have been the party of Britain in Europe for 30 years ... We have ensured that Britain is at the heart of Europe: a strong and respected partner.' It went on to emphasize the importance of the forthcoming British presidency of the EU, from July to December 1992, and to list as the first three priorities of that presidency negotiations for accession with the EFTA countries, development of the association agreements with Poland, Hungary and Czechoslovakia 'so that we can welcome them to full membership by the year 2000', and 'to conclude trade and cooperation agreements with the main republics of the former Soviet Union'. On defence, the manifesto promised 'to strengthen the Western European Union as the European Pillar of NATO', to 'press for a European reaction force', and to 'intensify the coordination of security policies within the Twelve'.[64]

Labour's manifesto left foreign policy to the end. The promise to 'seek to create the conditions in which, at the appropriate time, the new democracies of central and eastern Europe can join the Community' was the only reference to broader changes in European international politics. On defence it was even briefer: 'As the party which took Britain into NATO, Labour will base its defence policies on UK membership of the alliance.'[65] The Liberal Democrats, who had recovered to a level of 16–20 per cent in the opinion polls, were as in previous elections much more European in orientation: committing themselves to develop a common foreign and security policy, including 'the gradual integration of community members' armed forces under a joint military command', to increase economic assistance to central and east European countries and the CIS, even to 'develop a pan-European security framework' based upon both the OSCE and NATO.

International issues however played little part in the campaign; economic management, taxation and public expenditure were the dominant themes. Hesitations about Labour's commitment to raise taxes contributed to a fourth Conservative victory, with a reduced majority of 21 seats. The turnover of Conservative MPs also brought a new generation into Parliament, changing the party's internal balance; 'Thatcher's children', young men whose political careers had been made under her premiership and shared her views. The gradual disappearance of the government's majority over the five years of the Parliament, with a minority of intransigent anti-Europeans on the back-benches willing to combine with opposition parties to exploit the divisions within their own party, progressively weakened the government and undermined its attempt at a new departure in foreign policy.

Summer 1992, however, saw this new departure moving forward. In early May the Maastricht treaty was introduced for ratification in the House of Commons, comfortably approved after a two-day 'second reading' debate. The

Queen spoke to the European Parliament in Strasbourg, a symbolic gesture which would have been unthinkable under Margaret Thatcher. The following week John Major visited Warsaw, Prague, Bratislava and Budapest, acquiring an active interest in the region which was reflected in prime ministerial comments on foreign office papers for the rest of his time in office.[66] Relations with Helmut Kohl and the German Christian Democrats continued to improve, while the Bush–Major relationship remained strong.

Then, in the course of the British EU presidency, things fell apart. After the shock rejection of the Maastricht treaty in the Danish referendum on 2 June, the Prime Minister – a parliamentary whip by training and a party manager by instinct – announced that the process of ratification in the British Parliament would be temporarily suspended. Anti-Europeans within the Conservative Party, some of whom had been campaigning in Denmark, were thus prevented from exploiting the setback, but acquired additional stature from the government's evident concern over their potential influence. In September the pound was forced out of the exchange rate mechanism, after massive speculation and apparent confusion within the government. In November the government secured a majority of three on a motion to proceed with the ratification of Maastricht, due only to Liberal Democrat support, with 26 Conservative MPs voting against. Meanwhile the Conservatives had given advice to the Republican campaign in the USA, emphasizing techniques for attacking Bill Clinton. When in December after Clinton's election John Major went to Washington for a farewell visit to President Bush, the President-elect found time only for a telephone conversation. 'Mr Major's personal standing at present', Peter Riddell remarked in *The Times*, 'is not high either in the EC or in America'.[67]

The weakened government struggled on for four more years, periodically attempting to re-establish a framework for foreign policy within the constraints of a divided party and a hostile press. In September 1993, when the Maastricht treaty had at last cleared the Commons, John Major argued the case in *The Economist* for 'a new agenda' for Europe, to focus on eastern enlargement and the creation of a European pillar within NATO. It devoted more space however to dismissing the old agenda than to the detail of the new.[68] The key phrases of a compromise approach with which the Conservative government hoped to bridge the widening gap between its own supporters and continental governments were all included: 'new realities', 'practical decisions', 'subsidiarity', 'flexibility', 'diversity', and 'a Europe of nation states'. These phrases and themes were restated in a major speech in Leiden in September 1994, trailed as the British response to the Schäuble–Lamers paper, in which enlargement to the east and the reshaping of NATO were used to support an argument for variable geometry within 'a Union of increasing diversity' against a single core Europe.[69]

'The sense among politicians', a British official remarked in spring 1994, 'is that the niche which we occupied as a result of the Cold War is one which we can somehow continue to occupy; what they haven't realized is that the niche isn't there any longer, that the European theatre is where we have to play.'[70] Both Major and Douglas Hurd, his foreign secretary, were trying to edge Britain quietly back towards closer relations with Germany and France, without arousing domestic opposition; both were tacticians by temperament, rather than strategists or conceptualizers.[71] But competitors in the Cabinet – Michael Portillo, Michael Howard, Peter Lilley – were appealing to Thatcherite and nationalist sentiments within an increasingly divided party. Each party conference from 1993 to 1996 saw 'outbursts of xenophobia', with ministers outbidding each other to denigrate Brussels and to denounce the threat of 'a European superstate'.[72] At the 1995 party conference Douglas Hurd's successor as foreign secretary, Malcolm Rifkind, added his voice to 'the sceptical mood sweeping the Tory party', pressing for transatlantic free trade rather than further European integration.[73] But transatlantic relations had also been damaged over the previous two years, with Bosnia (as one British minister admitted) 'the real poison in the relationship'.[74]

British foreign policy, one disillusioned official remarked, was now being made in the Conservative Whips' office rather than the Foreign Office; the crucial question asked was whether any proposal would hold the Conservative Party together in the House of Commons, not whether it responded to international developments. Hardly surprisingly, long-term thinking on the reordering of Europe was abandoned. The British government approached the 1996–97 IGC roundly declaring that it would rather be isolated than compromise with further steps towards integration. Malcolm Rifkind travelled around the capitals of other major EU states in 1996, making a series of speeches which were announced as articulating the realistic and practical British approach to Europe, but which were universally greeted abroad and at home as marking his bid for the leadership of the Conservative Party after John Major's anticipated post-election resignation.[75]

Defence policy, too, was marked by a reluctance to look forward rather than back, and a preference for avoiding explanation to Parliament. 'Britain is revising its defence provision without an agreed rationale for doing so', one expert commentator noted in 1994; 'there is, at least at present, no source of British security policy of operational use'.[76] The House of Commons Defence Committee in its response to the 1993 Defence White Paper called for an opportunity to debate a rounded statement of the Government's security-policy goals', without gaining a reply.[77] Experience of Franco-British co-operation in Bosnia led to the development of a bilateral defence dialogue, in 1993–94: conducted in complete secrecy for the first twelve months, to avoid potential adverse reactions in either Parliament. The Labour Party approached the 1997 election promising to conduct 'a strategic defence and security review' to replace the drift of Conservative policy – but without declaring in advance the principles on which that review would rest.[78]

Labour had emerged from the 1992 election campaign badly shaken by its failure to win the fourth general election in succession, after leading the Conservatives in the opinion polls for most of the period from early 1989 to the campaign. As the Conservatives had moved away from a European commitment, Labour had moved towards one, but without spelling out in much detail what that commitment might imply. The anti-European right-wing press claimed to have won the election for the Conservatives; Labour was now anxious not to provoke hostile headlines as far as possible. For their leaders, too, the domestic debate about the EU crowded out consideration of the future shape of a wider Europe. Under the leadership both of John Smith (who died in 1994) and of Tony Blair, there was much active rethinking on domestic policy; foreign policy, however, was a secondary priority.

In an ideal world, the outside intellectual community would have filled the resulting gap, but without political access to government or to opposition and without active sponsorship within the media, there was little incentive to break into the policy debate. The Royal Institute of International Affairs embarked on a series of 'post-Soviet' studies, with financial support from companies; its only overall study of the politics of post-cold war Europe, however, was funded by the National Institute for Research Advancement in Tokyo.[79] The IISS published a number of papers and articles on 'European architecture', the future of NATO, and developments in south-eastern and eastern Europe. But its audience was as much international as domestic, and it paid in many ways more attention to the American foreign policy debate than the British.[80] Some academic centres – the Department of War Studies in King's College, London, the Department of Peace Studies at Bradford University – were active in examining the security dimensions of European transformation; some staff within the latter also advised the Labour Party on defence policy. But the international relations community as a whole focused more on theoretical developments than on the dynamics of regional change.[81] A larger number of economists, many associated with the Centre for Economic Policy Research, were working on economic transformation within central and eastern Europe; contributing some valuable analyses of developments within different countries as well as broader overviews of the policy process, though little read outside the expert economist community within Britain.

The new Labour government which signed the Treaty of Amsterdam, and agreed the enlargement of NATO, had come into office in May 1997, just in time for the end-game of the IGC negotiations. Other governments had been impatiently waiting for a political change in Britain, despairing of the obstructive attitude of he Conservative government. New Labour however was largely unbriefed about geopolitical change, understanding – like the incoming Major administration before it – that it must start rebuilding a European policy by coming to terms with Germany and leaving until later the definition of longer-term aims. Tony Blair's first major foreign policy speech as Prime Minister was not given until the Lord Mayor's dinner in November

1997. He spoke only in passing of EU enlargement and of Bosnia, did not mention NATO enlargement or Russia, and spoke most warmly of Britain's continuing role 'as a global player'. The contrast between the references to Europe and the US signalled the continuity of foreign policy assumptions with the British position of previous decades:

> Britain is part of Europe. It must play its full part in leading it. Not because there is no alternative. There is: we could go. But because it is in British national interests to stay. And as we are staying – let us do so with effect ...

> Our aim should be to deepen our relationship with the US at all levels. We are the bridge between the US and Europe. Let us use it. When Britain and America work together on the international scene, there is little we cannot achieve.[82]

The failure to adjust

The end of the cold war should have transformed Britain's foreign policy. In a divided Europe, dependent upon US commitment and potential reinforcement to guard against the Soviet threat, Britain was indeed the bridge between the continent and the USA: the advance base through which American reinforcements would flow. But in a reintegrating Europe, with Germany returning to its historic position as Europe's central power, Britain was again on its western edge, with its major markets and security interests on the European continent. The legacy of the Thatcher premiership, however, the culmination of thirty years of agonizing over whether national sovereignty and national identity were threatened by closer integration with the continent, had left both Conservatives and Labour too traumatized to lift their eyes to the broader picture. First Margaret Thatcher, then John Major, failed to develop consistent or coherent approaches to reunited Germany. That should have been the foundation for a redefinition of British policies to NATO, to the EU, to eastern enlargement, to Russia and to the USA.

The Major government attempted to begin a process of readjustment in 1991–92. But the domestic constraints were strong, even before forced exit from the European Monetary System destroyed its self-confidence. Margaret Thatcher remained a brooding presence, with many new and old Conservative MPs (and some ministers) who listened to her warnings; much of the press still preferred her robust nationalism to the more gentle expressions of national interest which characterized the approaches of Major and Hurd. The evidence suggests that the Major government had nevertheless intended to sidle gradually towards a stronger engagement with the continent and a more active role in rapprochement with central and eastern Europe, until setbacks abroad and party divisions at home forced them to retreat.

The absence of open political debate outside the embittered internal divisions within the Conservative Party reflected a mixture of conjunctural and structural factors. A confident opposition party might well have challenged the government, pursuing political alliances with parties across Europe and gaining domestic political capital from these connections. But Labour was immensely cautious about challenging the conventional wisdom after its failure in the 1992 election; and did not see foreign policy as a field in which any challenge would win it many votes. The shadow of the Murdoch press, in particular the tabloid *Sun*, hung over Labour's policymaking and presentation from 1992 to 1997 – staunchly anti-Communist during the cold war, staunchly anti-European both then and now. In some ways the press – the four Murdoch-owned papers, the *Telegraph* and the *Mail* – had acquired an effective veto over any redefinition of British foreign policy. The risk that they might whip up a nationalist campaign at its expense was not one which Labour Party managers were willing to take.

The Liberal Democrats, with 22 MPs out of 650 after the 1992 elections, lacked a sufficiently strong voice to get their more strategic approach to European order across to the public through a largely unsympathetic press.[83] The dominant role which the two front benches played in parliamentary business and debates made it difficult for the small group of foreign policy specialists across the parties to put forward any alternative view. The limited role, numbers and staff of parliamentary select committees left them without a basis for harnessing external expertise, or for exploring different approaches very far. The Lords played only a marginal role in foreign policy debate. Unlike the well-financed party institutes in Germany, the parties outside Parliament lacked money or staff to devote to foreign policy; the Labour Party dismissed its international officer as an economy measure after the 1992 election. The small Institute for Public Policy Research, set up with trade union funding to stimulate new ideas within the Labour Party, conducted only a handful of seminars on European and defence policy.

The intellectual community outside, in institutes and universities, thus lacked a direct entry to the policy debate. The weekly *Spectator*, the most widely-read forum for political debate in this period, was firmly Euro-sceptical; the Labour-leaning *New Statesman* did not command attention throughout the Labour Party. It is however not unfair to say that much of the expert community of International Relations scholars had retreated from policy debate, to the safer territories of theory and history; a survey of academic staff in the discipline in 1991 discovered that 'many academics feel excluded from the policymaking process', without knowing how to effect an entry.[84]

Academic salaries had shrunk in real terms during the 1980s, while universities had expanded and resources had been stretched more and more thinly. Chatham House's income and staff were shrinking in the early 1990s; the IISS was surviving by emphasizing its global orientation. Morale within a profession which had rapidly expanded in the 1960s and had coped with deteriorating circumstances since then was low. Some embattled officials within the Foreign Office adversely contrasted the 'anti-policy bias' of the British profession, its lack of ambition in the face of radical international change, with the self-confident writing and speaking of the American profession, which poured out a series of articles and volumes on Europe after the cold war, many of which were widely read in Britain.[85] But there was little of the traffic between universities, institutes and government which characterizes American careers, on which to build self-confidence in addressing the policy world.

The British foreign policy debate was self-absorbed throughout the transformation of European order between 1989 and 1997. Domination of policymaking and of Parliament by government was reinforced by the desire both of government ministers and of opposition spokespeople to discourage open discussion of difficult issues which might divide their parties. The ideological bias of much of the press inhibited political leaders from questioning established beliefs, and made it difficult for alternative arguments to gain a hearing. Conventional wisdom in London between 1994 and 1997 was that Britain still retained a special relationship with the USA, in spite of the temporary estrangement of the first Clinton administration, that European monetary union would not go ahead, and that eastern enlargement would make for a looser EU; such innovations as triangular summits between Germany, France and Russia, and between Germany, France and Poland, were barely reported. Meanwhile, other governments waited with growing impatience for the anticipated change of government, hoping that the learning curve of a new Labour government would be steep.

Notes

1. Percy Cradock, *In Pursuit of British Interests: reflections on foreign policy under Margaret Thatcher and John Major* (London: John Murray, 1997) p. 24.
2. Geoffrey Howe, *Conflict of Loyalty* (London: Macmillan, 1994) p. 538.
3. Cradock, op. cit., p. 10.
4. The most important of these seminars was in September 1983. Margaret Thatcher, *The Downing Street Years* (London: HarperCollins, 1993) pp. 451–9. See also Cradock, chapters 11–12. For a discussion of the role of intellectuals in shaping this particular policy shift see A.H. Brown, 'The leader of the prologue', *Times Literary Supplement*, 30 August 1990, p. 5.
5. Thatcher, *Downing Street Years*, op. cit. p. 746–8; Mrs Thatcher herself described the atmosphere as 'jolly, quaint, sentimental, and slightly overdone'; she 'took him to task' on the deployment of short-range nuclear weapons.
6. Speech given by the Prime Minister the Right Honourable Margaret Thatcher on 'Shaping A Global Community' to The Aspen Institute in Aspen, Colorado, USA on Sunday 5 August 1990.
7. Thatcher, *Downing Street Years*, op. cit. p. 791.

8. For a full text of the Bruges speech see Lawrence Freedman (ed.), *Europe Transformed: documents on the end of the Cold War* (London: Triservice Press, 1990) pp. 267–74.
9. *Boston Globe*, 18 November 1988; quoted in Philip Zelikow and Condoleeza Rice, *Germany United and Europe Transformed: a study in statecraft* (Cambridge, MA: Harvard University Press, 1995) p. 19.
10. Zelikow and Rice, pp. 96–8.
11. Paris European Council, 18 November 1989.
12. Quoted in 1990 Annual Conference of the European Democratic Union, Vienna, 30 September 1990, p. 5.
13. William Wallace, *The Foreign Policy-making Process in Britain* (London: Allen and Unwin, 1977).
14. Charles Carstairs and Richard Ware (eds), *Parliament and International Relations* (Milton Keynes: Open University Press, 1991). In the 1989–90 parliamentary session the Foreign Affairs Committee published reports on UNESCO, on the operation of the Single European Act, on UK policy towards South Africa, and FCO/ODA expenditure; it also took evidence, without publishing reports, on 'the status of the two German states' and the Gulf crisis, and met with ministers after each six-monthly European Council.
15. Stephen George, *Britain and Europe: the politics of semi-detachment* (Oxford: Clarendon Press, 1992).
16. See Steve Ludlam, 'The Spectre Haunting Conservatism: Europe and Backbench Rebellion', in Steve Ludlam and M.J. Smith, *Contemporary Conservatism* (Basingstoke: Macmillan, 1996) pp. 98–120.
17. This ethnic politics focus reflect the concentration of voters of Greek Cypriot origin in a number of marginal seats which Labour hoped to win.
18. The report of the party's policy review group on 'Britain in the World' is published in *Meet the challenge, make the change: a new agenda for Britain*, Labour Party, July 1989.
19. Ivor Crewe and Anthony King, *SDP: the birth, life and death of the Social Democratic Party* (Oxford: Oxford University Press, 1995).
20. Her Foreign Policy Adviser's memoir of this period provides an acerbic account of the atmosphere, in which 'it was sometimes … difficult to establish where Mrs Thatcher ended and Charles Powell began'; Cradock, *In Pursuit of British Interests*, op. cit. p. 14. Geoffrey Howe, in *Conflict of Loyalty* (London: Macmillan, 1994) chap. 35, describes the struggle between the two sides of Downing Street over the text of the Bruges speech, largely drafted by Charles Powell.
21. Brian Harrison, 'Mrs Thatcher and the Intellectuals', *Twentieth Century British History*, 5:2 (1994) pp. 206–45.
22. For the links between 'New Right' intellectuals and journalists see Maurice Cowling, 'Preface to the Second Edition', *Mill and Liberalism*, 2nd edn (Cambridge: Cambridge University Press, 1990) pp. ix–xlv; xxviii.
23. See for example Nora Beloff, 'Golden chances that keep going west', *The Times*, 19 July 1982. The lengthiest, and most hostile, article appeared in the *Sunday Telegraph* (15 May 1990) after the Berlin Wall had come down, in the form of a profile of 'Chatham House Man'.
24. William Wallace, 'Between two worlds: think-tanks and foreign policy', chap. 8 in Christopher Hill and Pamela Beshoff (eds), *Two Worlds of International Relations: academics, practitioners and the trade in ideas* (London: Routledge, 1994). See also Keith Webb, 'Academics and Practitioners: Britain', in Michel Girard and others, *Theory and Practice in Foreign Policy-making* (London: Pinter, 1994).

25. William Wallace, 'Foreign Policy and National Identity in the United Kingdom', *International Affairs*, January 1991, pp. 65–80.
26. *Le Nouvel Observateur*, no. 1307, 23–29 November 1989, p. 23 (authors' translation).
27. Thatcher, op. cit., p. 794; Zelikow and Rice, op. cit. pp. 115–16.
28. Some have argued that an actual back room deal took place between the French and the Germans, linking EMU with the outcome of the Two Plus Four Talks. See George Valence, 'Il'Engrenage Européenne', *L'Express*, 19 October 1990, p. 19; see also Alan Cafruny and Glenda Rosenthal, 'The State of the EC: Theory and Research in Post Maastricht Europe', in Rosenthal and Cafruny (eds), *The State of the European Community*, op. cit., pp. 7–8, and in the same volume Francoise de la Serre and Christian Lesquesne, 'France and the European Union', pp. 145–57; 146.
29. David Usborne, 'Political Union Now a Step Closer', *The Bulletin*, (Brussels: Ackroyd, 3 May 1990) p. 16.
30. *Europe* 5240, 22 April 1990.
31. For example in the Two Plus Four talks, Mrs Thatcher took a tough line and at one point looked likely to veto the whole process on the question of whether NATO exercises could take place in the former GDR after unification – a position that was not taken seriously by her negotiating partners. See Karl Kaiser, 'Germany's Unification', *Foreign Affairs*, 70:1, 1990–91, pp. 179–205.
32. See the comments by Nicholas Ridley, quoted in *The Spectator*, 14 July 1990, p. 8; for press report of the Chequers meeting see 'What the PM learnt about the Germans', *Independent on Sunday*, 15 July 1990. For Nigel Lawson's comments on Thatcher's crude anti-German sentiments see his *The View from No. 11* (London: Bantam, 1993) p. 923.
33. Quoted in Zelikow and Rice, op. cit. p. 367.
34. Alan Clark, *Diaries* (London: Weidenfeld, 1993) pp. 273–8.
35. *Defence Implications of Recent Events*, 10th Report of the House of Commons Defence Committee, 1989–90; HC-320, 11 July 1990.
36. The highly diverse group of contributors to this included Denis Healey, Francis Fukuyama, Eduard Shevardnadze, Theo Sommer, Noam Chomsky and J.K. Galbraith.
37. Lawson, *The View From No. 11*, op. cit., p. 1001. See also Bruce Anderson, *John Major: the making of the Prime Minister* (London: Fourth Estate, 1991); Alan Watkins, *A Conservative Coup: the fall of Margaret Thatcher* (London: Duckworth, 1991); see also the comments by William Waldegrave in Penny Junor, *The Major Enigma*, London, Michael Joseph, 1992, p. 310. See also Kenneth Baker (ed.), *The Faber Book of Conservatism* (London: Faber, 1993) p. 226.
38. Cradock, *In Pursuit of British Interests*, op. cit. p. 32. See also Ranelagh, *Thatcher's People* (London: Fontana, 1992) pp. 298–300. For the difference in style between Thatcher and Major see Sir Charles Powell, quoted in Junor, *The Major Enigma*, op. cit. pp. 209–10.
39. Wallace, 'Foreign Policy and National Identity', op. cit. p. 284.
40. 'My Friend Chris', *The Economist*, 20 April 1991; Michael Binyon, 'Farewell to an admirable fixer', *The Times*, 28 March 1995. Europe After Maastricht, House of Commons Foreign Affairs Committee, 1991–92, Second Report Vol. 2 (HC 223-II).
41. John Major, 'The Evolution of Europe', *Conservative Party News*, 11 March 1991. For an 'insiders' account of this speech see Hogg and Hill, *Too Close to Call*, op. cit., pp. 76–9. See also 'Turning to Germany', *The Times*, 9 March 1991.
42. Cradock, op. cit. p. 36.
43. Lawrence Freedman, 'Defence Policy', in Dennis Kavanagh and Anthony Seldon (eds), *The Major Effect* (London: Macmillan, 1994).

44. See the UK's non paper *Draft Treaty Provisions on CFSP*, 26 February 1991 (unpublished).

45. The Alliance summit in July 1990 had declined the British initiative to give NATO this out of area mandate. See the British government submission to the IGC–PU, 'Defence and Security in Europe', dated 15 December 1990, unpublished. These points were reiterated by Douglas Hurd in the Churchill Memorial Lecture, Luxembourg, 19 February 1991.

46. 'The Anglo-Italian Declaration' is reproduced in *Europe Documents*, Brussels, Agence Europe, no.1735, 5 October 1991.

47. I. Davidson and I. Dawnay, 'Major urges EC to admit east European states', *Financial Times*, 13 September 1991.

48. When, in 1986, the Spanish government had pressed for membership of WEU the British had insisted on drawing up a 'Declaration' which set out the principles which all members of WEU must accept. The strongest evidence that ministers were not paying attention to this part of the endgame was that no such conditions were demanded of Greece; compensation was offered afterwards by offering Turkey (and Norway) observer status as NATO members outside the EU.

49. See Anthony Forster, *Britain and the Maastricht Negotiations* (St Anthony's/ Macmillan, 1999) Chap. 3.

50. 'Against the current', *The Economist*, 8 June 1991, pp. 31–2.

51. In spring 1991 Peter Stodthart moved from Washington to London to take up his post as editor of *The Times*. He was reported to have been sympathetic to a policy of constructive engagement on European policy, but received clear instructions from Rupert Murdoch to take a strongly sceptical line (personal information).

52. For a flavour of the antagonism towards the 'Inertia, Euro-piety and Hurd Instinct' of the Foreign Office see Noel Malcolm, 'Dead hand of Mr Hurd', *Spectator*, 7 September 1991, p. 6.

53. These included J.M.C. Rollo, *The New Eastern Europe: Western Responses* (April 1990); Adrian Hyde-Price, *European Security beyond the Cold War: four scenarios for the year 2000* (July 1991); Judy Batt, *Central Europe from Reform to Transformation* (July 1991); and Chris Cviic, *Remaking the Balkans*, published just as the Yugoslav conflict was spreading in September 1991.

54. These included the editor of *The Economist* and the assistant foreign editor of the *Financial Times*, which were the only newspapers to comment on its discussions and conclusions. The only members of parliament there were Sir Geoffrey Howe, now a senior backbencher, and Cyril Townsend, a strongly pro-European Conservative 'wet', *Ditchley Conference Report* D90/10.

55. *Labour and Political Union*, Labour Party Press Office, 27 November 1991. It again included a warm reference to Cyprus as a candidate for EC membership, however.

56. 'Any ideas?' *The Economist*, 7 November 1992, p. 30.

57. See *Statement on the Defence Expenditures: Britain's Defence for the 1990s*, presented to Parliament by the Secretary of State for Defence, cmnd 1559–I, London, HMSO, 1991.

58. See Michael Evans, 'British troops to spearhead new NATO force' *The Times*, 25 May 1991, and Joseph Fitchett, 'The new NATO: A Mobile Force for Post-Cold War Era' *International Herald Tribune*, 27 May 1991. Richardson, 'British state strategies', op. cit., p. 160.

59. For press coverage of the presentation of the statement see Christopher Bellamy, 'Gulf Experience fails to halt defence cuts', *Independent*, 10 July 1991; 'Marching them down again', *The Economist*, 6 July 1991, p. 27; 'King's own Royal cutbacks',

The Economist, 13 July 1991, p. 28. For the paucity of the defence debate see the comments by a former serving officer, John Wilkinson MP, Parl. Deb. HC, 15 October 1991, col.205. For press comment see Edward Pearce, 'From the people who brought you the Somme', *New Statesman*, 18 October 1991, p. 23.

60. The UK's reduction in manpower of 20.1 per cent between 1990–95, was less than Italy, Germany and France. Defence expenditure in Britain (4.2 per cent) remaining higher than France (3.5 per cent) and Germany (2.6 per cent). The British 'peace dividend', amounting to 5.5 per cent reduction in defence spending in real terms planned for 1994–95, was markedly less than in America, France and Germany. See *Statement on Defence Estimates*, Cmnd 1981, HMSO, London, July 1992, p. 17 and 47. For the equipment orders announced between June and October see *Financial Times*, 15 October 1991.

61. The defect of the white paper, as the House of Commons Defence Committee noted, was its silence on the government's financial strategy over the coming decade, and the avoidance of a decision as to whether Britain should retain a comprehensive capability or should concentrate on doing fewer things well. See House of Commons Defence Committee, Eleventh Report 1990–91, HC 394, 24 July 1991, p. XI. See also Editorial, 'Defending the Defence Cuts', *The Times*, 10 July 1991; 'The Quiet Revolution', *Spectator*, 28 September 1991, p. 5; James Adams, 'Why Britain's forces are bleeding to death', *Sunday Times*, 10 November 1991.

62. These fears were compounded by criticisms by Prince Charles. Even The Queen was reported to have made her dismay clear to senior Tories. See 'Royal Family and generals unite to fight defence cuts' *Sunday Times*, 13 October 1991.

63. The references were made by Martin O'Neill, Parl. Deb. HC, 14 October 991, col. 69; Julian Amery, *ibid.*, col. 78; Bill Cash, *ibid.*, col. 92; John Wilkinson, Parl. Deb. HC, 15 October 1991, col. 204; John Cartwright, *ibid.*, col. 215. Only Cartwright and Cash directly referred to the IGC in the debates.

64. The party manifestos are reprinted in *The Times Guide to the House of Commons, April 1992*, London: HarperCollins, 1992.

65. Dan Keohane, 'The Approach of British Political Parties to a Defence Role for the European Community', *Government and Opposition*, 27:3 (Summer 1992) pp. 299–310.

66. Private information.

67. 'Will Clinton be "special"?', *The Times*, 7 December 1992.

68. 'Raise your eyes, there is a land beyond', *The Economist*, 5 September 1993. 'I have always believed Europe's ambition for monetary union later this decade was unrealistic … The vision of the founders of the Community was a fine one … But the new mood in Europe demands a new approach.'

69. John Major, 'Europe: A Future That Works', the Second William and Mary Lecture, Leiden, the Netherlands, 7 September 1994 (FCO Verbatim Service).

70. Interview.

71. Geoffrey Howe's comment on Douglas Hurd, his successor as foreign secretary, is telling: '… an excellent all-round professional, a wicket-keeper's wicket-keeper. If I was looking for reactive advice I would look no further.' Howe, *Conflict of Loyalty*, op. cit., p. 674.

72. The quotation is from Joe Rogaly in the *Financial Times*, 8 February 1994, 'An island swathed in fog', referring to the 1993 Conference; the language sharpened over the three following years. See also Helen Wallace, 'Britain out on a Limb?', *Political Quarterly*, 166:1 (1995) pp. 46–58.

73. *The Times*, 11 October 1995.

74. Quote by Philip Stephens, 'Political Notebook', *Financial Times*, 25 February 1994.
75. Meeting a group of British politicians in November 1997, Helmut Kohl went out of his way to recall his irritation at the style of Rifkind's speech in Bonn the previous winter. Private information.
76. Sherrard Cowper-Coles, 'From defence to security: British policy in transition', *Survival* 36:1 (Spring 1994) pp. 142, 152. Cowper-Coles wrote this paper while on attachment to the IISS from the British Foreign and Commonwealth Office.
77. Ninth Report of the House of Commons Defence Committee 1993–94, para. XX.
78. Labour Party manifesto, 1997, reprinted in *Times Book of the House of Commons* May 1997 (London: HarperCollins, 1997). One of the authors of this chapter discovered that a bilateral defence dialogue was under way while participating in a conference in Paris, in early 1994. Diplomats in the FCO confirmed its existence, but made clear that ministers were anxious to avoid Conservative members of the House of Commons Defence Committee discovering its existence.
79. See Hugh Miall, *Redefining Europe: new patterns of conflict and cooperation* (London: RIIA/Pinter, 1994).
80. Edward Mortimer, 'European Security After the Cold War: an assessment of the dangers to peace in Europe since the Soviet collapse, and of the Western responses they require', Adelphi Paper 271, Summer 1992.
81. William Wallace, 'Truth and Power, monks and technocrats: theory and practice in international relations', *Review of International Studies*, Summer 1996, pp. 301–21.
82. Prime Minister's speech to the Lord Mayor's banquet, 10 November 1997; Downing Street Press Office text.
83. A succession of policy documents set out a distinctive foreign policy approach between 1992 and 1997, in marked contrast to Labour's reticence; see for example, *Beyond the Nation State*, Liberal Publications July 1992 and *Shared Security*, Liberal Publications September 1994.
84. Keith Webb, 'Academics and professionals: Britain', in Michel Girard *et al.*, *Theory and Practice in Foreign Policy-making: national perspectives on academics and professionals in International Relations* (London: Pinter, 1994). See also Christopher Hill and Pamela Beshoff (eds), *Two Worlds of International Relations: academics, practitioners and the trade in ideas* (London: Routledge, 1994); and Wallace, 'Truth and Power', op. cit.
85. Personal information.

6

Coming to Terms with Germany: the Slow and Arduous Adjustment of Dutch Foreign Policy after 1989

Steven Everts *

> *What Victor Hugo said of God, might equally aptly be said of policy makers: they see the truth, but slowly.*
>
> R. Jervis[1]

Introduction

During the postwar period, the Netherlands was by and large a satisfied power.[2] As one observer rightly asserts: 'The Netherlands is a satisfied nation, despite the loss of its former greatness (at the end of the 17th century), the secession of Belgium (1830) and its demise as a colonial power (1949).'[3] The bipolar European order, the division of the continent and the multilateral institutional framework of the West that came with it, appeared to serve perceived Dutch interests and ideals quite well. US leadership of, and Holland's protection by, NATO together with the legal, supranational framework of the EC gave the Dutch a shielded place. The order that characterized European affairs for more than four decades was altogether seen as not too unfavourable.

Consequently, adjustment to the radically new circumstances of post 1989–91 Europe has been a slow and arduous process for the Dutch, albeit not only for them. The viscosity of established policy postures, the initial reluctance to engage in a fundamental rethinking of the established ideas and concepts was a result of this basic satisfaction with the postwar arrangements, as well as due to the general strength of the forces of inertia. Adaptation and reformulation always seem to be lengthy and sluggish processes, as can be witnessed throughout this book.

---

* I would like to thank Ph. P. Everts, A. Pijpers, P. Scheffer and A. van Staden for having read an earlier draft of this chapter. I am responsible for the many translations from Dutch into English in the text. Any errors of fact and/or judgement remain, as always, my responsibility.

In this chapter I will analyze how this process of coming to terms with a radically changed environment took place in the Netherlands. Before describing and analyzing the adjustment process as it occurred in Holland, a brief sketch of the main lines of Dutch foreign policy before 1989 will be given. After having laid out this starting position, it should be easier to ascertain and trace possible changes that took place afterwards.

Dutch foreign policy before 1989: the orthodoxies of Atlanticism and European federalism

The principal characteristics of the cold war European order, which are described in the introductory chapter, led the Dutch to adopt the double orthodoxy of Atlanticism and European federalism. The first meant the political primacy of NATO in all security affairs and demanded good relations with the US. The second, regarding economic integration in the EC, was simultaneously aimed at providing a legal and political structure in which Dutch exports could find their way into a vast market, as well as preventing the emergence of a directorate of the more powerful neighbouring states. The ultimate aim was to safeguard Holland from those continental conflicts and rivalries that in the not so distant past had been the main threat to its political independence.

If the two orthodoxies came into a collision, the Atlanticists had the right of way. The EC was undeniably important for economic growth and welfare and hence merited active Dutch engagement, but it was only NATO which, at the end of the day, could guarantee Dutch security. Staunch support for NATO and hence US involvement in Europe's security (Dutch diplomats and politicians were proud to describe themselves as America's most faithful ally!) was also motivated by the assessment that by keeping the Americans in, all the other European countries were relegated to the same second tier.[4]

Against this background, it should not be a surprise that Holland was often at odds with France, with which it disagreed on both the proper role for the US in European affairs and on the institutional make-up of the process of European integration. Where the French aimed at an independent, powerful Europe freed from superpower hegemony and led by France, the Dutch always emphasized the supremacy of transatlantic relations. Whereas France usually wanted European co-operation to remain an intergovernmental affair and hence always underlined the importance of the European Council, the Dutch, by contrast, preached the values of the Community-method and stressed the vital role for the Community's supranational institutions, such as the European Commission, the European Parliament and the European Court of Justice.

The motivations for these divergent strategies were, of course, strikingly similar: both France and the Netherlands believed that their particular approaches served their perceived national interests best. Since the law gives equal protection to the powerful and the weak, and since the power disparities were (believed to be) reduced in a supranational setting, it seemed logical for Holland to aim for the highest, 'purest' form of integration. This stance had an additional advantage: the Dutch could have a quite 'realistic' policy cloaked in quite 'idealistic' terms, portraying themselves as true believers, as the most Euro-enthusiast of the Community. Both at home and abroad, the Dutch choice for the federal route, and more in general their internationalist stance, was primarily defended in moral and ethical terms, rather than as defending the material interests of a vulnerable, open society. The ethical–legal form of argumentation conformed perfectly with pre-1945 Dutch foreign policy attitudes and with old self-perceptions of Holland being morally above the deplorable habits of continental power-politics; a 'lighthouse in a sea of darkness' as Prime Minister de Geer had said on the eve of the Second World War.

By constantly stressing the virtues of the Community method, and the legal equality of all member states that this implied, the Dutch sought to equalize the obvious power disparities between themselves and the larger EC member states. Equally, it was underscored that European integration was not, or at least should not, be made exclusively dependent on initiatives taken by the Franco-German couple. Time and again arguments could be heard against the 'hegemonic' aspects of any 'privileged' bilateral relationship in a multilateral setting. Although these main themes, or concepts, could count on near unanimous support in parliament and were consistently advocated over the years by a variety of coalition governments of different composition, it was not, unfortunately, a logically coherent strategy. Quite a few internal contradictions can be discerned.

To begin with, there was a gap between the federalist rhetoric and the precise positions taken by the Dutch at various instances in the pre-1989 period. For example, during the negotiations for the ECSC, the Dutch sought to place the High Authority under the political control of the Council of Ministers, whereas the French delegation wanted to maximize the supranational character of the future ECSC. In a way, these respective positions are a mirror image of the 'traditional' French preference for intergovernmental arrangements and 'eternal' Dutch preaching of the federal option. Furthermore, at the time of the negotiations that eventually led to the Treaty of Rome, the Dutch managed to maintain the national veto for decisions regarding the transport sector which was, and is, of prime economic importance to the Netherlands.[5]

Moreover, underneath the surface of the federalist rhetoric there was always a clear sensitivity to balance of power considerations. For example, if the Dutch were so keen to protect the supranational character of the EC, why did they so ardently support British membership, the so-called *préalable anglais*, when Britain's leadership had made no secret of their opposition to anything that went beyond intergovernmental co-operation? True, the British were likely to share the Dutch preference for free trade arrangements, as opposed to the French and other southern states' *dirigiste* and protectionist propensities, but beyond that there seemed very little they agreed upon in terms of European integration.[6] Advocacy of British membership and later efforts to be 'understanding' and forthcoming with regard to British reluctance inside the EC, had probably more to do with ideas of constructing a balance within the triangle of France, Germany and the United Kingdom, in the centre of which the Dutch found themselves. In other words, more than many Dutch officials cared to admit, the real consideration was with a balance of power.

On top of that, it seemed very 'consistent' to oppose arrangements in the field of political and security integration that were not based on the Community model. But this meant, of course, that nothing serious would come about. And perhaps this was just as well for Holland, since this meant that NATO supremacy in security affairs would be maintained.[7] That NATO was and is a purely intergovernmental organization did not reduce Dutch enthusiasm for it. Further proof of the essentially undesired expansion of European integration in the spheres of security and defence was the Dutch preference for maintaining the US nuclear monopoly for as long as possible, and hence their negative opinion of the British nuclear capability and, especially, the French *force de frappe*. When in 1974, NATO adopted a resolution in which the positive contribution that the British and French nuclear forces made to the Alliance's defence was welcomed, the Dutch strongly voiced their dissent.

Overall, there was a contradiction in the sense that Holland sought to establish a balance of power within the Atlantic framework, with the US as a European balancer, while at the same time, it strived to establish a legal, supranational order in the EC. In this way, the Dutch were hedging their bets, 'and as long as the Dutch were not forced to choose, they could combine the language of power with the language of the law.'[8] In this cold-war, Atlantic-oriented Europe, West Germany was contained; its economy was forcibly reoriented to the West, which conveniently meant that a great part of its imports and exports had to go through Rotterdam. Although Germany was self-evidently of prime economic importance as the main market for Dutch exports, these economic considerations were not translated into intimate political relations. Instead, the best political contacts were held with London and Washington, whose participation in European affairs was also needed since France could not realistically be expected to counterbalance the Germans on their own. Finally, political relations with Belgium and Luxembourg as well as, albeit for different reasons and in a different way, with the countries in central and eastern Europe, could best be described as a policy of 'benign neglect'.

One of the more important consequences of the cold war European order was that the Netherlands could entertain slightly illusory hopes as to its real political weight. Many foreign affairs officials in Holland considered it as the biggest of the small countries, or even the smallest of the big countries, and they would cite a range of economic statistics and historical facts to support their claim. And, of course, it is true that Holland *has* a relatively robust economy with a very stable currency, it is the world's third exporter of agricultural goods and it is the third foreign investor in the USA. It also possesses the world's largest port. Equally, the Netherlands has been one of Europe's principal imperial powers. More recently, there had been the exceptional period when the British were not yet members of the EC, when the Germans were still keeping a very low profile, thereby allowing the Dutch to fence with the French on de Gaulle's Fouchet Plan.[9] This was also the period when a disproportionate number of Dutch officials occupied leading positions in a variety of international organisations, for example van Lennep in the OECD and Luns in NATO. But all these statistics and claims were beside the point, since the Netherlands was not *perceived* as a key European player. As the Dutch historian Manning rightly observes: 'someone who takes the perspective of foreign observers must conclude that the Netherlands has never been a middle power. That has only been a claim in The Hague.'[10]

Dutch foreign policy during the cold war was a story of contradictory preferences, what has been called the Dutch split: the double orthodoxies of Atlanticism and European federalism. It may not have been consistent, but it seemed to work. In the postwar institutional setting that had emerged, with a legal/supranational EC that on the one hand reduced power disparities or made them less relevant and that was on the other hand ultimately overshadowed by the American-led Alliance, the Dutch had found a relatively sheltered place. It was largely a westward looking country, with its back turned against the continent. It saw itself more as part of the Atlantic bridge (together with the much admired British) than as existing on the western edge of the continent.

Inevitably, the end of the cold war threatened this sheltered position. It is a truism these days to state that the political, military, economic and social landscape of Europe has been fundamentally altered since the late 1980s and most dramatically since 1989–91. What will follow is an analytical description of Dutch perceptions of, and reactions to, those changes and developments.

The period since 1989 will be broken down into two phases. The first runs from the autumn of 1989 until December 1992. The main international events of this period were German unification, the Gulf war, the twin IGCs on EMU and EPU leading to the Maastricht treaty and the outbreak of the war in former Yugoslavia. In this first period relatively little rethinking took place at the official level and the little re-evaluation that did happen was small in scope and incremental in nature. The Dutch minister of foreign affairs during this phase was Hans van den Broek, the personification of prudence and a strong adherent to the double orthodoxy of Atlanticism and European federalism.

With his departure to the Commission in Brussels, in January 1993, the second phase starts, which ends in summer 1996. These were the years of the implementation problems of the Maastricht treaty, most easily witnessed in the EU's (in-)action in the former Yugoslavia, but not solely limited to problems in the second pillar. Across the board, European affairs seemed to have become more volatile. Enlargement of the EU and NATO reached a prominent place on the international agenda without this leading, however, to an international consensus of how to approach these challenges effectively. Finally, and of special importance for this chapter is the official review of Dutch foreign policy that took place towards the end of this second period.[11] Quite a number of adjustments took place during this second phase which can essentially be characterized as a less dogmatic interpretation of the twin orthodoxies. The ministers of foreign affairs in this period were, first, the Christian Democrat Peter Kooijmans and, second, the leader of the left-liberals D66, Hans van Mierlo. It was under the former that a much increased awareness of the pivotal role of Germany in the transformed European setting occurred, together with the desirability of a greater Dutch orientation towards Bonn. The review operation was an initiative taken by van Mierlo. It implied a strategic choice for a Europe which should be prepared for a much reduced and more selective US involvement, a Europe that would be a less transparent and orderly place. And, finally, it acknowledged that concessions would be required in the institutional make up of the EU in order to maintain its internal and external capacity to act.

The first phase: more of the same

In an article on the patterns of continuity and change in USA foreign policy, Rosati reviews the claims that adjustments to significant external changes are often subject to important forces opposing change. 'Despite the testimony of conventional wisdom in social theory, despite the first and abiding premise of social development, it is not change but persistence that is the "natural" or "normal" condition of any given social behaviour.'[12] Indeed, revolutions took place much faster on the streets of Leipzig or Prague than in the minds of policymakers in The Hague. The essential Dutch response to the revolution of 1989, at the official level at least, was cautious and conservative in character, both at the strategic and the tactical level. An example of this conservative reflex was Prime Minister Ruud Lubbers' open opposition to rapid German unification, as expressed during the informal Elysée dinner in November 1989.[13]

Confronted with a completely altered European environment, the Dutch government attempted to revert to the tried and tested axioms of Atlanticism and European federalism, which, so the argument ran, had served Holland and Europe so well in the past. Of course, the revolutionary character of the implosion of the communist regimes in central Europe was not denied as such, but these radical challenges to the status quo did not lead to a fundamental rethinking of known axioms, nor was such a reformulation deemed necessary.

Commenting on the implications of 1989, the former Dutch ambassador to Bonn said: 'plus que ça change, plus c'est la mème chose.'[14]

In a position paper by Minister van den Broek and State Secretary for European Affairs Dankert, sent to Parliament on 6 June 1990, the choice for more of the same was motivated as follows:

> the question is whether all these changes [German unification, democratisation of Central Europe etc ...] have changed in their essence the analysis, objectives and priorities as formulated in 1988 [which was the last government White Paper on European integration]. Or are these more new impulses for an even greater urgency in the realisation of previously defined objectives? On the whole, the choice has to be made primarily for the latter [...]. Behind the fundamental changes of the last year lies a lot of continuity. The necessity of further integration existed clearly in 1988. That necessity has only increased.[15]

Clearly, the Dutch government opted for an acceleration of West European integration – completion of the Single Market, IGCs on EMU and EPU – as the best answer to the central and east European revolutions. But the consequences of this *fuite en avant* for central Europe were not seen as problematic:

> the question is raised sometimes whether the Community might escape, by choosing so clearly the path of deepening of its own integration, its responsibilities *vis-à-vis* the countries in Central and Eastern Europe, shouldn't widening of the Community have priority over deepening? This question sits ill with the actual situation and deserves for that reason alone a negative answer ... further deepening does not only serve our interest, but also theirs.[16]

The developments in the east and particularly the prospect of a speedy realisation of German unification were seen as additional, powerful reasons to use the window of opportunity that seemed to have been created for a big leap forward towards the fulfilment of an old desire, namely a federal Europe, which could bind German irrevocably to its Western neighbours.

As to institutional preferences, the Dutch government reiterated its strong predisposition for the federal model, with a simultaneous strengthening of the democratic control and effectiveness of the Community's decisionmaking process:

> we have argued above why the Netherlands has always chosen, as it does now, for a federal vision on the further development of the EC. When, for instance, we will have to choose between a strengthening of the position of the European Commission and the European Parliament or the role of the Council, which naturally includes the European Council as well, that

choice cannot be made otherwise than for the first alternative ... the Netherlands aims for a federal Community.[17]

On numerous occasions these federal beliefs were professed when proposals were made for further decisionmaking in the Council through qualified majority, for further delegation of powers to the Commission, for increasing the role and powers of the European Court of Justice, for a communitarization of EPC. Countless references could be found to the value of the Community as a legal order voting, while all proposals that carried the danger of intergovernmentalism were, predictably, rejected out of hand.

This fundamental choice for a federal development of the Community was motivated, as it had been in the past, by the belief that 'in this way an institutional structure can be created that holds more safeguards for the position of smaller member-states.'[18] This motivation sits ill both with the argument that the federal route is in everybody's interest, which can also be found in government papers, and with the feelings of disappointment and irritation expressed in The Hague when others do not share Dutch federal preferences. Opposition to Dutch proposals by other member states was believed to be caused by 'the existence of illusions in a number of member-states as to the degree of sovereignty still at their disposal.'[19]

Analyzing the Dutch approach, Paul Scheffer, who is the chairman of the PvdA's (social democratic party) foreign policy committee and a commentator for the widely respected quality paper *NRC/Handelsblad*, has pointed to what he calls a blindness or myopia for 'national consciousness' in other states. Because the Dutch are so 'finished' and 'satisfied' as a nation, they have difficulty imagining that others consider themselves as independent sovereign states, and are keen on protecting what they consider their national separateness.

> The falling apart of Belgium does not affect us, since we are all Europeans now, England with its opposition against the EU strikes us as a strange anachronism; that a majority of the population in Denmark voted against that same Union came as a total surprise; and finally, France, which cultivates the idea of its national independence in political and security affairs, is considered no less than a great danger.[20]

When the formal negotiations for the twin IGCs on EMU and EPU began, with the meetings of the 'Group of personal representatives' in summer 1990, a new document was sent to parliament stating the Dutch starting position for these negotiations.'[21] In this paper the government repeated its strategic, fundamental choice for a federal Europe:

> 'as to the direction of the integration process, the Netherlands has always chosen the federal option ... The EPU must bring us a step further in this

direction. The length of this step is in principle less important than its direction.[22]

This last sentence is, as we shall see, crucial in explaining Dutch attitudes during the IGCs. The Dutch government declared that it would place, in the negotiations, 'greatest emphasis on democratisation of the decision making process'.[23] Yet, the progress made at Maastricht in terms of further democratic powers for the European Parliament was rather modest. Not only were Dutch priorities in this respect not shared by others, but there were other, arguably more important, areas in which Dutch preferences were significantly out of tune with the ideas of its principal European partners.

In the negotiations on external actions of the future EPU to establish a Common Foreign and Security Policy, the Netherlands largely stuck to its (contradictory) dogmas. It resisted attempts to construct this CFSP on an intergovernmental basis, while simultaneously stressing that steps towards a European defence policy should not lead to a reduction of the central role of NATO. 'The negotiation position can be described as follows: France and Germany, supported by Greece, Italy, Spain, Belgium and Luxembourg want a CFSP in the EU on an intergovernmental basis ... The Netherlands with the United Kingdom, Denmark, Ireland and Portugal do not share that view.'[24]

In the same period Holland also resisted French proposals to place the WEU under the political control of the European Council. Again, they found themselves in a coalition of similarly Atlantic-oriented states, namely the United Kingdom, Portugal and Denmark.[25] A true guardian of transatlantic co-operation, the Dutch government emphasized the need to keep the USA politically and militarily involved in European security. Consequently, it considered the reservations that the American government had expressed regarding plans to put the WEU under the European Council 'self evidently of great importance' for the Dutch position.[26] If there was any role for the WEU, it had to be 'complementary' to NATO and limited to out-of-area activities only.[27] In short, Dutch attitudes in this period were entirely consistent with the two dogmas of Atlanticism and European federalism. The latter dogma was used, tactically or sincerely, to uphold and maintain the former. Scheffer expresses a harsh, but accurate, judgement on Dutch policies in this period:

whoever looks at the partners of the Netherlands in the debate on the security side of the Political Union is taken aback: the United Kingdom, Ireland, Denmark and Portugal. There is really nothing further West in Europe. On the mental and political map, we behave as if we are also an island, or at least a peninsula. It is a coalition of peripheral nations in which the Netherlands feels at home, despite all European rhetoric. And it has to be clear that this anti-continental attitude has no chance at all to be successful after 1989. Our centre of gravity no longer lies 'at and overseas'.[28]

The rejection of the Dutch proposals for a federal Europe on 'Black Monday': a pivotal event

Between the negotiations and the final agreement on EPU and EMU, Dutch diplomacy suffered a major humiliation on what came to be known in Dutch diplomatic history as 'Black Monday'. On their predecessors, 30 September 1991, the Dutch as EC president-in-office, having pushed aside the proposals by Luxembourg for an EPU based on the 'pillar-structure' (which had been supported by a large majority of member states), presented their proposals based on federal principles, including full communitarization of CFSP, a strong increase of the powers and role of the Commission and Parliament, and so on.[29] Due either to sheer incompetence or to excessive wishful thinking (or both), but in any case unaware that sufficient support for these proposals was lacking, the day ended in a catastrophe: only Belgium and the Commission expressed their agreement. Not for the first time, Holland had overestimated support for its plans in other countries, especially in key capitals such as Paris and Bonn.[30] It may have been true that Germany was not against the proposals as such, and may even have expressed serious interest, but the Dutch should have known that Germany will always, when push comes to shove, side with France. That van den Broek was hardly on speaking terms with two of his main continental colleagues, Genscher and Dumas, and busy with brokering cease fires in the Yugoslav war, clearly did not help.[31] After the brutal rejection of their own proposals, the Dutch could do nothing but go back to the Luxembourg proposals, the proposals they had criticized so much and use the pillar structure as the basis for the final negotiations of the Maastricht treaty.

With hindsight, it seems that these painful days in September 1991 have played a pivotal role in the process of adjustment of Dutch foreign policy after 1989.

> The Netherlands really thought that history was on its side and that it formed an *avant-garde* in Europe. It might take a long time, but that Europe would ultimately form itself according to the Dutch self-image was essentially undisputed. Little by little, people really started to believe that increasing economic and cultural interdependence would create, spontaneously, a supranational order.[32]

After Black Monday there was really no way the Dutch could entertain any illusions as to the degree of support in other countries for their federal ideals. A whole intellectual tradition, a whole conceptual approach to European order had suffered a major defeat. The Dutch had stuck to their tried and tested formula of Atlanticism and federalism and the result had been a failure. Put against the initial Dutch position – the length of that step is in principle less important than its direction – the final agreement at Maastricht was obviously considered somewhat meagre and insufficient. In a debate just before the European summit, Lubbers acknowledged that the final result 'might not be entirely what Holland has wanted initially, but this should not be a reason to reject the treaty. The best should not become an enemy of the good.'[33] Evidently, Dutch dispositions and preferences are still considered the best, but sadly lacking in support.

Nearly one year later, in a speech in Leiden that was announced as a major re-evaluation of Dutch foreign policy, van den Broek again denied or at least belittled the need for different priorities and new ideas to guide Holland through post-cold war Europe. It was somewhat disconcerting to hear a West European foreign minister declare three years after the fall of the Berlin Wall that 'we can and must continue the main lines of our post-war policies.' This extreme reluctance on his part to shed established policies did not go unnoticed and was severely criticized by outside commentators.

The Netherlands, it should be said, has a relatively small, closely knit foreign policy 'élite', with a fairly important role and opportunity for outsiders to influence government policy. The role played by various study groups and advisory commissions, such as the Advisory Council for Peace and Security, which is composed of both academics, former diplomats and retired military men, or certain study groups of the Atlantic Commission as well as the Scientific Council for Government Policy, seems particularly crucial in understanding the foreign policy process in the Netherlands. In accordance with the consensus seeking and depoliticising style of Dutch politics in general, these commissions tend to be filled with people from all the major political parties. In a sense, they represent institutionalized, though imperfect, channels of communication between the political and diplomatic élites and a wider circle of academics, journalists, political commentators and representatives of NGOs.[34]

By now, the chorus of academics and other commentators who had underlined that a continentalization of Dutch foreign policy was necessary, had become a crescendo. For Maarten Brands, a professor of modern history at the University of Amsterdam 'the evening in Leiden was grotesque, as if the revolution of 1989/90 does not affect us. Although it was 17 September 1992, large sections of the minister's speech fitted just as well, or even better, in the era before the great revolution of 1989.'[35] Continuity was the core concept of his speech.

> What was so conspicuously absent in his speech, was a realisation of phenomena such as what is called the 'return of history', how developments in Eastern Europe have started to interfere in West European integration, the German Question in its new form and the like and, more importantly, what could be the answer to this from the Netherlands. Of course he also does not know the answers to all these questions ... but the minister could at least have integrated these questions more prominently into his analysis.'[36]

Other commentators also expressed their doubts as to whether, in the changed strategic–political environment, reflexive Atlanticist rejections of, for example, the Franco-German Eurocorps were tenable. Holland's position had clearly weakened in a more volatile Europe, where power disparities were becoming more pronounced, where USA involvement in European affairs had shrunk or at least become more selective, and where the disciplining force of the Soviet threat had disappeared after the implosion of the Soviet Union at the end of 1991. Europe had become a messier place with a resurgence of national rivalries in central and eastern Europe, but also in Western Europe.

Bob van den Bos, previously a researcher at Clingendael (the Netherlands Institute of International Relations) and by this time an MP for the left-liberals D66, concluded that 'by upholding our striving for a federal Europe, linked to absolute Atlantic priority, we will guarantee our international "recognisability" but not our success'. He argued for a greater flexibility in Dutch foreign policy, necessitated by both the events of 1989 and the concomitant weakening of Holland's strategic position, as well as the changing policy positions of the US and the surrounding European partners. 'There is really no reason anymore for the panic fear of all post-war cabinets about the formation of a European block formation within NATO.' Certain unchanged Dutch interests justified upholding a number of traditional orientations, principally in the field of democratic control and transparency in EU decision making, but a major change in emphasis was required, notably from the Atlantic to the European framework. On the tactical level, he urged the Dutch to modify their tone drastically. 'The ethical–legal form of argument will have to be replaced largely by political arguments that correspond better with what our bigger partners consider their national interest too. It is also desirable to stop useless rear-guard actions against a too powerful European Council.'[37]

> Our European policy will have to be much more flexible. Therefore it is highly desirable to strip the traditional European doctrines of their nearly dogmatic character. The new situation requires an exceptionally active and mobile diplomacy. The Netherlands will have to make much more use of variable coalitions. We cannot afford anymore to fly on the automatic pilots of Atlanticism and federalism. On the 'monkey hill' [the nickname for the Ministry of Foreign Affairs], imagination should rule.[38]

Brands had voiced a similar plea for a less dogmatic approach. 'In any case, the Netherlands can no longer afford the role of "calibrator" of Europe, with the self-imposed task of assessing whether the Atlantic content of new proposals is acceptable and how much progress is made in reducing the democratic deficit.'[39]

If a more 'sober', pragmatic, flexible and continental approach was necessary after the Indian summer of Dutch foreign policy before 1989, van den Broek did not seem the best person to carry out these changes. Having been in the job for nearly ten years, he had become the personification of the twin dogmas of Atlanticism and federalism. Due to his cautious character and his somewhat pedantic, haughty behaviour, he had limited the number of advisers to a group that could easily fit, as the story went, in a single toilet. 'He does not suffer fools gladly', former minister of foreign affairs van der Stoel once said. Many MPs complained that parliamentary debates had turned into lectures. But in January 1993 van den Broek moved to the European Commission and a new Christian Democratic minister, Peter Kooijmans, took over.[40] It is tempting to attribute most of the changes in emphasis that would take place later to van den Broek's departure alone. Such a conclusion does not seem warranted, however. Van den Broek may have been overly attached to the old orthodoxies, but his professionalism was undisputed. Moreover, he was backed by near-unanimous support on the main lines of his policy. It was only after 1991 that serious pleas, first from outside but later also inside parliament, for a reorientation towards Holland's continental partners gained a more prominent place.

Furthermore, the outside world had continued to evolve in important respects which only increased the necessity of more than merely incremental and piecemeal adjustments. The EU's involvement in former Yugoslavia had made the persistence of divergent national strategies and particularities in Western Europe, and hence the extreme difficulty in arriving at a truly common approach, painfully clear. A new American administration had taken office that had made no secret of its intention to put domestic economic considerations first. And an increasing number of people doubted whether institutional relations with the new democracies in central Europe could be based indefinitely on incrementalist and predominantly noncommital adjustments such as the Europe agreements or the NACC. The question of enlarging both the EU and NATO could not be avoided or dealt with forever by temporizing initiatives like the Partnership for Peace.[41] Enlargement to the east was also considered vital in Holland for the stabilization of that region, but at the same time it would mean an end to the institutional system to which the Dutch had grown so accustomed and which had served them so well. What would the implications be and how could possible negative consequences best be avoided? The continuing movement of events showed that international developments were continuously ahead of the concepts used to deal with them, in Holland as well as elsewhere. New answers were needed, new ideas, new priorities and new strategies. The choice was not, as the famous slogan went, between a 'Brusselization' of Eastern Europe or a Balkaniz-ation of Western Europe. What was needed were workable arrangements that would assure the first while avoiding the second. With existing policies Europe, and Holland, seemed on their way to obtaining the latter while forgoing the former.

The second phase, 1993–97: the relaxation of the twin orthodoxies

1. Bandwagoning with Germany

One of the most important developments in post-1989 Dutch foreign policy has been its 'discovery' of Germany. To argue for a greater foreign policy orientation on Bonn became fashionable in Holland; Germany was definitively 'in' now in policy circles. And if Germany was in, then Britain was out.[42] Although the importance of West Germany for Dutch exports had always been recognized – trade between Holland and Germany constitutes the fourth largest bilateral trade flow in the world – there had been no real affinity with the (West) Germans. Perhaps illustrative of this attitude are the titles of two important post war studies of Dutch–German relations: 'Suspicion and Profit' and 'Partner out of necessity'.[43] The Dutch preferred to stand with their back against the continent, to look westwards, to the sea, to their friends the British with whom contact was so easy and further West to Washington.[44] Since American involvement had become visibly reduced, and because the British Conservative government continued its minimalist stance on Europe, the Dutch realized that whatever designs they may have had for a European order, it would have to be constructed with their continental neighbours. Predominant feelings towards Britain were no longer those of affection and understanding; they were at this stage best described as increased irritation and disappointment about so much self-congratulatory negativism and obstructionism.

However, the shift towards a strategic orientation on Bonn was not just the result of the gradual disappearance of Holland's traditional friends, it clearly also occurred because in European affairs, Germany was seen to have become the central player. It has now become a truism in the Netherlands to acknowledge Germany's pivotal role in any European order, to stress the country's transformation from a state at the periphery to a state at the heart of Europe, to emphasize the country's refound sovereignty after its unification, to point out the destabilizing and centrifugal forces of central Europe that affect Germany more than any other European country – the mix of interests and special responsibilities that ties Germany to the east and makes Germany the main advocate of speedy accession for the Visegrad countries to both the EU and NATO – and, finally, to draw attention to the on-going, self-searching debate in Germany itself on the new role it can and should strive for.

In one of its more influential reports, the Dutch government's Advisory Council on Peace and Security also made the case for a greater foreign policy orientation on Germany.[45] It stressed that the Netherlands and Germany had a lot in common with regard to basic foreign policy objectives. In fact, agreement on major Dutch priorities – a democratic European Union with an effective CFSP and a 'hard' EMU, while preserving ties with the USA through a reformed NATO – could surely be more easily achieved with the Germans than with any other large European country. Better contacts with Bonn were therefore not only necessary because of the new, central position of Germany in Europe – a phenomenon that could perhaps be described as bandwagoning – but also because Germany and Holland had remarkably similar outlooks and objectives. This had, of course, also been true throughout the period of the cold war, but had not received due attention from The Hague. Co-operation had therefore been largely reserved to discussions in multilateral fora such as the EC and NATO.

What the Advisory Council and others proposed was an upgrade of, and increased investment of political energy into, bilateral contacts with Bonn.[46] A similar plea had come from Ben Knapen, the editor in chief of *NRC/ Handelsblad*, who also had made the more general point that in the new, rougher European constellation, a 'revaluation of especially the bilateral ties with our closest neighbours is highly desirable'.[47] This new stress on bilateral contacts with Germany, together with a revival of the Benelux, required quite a mental leap for Dutch policymakers, who had always emphasized the virtues of multilateralism and who had decried exclusive or privileged bilateral relationships within a multilateral framework, the classic case in point being the 'hegemonic' Franco-German couple.

If the need for a greater orientation towards Germany was at last acknowledged across the political spectrum, the concrete implications and possible disadvantages of this shift were subject to more debate. To begin with, the political–psychological relationship with Germany had never been an easy one. The continued existence of the psychologically charged character of that relationship has, to my mind, as much to do with the essentially asymmetrical nature of that relationship, as with the continued, somewhat cultivated, importance attached to the memories of German occupation during the Second World War.[48] Prime Minister Lubbers expressed this line of thinking in an article in *NRC/Handelsblad* on 1st July 1994: 'It will always be the case that the Netherlands and Germany will resemble each other, but we are not a "deutsch land". We are not one of the German Länder, we have our own identity.'[49]

That said, at the same time it seems true that the extent of supposed anti-German feelings at the mass level were often exaggerated, by foreigners and Dutch alike, and many opinion polls bear this out.[50] Although it is true that 'Germany' still did not always evoke high levels of enthusiasm in the Netherlands, the dominant Dutch attitude could perhaps best be found in Professor Brands' frequently repeated advice: 'you don't have to like the Germans particularly, but they matter'. And if the Germans mattered before 1989, they certainly mattered even more thereafter.

A strategic reorientation towards united Germany would have a price. The Advisory Council made a specific plea for greater Dutch understanding of German concerns, notably the possible consequences of increased instability on its eastern borders. The Council therefore urged both the Western multilateral organisations and the Netherlands not to leave the Germans alone in carrying the burden of restructuring the new democracies in the east. If the Netherlands wanted to be heard in Bonn it would surely help if it expressed explicit support for Germany's campaign to bring these countries as soon as possible into NATO and the EU. So would an expansion of its own efforts, financially and otherwise, in that region. Illustrative for the traditionally low priority attached to the 'east' was the fact that even in 1994 the Netherlands did still not possess a large or even middle-range diplomatic mission in any east European or former Soviet capital; the Dutch embassy in New Delhi still remained larger than the embassy in Moscow.[51]

The Advisory Council proposed no less than a doubling of Dutch aid to the region. This substantial increase in aid was deemed necessary both because of the need to ward off increased fragmentation in central Europe and as a political signal to Germany that its concerns were considered legitimate, and that the Netherlands wanted to help. It had to be avoided at all costs that the effective and preferred answer to the German question for the past forty years, namely its *Westbindung* and its active membership of NATO and the EU, would become a problem for Germany. That situation might occur if these organisations' policies towards central Europe would (continue to) be piecemeal and incremental, which in turn could force the Germans to look for arrangements outside these multilateral institutions.

Related to, while at the same time a means for obtaining, the desired rapprochement with Germany was the plea for a more positive attitude towards the previously much vilified 'hegemonic' Franco-German axis. An example of the classic Dutch view of distrust of France and opposition to the Franco-German axis was given in an overview article by Lubbers: 'Europe will be more successful if Paris would opt for Europe and not only for an axis Paris–Bonn, however useful that axis was.'[52] Especially the use of the past tense is interesting. Franco-German initiatives had been useful in the past, but apparently were not any longer. However, since any progress in the field of European integration was, by now, widely considered to be dependent on prior agreement between Bonn and Paris and since such progress (which was also desired by Holland) had visibly become more difficult to achieve after 1989, a more realistic assessment of its political importance and a generally more favourable Dutch posture were required.

If the case for a greater alignment with Germany could be considered as proof that Holland had drawn some belated conclusions about the end of the cold war, and if it is reasonable to argue that indeed it was one of the most remarkable features of post-1989 adjustment, both the strategic implications as well as the tactical means to obtain it were not undisputed.

To begin with, the strategic choice for Bonn clashed with the views of those who argued that in the new, more volatile European constellation the Netherlands would have to find its way among ever-changing coalitions, and should hence not opt for an exclusive or strategic choice for Germany.[53]

Furthermore, due to the sizeable power disparities, an overly-eager Holland could very well be taken for granted by Germany. Each time The Hague would express its desire for closer co-operation with Bonn, the German need to incorporate Dutch views – never great to begin with – would be reduced, while at the same time, by opting so openly for Bonn, Holland could lose out on support from other capitals.[54] Others expressed their concern that, against the background of an already considerable economic dependence on Germany, it would be unwise to further increase that dependency through a strong political orientation on the neighbour to the east. Finally, the question was raised whether Holland could derive certainty from a highly uncertain nation. It was stressed that Germany was facing a nearly insurmountable, complex cluster of internal and external problems and challenges and that since unification it had been going through a highly introspective phase.

No matter how pertinent these questions may be, they could not dissimulate the main point: which is that, slowly and hesitantly, Holland started to shed one of its principal axioms of the postwar period, namely its anti-continentalism. Throughout the cold war era, Dutch policymakers had thought and behaved as if the centre of gravity of European affairs had been off-shore. German unification undid the division of the continent, it accelerated the on-going continentalization of European politics, and it made it unmistakably clear that the European epicentre had moved east. This fundamental shift had to be incorporated in the mental map of Dutch politicians, which was not easy, as could also be witnessed in Lubbers' encouraging advice: 'however, let us try, above all, to see the positive sides of this'. Apparently, these positive aspects were yet to be discovered and not immediately self-evident.[55]

2. Europe: water in the federalist wine

Rethinking of Dutch foreign policy assumptions was not, however, limited to its relations with Germany or to the axiom of anti-continentalism. The coming to terms with Germany should be seen in the wider context of a revaluation of Holland's general European policy. In this wider debate, commentators urged the government to draw its conclusions from the debacle of Black Monday. We have already seen that the prevailing reluctance and inability on the Dutch side to accept that concepts such as 'national consciousness' mattered for other member states, led them to believe, incorrectly as it turned out, that Dutch preferences for a European federation were widely shared. 'We are open to everything and everyone, except for the view that this virtue [the rejection of national consciousness] was born in the first place out of necessity.'[56] At any rate, the cosmopolitan pleas for a federal legal order had clearly not found a favourable response in other member states, at least not in the politically more important ones, and many now argued for a more pragmatic posture. This disenchantment was undoubtedly painful and required substantial mental efforts, but especially after 1993 its consequences for Dutch thinking and acting were becoming ever more apparent. Broadly speaking, they led to three important changes in the underlying assumptions that would guide daily diplomacy:

1. A strategic choice was made for Europe. The semi-theological disputes between Atlanticists and Europeanists had been decided in favour of the latter. This change was, of course, facilitated by international developments which had taken off the rougher edges of the previously diametrically opposed positions of the Atlanticists and the Europeanists, such as the gradual French rapprochement with NATO. Even the most ardent defenders of the transatlantic bond now agreed that ESDI and NATO should no longer be seen as a zero-sum game. Throughout the mid 1990s the Dutch government became increasingly supportive of CJTF and its 'separable but not separate' formulas. At the Amsterdam summit in June 1997, it appeared that the Dutch were prepared to go even further, since they were no longer in the group of countries, led by the United Kingdom, that was opposed to merging the WEU with the EU. This was in marked contrast with the Dutch position during the previous IGC.
2. Within Europe, the Netherlands would concentrate its efforts on the 'near abroad'. This not only implied a greater political investment in bilateral relations with Germany, but also with France, no matter how difficult that would be, and with it the Franco-German axis; while, finally, an effort was made to revitalize the political importance of the Benelux.[57] This revival of the Benelux as a forum to co-ordinate policies and hammer out common approaches fits in well with the trend that can be witnessed where certain 'regional groups' are formed within the EU; the Scandinavians, the Mediterraneans and, after their accession perhaps also the Central Europeans. The real importance of these caucuses should not be exaggerated, but more political investment in the Benelux could be quite interesting for Holland since the Benelux collectively casts more QMV-votes than either France or Germany.[58]
3. As to the institutional make up, a much more flexible approach to its federalist ideals was deemed essential, as much as new institutional arrangements in which the larger and more powerful states would have a bigger say were considered inevitable. In fact, the acceptance of population-weighted 'double majorities' in matters where decisions would be made by QMV has now become official policy. The Dutch government has also shown some initial interest in a 'team presidency' of the EU.[59]

One of the concrete results of this endeavour was the combined Benelux Memorandum for the 1996 IGC.[60] Sadly, Belgium and the Netherlands fell out openly at the Amsterdam summit regarding a topic that should have made them natural allies, the issue of changing the weighting of votes in the Council of Ministers. An injudicious Dutch proposal had, for the first time in the history of the EC/EU given more QMV-votes to the Netherlands, than to Belgium, something which was difficult to justify and politically impossible to sell to the Belgians, even if the Netherlands does have significantly more inhabitants.

At the same time, the acceptance of a differentiation in integration levels and the whole discussion around 'multi-speed' and 'variable geometry' that came with it, was increasingly seen as the lesser evil compared to a complete standstill in European integration. Nonetheless, the fragmentation that multi-speed would cause was not applauded. In the various memoranda published before the 1996 IGC, the government expressed cautious support for multi-speed arrangements, provided that the role of the Community's institutional framework, in particular the central role of the Commission, would not be negatively affected: in other words that the *acquis communautaire* would be safeguarded. That said, multi-speed might turn out to be a blessing in disguise, since Holland could realistically be expected to join any core group that might emerge, especially a monetary core group, and its influence would probably be greater inside than outside.

The bottom line was still the same: the Indian summer that the cold war had been for Dutch foreign policy was over. From now on it would be thrown back to its true size and importance, which had proven far less than many in The Hague had believed instrumental in driving home this message. A long list of failed Dutch candidates for important international positions had also been. Finance Minister Ruding did not get the top job at the IMF, which went to Camdessus; he also did not become the director of the EBRD, which was set up in London instead of Amsterdam. Furthermore, Holland did not get the European Monetary Institute despite the candidacy of, again, Amsterdam, and Lubbers failed in both his attempts to lead, first, the European Commission and, second, NATO. As if this was not enough, Holland was also not a member of the Contact Group on Bosnia, in spite of being the third largest European contributor to UNPROFOR and its successor IFOR.[61]

The significance of these disappointments for the conceptual rethinking in Holland may have been limited, but it was important in dispelling the myth that the Netherlands is much more than a small country. It also pointed to a tradition of self-delusion in the Netherlands as to its international influence and the level of international support for its ideas, just as Black Monday had done before. It is worth quoting Scheffer again at greater length, because in his essay he has deconstructed perceptively the *problematique* of Dutch foreign policy after 1989–91:

> We cannot escape the unpleasant question of what is the greater risk in Europe: a strong revival of national particularities or a form of political co-operation in which power disparities will remain palpable … Inasmuch as the Netherlands has anything to choose, the choice is not between a Europe on its way to a federation or else nothing at all, but rather between a hesitatingly co-operating Europe or a Europe of impassioned rivalries.[62]

> The Netherlands can either co-operate actively in a mild form of a directorate of the middle powers inside the EC or it will contribute, unwillingly, to the fact that an overstrained ideal of equality will lead to a raw form of directorate outside the EC, or worse that an 'Alleingang' of the UK, France and Germany is provoked.[63]

This conclusion may be slightly exaggerated, but it does seem true that Dutch foreign policy will, to an ever decreasing extent, be characterized by open policy options and more and more by dilemmas, by choices between two evils. This point was, among others, also made by the so-called Scientific Council for Government Policy in its study 'Stability and Security in Europe', to which a great number of Dutch and some foreign specialists made specific contributions.[64] This report together with a rather broad public discussion with numerous contributions from a great variety of authors formed the background of the official review of Holland's foreign policy that had been initiated by the new coalition government that took office in summer 1994.[65]

3. The official review of Dutch foreign policy: much ado about nothing?

In its government programme the so-called 'purple' coalition, the first Dutch government since 1917 formed without the participation of the Christian Democrats, made it clear that within the three traditional orientations of Dutch foreign policy (the Atlanticist, the globalist and the Europeanist) the last would get the greatest emphasis. 'Without neglecting old ties, the Netherlands will concentrate on its position within Europe and on the realization of an enlarged EU in which it can play its own role.'[66] Behind these rather noncommittal phrases lay an important shift, through which the government took over, albeit somewhat slowly and hesitantly, outside pleas for a reorientation towards the European continent. In autumn 1994, during the annual parliamentary debate on foreign policy, the new Minister of Foreign Affairs, Hans van Mierlo, clearly indicated that he had realized the extent of changes that had taken place in Europe after 1989. His words echoed concerns and conclusions that had been voiced by others before. 'The centrifugal forces that opened out in 1989 have not left the multilateral institutions, on which our position was based to a very great extent, unaffected. In a Europe without blocs, we are thrown back at our own power and our own size. And in the open political market, own power and own size prevail more and more.' After referring to the changed roles of several relevant actors, most importantly Germany and the USA, he concluded that 'under these conditions, a more continent-friendly orientation of our country was and is logical.'[67]

His assertion that 'a smooth and effective multilateral consultation machine' is a requirement in itself, but that 'it can also help prevent the big countries from managing important affairs among themselves, outside the multilateral fora' was revealing in two respects. It brought the accumulated irritation of being excluded from policymaking bodies such as the Contact Group on Yugoslavia to the surface, which had made the Srebrenica debacle – when the Dutch rightly felt they had been left in an untenable position by their more powerful partners – all the more painful. But it was at the same time a realization that Scheffer's scenario, although overly negative, was not entirely wrong. And even more important was the acceptance by the government that the Netherlands would have to pay a price to forestall this danger.

The Advisory Council had argued along similar lines, in its report for the 1996 IGC. Among a host of more detailed comments and recommendations, the main thrust of the report was that a greater role for coalitions of the willing, able to operate within the institutional framework of a more effective CFSP, was required. In this context it explicitly referred to the larger member states. At the same time these countries were then expected to develop this CFSP within the EU, and no longer in *ad hoc* groups outside the Union. In order to enhance the effectiveness of the EU's CFSP it advocated an increased use of QMV, based on the principle of 'double majorities'. It also argued for a greater role for bigger member states in terms of the presidency of the Council of Ministers in general and the troika in particular. Similarly, the Council urged the government to think about possible future arrangements in an ever expanding union in which not every member state, and certainly not all smaller states, could have its 'own' Commissioner.[68] In short, an ever greater realization had emerged that in order to maintain and certainly to increase the EU's capacity to act, the Dutch would have to come down a peg or two in institutional terms. Moreover, an enlargement of the EU, without reforming the current decision making procedure and institutional arrangements would, as the received wisdom ran, not only lead to an unacceptable change in the fragile balance between big and small states in the EU, but it would also lead to near complete standstill and deadlock of its decision making capacity.

The official review of Dutch foreign policy had, nonetheless, not found its principal origins in a conscious realization that post-1989 Europe required a new rationale for Dutch foreign policy, but in a rather trivial budget disagreement between the Conservative VVD and the social–democratic PvdA. Essentially, the former wanted budget cuts to be found by reducing Holland's ODA, while the latter wanted to take the money from defence. An immediate decision was postponed, but the hope was expressed that a solution would be found during the review. In the 'government agreement', a fundamental policy evaluation was also announced. For a good six months nearly everyone who had anything to say on Dutch foreign policy did so in the many articles, academic and other, published in the national press and elsewhere. This wide-ranging national debate on the content of Dutch foreign policy was, as these debates often tend to be, largely unstructured and without real engagement, since most authors preferred not to deal with more thorny questions like priority formation and dilemma resolution. That said, three recurring themes were discernible:

1. The first was essentially a debate on whether Dutch freedom of manoeuvre had increased or decreased since 1989. Some argued that the new Europe, with its heightened volatility, had actually opened up possibilities for Dutch initiatives that had not existed during the cold war. As a consequence, its freedom of movement could be augmented. Others, and on balance this seemed to be the majority view, argued the opposite. For them, more volatility and a resurgence of national rivalries, especially among the bigger states, meant smaller margins for the Dutch. This was also the line taken by the Scientific Council, which had urged the government to concentrate its efforts on strengthening the 'cohesive elements' in Europe and, in terms of policy, to reduce Dutch deviations from German and French thinking as much as possible. Their reasoning seemed to be 'rather a Franco-German Europe than none at all'. Others again criticized these pleas, labelling them as 'neo-neutralism' and saying that if adopted they would effectively end Dutch foreign policy as a distinct activity and turn Holland from a satisfied nation into an invisible nation.[69]

2. Second, there was an increased awareness that Holland, as an open society, had become more vulnerable as a consequence of ever increasing global interdependence and of the erosion of international frameworks that had previously shielded and protected the Netherlands. Most commentators now agreed that more financial and political efforts were called for to maintain, and where possible strengthen, these international frameworks.

3. Finally, there was the sub-discussion on the usefulness of the concept of the 'national interest', put into the singular or plural, enlightened or not, as a guidance for policy. The leader of the VVD, Frits Bolkestein had argued in a rather populist way that Holland had been naive in the past, neglecting its financial and other interests. What was needed was no less than a change of 'culture' in its thinking about foreign policy. He urged the Dutch to fight much harder for their 'national interest'. His alarmist speech was criticized by a great number of people, his coalition partners Prime Minister Kok and van Mierlo among them. His questionable historical analogies, as well as the usefulness of the concept of national interest, were subject to severe criticism from other parties.

To a considerable extent, this public discussion was disconnected from the evolution of policy within the ministries. Early on van Mierlo had declared that 'it is a misunderstanding to expect a discussion of the content of the review. *The review is not principally about the content of policy.* It is more about an attempt to look at various international issues in their respective interconnection and where to put the accents of policy.'[70] The final outcome of the whole review saga was disappointing. Having stifled a real debate on Holland's place in Europe and the wider global setting, that is a discussion on priorities and strategies, and having resolved the initial budget disagreement in a classic 'split the difference' approach, the whole operation went out like a snuffed candle. With hindsight, the whole public discussion looks like much ado about nothing. The organizational changes that were announced, namely the establishment of integrated regional directorates, were rather non-controversial.[71] The essential governmental answer to all post-1989 problems seemed to be: more co-ordination and coherence.

What the above mentioned public discussion did reveal, however, was the end of the Euro-enthusiast national consensus. The VVD, and especially its leader Bolkestein, started to mark out some distance from the three other big political parties. It expressed its opposition to the Social Chapter of Maastricht, it emphasized its hostility towards a single core group, it argued against a communitarization of the second and the third pillar, and instead of putting greater stress on relations with Bonn, Brussels and Paris, Bolkestein emphasized the need not to isolate London and Moscow. But also in the PvdA, a lively discussion about the federal dream broke out after the publication, in September 1996, of a controversial report on the future of Dutch foreign policy. In it, the authors, after concluding that 'the classic federal idea of a United States of Europe is hardly supported by anyone anymore', argued that:

> we want to go ahead with further active integration, even if that process does not proceed according to our wishes because of the lack of truly democratic control. When faced with the choice: first more democracy, or first more effective policy, we opt for the latter. That is a practical choice. Of course, we also believe that more transparency and control is needed on the international market and European decision-making, but we cannot always wait for that.[72]

The point, however, that received most public attention was the issue of Holland's recently acquired status as a major net contributor to the EU budget. Its position as the largest *per capita* contributor attracted a considerable amount of political attention, with a developing perception, justified or not, that the Netherlands' membership of the EU is much less advantageous than in the past. This particular focus on the budgetary implications of the EU is all the more interesting since Dutch leaders had for years pledged their moral commitment to European integration, without admitting openly the incongruity of being a net beneficiary from the EC budget. The Dutch, too, had been quite happy to let the Germans pay.

Conclusion

Essentially, the story of the Dutch debate on a new European order is one of coming to terms with a (perceived) gradual reduction of Dutch influence in a widening, rougher and more volatile Europe.[73] Since the Netherlands had had it 'so good' during the cold war era, a strong reluctance to engage in a fundamental rethinking of the two core concepts that guided the Dutch through the four postwar decades, Atlanticism and European federalism, was understandable. For more than three years after 1989, the principal Dutch reaction was 'let's try to preserve what we had before'. These conservative reflexes not only sprang from a general obstinacy and aversion to fundamental rethinking that can be witnessed across Western Europe, it was also a result of the basic satisfaction with the cold war order which had served and shielded the Dutch so well. Between 1989 and 1993, the viscosity of established ways of thinking and a certain nostalgia prevailed over most attempts to adjust to, let alone anticipate, developments inside and outside Europe. The principal Dutch approach to the post-1989 world seemed to be consistent with the saying: 'I have made up my mind, don't confuse me with the facts.'

When this posture of denial became increasingly ineffective, a slow and arduous process of re-evaluation and adaptation of key concepts became unavoidable. Characteristically, outside commentators and observers would point to the impossibility of maintaining the two orthodoxies in a drastically changed world, and would argue for certain specific changes at both the strategic and the tactical level. Later on, some of these recommendations would find their echo in new governmental declarations and white papers. It should be stressed that, as stated as one of the hypotheses in the introduction, whatever debate there was, it was a primarily domestic one, with only occasional participation of foreign observers and specialists.

In the second phase after 1993, a slow process of disillusionment led to a reassessment of principles that had previously been perceived as sacrosanct. It involved, as we have seen, a strategic choice for Europe, a greater orientation on Germany and an enhanced political investment in bilateral ties with the near-abroad, the Benelux especially. Moving gradually towards the acknowledgement that Holland is a small country – although quite a bit of 'status ambivalence' remained and will endure for some time to come – the government declared that it would concentrate its efforts on the expansion of the EU's internal and external capacity to act. Ministers realized that increasingly Holland would not have the luxury of several policy options, but that given a choice between two unattractive options, it could only choose the lesser evil. It does seem likely that the Dutch will have to get used more and more to policy defeats or situations in which real power disparities will prevail over the desired legal equality of the treaties.

In some respects, the first seven years after the end of the cold war led to a decline in what could be called the 'foreign policy distinctiveness' with which, for a variety of reasons, smaller states with a history of a very active and visible foreign policy, like Holland and Sweden, have had to struggle. In a sense, they were forced to accept a certain 'marginalization' process in Europe, having to find their place in a European order that was opening to the east and the south. The response of the idealist tradition in Dutch foreign policy has been to argue that the future of Dutch foreign policy should lie, thematically, in the so-called 'soft sector' (human rights, environmental issues and so on), and geographically, in the extra-European arena.[74] This could also be combined with a certain aloofness and resignation inside the EU, since the freedom of manoeuvre for Holland in that respect has become significantly reduced. On the other hand, realists have argued that such an 'escapist' move would cause grave harm to vital Dutch interests and that it would represent a negation of the forces underlying the painful adaptation process that Dutch foreign policy had undergone since 1989.

From the perspective of the summer of 1997 two additional conclusions had emerged. First, the high tide of European federalism was over. There had been a gradual disenchantment in Holland with the federalist agenda. The day after the Amsterdam summit, the editorial in the *Independent* rightly stated that 'we are all Eurosceptics now'.[75] In a sense the meagre results of Amsterdam allowed the Dutch, just as it allowed everybody else, to postpone a decision on whether they were really willing and prepared to make the Great Leap forward to a European federation.

Second, the latter half of the 1990s showed a reduction in the strategic centrality and dominance of the Franco-German axis, a development that found its confirmation at Amsterdam. The choice was no longer between a Franco-German Europe or else nothing at all; hence the pleas for a greater orientation on that now less effective axis lost some of their appeal and urgency. This in effect removed one of the dilemmas that the Dutch government had had to struggle with over the past seven years. No matter how logical and reasonable the arguments were that Brands and others used for a greater orientation on the Franco-German axis, the truth was that all attempts at a rapprochement with the Parisian side of that axis had been singularly unsuccessful. The differences in fundamental policy assumptions and preferences simply seem too great to overcome, whether it regards EMU, Bosnia, Iraq, NATO reform and enlargement, or the 1996 war of words between Paris and The Hague on drugs.

The change of government in London in May 1997 opened up interesting new possibilities for the Dutch. Despite a lot of continuity, 'pragmatic' New Labour seemed less gripped by an ideologically and emotionally motivated 'fear and loathing' attitude than the previous Conservative government. From the Dutch perspective, Britain had become a player again. The problem was, of course, that this British government had nevertheless excluded itself from Europe's commanding project: EMU. In that respect, the Dutch would have to come to terms, at least for the time being, with a Franco-German dominated EMU Europe. In all likelihood, the Dutch government will want to hedge its bets, and both cultivate the potential of a shared British–Dutch agenda and come to terms, meanwhile with Franco-German hegemony. Not having to choose is after all often the most appealing option for politicians.[76]

Notes

1. Cited in P.E. Tetlock 'Learning in US and Soviet Foreign Policy: in search for an elusive concept' in: G.W. Breslauer and P.E. Tetlock (eds), *Learning in US and Soviet Foreign Policy* (Boulder, CO: Westview Press, 1991) p. 38.
2. In this chapter I will use the terms 'the Netherlands' and 'Holland' interchangeably, although I am quite aware that to do so is, in fact, inaccurate. Moreover, I will deal mainly with Dutch attitudes concerning European order, which leaves out very important parts of Dutch foreign policy. The global side of Dutch foreign policy is expressed in an active Dutch role in the UN and its functional organisations, the relatively great importance attached to human rights issues – albeit far from superseding other, mainly economic, considerations, as well as in the significant resources dedicated to overseas development aid. The annual amount of money spent on development aid is US $3.6 billion, which is more, both in absolute and relative terms, than, for example, the United Kingdom.
3. Paul Scheffer makes this point in one of the best essays written on Dutch foreign policy after the end of the cold war entitled 'Nederland in een gebroken rechtsorde' in a book of essays collected by the Atlantic Commission in The Hague: L. Sprangers, A. van Staden and A. Venema (eds), *Een continent op drift. Over de veiligheid van Europa* (Amsterdam: G.A. van Oorschot, 1994), p. 202.
4. See A. van Staden, *Een trouwe bondgenoot. Nederland en het Atlantisch Bondgenootschap* (Baarn: Anthos, 1974). Van Staden has characterized the Dutch adoption of the two orthodoxies as a typical 'small state strategy', since both the Atlanticist and the European federalist line of thinking were expected – rightly or wrongly – to function as a 'level off' mechanism of the power disparities in Europe. See his 'Small State Strategies in Alliances, the Case of the Netherlands', *Cooperation and Conflict*, 30:1, 1995.
5. These two examples are taken from R.T. Griffiths (ed.), *The Netherlands and the Integration of Europe 1945–1957* (Amsterdam: NEHA, 1990), quoted in Scheffer, 1995, op. cit., pp. 52–3. To these examples another could be added, which is that Holland has also successfully blocked any attempts at giving the EC a significant role in the energy sector.
6. The official rationalization was that if the Netherlands was forced to accept an intergovernmentally structured EC, then there would no longer be a reason to keep the United Kingdom out.
7. See M. Kwast van Duursen's essay 'Nederland en een federaal Europa: kleine landen politiek of ideaal van beleid?' This essay was published in one of the first serious studies into the consequences of 1989 for Dutch foreign policy: Ph.P. Everts (ed.), *Nederland in een veranderende wereld. De toekomst van het buitenlands beleid* (Assen: Van Gorcum, 1991) pp. 60–78.
8. P. Scheffer, *Machtsverschil en rechtsgelijkheid in de Europese Unie* (Werkdocumenten, Wetenschappelijke Raad voor het Regeringsbeleid, Den Haag, June 1995) p. 10.
9. B. Knapen, *Nederland en omstreken. Opstellen over desoriëntatie en democratie*, (Amsterdam: Prometheus, 1995).
10. A.F. Manning, 'De buitenlandse politiek en internationale positie', in P. Luykx and N. Bootsma (eds), *De laatste tijd. Geschiedschrijving over Nederland in de 20e eeuw* (Utrecht: Agon, 1988) p. 289.
11. It is perhaps worth noting that the English word 'review' does not quite match the rather grandiose expectations that the Dutch word 'herijking' implies. But 'review' is the official English translation, 're-evaluation' is the French, and

'Neubestimmung' the German translation. Those two reflect better the more ambitious plans that many had hoped for, or had considered necessary, and that the Dutch term 'herijking' had suggested.

12. Robert Nisbet is cited in J.A. Rosati, 'Cycles in Foreign Policy Restructuring: the Politics of Continuity and Change in US foreign policy', in J.A. Rosati, J.D. Hagan and M.W. Sampson (eds), *Foreign Policy Restructuring: How Governments Respond to Global Change* (Columbia, SC: University of South Carolina Press, 1994) p. 226.

13. See among others H. Teltschik, *329 Tage, Innenansichten der Einigung* (Berlin: Siedler, 1991). This opposition put a great strain on the relations between Kohl and Lubbers and is generally considered to have induced the former to veto Lubbers' candidacy for the Commission's Presidency after the departure of Delors.

14. Interview with the Dutch ambassador in Bonn between 1986–1991, J. Van der Tas, The Hague, 7 September 1995.

15. *De voltooiing van de interne markt, brief van de minister en staatssecretaris van buitenlandse zaken,* Tweede Kamer der Staten Generaal (Second Chamber of Parliament), Vergaderjaar 1989–90, 6 June 1990, 20 596, no. 26, pp. 2 and 5.

16. *Ibid.*, pp. 4 and 5.

17. *Ibid.*, p. 12.

18. *Ibid.*, p. 14.

19. *Ibid.*, p. 10.

20. Scheffer, 1994, op. cit., p. 203.

21. *De Nederlandse standpuntbepaling ten aanzien van de Europese Politieke Unie, brief van de minister en de staatssecretaris van buitenlandse zaken,* Tweede Kamer der Staten Generaal (Second Chamber of Parliament), Vergaderjaar 1990–91, 26 October 1990, 20 596, no. 32, p. 32.

22. *Ibid.*, pp. 4–5.

23. *Ibid.*, pp. 3–4.

24. The Dutch government justified its rejection of the Luxembourg proposals on CFSP by invoking its classical objections to anything short of full communautarisation: '... decision-making by qualified majority is introduced in what remains a purely intergovernmental form of co-operation ... it has been crucial [for the Dutch government] to search for a fair balance between the upholding of the transatlantic relationship and the further development of the European integration in a federal direction', *Europese Politieke Unie: een bestandsopname, brief van de minister en staatssecretaris van buitenlandse zaken,* Tweede Kamer der Staten Generaal (Second Chamber of Parliament), Vergaderjaar 1990–91, 14 May 1991, 21 952, no. 19, pp. 3–4.

25. *Notitie aan de Tweede Kamer inzake EPU, WEU en NAVO, brief van de ministers van buitenlandse zaken en defensie,* Tweede Kamer der Staten Generaal (Second Chamber of Parliament), Vergaderjaar 1990-91, 22 May 1991, 21 952, no. 20, p. 5.

26. *Ibid.*, p. 6.

27. *Ibid.*, p. 10.

28. Scheffer, 1994, op. cit., pp. 222–3.

29. This is the dominant view. For an alternative view: S. Rozemond, 'Met de rug naar het continent', *Internationale Spectator*, 48:12, December 1994, pp. 588–9.

30. For any deal in Europe full support of at least two of the larger member-states is necessary. But the federal character of the Dutch proposal was, of course, in direct conflict with long-standing British and French institutional preferences. In addition, the emphasis put on maintaining NATO supremacy in security affairs was, predictably, rejected by France. No proposal that, in fundamental respects,

goes against the wishes of two leading EC-members will ever be accepted, and that should have been clear from the start. However, there is also a domestic side to this story. Due to prolonged interdepartmental co-ordination in Holland over the summer, the draft EPU-proposal was made available at a very late stage, which left very little time (too little as it turned out) to gather the necessary international support. This problem was worsened by the absence of effective political co-ordination: Prime Minister Lubbers was busy defusing a political crisis linked to the restructuring of certain welfare provisions, van den Broek was engaged in the quagmire of former Yugoslavia, which gave the committed federalist Dankert (state secretary for European affairs) more or less a free hand. In any case, clear warnings from the Dutch permanent represenation in Brussels that adequate support from other governments was lacking, were ignored by all, which eventually proved to be fatal.

31. This point was made in an interview with the editor in chief of *NRC/Handelsblad*, Dr Ben Knapen, 8 January 1996.
32. Scheffer, 1994, op. cit., p. 206.
33. *Europese Politieke Unie en Economische en Monetaire Unie, verslag van een mondeling overleg*, Tweede Kamer der Staten Generaal (Second Chamber of Parliament), Vergaderjaar 1991–92, 21 952, no. 39, p. 9.
34. See Ph.P. Everts, 'Academic experts as foreign policy advisers: The function of government advisory councils in the Netherlands' in M. Girard, W. Eberwein, and K. Webb, (eds), *Theory and Practice in Foreign Policymaking: National Perspectives on Academics and Professionals in International Relations* (London: Pinter, 1994).
35. M.C. Brands, 'Vanuit de luwte in de drup, noodzaak van een beweeglijker Nederlands buitenlands beleid na de revolutie van 1989', *Internationale Spectator*, 47, January 1993, p. 12.
36. Brands, op. cit., 1993, p. 7.
37. B. van den Bos, 'De noodzaak van een Europese verankering. Waarom Nederland het moeilijk krijgt in Europa', *Internationale Spectator*, 47, January 1993, pp. 13–17.
38. Van den Bos, op. cit., 1993, p. 16.
39. Brands, op. cit., 1993, p. 11.
40. It is somewhat ironic that van den Broek, the Atlanticist *pur sang*, took up the position of Commissioner responsible for external relations of the EU. In some respects he was going to prepare and implement policies that he as a minister had always believed should have been the exclusive competence of NATO!
41. Critics of Partnership for Peace claimed that its acronym, PfP, stood in fact for Postponement of Policy.
42. See Ben Knapen's excellent article on Anglo-Dutch relations, 'Het is tijd dat de mist in het Kanaal optrekt', *NRC/Handelsblad*, 12 November 1994.
43. H. Beunders and H. Selier, *Argwaan en profijt. Nederland en West-Duitsland 1945–1981*, (Amsterdam: Universiteit van Amsterdam, 1983) and F. Wielenga, *West-Duitsland: partner uit noodzaak. Nederland en de Bondsrepubliek 1949–1955* (Utrecht: Het Spectrum, 1989).
44. A good illustration of the reflexive impulses on the part of Holland's foreign policy elite always to consult and seek approval by the Americans could be witnessed when a proposal that was made in The Hague for further co-operation in the Caribbean area was sent to the Dutch embassies of that region. One ambassador gave a very quick reply. Strikingly, he did not analyze the pros and cons of the proposal at all, nor did he give his personal view. The telegram contained just one line: 'Does Washington know about this?'. Anecdote taken from Ph. P. Everts,

'Weet Washington hiervan?' Onderzoek naar de internationale involved van Nederland in: H.J.M. Claessen (ed.), *De chaos getemd* (Rijksuniversiteit Leiden: Faculteit der Sociale Wetenschappen, 1991) p. 63.
45. Adviesraad Vrede en Veligheid, *Duitsland als partner*, Den Haag, March 1994.
46. This has now resulted in a Königswinter-style conference where Dutch and German politicians, officials, commentators and businesspeople meet to discuss a whole range of European issues.
47. Knapen, op. cit., 1995.
48. That Belgium has suffered much more at German hands – it had been invaded twice this century, whereas the Netherlands was not, due to its neutrality in the First World War – but does not seem to have developed similar hang ups only proves by how little serious drama the Netherlands had been struck by in the last few centuries, and hence how satisfied it had been. More generally, it seems true to say that the fewer commemoration events are organized in a country, the happier and more at ease with itself and its past, that country is.
49. Lubbers in *NRC/Handelsbad*, 1 July 1994. The quibble he made in Dutch does not work in English unfortunately. But since the play upon words is possible in German I have put those two words 'deutsch land' in German.
50. See for instance the Annexe 3 to the Advisory Council's report *Germany as Partner*: Ph. P. Everts, 'Meningen in Nederland over Duitsland'.
51. As is pointed out by A. Pijpers, 'The Netherlands: the weakening pull of Atlanticism', in C. Hill (ed.), *The Actors in Europe's Foreign Policy* (London: Routledge, 1996) p. 260.
52. R. Lubbers, 'Europa's akkers liggen open', *NRC/Handelsblad*, 2 August 1990.
53. Strikingly, pleas for both, mutually exclusive strategies were coming from Maarten Brands, who has argued for both the increased usage of variable coalitions and a strategic choice for Bonn and the Franco-German axis. See Brands, op. cit.,1993 and his 1995 article ' "Rauwe" of "gekookte" integratie van Europa. Stabiliteit en veiligheid en de EU-Kerngroep', *International Spectator*, 49:9, September 1995, pp. 441–7.
54. This is of course a classic discussion, comparable to the one about the merits of the close alignment of the Netherlands with the USA, and to a lesser degree with the UK, during the cold war. The ultimate judgement of whether such a strategy is worthwhile depends on the – largely subjective and arbitrary – estimate of costs and benefits that such a strategic choice entails.
55. Lubbers, op. cit., 1990. It is quite remarkable how a pragmatically oriented, Christian Democratic politician like Lubbers could have such poor working relations with fellow Christian democrat Kohl and such excellent contacts with Thatcher, who in turn made no secret of her appreciation and liking of Lubbers. These largely dormant feelings of affinity and aversion came to the surface at that moment of truth when in the autumn of 1989 the prospects of speedy German unification were realized. Not entirely surprisingly Thatcher and Lubbers were among the most vocal critics of Kohl. But also more generally speaking, it seems true that Lubbers was very keen on keeping the British 'in'. It was partly at his insistence at the Maastricht summit that the two British opt-outs were proposed.
56. Scheffer, op. cit., 1994, p. 204.
57. Policymakers took care, however, not to advertise this renaissance of the Benelux too much. It was feared, with some justification, that if the three would act jointly too overtly, they would be perceived too much as one entity by the larger states, which could then lead to demands from those countries to allocate, for example just one Commissioner to the three Benelux countries.

58. As is pointed out in Scheffer, op. cit., 1995, p. 41.
59. *Memorandum on institutional reform of the European Union*, The Hague, July 1995.
60. *Memorandum en vue de la CIG*, Brussels, 8 May 1996.
61. This 'long list of failures' seemed to have come to an end in 1996 with the successful candidature of W. Duisenberg, long time president of Holland's central bank, to succeed Mr Lamfalussy as president of the European Monetary Institute in Frankfurt, the precursor to the European Central Bank of EMU.
62. Scheffer, op. cit., 1994, p. 223
63. Scheffer, op. cit., 1994, p. 226
64. Wetenschappelijke Raad voor het Regeringsbeleid, *Stabiliteit en veiligheid in Europa. Het veranderende krachtenveld voor het buitenlands beleid*, Den Haag, 1995. One of the editors of the volume, William Wallace, participated (with Helen Wallace) in this study, which also included two French participants and one German (Christoph Bertram, from *Die Zeit*).
65. The new government was called 'purple' because that is the colour one gets when one blends the three respective colours of the three parties, red (PvdA: social-democrats), blue (VVD: liberal conservatives) and green (D66: left liberals).
66. *Regeerakkoord*, Den Haag, August 1994.
67. Van Mierlo, Tweede Kamer, 30 November 1994, 29–1830, p. 5.
68. Advisory Council on Peace and Security, *Een nieuwe uitdaging-Europa 1996*, The Hague, May 1995.
69. See J. Rood, 'Het neo-neutralisme van de WRR' *Internationale Spectator*, 49:9, September 1995, pp. 447–52.
70. Van Mierlo in *De Volkskrant*, 13 March 1995 (emphasis added).
71. Before the official review, the Foreign Office had two types of regional directorates: the 'political' ones that dealt with 'traditional' diplomatic issues and which fell under the Directorate General Political Affairs (DGPZ) and those that belonged to the Directorate General International Co-operation (DGIS), which were responsible for Holland's ODA. In addition, the Economics Ministry, which is responsible for foreign economic relations, also had regional directorates. Now, all these different regional directorates are put together to facilitate co-ordination at all levels of policymaking, implementation and evaluation.
72. *Het buitenland van de PvdA. Voorbij de waterlinie* (Den Haag: Partij van de Arbeid, September 1996) p. 8.
73. It is worth noting that in the Dutch debate the status of the Netherlands is measured mostly in the number of Dutch citizens on influential posts in various international organizations, and nearly all those who claim that Dutch influence has diminished refer to the glorious days of the 1950s to support their claim.
74. See for instance P.R. Baehr, 'De "zachte sector" in het buitenlands beleid: een afweging van prioriteiten', in Ph.P. Everts, 1991, op. cit., pp. 78–92.
75. *The Independent*, 19 June 1998.
76. I have developed this theme in more detail in 'New Labour, New Britain, New Europe? De eerste honderd dagen van de nieuwe Britse regering', *Internationale Spectator*, 51:9, September 1997, pp. 495–501.

7
An End to Neutrality? Continuity and Change in Swedish Foreign Policy

Lisbeth Aggestam

Introduction

With the fall of the Berlin Wall, the perceived certainty and predictability of 'us' and 'them' – 'east' and 'west' started to crumble. For Sweden, whose identity in the international arena has largely been fashioned around a policy of 'non-alignment in peace and neutrality in war', the end of the cold war challenged a deeply held belief system. It initiated a debate about the *rationale* of pursuing a policy of neutrality in a Europe no longer characterized by bipolarity.

This chapter aims to explore how the end of the cold war has been perceived in Sweden, and the way in which it influenced a major re-orientation of Swedish foreign policy – that of becoming a member of the European Union. From an academic point of view, the analysis of Swedish responses to the end of the cold war raises the wider theoretical question of how international structural changes affect and are perceived by a small state.

The chapter emphasizes the ideational dimension of foreign policy. It highlights how identity and political beliefs shape the way in which new information and situations are interpreted and defined. As Boulding pointed out many years ago, '[i]t is what we think the world is like, not what it is really like, that determines our behavior.'[1] Continuity and change in Swedish foreign policy will be explored through a focus on the meanings attributed to neutrality and non-alignment in post-cold war Europe.

'The roots of Swedish neutrality'

Few analysts would argue against the view that the policy of neutrality has had a profound impact on Swedish foreign policy. This chapter therefore starts with a brief historical exposé of how Swedish foreign and security policy has been informed by the *dictum* of non-alignment in peace and a declared ambition to remain neutral in the event of war. As a prominent interpreter of Swedish foreign policy has stated, '[t]he collective experience of a nation cannot be defined with certainty, but anyone who wishes to understand current Swedish foreign policy ought not to be ignorant of the roots of Swedish neutrality'.[2]

The roots of Swedish neutrality date back to the early 19th century. It is not uncommon, even today, to find arguments in the political discourse that stress the fact that Sweden has not been involved in any military wars since the Congress of Vienna (a frequent argument, for example, in the referendum on EU membership in 1994). As the foreign minister, Östen Undén, declared shortly after the Second World War:

> The fact that Sweden has been able to remain at peace for 135 years has undoubtedly had a strong psychological effect on the attitude of the Swedish public towards the problem of security. During this long period Europe has been shaken by mighty conflicts but our country has never become involved. Whatever the explanation may be for our avoidance of war, our people cannot easily be convinced that their security now requires the abandonment of neutrality as an ineffective and out-of-date policy.[3]

Sweden's policy of neutrality has never been specified in any international agreements or treaties (unlike, for example, Austrian and Swiss neutrality) and is thus 'self-imposed'. The precise interpretation and understanding of neutrality has been the preserve of the Swedish foreign policy élite, particularly the ministry of foreign affairs. In the postwar period, Swedish neutrality was understood in a significantly different way from other periods, as it was closely moulded to the conditions of bipolarity and the Europe of Yalta.

Apart from a brief flirtation with thoughts of a Scandinavian defence alliance in 1948–49,[4] Swedish postwar foreign policy appears to have been influenced by the combination of two schools of thought: small state realism, and liberal internationalism. After the Second World War, small state realism was expressed through a preoccupation with 'national survival'. Modernity and neutrality evolved as two essential components of a Swedish postwar identity.[5] Self-conceptions relating to modernity were expressed in terms of the 'Swedish progressive model' (a corporate economic system). The means by which to safeguard Swedish sovereignty was the pursuit of a policy of neutrality, as 'an instrument by which the state sought to remain outside any armed confrontation in its vicinity'.[6] A substantial territorial army (based on conscription) should ensure that any transgression of Swedish territory would inflict serious costs on the aggressor. In peacetime, Swedish non-alignment was thought to contribute to stability and confidence-building between the blocs in the strategically sensitive northern flank of Europe.[7]

Swedish foreign and security policy should therefore stay clear of any formal commitments and alignments that could compromise Swedish independence and freedom of action. This position excluded Swedish membership of the

European Community. In a landmark speech of 1961, the Swedish Prime Minister, Tage Erlander, declared that Swedish membership in the EC was not compatible with a credible policy of non-alignment.[8] This became official policy for the following three decades. The supranational character of the EC, particularly the common trade policy and (from the 1970s) the evolving foreign policy cooperation (EPC), excluded economic integration which in any way had undertones of political integration.[9] Thus, West European economic co-operation was sought through a free trade agreement with the EC and through the explicitly intergovernmental framework of EFTA, from 1960. This was considered compatible with a policy of neutrality.

EC membership was not a partisan political issue. In 1971, the Swedish Parliament passed a resolution with an overwhelming majority rejecting the prospect of Swedish EC membership. While, on the right, the Moderate (conservative) party and the Liberals were generally more positively inclined towards EC membership, the Centre (agrarian) party and the Communists were influenced by traditions of outright hostility to membership. The Social Democratic party contained both pro- and contra-EC factions. However, in discussions of EC membership and the policy of neutrality, the Social Democratic party tended to view itself as the 'protector against potential deviations to the left or right'.[10]

Nordic co-operation, on the other hand, enjoyed great support and legitimacy throughout the postwar period, based as it was on explicitly intergovernmental institutions such as the Nordic Council and the Nordic Council of Ministers. The Nordic countries developed a loose form of union characterized by a free movement of labour, a set of common social conventions and passport freedom. However, on the question of how to safeguard their own security, the Nordic states diverged. Denmark, Iceland and Norway chose NATO membership, while Finland and Sweden chose the course of non-alignment. Yet, in response to the superpower confrontation during the cold war, the impetus was created to attempt to act as a unit by co-ordinating their foreign policies in international fora, such as the UN, the CSCE and the Council of Europe. In the Nordic region itself, they shared an interest in attempting to delimit the influence of the superpowers by making *Norden* a low tension area – what used to be called the 'Nordic balance'.[11]

Some analysts have suggested that the attempt to articulate a credible Swedish neutrality policy soon became a goal in itself, rather than simply an instrument of Swedish security policy.[12] A 'security culture' evolved, characterized by an increasingly closed belief system. Over a number of years, the policy of neutrality became institutionalized and legitimized by a broad political consensus, both across the parties and throughout the wider public. Conducive to this development was the consensual political model characteristic of Nordic parliamentary democracies, particularly in foreign affairs.

Against this strictly formulated policy of neutrality, however, it should be reiterated that Swedish neutrality is self-defined and has thus, at times, exhibited a certain pragmatism. In 1994, a commission reviewing the Swedish policy of neutrality in the 1950s and 1960s revealed how, unknown to the Swedish public, extensive contacts had developed with NATO. Neutrality in conflict and war in Sweden's vicinity remained the primary goal, yet, if attacked, preventive measures with NATO had been negotiated.[13]

Nonetheless, it could be argued that neutrality became a cornerstone in the postwar 'ideology' of Swedish foreign policy.[14] As Northedge has stated, ideology may promote greater political cohesion within a state by providing 'a scale of values by which its people may know what to strive for and what to repudiate', but more importantly, it tends to work as a filter or 'prism through which states perceive the international realities on which their foreign policy must work'.[15] With such a degree of internalization, the concept of neutrality became increasingly merged with the political culture of Swedish foreign policy.[16]

However, the policy of neutrality did not mean that the Swedish government pursued a foreign policy of 'splendid isolation'. From the 1960s onwards, an active foreign policy with strong tenets of liberal internationalism was pursued, particularly through the United Nations framework. Sweden was for a long time a substantial contributor of international development aid in an effort to improve social and economic equality in the international system; actively involved in UN peacekeeping; and worked particularly intensively in supporting small states in the international system. This idealistic dimension of foreign policy was oriented on extra-European issues, apart from the support of confidence-building and disarmament within the 'UN of Europe' – the CSCE.[17]

Swedish democracy since the Second World War has been highly consensual, with an educated electorate committed to the superiority of the 'Swedish model' both in domestic and in foreign policy. Changes in policy have largely been incremental, with political leaders recognizing the need to carry public sentiment with them. The definition and redefinition of foreign policy remained very largely the responsibility of political leaders in government. The small outside community of International Relations experts, including Stockholm's small international institutes, had focused more on global than on European issues, let alone Swedish foreign policy. 'The typical Swedish' International Relations scholar, Bertil Nygren remarked from a survey at the end of the 1980s, 'is a passively and leisurely interested observer of world affairs.'[18] Neither parliamentarians nor parties sought outside advice, or sought to question the assumptions of foreign policy. Policy planning, together with such reformulation of concepts as might from time to time be thought desirable, therefore remained firmly in the hands of ministers and officials – of the governing élite.

Continuity and change

In theories on the foreign policy of small states, there is an implicit or explicit assumption that small states are sensitive and adaptive to changes in international structures.[19] In addition, academic research on cognition indicates that (i) in times of great transformation, such as the end of the cold war, it is reasonable to assume that changes in the international environment may bring a certain 'cognitive dissonance' to foreign policy perceptions and beliefs. However, it is also suggested that (ii) beliefs are inherently stable and that new information tends to be interpreted and adopted in view of pre-existing beliefs.[20]

This section seeks to explore the spectrum between the two poles of foreign policy: continuity and change. When the superpower confrontation changed towards *détente* and the transformations in eastern Europe gathered speed, the question about the costs and benefits of pursuing a policy of neutrality became more pressing in Sweden. Swedish responses to the end of the cold war revolve around the redefinition of a number of key concepts closely interlinked with neutrality, such as sovereignty, identity and security. But they were also influenced by the parallel debate over Swedish economic development. Swedish companies during the 1980s had become more and more convinced that they needed to operate within an integrated European market in order to gain the economies of scale to cope with global competition and technological change. Per Gyllenhammar, one of Sweden's leading industrialists, had been a moving spirit in establishing the European Round Table of Industrialists to press for Community-wide deregulation. Sweden's major companies thus moved to invest inside the European single market, without the Swedish economy benefiting from a balancing flow of inward investment from foreign multinationals. Popular faith in the 'Swedish model' was also faltering, as high taxation and low growth threatened full employment. Perceptions of changing economic costs and benefits were thus entangled with perceptions of national identity and security in the Swedish post-1989 debate.

Reconceptualizing sovereignty

Throughout the cold war period, the Swedish government had to manage a balancing act between upholding a credible policy of non-alignment and the economic demands and pressures stemming from a heavy reliance on foreign exports. The idea of free trade has, therefore, strong support in Sweden due to its open and export-oriented economy.

To understand the momentum of change in Swedish policy towards Europe, it is important to trace the seeds of transformation back to the early 1980s, when the EFTA members began to negotiate a free trade area with the European Community – a European Economic Space (EES). The fundamental impetus for rethinking Swedish policy towards Europe came with the EC decision in 1985 to create a Single Market. By the end of 1987, the response was formulated in an affirmative policy paper by the Social Democratic government, emphasizing Sweden's European identity.

> Sweden is a part of Europe. That is where we are situated geographically. That is where we have our historical and cultural roots. Developments in Europe are of great importance when we draw up today's and tomorrow's policies.[21]

This paper, presented to the Swedish Riksdag (parliament), demonstrated the 'spill-over' effect of the Single Act on a non-EC member state. Yet, the framework of foreign policy co-operation between EC member states (EPC), which became treaty based with the Single European Act, prevented full consideration of Swedish EC membership.

Nonetheless, the thrust of economic integration proceeded. In 1988, the Swedish currency (*krona*) was linked to the ecu and in 1989, restrictions on free capital movements were lifted. Rethinking the basis of Swedish sovereignty and independence was closely interlinked with the way in which the Swedish economy started to decline in the late 1980s. In line with Milward's thesis of integration, the Swedish government appeared to seek closer co-operation in Europe as a way to satisfy domestic goals and demands.[22]

In policy influential circles, the view emerged that efforts to preserve every inch of *formal* sovereignty to maintain a credible neutrality policy undermined Swedish *effective* sovereignty. A number of political scientists and economists stressed that the multi-layered development of an increasingly international-ized economy, interwoven by complex transnational relations, required a reconceptualization of sovereignty in relation to actual political influence. According to this perspective, processes of informal integration were continually debasing the state-centric view implicit in the concept of neutrality.[23]

When the EC–EFTA negotiations were initiated in 1989, on what was now called the European Economic Area (EEA), the contrasting arguments on formal and effective sovereignty became more apparent. The EEA promised Sweden important access to the Single Market, but without political influence on the decisions relating to it. Thus, a new consensus started to evolve between the élites of industry, trade unions and political parties that Sweden's extensive economic dependence on the European market had to be matched by an increase in Swedish political influence over that market through full membership of the European Community. With this view followed a more 'open' and frank questioning of the policy of neutrality.[24] In the immediate aftermath of the end of the cold war, the Social Democratic government continued to reiterate that the credibility of the policy of neutrality still prevented Sweden from applying for full EC membership.[25] However, this position became increasingly politicized. The more pro-European parties, the Liberals and Moderates, saw a 'window of opportunity' opening up for a potential full membership of the EC, as the cold war divisions in Europe started to crumble. At the time, this view enjoyed broad support from the Swedish public. Opinion polls reflected a positive view of Swedish EC membership – months in advance of any government declaration.[26]

In October 1990, Prime Minister Ingvar Carlsson set out his vision of an undivided Europe built upon an evolving new peace order. If such a new Europe emerged, he stated, it would be possible to combine Swedish EC membership with a continued neutrality policy. With this vision and the state of the Swedish economy in mind, Carlsson declared that the Swedish government had the *ambition* to join the European Community.[27] Two months later, a substantial majority of politicians in the Swedish parliament supported this declaration; and even went one step further by determining that Sweden intended to seek EC membership. Characteristic for Nordic consensual democracy, this position enjoyed the support of all political parties, except from the Left (former Communist party) and Green parties.

Thirty years after Erlander's speech, the balancing act between economic and security interests had thus tilted towards Swedish membership of the European Community. While the economic realities since the early 1980s had pushed Sweden into this direction, however, this fundamental reassessment of policy would not have been feasible without the systemic transformations underway in Europe – at least not at this pace. With the end of the cold war, beliefs about the benefits of pursuing a policy of neutrality became more open to challenge, thus encouraging new thinking on foreign policy.

Reformulating neutrality

German reunification in 1990 was widely seen in Sweden as showing that the old order had lost its stifling grip. The emergence of an economically powerful Germany at the centre of Europe and the European Community impressed Swedish policymakers. The overwhelming parliamentary support for Swedish membership of the EC must be viewed in the light of German unification and of the signing of the pan-European CSCE Charter of Paris.[28] At each stage in the process of considering EC membership, however, the security situation in the 'new Europe' was re-evaluated by the Swedish ministry of foreign affairs. Amidst the spontaneous initial euphoria of the end of the cold war, there was considerable uncertainty among Swedish foreign policymakers about the stability of the new developments in Eastern Europe, the Baltics and the Soviet Union. This did not encourage an immediate abandonment of the policy of neutrality.[29]

The legacy of neutrality seems to have been a constraining element in how Swedish policymakers perceived the new developments in Europe. In the Swedish ministry of foreign affairs – the long-standing articulator of the neutrality policy – there appeared to be a number of conflicting views of how to define and interpret neutrality at a time characterised by great flux and unpredictability.[30]

When the Soviet Union finally disintegrated and the Warsaw Pact dissolved, however, the strategic situation in Northern Europe was transformed, with a considerably reduced level of military threats and risks, allowing for a more flexible interpretation of non-alignment and neutrality. In the spring of 1991, the ministry of foreign affairs made an assessment that emphasized the *opportunities* to be grasped in the 'new Europe' rather than stressing the *risks* involved in pursuing a re-orientation of foreign policy.[31]

On the first of July 1991 – less than a year after stating the ambition – the Swedish government *formally* submitted its application for full membership in the European Community. It was, however, made clear that Sweden had no intention of abandoning its neutrality at this stage.[32]

The election which followed in autumn 1991 brought a new centre-right coalition government to power, with Carl Bildt (of the Moderate party) as prime minister. This change of government allowed for a somewhat different emphasis in Swedish foreign and security policy. Carl Bildt introduced a more restrictive formulation of neutrality, by characterizing the parameters of Swedish foreign policy in terms of 'military non-alignment combined with a European identity'.[33] Non-alignment, he argued, should be interpreted as denoting the military hard core of Swedish defence policy. Sweden would continue to take full responsibility of its own defence.

The policy of non-alignment represents a strong element of continuity in Swedish foreign policy. In early 1992, however, Carl Bildt indicated on a number of occasions that he considered 'neutrality' an obsolete term in post-cold war Europe.[34] This gave rise to criticism from other parties, particularly from Social Democrats, who emphasized the continued relevance of the policy of neutrality until such time that genuine common security was achieved in a pan-European peace order.[35] In spring 1992, a compromise was reached between the political parties (except the Left party) which again restated the policy of non-alignment, but also underlined Swedish active involvement in European security co-operation. The credibility of Swedish neutrality in the event of war was weakened by the statement that Sweden would only *attempt* to stay neutral in a European conflict.[36]

This modified line of policy continued to be further qualified in the course of the European Commission's scrutiny of the Swedish membership application (which indicated that Swedish neutrality could raise difficulties). Thus, any lingering notions of the traditional neutrality *dictum* was deleted in the government declaration of October 1992 which only stated that 'Sweden stands outside of military alliances'.[37] While the reformulation of neutrality was a response to the end of the cold war, the pace at which it was done was thus heavily influenced by the fact that Sweden was about to start its membership negotiations with the European Union. Economic interests and the redefinition of security policy were thus closely linked. The end of the cold war had, for most Swedes, lessened the political obstacles to full EU membership. Perceptions of economic vulnerability increased the attractions of EU membership. But popular acceptability of EU membership depended on successful reformulation of the Swedish consensus on non-alignment as the underlying principle of foreign policy.

Foreign policy with a European identity

The government under the stewardship of Bildt set out with the aim of redefining Swedish foreign policy with a 'European identity'. According to Bildt, the fundamental transformation of European security and the evolving processes of European integration presented Sweden with opportunities to become involved in an unprecedented way with its European neighbours.[38] While the precise definition of a European identity was left unclear, it symbolized the priority attributed to carving out an active role for Sweden in the evolving security structure of post-cold war Europe. Furthermore, this emphasis on a European identity was intended to signal a re-orientation of Swedish foreign policy towards Brussels – and indeed, it was noted in the EC Commission opinion on Swedish membership.[39]

Sweden, according to this reformulation, should actively participate in efforts to reunite Europe through diplomatic and economics means, for example in the Baltic republics, but also militarily by participating in the Nordic UN battalion in Bosnia. The view evolved in the higher echelons of the ministry of foreign affairs, that a policy of neutrality had become 'an irrelevant and misleading label'.[40] Sweden should aim to become enmeshed in the European integration process, with a clear European identity attached to its foreign policy. Neutrality should thus only be seen as a security option.[41]

This European reorientation of Swedish foreign policy seemed to resonate with public opinion at the time. Opinion surveys in 1992 indicated that the Swedish public had also moved towards the view that Swedish foreign policy should mainly be concerned with its more immediate external environment, such as the Nordic region and Europe.[42] On the more specific issue of EC membership, however, the enthusiasm of the early 1990s declined when the conflict broke out in Bosnia and the Maastricht referenda in Denmark and France proved so contentious.

In the Swedish referendum on EU membership, in autumn 1994, the Left and Green parties opposed Swedish membership, while the other political parties, with varying degrees of enthusiasm, supported Ja/Yes (the Social Democrats, the Centre party, and the Christian Democrats contained substantial numbers of Eurosceptics within their parties).

Swedish politicians and policymakers deliberately played down the security implications of EU membership, except for stressing that the EU represented the best platform for the maintenance of peace in Europe. The main arguments proposed in favour of membership were socioeconomic, while the consequences of joining a Union with a treaty article (J.4.) stipulating the 'eventual framing of a common defence policy, which might lead to a common defence' were less discussed.[43] Neither was there a thorough debate on the consequences of the *acquis politique* and the *finalités politiques*, which the European Minister, Ulf Dinkelspiel, signed up to on behalf of the Swedish government in February 1993.[44]

Champions of the EU stressed that membership did not involve hard core defence issues, but only the more limited, intergovernmental foreign policy co-operation on wider international dimensions of security.[45] The EU-sceptics contended that membership was incompatible with Swedish non-alignment and neutrality. The development of 'an ever-increasing union' was interpreted in terms of 'a military superpower in the making'.[46] Considering the continued support for Swedish neutrality among the general public, proponents of EU membership did not want to encourage a wider and more in-depth discussion of the security implications which could run the risk of tilting the majority of voters towards *Nej/No*.[47]

Two months after the national election (which saw the return of a Social Democratic minority government), the turnout in the 1994 referendum showed that only 52.2 per cent of the Swedish electorate were convinced that becoming a citizen of the European Union was a good thing.[48] This trend towards Euroscepticism, which has strengthened since 1994 corresponded poorly to the views of the Swedish political establishment. EU membership became linked in an unfortunate way with wider processes of change, including a severe economic crisis in Sweden that undermined two of the key components of the Swedish postwar identity – modernity and neutrality. The debate in the Swedish referendum campaign demonstrated how difficult the political élites found it to articulate views of European integration that were perceived as compatible with popular conceptions of nationhood and national identity.

Rethinking security

In a time of great change and turbulence, the continued emphasis on military non-alignment provided some sense of stability in Swedish foreign and security policy. The consensual politics that surrounded the redirection towards EU membership strengthened this stability. It is symbolic that the EU application was delivered to Brussels by the Social Democratics; that a centre-right government negotiated and concluded the accession; and that a Social Democratic government returned to power two months before the referendum and ensured the parliamentary ratification to become a member of the European Union by 1 January 1995.

The end of the cold war has broadened the concept of security to include social, economic and environmental dimensions. In Sweden, the concept of 'security policy', even before the end of the cold war, had a dual connotation. In a narrow definition, it referred to national defence and military non-alignment. The broader notion related to aspects of international security that do not involve territorial defence, such as peacekeeping, foreign aid and global disarmament.[49] 'Sustainable security' surfaced as a new concept in speeches by the Social Democratic government in 1996–97. Broadly, it connoted support for a deepening of democracy, social and economic development in the states that emerged from behind the Iron Curtain.[50] Yet, perhaps more than the previous government, the broader notion of security was still linked to the reiteration of Swedish military non-alignment, informed by the belief that the policy of non-alignment remained the best means to secure stability in Northern Europe, and to provide Sweden with credibility in its efforts to build common security in Europe and the wider world.[51]

Although policymakers insisted that Swedish membership of the EU had no direct military implications, a certain sense of security flowed from membership. This was clearly expressed by the deputy Foreign Minister, Pierre Schori, who stressed that EU membership constituted the most important security factor for Sweden – 'the EU is in itself security policy': it was not likely that the EU would remain indifferent if one of its members was under threat and attacked.[52] According to Schori, EU membership was therefore the first stepping stone towards common security in Europe.

Some high-ranking officials in the Swedish armed forces, however, disputed this image of an implied security guarantee. From a geopolitical perspective, the former Supreme Commander of the Swedish armed forces, General Bengt Gustafsson, expressed doubt about the political will of the European continental states to come to 'rescue' in the event of an attack against Sweden.

> The US, Canada, and the UK with their Northern and maritime orientation, have greater incentive to support a stable Nordic area in order to safeguard their own security interests in the Atlantic. It is, moreover, in reality only the US that has the necessary disposable military resources to balance a strong Russia in the Nordic area.[53]

While the Swedish government continued to reiterate its military non-alignment, a much more flexible and broader interpretation of security nevertheless evolved, which permitted more active participation in a number of security and defence organizations. In 1994, Sweden became involved in NATO's Partnership for Peace (PfP). When Sweden acceded to the European Union in January 1995, observer status in the Western European Union (WEU) followed.

The use of military forces for the purposes of conflict prevention and crisis management has increased in post-cold war Europe. Sweden had extensive experience to draw upon in this regard with its long tradition of UN peacekeeping. Swedish troops, for example, were actively involved in Bosnia, first through the UNPROFOR Nordic battalion, and later in the Implementation Force (IFOR) and the Stabilisation Force (SFOR) authorized by the UN Security Council under NATO command.

Swedish participation in the PfP programme meant that Sweden had initiated a formalized link with NATO – something that would hardly have been an option during the cold war. PfP involves no security guarantees or commitments, but in the event of a military attack, political consultation may be sought. For Sweden, the PfP provided a useful forum of contacts and consultation, primarily regarding peacekeeping operations, but also in other issue areas such as civil preparedness.[54] PfP involved, however, direct military co-operation with NATO, in terms of a minimum level of interoperability to facilitate multinational efforts in peacekeeping missions.

Participation in PfP was not marked by any domestic controversy, since it was presented as a specific Swedish effort to contribute to European peace and stability. Peacekeeping operations under the mandate of the UN or OSCE have enjoyed widespread support in Sweden. However, it should be recognized that close cooperation with a military alliance could bring a non-aligned state, such as Sweden, into politically sensitive situations, as the definition of 'peace-keeping activities' may not always be clear-cut.

In principle, therefore, Swedish military doctrine had remained largely unchanged since the end of the cold war. The primary task of the Swedish armed forces was still to defend Swedish territory, independent of any alliance, its secondary task to contribute to international peacekeeping. In practice, not only participation in PfP but also the 'Europeanization' of Sweden's armaments industry were further limiting Swedish autonomy. The economic and financial difficulties Sweden had faced in the early 1990s had squeezed the defence budget; shrinking export markets for arms, and the rising costs of research and development, were forcing Swedish producers into closer international links, with British Aerospace in particular. Swedish membership of the Western European Armaments Group (WEAG) would have been unthinkable during the cold war, as representing alignment with the Western alliance; collaboration in arms production would have infringed Swedish controls over arms exports. But it had become a necessary part of Swedish industry's adaptive strategy in the 1990s.[55]

Images of a pan-European order

This chapter has so far attempted to illuminate the elements of continuity and change that have characterized Swedish foreign policy since the end of the cold war. The reconceptualizations of sovereignty, identity and security meant that a strict interpretation of neutrality was abandoned as a response to the end of bipolarity in Europe, and in pursuit of Sweden's perceived economic interests. From this observation arises the question of what, if any, new images of European order had been developed which might influence ideas of how Swedish foreign policy should be charted in the future.

Swedish visions of European order have been broadly informed by the notion of common security within the framework of the Organization for Security and Cooperation in Europe (OSCE). The report of the Palme Commission on Disarmament and Security issues in 1982, chaired by the chairman of the Swedish Social Democratic Party (and former prime minister), had played an active part in shaping the concept of common security as an alternative to competitive security, and had done a great deal to popularize it.[56] The view of the OSCE as the 'normative superstructure' predated the end of the cold war. It built on a tradition in Swedish thinking of the OSCE (previously CSCE) as the 'UN of Europe' – the forum in which to pursue strategies of conflict management and confidence-building.[57] The OSCE enjoyed a high degree of legitimacy in Sweden as the overall, all-embracing European security organization, as it included both the United States and Russia as members.[58]

However, whereas the OSCE may be seen as the 'superstructure' in a new European order, more concrete proposals have concerned the 'building blocs' of this structure, particularly ideas of how to develop the EU/WEU and NATO. These views were, in turn, linked to how new co-operative sub-regional arrangements should be constructed, for example, in the Baltic Sea region. Swedish perceptions of a post-cold war European order are analyzed here by delineating three foreign policy role conceptions:

i   *pragmatic minimalist* (the European Union);
ii *bridge-builder* (the Baltic Sea region); and
iii *non-aligned collaborator* (NATO).

Role conceptions contain normative political ideas about the appropriate and expected foreign policy behaviour of the state. They can be thought of as cognitive 'road maps' that foreign policymakers rely on to navigate through a complex political reality.[59]

Pragmatic minimalist

A key theme for Swedish politicians (both left and right) since the end of the cold war, was of European integration as the motor that will enable a new peaceful European order to develop. However, Swedish images of a European order built around the EU were not translated into any commitment to a federal Europe. This was clearly stated in the government paper on 'Sweden's principal interests' in the 1996 intergovernmental conference (IGC): 'We do not want the EU to develop in a federal direction'.[60]

The Swedish government was still preoccupied in pursuing what it regarded as the national interests of Sweden, arguing that the means to fulfil these national objectives had now to be sought through membership of the EU. The 1994 government commission on 'Sovereignty and Democracy' concluded that formal sovereignty could be 'pooled' to become more effective.[61] However, in similar fashion to the legal arguments in the German constitutional ruling of 1993 on the Maastricht treaty, the Swedish approach to European integration was broadly informed by the idea that democracy is and will remain national and that membership of the EU is essentially a co-operation between sovereign states, which determine the pace of integration.[62]

The major parties in Sweden broadly converged on the view that the key to transforming Europe lay in enlarging the European Union, to safeguard democracy and prevent instability in Eastern Europe. Pierre Schori, a prominent articulator of Swedish foreign policy within the Social Democratic party, wrote in 1992 that the dissolution of communism and the disintegration of the Soviet Union represented the second phase of liberation in Europe. Schori argued that it was imperative that Sweden became involved and supported European integration as a stepping stone in the creation of a lasting peace in Europe.[63]

In a speech in Brussels in 1993, Carl Bildt spoke of four historical sources of tensions and conflicts that had marked the history of Europe. Two of these he considered resolved – the enmity between France and Germany, and Poland's relations with its neighbours. The third source of tension in Europe was Russia's imperial ambitions – a problem that Bildt thought only could be overcome by incorporating Russia into European co-operative security structures and frameworks. The fourth problem that Bildt pointed to as a source of instability on the European continent was the precarious situation in the Balkans.[64]

The primary expression of this image of a pan-European Union lay in the high priority that was given to the issue of EU enlargement in Sweden, once Sweden itself was accepted into the EU. While the Swedish government exhibited a considerable degree of ambivalence to NATO enlargement in 1995–97, the extension of the EU to include the states of eastern Europe and the Baltic was considered of crucial importance in the process of strengthening stable and peaceful developments in Europe. This commitment was demonstrated in the post specially created in the Swedish ministry of foreign affairs to support and share experience with the three Baltic states and Poland on negotiating accession to the EU.[65]

It was, however, recognized that enlargement raised internal problems for the EU. In the period leading up to the EU 1996 intergovernmental conference, the Swedish government and parliament encouraged a wider debate on institutional reform, especially by commissioning a number of expert reports. To use government reports and commissions has a long tradition in Sweden as a way to build consensus and support for future decisions of crucial importance.[66]

Yet, the underlying question as to how the Swedish government and political parties viewed the commitment to non-alignment in a Union with ambitious aspirations to develop a common security and defence policy had not been fully addressed; as no major developments were expected regarding 'common defence'. Nonetheless, the Swedish concept of a minimalist role did not necessarily imply passivity and a preference for the status quo. An experienced Swedish diplomat expressed the following view just before EU accession:

> Sweden will be an active and committed participant in the evolution of the Common Foreign and Security Policy. Foreign observers who think otherwise have not really understood the Lutheran Swedish mentality. When we join in international cooperation we intend to have an influence, and we want to make a difference.[67]

The Swedish government, though still a very new member of the EU, made a number of proposals to strengthen the effectiveness of the Common Foreign and Security Policy (CFSP) in the run-up to the 1996–97 IGC. It indicated that some decisions might be open to qualified majority voting; it supported the establishment of a planning and evaluation unit, provided that its functions were tightly defined so as not to intrude on reserved national responsibilities.[68] A joint Swedish–Finnish paper, published April 1996, proposed a more formal link between the WEU and the EU to improve the credibility of CFSP in crisis management: the 'Petersberg tasks' of peacekeeping and humanitarian missions.[69] Yet the paper argued against any moves beyond this to merge the two organizations. Any suggestion that the EU was taking on a more direct security and defence role, it was feared, might provoke Russia to raise objections to the inclusion of the Baltic states within the EU, on similar grounds to its resistance to NATO enlargement.[70]

Whatever the ambitions of the Swedish government and administration to play an active role in the further development of the EU, however, their freedom of manoeuvre was limited by the sceptical attitudes of a substantial proportion of the Swedish public. Swedish officials in Brussels during the final stages of the IGC indeed complained that their country's reputation as a 'reluctant' EU member had damaged Sweden's influence over the negotiations.[71] There was little popular support within Sweden for any further transfers of sovereignty to the EU level, beyond those which the government had formally accepted in the accession treaty. The attitude which the Social Democratic government adopted to participation in the single currency was heavily influenced by this gap between the ambitions and assumptions of the élite and the hesitations and anxieties of the public. Göran Persson, the prime minister, referred to EMU as a 'risky project', while carefully leaving open the possibility that Sweden might join at a later stage.[72] This 'wait and see' position was sharply criticized from both sides by other political parties, some arguing that it failed to exclude entry altogether, others that preparations to join should be set in train. Some academics also criticized the government's hesitation. Sweden's 'Achilles heel' as an EU member, Magnus Jerneck argued, was the historical baggage it carried, which handicapped every step it took towards closer integration.[73]

The decision to 'wait and see' how monetary union developed meant that the Swedish government in practice accepted the development of a multi-speed Europe. This represented a retreat from the Swedish position at the start of the 1996 IGC negotiations, when the concept of an integration process *à la carte* had been unequivocally rejected.[74]

Bridge-builder

With the end of the cold war, various forms of sub-regional co-operation were given a new impetus. In the Baltic Sea region, the dissolution of the Soviet Union changed the political geography of Northern Europe. Sweden supported the efforts and aspirations of the Baltic states and Poland to join the EU, and provided extensive aid to these states. Sweden was, for example, involved in the negotiations concerning the withdrawal of remaining Russian troops and supplied equipment and training for a Baltic peacekeeping unit (BALTBAT).

As part of the building of new bridges of a pan-European order that did not isolate Russia, the Nordic countries worked actively in achieving stable and peaceful relations in northern Europe – extending the 'zone of peace' further eastwards.[75] Sweden self-consciously acted as a 'bridge-builder' in these efforts.[76] Baltic Sea cooperation can be viewed as an attempt to create a 'security community' – acting on the assumption that the more communications and transactions are developed, the more states and societies become aware of their common interests.[77] The influence of this transactionalist perspective, combined with the concept of 'sustainable security', guided Swedish policy towards the Baltic Sea region.

> Our aim is to create a tightly knit fabric of regional ties in areas such as the building of democracy, human rights, trade, industry, environmental protection, people-to-people contacts, combating of cross-border crime, etc., thereby promoting the development of a democratic, stable and prosperous region. Such a network of cooperation indeed is an essential component of security.[78]

The end of the cold war thus presented a 'window of opportunity' to build new co-operative structures and stability in the Baltic Sea region. Military activity in the region declined, and peaceful conflict resolution was accepted as the means by which to solve potential differences between the states around the Baltic Sea.

Following the Nordic pattern of pragmatic intergovernmental co-operation and institution-building, a Baltic Sea Cooperation Council was established. Though this co-operation did not include security issues *per se*, it was an effort to create alternative confidence-building measures to secure stability around the Baltic Sea area, as well as a practical attempt to involve Russia in cooperative European structures. The Baltic co-operation programme included issues of economy, infrastructure, environment and civil preparedness. One important aspect of this co-operation was to draw political attention to the needs of this region, particularly in the EU context. It was, for example, argued that for a country like Poland, 'such regional cooperation provides another pathway back to Europe'.[79]

The direct link between Swedish security and developments in the Baltic states was spelled out in 1993, when Carl Bildt floated the idea that if the Baltic republics were attacked, Sweden would not remain neutral according to international law.[80] This statement provoked political controversy, as it deviated from the multi-party consensus of 1992 on non-alignment. The Social Democrats insisted that Swedish non-alignment was not compatible with military commitments of any kind.[81] The official formula that was forged after this dissension was a continued emphasis on Swedish non-alignment, yet, with the qualification that Sweden would not remain 'indifferent' to aggression in the Baltic.[82]

The controversial statement by former British Foreign Secretary Douglas Hurd, that the security of the Baltic republics was a special responsibility for Sweden and Finland, however, encouraged a change of tone in statements about the Baltic states' aspirations for NATO membership. The Swedish government was quick to respond by stating that Sweden could not, and would not, extend any security guarantees to the Baltic states. Foreign Minister Lena Hjclm-Wallén stated clearly in parliament that the security around the Baltic Sea was a responsibility for Europe as a whole.[83] 'Bridge-builder' was not intended to mean 'security-guarantor'.[84] Following on from this, in 1996–97, the Swedish government started to signal support for the Baltic states' aspiration to seek NATO membership. While actively being engaged in a deepening of Baltic Sea co-operation, it stressed that regional security must be a responsibility of the USA and Europe as a whole. As the Swedish foreign minister stated, 'the security of Europe is indivisible'.[85] This may be interpreted as a Swedish recognition that transatlantic security through NATO would remain a key component in the evolving European security architecture.

Non-aligned collaborator

While neutrality as a central component in Swedish security policy had been diluted, a key symbol of continued military non-alignment remained non-membership of NATO. However, throughout the post-cold war period, a gradual re-evaluation of NATO and USA involvement in Europe was under-way, which brought Sweden into close collaboration with NATO. NATO's greater emphasis on crisis management and security co-operation – such as the Partnership for Peace (PfP) – facilitated active Swedish involvement in peacekeeping efforts under NATO command. In Bosnia, for example, Sweden was engaged in peacekeeping activities jointly with Nordic NATO member states. The end of the cold war had made it less sensitive for Sweden to seek closer security co-operation with the three Nordic NATO members.[86]

The flexibility of PfP was an argument that the Swedish government initially used against NATO eastward expansion. For some time, the Swedish government held the view that the Baltic and eastern European states should not primarily seek military security guarantees through NATO, but should be encouraged to pursue stable political and economic relations through membership of the European Union.[87] Apart from an awareness of Russian objections, NATO enlargement was seen as running the risk of creating new divisions and instability in Europe.[88] The Swedish government, however, recognized that NATO had changed considerably since the cold war. From the mid-1990s onwards, it has been acknowledged that both NATO and US engagement are vital to European security. As the deputy Foreign Minister stated in 1995, '[t]he continued vitality of NATO, with a significant American military presence in Europe, is also in Sweden's interest'.[89]

From a Swedish perspective, PfP served as a useful vehicle to involve NATO in the Baltic region. The idea of a 'North European PfP' was floated in a meeting between the Swedish Prime Minister and the US President.[90] In response to the exclusion of the Baltic states from the first wave of new NATO members, Carl Bildt argued along similar lines, proposing a common international force for crisis management in northern Europe that would include Russia.[91]

Swedish collaboration with the military forces of other states meant that a certain 'internationalization' of the Swedish armed forces has been taking place. For example, in May 1997, Sweden hosted a major PfP exercise – 'Cooperative Banners' – involving 4000 troops from 18 different states.[92] It could be argued that while NATO has become 'Europeanized', non-members like Sweden have become increasingly 'NATOized' in the post-cold war period. To be involved in these processes requires a certain 'balancing act' – something that both the Swedish foreign and defence ministers have acknowledged.[93]

The question whether Sweden at all should consider NATO membership became a political issue in spring 1995, when the framework for the next Swedish defence plan was discussed in the parliamentary defence committee. The Social Democratic defence minister at the time, Tage Pettersson, did not want NATO membership to be a consideration in any discussion on the future of Swedish defence. The Liberal and Moderate parties, however, wanted to include potential membership as part of an evaluation of the consequences of NATO enlargement.[94]

The decision that emerged from the defence review in 1996 was that Sweden should remain militarily non-aligned. This was, however, further qualified in government comments suggesting that this policy is not 'a given, once and for all'.[95] If NATO were to enlarge to include the Baltic states, it was becoming widely recognized in Swedish political circles that the strategic position of Sweden would fundamentally change. In the beginning of 1996, the Social Democratic government indicated its openness to future Swedish NATO membership within the next decade, *if* indeed NATO became the central hub of common security in Europe.[96] Against this opening towards NATO membership, it should be pointed out that few politicians and policymakers rejected Sweden's policy of non-alignment entirely, partly because it still enjoyed such substantial support among the Swedish public.[97] The 'non-aligned idealism' that became rooted among the Swedish populace in the cold war still continued to thrive[98] – perhaps partly also because foreign ministry officials continued to talk of Swedish security policy almost as if the cold war had not ended.

> ...the fact remains: Sweden has not been at war since 1814. A country's security policy has a great deal to do with history. The good results that Sweden's policy has achieved means that our non-participation in military alliances has broad support in public opinion. This is of fundamental importance for understanding the Swedish position. We believe that our security policy, based on military non-alignment and supported by a strong defense, continues to contribute to peace and stability not only for our own country but for Europe as a whole. We believe that this was the case during the Cold War and that this is still the case.[99]

Among Swedish political parties, only the Liberal party had openly declared its support for membership in an enlarged NATO, in 1996. The Moderate party said 'yes' in principle, but not at that moment in time.[100] The two largest quality morning papers in Sweden supported these positions on NATO membership.[101] There is an interesting parallel to draw between the way in which Sweden moved towards EU membership in the 1980s and how Sweden was moving closer to NATO membership in the late 1990s – in practice, if not in the political rhetoric.

At the crossroads

Changes in foreign policy role conceptions are likely to occur when key foreign policy ideas lose their salience and credibility among the foreign policy élite. Swedish postwar neutrality was 'custom made' to fit the cold war conditions. When these changed, the niche that neutral Sweden had carved for itself in bipolar Europe was lost. The trigger that challenged the sacrosanct policy of neutrality was thus the end of the cold war. Yet the pace at which this process of rethinking took place was instrumentally determined by the setting of another goal: Swedish membership of the EU. European Union membership is a symbolic expression of Swedish adaptation to changes in European international relations.

The different stages in the process of adaptation have been analyzed in a number of reports commissioned by the Swedish government. The academic input in these reports to interpret the new developments in post-cold war Europe was considerable. While Swedish political scientists have had a tendency to view their own importance as marginal to policymaking,[102] there was a noticeable increase in academic interaction with 'practitioners' in the

1990s. Research on European politics and the Baltic Sea was particularly encouraged with the support of various government grants.[103]

Increasing academic involvement indicated that the debate on Swedish foreign policy was at last becoming more open. It was also becoming more politicized. The two largest parties in Swedish politics – the Social Democrats and the Moderates – had begun to question the precise meaning of Swedish non-alignment in post-cold war Europe. The former party adopted a cautious position, while Carl Bildt of the Moderate party attempted to stretch the boundaries of debate. Neutrality has been abandoned as a guiding principle in Swedish foreign policy. What remains of this 'ideology' is the hard core of military non-alignment.

Three underlying foreign policy role conceptions have been outlined in this chapter to illustrate the elements of continuity and change in Sweden's post-cold war foreign policy. Despite the fact that Swedish membership of the European Union may be viewed as a pragmatic recognition of the changing patterns of international relations in Europe, its minimalist position on some key policy issues illustrates how traditionalist tenets have continued to influence Swedish approaches to European integration. The notion of bridge-builder between the states around the Baltic Sea is founded on a belief that Swedish non-alignment brings stability to northern Europe. Non-alignment is thought to provide Sweden with a capital of trust to pursue the building of 'a sense of community' among the Baltic states.

Sweden's strategy of a closer collaboration with NATO while remaining non-aligned signified the active involvement of Sweden in European security affairs without abandoning the historic traditions of Swedish foreign policy. This compromise, however, was already under challenge in 1996–97, with the question of eventual NATO membership open for discussion among the policy élite.

In the case of EU membership, the Swedish government proved capable of a rapid redirection of Swedish foreign policy. In defence and security policy, however, there continued to be substantial resistance to abandoning the last strands of non-alignment. The domestication of neutrality in Swedish political culture was indeed a success story. The policy of non-alignment has continued to enjoy substantial legitimacy among the Swedish public throughout the years of transition after the end of the cold war.

External developments are of crucial importance to a small state like Sweden. Yet domestic constraints have proved extremely powerful in holding Sweden's foreign policy élite back from spelling out the implications of this transformed international environment. This raises the delicate question of how far government and political élites should lead, rather than be limited by, public opinion. Political leaders were edging forward in 1995–97, testing the limits of public acceptability and hinting at the need for further readjustment. The redefinition of Swedish foreign policy was thus proceeding through a two-level game, in which foreign policymakers maintained a precarious balance between international and domestic demands.

Notes

1. K. Boulding, 'National Images and International Systems' in J. Rosenau (ed.), *International Politics and Foreign Policy: A Reader in Research and Theory* (New York: The Free Press, 1968) p. 391.
2. K. Wahlbäck, *The Roots of Swedish Neutrality* (Stockholm: The Swedish Institute, 1986) p. 80.
3. Undén, quoted in K. Wahlbäck 1986, op. cit. p. 80.
4. See further, N. Andrén, *Maktbalans och Alliansfrihet: Svensk utrikespolitik under 1990-talet* (Stockholm: Norstedts, 1996) pp. 74–9; B. Schiller, 'At Gun Point: a critical perspective on the attempts of the Nordic governments to achieve unity after the Second World War', *Scandinavian Journal of History*, 9:3 (1984) p. 236.
5. A. Johansson, 'Gör upp med neutralitetsmyten' *Dagens Nyheter*, 20 February 1996.
6. B. Sundelius, 'When Sweden chose to join the European Community', in W. Carlsnaes and S. Smith (eds), *European Foreign Policy: The EC and Changing Perspectives in Europe* (London: Sage, 1994) p. 178.
7. B. Huldt, 'New Thinking in Sweden? The Public Debate on Security and Defense 1979–1995', in *New Thinking in International Relations: Swedish Perspectives*, 1994–1995 Yearbook of the Swedish Institute of International Affairs (Stockholm: Swedish Institute of International Affairs, 1995) p. 142.
8. R. Lindahl, 'Towards an Ever Closer Relation: Swedish Foreign and Security Policy and the European Integration Process', in *New Thinking in International Relations: Swedish Perspectives*. 1994–1995 Yearbook of The Swedish Institute of International Affairs (Stockholm: Swedish Institute of International Affairs, 1995) p. 165.
9. See M. Bergquist, *Sverige och EEC: En statsvetenskaplig studie av fyra åsiktsriktningars syn på svensk marknadspolitik 1961–1962*. Doct. diss., Lund Political Studies 11 (Stockholm: Norstedt and Söners förlag, 1970); C-E. Stålvant and C. Hamilton, 'Sweden' in H. Wallace (ed.), *The Wider Western Europe: Reshaping the EC/EFTA Relationship* (London: Pinter, 1991) p. 211.
10. Sundelius, 1994, op. cit., p. 179.
11. This is the reason why, for example, Norway and Denmark have stipulated in their membership of NATO that no foreign bases are to be permanently stationed on their territory in peacetime. See further, B. Sundelius (ed.), *Foreign Policies of Northern Europe* (Boulder, CO: Westview Press, 1982).
12. See for example, W. Agrell, *Alliansfri – tills vidare: Ett svenskt säkerhetsdilemma* (Stockholm: Natur och Kultur, 1994) pp. 26–7.
13. 'Om kriget kommit … Förberedelser för mottagande av militärt bistånd 1949–1969' SOU 1994: 11 (Stockholm: Fritzes, 1994) [Swedish government official report].
14. On the ideology of foreign policy, see for example, C. Jönsson, *Superpower: Comparing American and Soviet Foreign Policy* (London: Pinter, 1984) p. 43.
15. F. Northedge, 'The Nature of Foreign Policy', in F. Northedge (ed.), *The Foreign Policies of the Powers* (London: Faber and Faber, 1974) p. 15.
16. Culture is in this context characterized by 'broad and general beliefs and attitudes about one's own nation, about other nations, and about the relationships that actually obtain or that they should obtain between the self and other actors in the international arena'. See Y. Vertzberger, *The World in Their Minds: Information Processing, Cognition, and Perception in Foreign Policy Decisionmaking* (Stanford: Stanford University Press, 1990) p. 268.
17. See Huldt, 1995, op. cit., p. 140.

18. See B. Nygren, 'The Role Perceptions of Swedish Academics *vis-à-vis* Foreign Policy Practioners', in M. Girard, W-B. Eberwein and K. Webb, *Theory and Practice in Foreign Policy-Making: National Perspectives on Academics and Professionals in International Relations* (London: Pinter, 1994) p. 98.
19. See for example, A. Baker Fox, *The Power of Small States: Diplomacy in World War II* (Chicago: University of Chicago Press, 1959); M. Kelstrup, 'Small States and European Political Integration', in I. Petersen and T. Tilikainen (eds), *The Nordic Countries and the EC* (Copenhagen: Copenhagen Political Studies Press, 1993); Sundelius, 1994, op. cit.
20. See for example M. Brecher, *The Foreign Policy System of Israel: Setting, Images, Process* (London: Oxford University Press, 1972); R. Jervis, *Perception and Misperception in International Politics* (Princeton: Princeton University Press, 1976); L. Festinger, *A Theory of Cognitive Dissonance* (Stanford: Stanford University Press, 1957); H. Sprout and M. Sprout, *Ecological Perspective on Human Affairs* (Princeton: Princeton University Press, 1965); J. Steinbruner, *The Cybernetic Theory of Decision* (Princeton: Princeton University Press, 1974); Vertzberger, 1990, op. cit..
21. *Sverige och den västeuropeiska integration*, Prop. 1987/88: 66 (government bill), Stockholm, December 1987, quoted in, C-E. Stålvant and C. Hamilton, 1991, op. cit., p. 201.
22. A. Milward, *The European Rescue of the Nation-State* (London: Routledge, 1992).
23. See for example, G. Hansson and L-G. Stenelo (eds), *Makt och Internationalisering* (Stockholm: Carlssons, 1990); U. Nordlöf-Lagerkranz (ed.), *Svensk Neutralitet, Europa och EG* (Stockholm: Institute of International Afffairs, 1990).
24. See for example the anthology, *Tjugo Röster om Europa* (Kristianstad: ABF, 1990).
25. See I. Carlsson, *Dagens Nyheter*, 27 May 1990.
26. See Lindahl, 1995, op. cit., p. 168.
27. See Riksdagstryck, 2 October 1990 (Swedish Parliament Record); Regeringsskrivelse 1990–91 (official letter from the government to parliament).
28. L. Karvonen and B. Sundelius, 'The Nordic Neutrals: Facing the European Union', in L. Miles (ed.), *The European Union and the Nordic Countries* (London: Routledge, 1996) p. 247.
29. See Andrén, 1996, op. cit., p. 162.
30. Sundelius, 1994, op. cit., p. 187.
31. Sundelius, 1994, op. cit., pp. 192–3.
32. Utrikesfrågor 1991 [official documentation concerning important questions of Swedish foreign policy] (Stockholm: Ministiry of Foreign Affairs, 1991).
33. See Government policy presented to Parliament by the Prime Minister, Carl Bildt, 4 October 1991; Proposition 1991/2: 102 (governmental bill).
34. See for example, interview in *Svenska Dagbladet*, 19 January 1992.
35. P. Schori, 'Neutralitetspolitiken kan omprövas', *Dagens Nyheter*, 14 January 1992.
36. See 'Säkerhet och Nedrustning', Riksdagen, Stockholm, 28 April 1992. Utrikesutskottetsbetänkande 1991/92: UU19 [Report from the Parliament's Standing Committee on Foreign Affairs].
37. Karvonen and Sundelius, 1996, op. cit., p. 252; see also Andrén, 1996, op. cit., p. 164.
38. See Carl Bildt, *Hallänning, Svensk, Europé* (Uddevalla: Bonniers, 1991); see also the Government budgetary bill of January 1992.
39. See European Commission, 'Sweden's Application for Membership: Opinion of the Commission', SEC (92), Brussels, 7 August 1992.

40. K. Wahlbäck, quoted in P. Luif, *On the Road to Brussels: The Political Dimension of Austria's, Finland's and Sweden's Accession to the European Union* (Vienna: Braumüller, 1995) p. 249.

41. Andrén, 1996, op. cit., pp. 164–5.

42. During the cold war, opinion surveys indicated less of a regional focus and more of a global concern for east–west relations, disarmament and the 'moral dimensions' of foreign policy. See U. Bjereld and M. Demker, *Utrikespolitiken som Slagfält: De svenska partierna och utrikesfrågorna* (Stockholm: Nerenius and Santérus, 1995) pp. 62–3.

43. Except for a brief report commissioned by the government. 'Historiskt Vägval', SOU 1994: 8 [Swedish government official report] (Stockholm: Fritzes, 1994).

44. U. Dinkelspiel, *Dagens Nyheter*, 7 February 1993; U. Hammarström, 'Sweden' in A. Krohn (ed.), *The Baltic Sea Region: National and International Security Perspectives*. (Baden-Baden: Nomo's Verlagsgesellschaft, 1996) p. 143.

45. This argument was in line with the conclusions that had been drawn in a report by the Swedish ministry of foreign affairs. See, *Sverige, EG och den säkerhetspolitiska utvecklingen i Europa* (Stockholm: UD informerar, 1991).

46. In particular, the Green and Left parties used this argument.; Cf. J. Galtung, *The European Community: A Superpower in the Making* (London: George Allen and Unwin, 1973).

47. See for example, P. Schori, *Dagens Nyheter*, 12 June 1992.

48. T. Bjørklund, 'The Three Nordic 1994 Referenda Concerning Membership in the EU'. *Cooperation and Conflict*, 31:1 (1996) p. 15.

49. Huldt, 1995, op. cit., p. 155.

50. P. Schori, 'Hållbar Säkerhet kring Östersjön', Briefing from UD 2/97 (Stockholm: the Swedish Ministry of Foreign Affairs, 1997) p. 7.

51. Andrén, 1996, op. cit., p. 172.

52. Schori, 1997, op. cit., p. 4.

53. B. Gustafsson, 'Widening Horizons in Swedish Security Analysis', in *New Thinking in International Relations: Swedish Perspectives*. 1994–95 Yearbook of the Swedish Institute of International Affairs (Stockholm: The Swedish Institute of International Affairs, 1995) p. 130.

54. L. Aggestam, 'NATO och NATOs Civila Beredskap', Report No. 11 (Stockholm: The Swedish National Board for Civil Preparedness, 1995).

55. Some academics have argued that Swedish membership of WEAG reduces the credibility and aim of Sweden to remain militarily non-aligned. See U. Bjereld and P. Cramér, 'Vapensamarbete försvagar svensk trovärdighet', *Svenska Dagbladet*, 28 September 1996.

56. *Common Security: a programme for disarmament*, report of the Independent Commission on Disarmament and Security Issues (London: Pan, 1982). This group included three other former prime ministers, one former head of state, and five former foreign ministers among its 17 members. Like the prior Brandt Commission and the later Brundtland Commission, its aim was to reshape ideas about world order.

57. Huldt, 1995, op. cit., p. 149.

58. See for example, Schori, 1997, op. cit. .

59. For a more extensive discussion of the concept of role – see L. Aggestam, 'Role Conceptions and the Politics of Identity in Foreign Policy', *Arena Working Paper* No. 8, (Oslo: Arena, 1999).

60. 'Sweden's principal interests in view of the 1996 EU Intergovernmental Conference'. (Stockholm: The Cabinet Office, July 1995).

61. SOU 1994: 12 (Swedish government official report), *Suveränitet och Demokrati.* (Stockholm: Fritzes, 1994).
62. The main arguments on this can be found in the government bill on EU membership – Proposition 1994/5: 19.
63. P. Schori, *Dokument Inifrån: Sverige och Storpolitiken i Omvälvningarnas Tid* (Stockholm: Tidens Förlag, 1992).
64. Address by Prime Minister Carl Bildt to 'La Fondation Paul-Henri Spaak', Palais des Académies, Brussels, 16 September 1993; see also C. Bildt, *Hallännng, Svensk, Europé* (Uddevalla: Bonniers, 1991).
65. Schori, 1997, op. cit., p. 7; the Swedish view was that negotiations with new potential members should start at the same time, while it was recognized that differentiation would take place along the way and that new members might accede to the EU at different times.
66. See 'Sweden's principal interests …' 1995, op. cit.; 'Utvidgning och Samspel', SOU 1995: 132; 'Union för både Öst och Väst', SOU 1996: 15; 'Sverige, EU och Framtiden', SOU 1996: 19. (Swedish government official reports).
67. I. Karlsson, 'A Role for the Scandinavian Countries Adjacent to NATO', in Goldstein (ed.) *Security in Europe: the role of NATO after the cold war*, (London: Brasseys, 1994), p. 55.
68. See G. Herolf and R. Lindahl, 'Av Vitalt Intresse: EU:s Utrikes-och Säkerhetspolitik inför Regeringskonferensen', SOU 1996: 7 [Swedish government official report] (Stockholm: the Ministry of Foreign Affairs); R. Lindahl, 'The Swedish Debate', in *The 1996 IGC – National Debates (2)*, RIIA discussion paper No. 67 (London: Royal Institute of International Affairs, 1996).
69. L. Hjelm-Wallén and T. Halonen, 'Svensk–Finsk WEU-aktion', *Dagens Nyheter*, 21 April 1996; 'The IGC and the Security and Defence Dimension towards an Enhanced EU Role in Crisis Management', Memorandum from Finland and Sweden, 25 April 1996.
70. *Svenska Dagbladet*, 25 March 1997; 'EU:s koppling till VEU svårast för Göran Persson', *Svenska Dagbladet*, 14 June 1997.
71. Interview with G. Lund, 'Hopp om nytt EU-fördrag inom kort', *Svenska Dagbladet*, 5 May 1997; 'Sverige på väg bli bromskloss', *Svenska Dagbladet*, 24 November 1996.
72. *Svenska Dagbladet*, 29 May 1997, 5 June 1997, 9 June 1997. It should be noted that the Social Democratic government included a number of ministers who openly supported Swedish entry into the EMU.
73. M. Jerneck, 'EMU mer än valutaunion', *Sydsvenska Dagbladet*, 10 June 1997.
74. Cf. '… it is in Sweden's interests that continued integration – in an enlargement perspective also – should be based as far as possible on cohesive co-operation within an uniform institutional framework. An *à la carte* Europe is not in our interests, as it would undermine possibilities of realizing the advantages of the single market.' See 'Sweden's principal interests …', 1995, op. cit.
75. Cf. C. Archer, 'The Nordic Area as a "Zone of Peace"', *Journal of Peace Research*, 33:4 (1996).
76. T. Gür, 'Sverige – "aktiv" men (absolut) inte "ledande"', *Svenska Dagbladet*, 8 September 1996.
77. The pioneering work on this idea was done by K. Deutsch *et al. Political Community in the Northern Atlantic Area* (Princeton: Princeton University Press, 1957) pp. 5–7.
78. U. Hjertsson, 'Sweden and Security in the Baltic Sea Region', in *1st Annual Stockholm Conference on Baltic Sea Security and Cooperation* (Stockholm: The Swedish Institute of International Affairs, 1997) p. 59.

79. A. Hyde–Price, *The International Politics of East Central Europe* (Manchester: Manchester University Press, 1996) p. 118.
80. This has always been a particularly sensitive issue in Swedish foreign policy, as Sweden formally recognized the incorporation of the three Baltic states into the Soviet Union in 1940.
81. P. Schori, *Dagens Nyheter*, 15 November 1993.
82. See for example, the Foreign Minister Lena Hjelm-Wallén, *Dagens Nyheter*, 22 February 1995.
83. *Dagens Nyheter*, 22 April 1996; *Svenska Dagbladet*, 2 May 1996.
84. Cf. Andrén, 1996, op. cit., p. 174.
85. T. Halonen and L. Hjelm-Wallén, 'Sverige och Finland har inget behov av Natomedlemskap', *Svenska Dagbladet*, 15 March 1997.
86. The Nordic NATO member states are Denmark, Norway and Iceland.
87. See for example Schori, 1995, op. cit., pp. 12–16.
88. See Huldt, 1995, op. cit., p. 157.
89. P. Schori, 1995, op. cit., p. 15.
90. Hjertsson, 1997, op. cit., p. 59; see also, Hammarström, 1996, op. cit., p. 162.
91. 'Bildt vill ha militärt nätverk för fred', *Svenska Dagbladet*, 4 September 1996. The idea of a 'Nordic PfP' has not been embraced by the Baltic states themselves, because they do not want to see this development as an alternative to NATO membership.
92. *Svenska Dagbladet*, 28 May 1997.
93. T. Pettersson and L. Hjelm-Wallén, *Dagens Nyheter*, 13 June 1996; see also, 'Planer på Natoövning retar Persson', *Svenska Dagbladet*, 23 April 1997; 'Sverige i allt tätare allians med Nato', *Svenska Dagbladet*, 9 June 1997.
94. Karvonen and Sundelius, 1996, op. cit., p. 259.
95. T. Halonen and L. Hjelm-Wallén, 'Sverige och Finland har inget behov av Natomedlemskap', *Svenska Dagbladet*, 15 March 1997; see also, interview with Björn von Sydow (defence minister), 'Gärna NATO – men inget medlemskap', *Svenska Dagbladet*, 18 February 1997; Schori, 1997, op. cit., p. 8.
96. See Schori, 1997, op. cit., p. 5; Andrén, 1996, op. cit., p. 175.
97. In a study of public opinion in 1996, there was still a substantial majority – 69 per cent – who supported a policy of non-alignment aiming to be neutral in the event of war. See, 'Fortsatt tvekan till Nato', *Svenska Dagbladet*, 8 February 1997.
98. See Karlsson, 1994, op. cit., p. 52.
99. Hjertsson, 1997, op. cit., p. 62.
100. 'Fp vill att Sverige går in i Nato', *Svenska Dagbladet*, 5 October 1996; 'M vill skynda långsamt mot Nato', *Svenska Dagbladet*, 6 October 1996.
101. *Dagens Nyheter* (independent liberal) and *Svenska Dagbladet* (independent conservative)
102. B. Nygren, 'The role perceptions of Swedish academics *vis-à-vis* foreign policy practitioners', in Girard, Eberwein and Webb, *Theory and practice in foreign policy making: national perspectives on Academics and Professionals in International Relations* (London: Pinter, 1997) p. 102.
103. K. Salomon, 'Universiteten följsamma mot politiska konjunkturer', *Svenska Dagbladet*, 9 June 1997.

8
Spain and European Order after the Cold War

*Robin Niblett**

Introduction

The Spanish people experienced the end of the cold war from a distinct and distant vantage point. Having chosen neutrality during the Second World War, Spain was neither invaded by the axis nor liberated by the allies, as were most other states on the European continent. Nor was Spain invited to play a role in constructing the post-1945 European order. On the contrary, under the authoritarian regime of General Franco, Spain was excluded from the Marshall Plan and then from membership of Western Europe's two central institutions, the European Community (EC) and NATO, until after the General's death in 1975. As a result, few Spaniards had any affinity with the bipolar order which overshadowed the European continent after 1945. By the mid-1980s, the east–west stand-off was widely perceived as a dangerous anachronism, in which both superpowers shared equally the responsibility for a possible outbreak into nuclear conflict.

Spanish observers followed the end of the cold war and the collapse of communism in eastern Europe with a mixture of delight and apprehension. The fall of the Berlin Wall in November 1989 was an unexpected external after-shock to Spain's own internal revolution. Having become a member of the European Community in January 1986, Spain had just begun to adapt its economy to the full rigours of European economic integration. The Spanish government only started finalising the terms of Spain's membership in NATO in December 1988, two years after the referendum that secured a narrow popular approval for Spain joining the Atlantic alliance. In 1989, after more than one hundred years of self-imposed isolation on the periphery of Europe, Spain was in the last stages of incorporating itself into a cold war European order when that order was on the verge of collapse.[1] Spain's reconciliation with its 'natural and historic project'[2] occurred just as the bases of the 'project' appeared to be unsustainable.

---

* I would like to thank Charles Powell and Esther Barbé for their comments on early drafts of this chapter.

This chapter first assesses the reasons behind Spain's ardent support for the process of West European integration, and describes the challenges that the end of the cold war posed to Spain's vision for this process. The following sections explain the Spanish government's approach to German unification and the Maastricht negotiation. The chapter then assesses how Spanish policymakers reacted to the post-Maastricht crisis of confidence in Europe, with particular attention to the Spanish EU presidency in 1995. The final sections point to Spain's European Achilles heel – its economy – and describe the ways that both the Gonzalez and Aznar governments tried to overcome this handicap while battling to remain at the core of the new Europe being built around the EU's Economic and Monetary Union (EMU).

Committed Europeans

Spanish conceptions of European order after the cold war were intertwined with the ambition of Spanish policymakers since the early 1980s to sustain Spain's economic and diplomatic renaissance within the European community. The reasons for this European focus were a mixture of the political and the material. Politically, Spain's integration into the European community underpinned the post-1976 transformation of Spanish society and guaranteed that democracy would take firm root. The European community provided an important framework for national reconciliation, by helping to legitimize the relationship between Madrid and the governments of Spain's autonomous regions. Catalans and Basques, for example, could hope that Madrid might become a link in the chain of governance between Spain's autonomous regions and the community; with Brussels, not Madrid at the apex. As Andres Ortega, one of Gonzalez's main advisers during the post-cold war period, concluded,

> today, being a 'member state' (of the EU) is as important for Spain's national identity as being a nation-state. … Without a European perspective, Spain could come under severe tensions, leading even to its rupture.[3]

At a deeper, cultural level, integration into the EC also promised to sweep away the last vestiges of anti-reformism which the Spanish writer Unamuno, among others, had championed for Spain at the turn of the century. The seemingly irreversible tide of Spanish decline since 1898, capped by forty years of failed particularism under Franco, had discredited policies of separation from the rest of Europe. The 'Pireneico' instinct (meaning, literally, 'of the Pyrenees') and the perverse pride in being 'castizo' (backward) had come to be seen simply as symptoms of defeatism. In their place, 'Europe' offered Spain the chance to rejoin the society of modern industrialized and democratic states and, ultimately, to regain its historical position as a leading European and international power.[4] Spaniards rallied to Ortega and Gasset's dictum that, 'solo desde Europa puede hacerse España', – 'Spain can only further itself through Europe'.

From a more practical perspective, EC membership offered the only route to a rapid modernization of the Spanish economy. EC membership enabled Spain to trade freely in other EC markets and to secure EC financial grants to assist with the country's economic reconstruction. Despite the added competitive pressures that the Single Market placed on the Spanish economy, a borderless Europe also increased the attractiveness of low-wage Spain as a destination for foreign investment, while dismantling the persistent non-tariff barriers to Spain's trade with other EC states. Between 1986 and 1991, an estimated \$80 billion entered Spain, half of it foreign direct investment.[5] Thanks to the removal of most EC tariff barriers and the rise in foreign investment, Spain had enjoyed the fastest rate of GDP growth in the community between 1986–89, averaging 6 per cent per annum.

This combination of political and practical benefits meant that, after its accession, Spain quickly became an enthusiastic supporter of all aspects of European integration. The government strongly endorsed the 1988 Delors Plan for Economic and Monetary Union,[6] seeing it as an additional spur to accelerate the convergence of the Spanish economy with its EC partners. The Socialist government also placed great emphasis on the social aspects of European integration, hoping to underpin at the EC level social and worker rights that it had recently introduced in Spain. The proposal for an EC Social Charter was one of the main policy priorities of the first Spanish EC presidency between January and June 1989. Spanish politicians were strong supporters of European Political Cooperation (EPC), the process whereby EC member states co-ordinated their foreign policies, for equally self-interested reasons. On the one hand, EPC offered to Spain the same benefits as it did to all smaller EC member states: access to privileged information, the opportunity to monitor and comment upon the foreign policies of the Community's 'big three', and the opportunity, through chairmanship of the EC presidency and participation in the rolling troika, to take a leading role in international affairs over a period of eighteen months.[7] On the other hand, Spain also saw EPC from the perspective of a former 'world power'. EPC allowed Spain to tackle problems in its two areas of political interest – Latin America and North Africa – from a new and powerful vantage point.[8] Spanish influence in these regions could only be enhanced through its linkage to an increasingly assertive European Community.

Felipe Gonzalez and his cabinet took a similarly positive approach to the question of developing a defence dimension to European integration. The pragmatists within the socialist government, including Gonzalez, the Defence Minister Narcis Serra and Manuel Marin, Secretary of State for European Affairs and later one of Spain's two European Commissioners, had justified their switch to supporting Spain's NATO membership as a means to lever Spain into

Western Europe's main institutions, the EC and WEU. This pragmatism towards NATO did not temper, however, their conviction that for Europe to have international influence it would need to develop an autonomous defence identity. Nor did their pragmatism and the pro-NATO referendum vote quash the widespread public antipathy in Spain towards NATO and the United States, an antipathy shared by all socialist parliamentarians if not by most members of the opposition Partido Popular.[9] For the majority of Spaniards, NATO was not an organization that defended freedom and national sovereignty, as was the case for other west European countries. Instead, popular perceptions of NATO remained intertwined with American support for the repressive Franco regime. As a result, the United States was not perceived as a 'liberator', but, in the words of one foreign ministry official, as 'the ally of a dictator in the face of a non-specific threat'. Spanish mistrust of the Atlantic alliance was fed by strong public support for Spain to maintain its neutral status. This support for neutrality had its roots in Spain's exclusion from the great European conflicts since the Napoleonic era, and in the sharp memory of the colonial and civil wars which had carried such a high cost for Spanish lives in the recent past.[10]

Although physically situated on the edge of Europe and, with a proud but distant history as one of Europe's imperial powers, the years in the wilderness had swept away any illusions that Spain could raise its economic prosperity and regain political influence outside the framework of west European institutions. Spaniards had been forced to abandon the delusions of grandeur and sense of insular autonomy that still resonated in that other former Great Power on Europe's periphery – the United Kingdom. In short, Spanish policymakers soon realized that lending their unequivocal support to the process of European integration was the surest and most realistic means for Spain to achieve its domestic and international goals. As Felipe Gonzalez stated towards the end of his premiership, 'I have a certain passion for European construction, but it is never abstract, it is tied to my country, because it is fundamental for Spain.'[11]

Challenges for Spain at the end of the cold war

Spanish concerns at the end of the cold war did not have at their root the fear of a potential return to historical enmities among the core countries of Western Europe, as was the case for many in the European community. The main danger to Spain could be encapsulated in one phrase – 're-peripheralization'. On the one hand, Spain risked being banished again to Europe's periphery by the sudden acceleration, in 1990, of plans for west European economic integration, specifically the desire to move to a single currency in as short a time-frame as possible. Despite its impressive economic growth since 1986, Spanish GDP per capita remained at roughly 75 per cent of the European average, while unemployment had jumped to 15 per cent of the workforce by 1990. Economic convergence with its EU partners was still a long-term ambition. As the desire to contain a united Germany's economic power brought forward the date of European Monetary Union, Spain faced an unenviable choice. It could strive to join the single currency before it had achieved sufficient economic convergence and risk the consequences. Alternatively, as Carlos Zaldivar, a close adviser to Gonzalez and the head of the Prime Minister's Planning Staff in the Moncloa Palace in 1990, concluded, Spain could sit back and watch Europe split into two groups: those on the fast track to economic integration and those, like Spain, left on the periphery.[12]

The second source of concern for the Spanish government centred upon the community's efforts to support the reform process in central and eastern Europe after 1989. Germany had played a vital role in Spain's political reintegration and economic renaissance. It was Helmut Kohl who had provided the political muscle at the Stuttgart summit in 1983 to break the negotiating deadlock with France over Spanish accession to the EC. It was also German companies, such as Volkswagen, who were the largest foreign investors in the Spanish economy. While Spanish policymakers did not share the widespread concerns about Germany reasserting a hegemony over central Europe, they nevertheless feared that Germany's and the EC's political and economic energies would now refocus away from Spain and towards the east.

The European Commission's decision, in August 1990, rapidly to upgrade the restrictive Trade and Cooperation Agreements with Poland, Hungary and Czechoslovakia to fully-blown Association Agreements highlighted the potential costs to Spain of the EU's opening to the east. The Commission's proposals undermined Spain's preferential terms of trade and its privileged position as the low-cost production base within the EC. During 1991, a majority of EC member states insisted on making the key concessions necessary to complete the 'Europe Agreements' in sectors of direct interest to Spain and Portugal, such as steel, textiles, fruit and vegetables, rather than in sectors such as beef and dairy products that were of domestic interest to the core EC members. This decision undercut the comparative advantage of important Spanish products in EC markets while Spain was still running trading deficits with its EC partners. At the same time, incentives in the Europe Agreements to encourage and protect EU investment in the CEECs endangered the flow of foreign direct investment by EC multinationals into Spain.

The decisions by the European Council after Maastricht to enlarge the European Union to EFTA members, and to accept eventual EU expansion to the Europe Agreement countries, intensified the strategic danger for Spain. The EU Mediterranean group of Spain, Portugal, Greece, Italy and France would carry far less weight in an EU of twenty members than it did in one of twelve members. EU enlargement to the north and east would make it harder for Spain to defend its sectoral interests in the Council of Ministers, at the same time as deflecting the Spanish government's longer-term ambition gradually to extend the focus of the EU's external relations more towards areas of Spanish interest in Latin America and North Africa.[13]

The third source of concern for the Spanish government was that the end of the cold war might lead to a renationalization of its partners' attitudes towards Europe and to a cooling down of the pace of west European political and social integration, EMU apart. The Spanish political élite, saw no alternative other than west European integration for the pursuit of its economic and diplomatic interests. A weaker Europe, whether in terms of completing the Single Market, distributing structural funds, or developing common foreign policies, would mean a weaker and more marginalized Spain. Ever sensitive to the latent nationalisms within Spain, the central government was also alarmed that European integration would weaken just as the collapse of communism in the east had released a wave of disaffected nationalist movements around the EU's periphery, not least in Yugoslavia.[14]

Despite these concerns, the end of the cold war in Europe at least found Spain in a position to be involved from the outset in laying the foundations for a new European order. Having been excluded not only from the post-1945 deliberations, but also from Versailles and the Concert of Europe beforehand, the Spanish government and foreign policy establishment now had a chance to influence the shape of any new arrangements as well as to secure Spain's position in this wider Europe.

A strong domestic political base

The Socialist government headed by Felipe Gonzalez enjoyed a solid domestic political platform at the end of the cold war. In 1989 it still retained, after its third, successive election victory, a healthy parliamentary majority. This majority gave the Gonzalez government great freedom of action in its European policymaking. Since the return to democracy, political parties in Spain still have not evolved much beyond their role as electoral machines. After victory at the polls, nominations to the Cabinet tend to strip the governing party of its most talented elected members, leaving it as a shell that awaits the next election. During this period, a high premium is placed on party loyalty. Critics of Gonzalez from the leftist wing of the Socialist Party (PSOE), for example, were eventually ejected and set up their own separate party, the Izquierda Unida.

Within the government, Gonzalez could exert strong executive control over his Cabinet, owing to his constitutional position as president of the government. His freedom of action was most pronounced in the area of foreign policy where, despite the high reputations of Francisco Fernandez Ordoñez and Javier Solana (foreign ministers from 1985–92 and 1992–96 respectively), a combination of the legacy of Spain's one-hundred year exclusion from international politics, the Spanish electorate's ignorance and apathy towards international affairs, and the need to set bold new parameters for Spanish foreign policy favoured a 'personalization' of Spain's external relations.[15] By the same token, Gonzalez adopted an active role in Europe in order to enhance his credibility at home.

Although vocal in its criticism of the government on domestic issues, there was no fundamental divergence between the views of the main opposition party, the conservative Partido Popular (PP) led by José-Maria Aznar and the PSOE on the broad thrust of Spain's strategy towards Europe during the post-cold war period. Criticism focused usually on the alleged failure of the Socialist government to protect Spanish national and sectoral interests sufficiently robustly in Brussels. On matters of European 'high policy', such as the Single Market, plans for monetary union and European foreign policy, Gonzalez could be confident of parliamentary support from the PP. And whatever the differences the main regional parties (the Catalan Convergencia i Union [CiU] and the Partido Nacional Vasco [PNV]) may have had with the socialist government on constitutional or economic issues, the one area where their interests converged was 'Europe'. In their view, deepening the process of European integration made the position of the central government less dominant within Spain.[16] The parliamentary consensus in favour of European integration reflected one of the most pro-European publics in the EC. In 1989, 81 per cent of Spaniards supported a European Union; 67 per cent favoured monetary union and 57 per cent the creation of a European government.[17]

Popular support for European integration was mirrored within the Spanish foreign policy establishment. Spain's policy towards Europe benefited from being concentrated in the hands of a small, highly experienced 'clique' of civil servants that had specialized throughout their careers in EU affairs. By 1989, many of the officials who had negotiated Spain's accession to the community had risen to key positions either in the Commission, in the Palacio de la Trinidad in Madrid – the foreign ministry's separate and exclusive European secretariat –, or in Spain's Permanent Representation in Brussels, which became Spain's largest overseas representation, larger even than its Washington Embassy.[18] These officials were convinced that Spain's continued political and economic renaissance depended upon maintaining the momentum of west European integration. But after the bruising experience of Spain's accession negotiations, they were acutely conscious of the relative gains and losses attached to each EU policy decision. Negotiations in Brussels became Spain's 'highest form of foreign policy',[19] and officials in the Palacio de la Trinidad and Brussels representation prided themselves on being tougher negotiators than their colleagues from the national sectoral ministries. Regular inter-ministerial co-ordination, backed by the constant exchange of personnel and ideas between the Brussels representation and the Trinidad, secured a high reputation for Spain within EU policymaking circles.

Concentrated within the tightly-knit Moncloa–Trinidad–Brussels triangle, Spain's European élite were able to develop their ideas towards European integration in a politically enclosed environment. The absence of democratic politics and open civil society in Spain until the late 1970s meant the absence of informed debate outside government concerning international relations. In 1989–92, no Spanish research institutes existed to snipe away at Spanish foreign policy from the sidelines and demand fundamental rethinks of policy towards the EU.[20] Nor was there much academic commentary on conceptual approaches to Europe from the universities. Political science remained, even in 1989–96, a neglected subject in comparison to the popular focus of Spanish teaching and students on law and economics.[21] The main daily papers – *El Pais* and *ABC* – covered European issues in considerable detail, but had no popular nor conceptual basis from which to challenge the prevailing pro-European orthodoxy.[22] In sum, throughout the upheavals of the post-cold war years, the Spanish government enjoyed great freedom of manoeuvre to develop its Europe policies and to carry them through.

Opportunities for progress: 1989–92

Gonzalez was one of the first European leaders to congratulate Helmut Kohl after the collapse of the Berlin Wall in November 1989, a step which cemented their close personal relationship.[23] This show of support reciprocated West Germany's long-standing support of Spain and its own democratic transition.[24] Gonzalez was also aware that if he was to safeguard Spain's recently won economic gains and prevent its marginalization in the wider, post-cold war Europe, then his government would have to work harder than ever to nurture the Spanish–German bilateral relationship in the years to come. Fortunately, Spanish concerns that German unification might slow the process of west European integration were shared both by the German government and by the majority of its EU partners. As a result, Gonzalez was able to stand shoulder to shoulder with Kohl and Mitterrand in supporting the Franco-German strategy for an IGC on European Political Union, and in arguing that the EU should use German unification as a spur to accelerate and deepen the process of west European integration.[25] The challenge for the Spanish government was a tactical one: it had to assess how the raft of proposals in the IGC would affect Spain's particular national interests and weave the defence of those interests into the negotiations. Ultimately, Carlos Zaldivar noted that 'there were no zigzags in the Spanish position'. In each case, it supported or introduced proposals that had the dual objective of 'deepening' European integration while also furthering Spanish national interests.[26]

The Spanish government's first and most cherished proposal called for a formal linkage between the European citizen and the Union, enshrining specific citizens' rights in the Treaty on European Union (TEU), such as freedom of movement and abode within the EU and the right to vote in local and European elections in one's place of residence. Spain had the largest number of nationals of any EU member state working elsewhere in the Union.

Extending social protection beyond Spanish borders to their citizens was a priority. The idea of European citizenship also reflected the shared view of both government officials and the Spanish public that the process of European integration should provide a further underpinning for human rights in Europe. Spaniards had long equated the idea of Europe with social and political freedom. Their newly-gained individual freedoms could only benefit from being anchored at the European, supranational level.

The Spanish government strongly supported bringing 'home and justice affairs' under the EU umbrella, reflecting again the pursuit of specific national concerns. Closer co-ordination of immigration and visa policies would help dissuade North African immigrants from using Spain as a staging post into richer EU countries. Anti-terrorism co-operation could also help curb the operations of the Basque separatist group ETA, which has been such a painful thorn in the side of Spain's young democracy. Despite the savagery of its terrorist campaign, ETA retained pockets of sympathizers outside Spain, who still saw it as fighting against the fascist centralism of the Franco era. Co-ordination of anti-terrorist programmes and extradition policies at the EU level would provide a formal mechanism for overcoming the ambivalence that was occasionally displayed towards ETA within the EU.

The Spanish government was also a strong, if pragmatic supporter of upgrading European Political Cooperation into a Common Foreign and Security Policy (CFSP). From the Spanish perspective, the artificial division between the 'political and economic aspects of security' and its more traditional 'defence' dimension weakened the EU's capacity for autonomous action on the world stage. Spanish policymakers saw a new confluence between their national interests and the EU's broader strategic goals. The disappearance of a tangible security threat from the Eastern bloc had given Spanish concerns about political instability in the Maghreb greater salience for the EU. The EU was also in a better position to become actively involved in the political and economic development of central and southern America, now that the region was no longer a stage for US–Soviet competition. At the same time, Spanish officials were wary that the end of the cold war might encourage larger EU member states to revert to more nationalistic foreign policies. Like other smaller EU members, Spain saw a maximalist CFSP as a means to circumscribe this process. The government therefore supported the Franco-German proposals to use qualified majority voting to adopt 'common actions' under the CFSP. However, Spain's continuing national interests in Latin America and North Africa meant that the government did not advocate drawing CFSP fully under EU competence, nor diluting the ability of individual states to oppose common policies on the grounds of 'vital' national interest.[27]

Still, the Spanish government would have preferred the inclusion of some defence dimension to the EU under the CFSP provisions. Gonzalez sought to overcome the ingrained neutralism of the Spanish people and enable Spain to play a constructive role in the post-cold war European order. Domestic support for sending Spanish troops abroad would be far more forthcoming in the context of an EU or WEU operation than as part of a US-led, NATO operation.[28] Gonzalez and Narcis Serra publicly supported, therefore, the Mitterrand–Kohl initiative in October 1991, which called for the creation of a European Defence Identity as part of the Maastricht IGC. Within NATO, Spanish officials argued that NATO had to renounce quickly the cold war doctrines of forward defence and flexible response if it wanted to retain its relevance. The essence of the Spanish approach was that NATO should adapt and become compatible with the evolution of the EU and not vice versa. Although supportive of a continued US presence in Europe, both the defence ministry and Gonzalez as prime minister believed that NATO was not relevant for the post-cold war crises that were likely to arise in the Balkans, Middle East, and Maghreb.[29] It was essential that Europe develop instead structures of 'co-operative security' that were inclusive by design, like the Conference on Security and Cooperation in Europe (CSCE), alongside the defensive and deterrent structures of the Atlantic alliance. The most obvious manifestation of this ambition was the Spanish government's proposal, alongside Italy, at the CSCE meeting in Majorca in September 1990 for the creation of a parallel Conference on Security and Cooperation in the Mediterranean (CSCM).[30]

Irrespective of the progress made in modernizing the EU politically during the IGC, Spanish ministers and officials were acutely conscious that the parallel negotiations on EMU carried the most profound implications for Europe after the cold war, and for Spain's ultimate position within it. Spain had good reason, as noted above, to fear rapid progress to a single currency. However, Gonzalez had no desire to block EMU. On the contrary, he saw EMU as constituting for the EU 'the most transcendent step forward since its creation'. EMU removed the risk of political and economic dilution that could accompany further EU enlargement and would, *de facto*, lead to a form of European Political Union. The priority for Spain was to ensure that it succeeded in forming part of this 'nucleo central Europeo' and did not end up 'descolgado' (detached) from the mainstream of post-cold war European integration.[31]

Gonzalez and his government concentrated their efforts on two fronts. On the one hand, they made every effort to ensure that the convergence criteria for EMU did not discriminate unduly against Spain. Finance Minister Solchaga succeeded in blocking the inclusion of current account and unemployment criteria from the list of EMU targets, and he was instrumental in the creation of the two-step timetable, which designated 1999 as the point of no return for Monetary Union, giving less prepared countries an additional two years of preparation beyond the optional target date of 1997.[32] On the other hand, Gonzalez and his advisers were determined to offset the expected costs to Spain of keeping up with the new pace of European economic integration. Having accepted restrictive terms for EC accession in 1986 as the economic price for a political return to Europe, Maastricht now offered Spain the opportunity to renegotiate a more advantageous economic package.[33] Gonzalez argued unceasingly that the European Union required the budgetary mechanisms to support its poorer members as they ceded national control over their economies and struggled to converge with their EU partners.[34] Spanish proposals during 1991 for the 'principle of sufficiency of means' and for a more progressive system of member state contributions to the EU budget, linked to GNP per capita, were rejected. In the end, however, Gonzalez tied Spanish approval of EMU to the establishment of a new EU 'Cohesion Fund' and succeeded in incorporating the Fund in the TEU.[35] Overall, Spanish politicians were able to look upon the results of the Maastricht IGC with some satisfaction.[36]

Holding course through the storm: 1992–96

The optimism engendered by the signing of the TEU in March 1992 and the Spanish parliament's rapid ratification of the Treaty was quickly punctured, in Spain as in other EU member states.[37] The onset of economic recession throughout the EU in early 1992 was keenly felt in Spain. The peseta was forced to devalue three times after June 1992, losing 22 per cent of its value in the process. Unemployment climbed to 18 per cent, the highest level in the EU, while the budget deficit rose to 6.1 per cent of GDP. Buffeted by the worsening economic conditions, the PSOE lost its parliamentary majority in the 6 June, 1993 elections. With economic recession came a loss of domestic support for European integration in most EU member states. No where was this turnaround as seemingly abrupt as in Spain, where strong support for the EU in 1992 (64 per cent favoured TEU ratification) turned 180-degrees by 1995. A series of conflicts over Spanish fishing rights in 1993–95 compounded and inflamed anti-EU sentiment among the Spanish public.[38]

Economic recession exacerbated the Spanish fear that EMU would leave Spain isolated on the periphery of a two-speed Europe. By the end of 1992, the Spanish government faced a stark dilemma. The concept of an enlarged but more loosely integrated EU implied a dangerous dilution of Spain's voice in EU affairs. On the other hand, while a post-cold war EU built around a core of west European states would guarantee continued west European political and economic integration, Spain risked exclusion from this new EU core by dint of its economic weakness. Despite this risk, Gonzalez revealed his preference for a west European core when he supported, in March 1992, the suggestion by a German MEP that a five to six member EU 'directoire' should take charge of the future course of EU integration.[39] In order to prepare itself for the possible split into a two-speed Europe, the Gonzalez government adapted its European strategy in two ways. First, it took a more hard-nosed approach within the EU, defending its economic and political interests more strongly than ever so as to ensure that Spain stood the best possible chance of entering into the EU's 'nucleo duro'. Secondly, it tried to compensate for its economic handicap by proving to core countries such as France and Germany that Spain was of sufficient political stature and importance not to be excluded. Three episodes over the following three years illustrated the Spanish approach.

First, at the European Council in Edinburgh in December 1992, Gonzalez threatened to veto the opening of enlargement negotiations with the EFTA countries unless his wavering EU colleagues met their financial commitments to the Cohesion Fund within the agreed timetable.[40] After reaching an acceptable compromise, Gonzalez was able to come away from the summit having demonstrated that Spain was a country whose interests had to be taken seriously within the EU. Second, one year later, during the winter of 1993–94, the Spanish government put up an equally robust defence of its voting weight in the EU Council of Ministers, which threatened to be diluted by the accession of Norway, Sweden, Finland and Austria.[41] France and Germany shared the Spanish concern that, without reform, the accession of these four 'small' countries (with a combined population of 26 million, as compared to Spain's population of 39 million) would further weaken the voice of states with larger populations. But they were willing to leave debate of the issue until the 1996 IGC; only the British lined up alongside Spain. After a series of highly publicized deadlocks in the Council of Ministers, the Spanish government relented, after securing a commitment from the Commission that the existing blocking minority under QMV would only be overruled by the new majority after a period of extended consultation. By precipitating this crisis, in the style of de Gaulle and Thatcher, Spain once again underscored its determination not to see its status or interests compromised by EU enlargement, as well as its claim to be one of the EU's 'big powers'.

Third, the Spanish government insisted from 1990 onwards that the EU develop a more proactive and structured relationship with its Mediterranean neighbours. Spanish policymakers argued that European order after the cold war was not simply a matter of reuniting east and west. European order could only be secured if the Union looked south and supported the political and economic stabilization of its whole periphery. Spanish politicians and academics pointed out that the price for neglecting its southern neighbours would be high, in terms of political instability, migratory pressures, the threat to energy supplies and lost markets.[42] Of course, Spain's particular national interests in the region (immigration from Morocco; the fate of Ceuta and Melilla; Libya's status as Spain's second largest oil supplier; and, perhaps most important, the planned gas pipeline from Algeria, through Morocco to Spain) made the government all the more determined to balance the EU's initiatives towards eastern Europe with a new approach towards north Africa.

After the EU's failure to follow through on the ambitious agenda of the CSCM conference in Majorca, the two Spanish EU Commissioners, Abel Matutes and Manuel Marin, working in close consultation with Madrid, gradually forced the Mediterranean issue onto the EU agenda. During the

Corfu and Essen EU summits, in June and December 1994, Spanish officials made it clear that Spain would not approve the new five-year 'Phare' financial package for central and eastern Europe unless a package of similar weight and structure was approved for the EU's Mediterranean neighbours.[43] Despite strong opposition from other EU member states, Gonzalez succeeded in unblocking the funds, after appealing directly to Helmut Kohl and his Finance Minister, Theo Waigel, during a private meeting on the margins of the Cannes summit in June 1995. Yet again, the Spanish government had combined the pursuit of its national concerns with raising the country's political profile within the EU.[44]

Sticking to the mainstream

At no point during the bleak years that followed Maastricht, however, did Spanish policymakers consider translating their increasingly stout defence of national interests into a more sceptical strategy towards the concept of deeper European integration – nor was there internal domestic pressure to do so. Instead, in keeping with the 'orteguian' orthodoxy, Gonzalez and Solana argued at every turn that far from European integration being the source of Spain's problems, Europe was in fact the solution and 'mas europa' (more Europe) the only viable strategy.[45] As Esther Barbé has pointed out, the government's approach reflected a continuity not only in its strategy towards integration but also in its underlying political philosophy.

The reasons for this conceptual constancy were twofold. Spain's influence upon the course of European integration, and its ability to defend its specific national interests, depended upon securing a place in the core of the European Union. Spain also had no other option but to swim with the European mainstream. The idea that Spain should respond to enlargement of the Union by building alternative alliances was discarded. Officials within the foreign ministry could point to the many similarities between Spain's position in the EU and that of the United Kingdom. Both have global interests; both sit uneasily on the periphery of the European continent; both came late to the Community and under what they saw as punitive economic terms. Those same officials recognized, however, the inherent difficulties in building closer ties with the UK. Gibraltar remained the fundamental stumbling block, souring popular Spanish perceptions of Britain and holding as a hostage to fortune any attempts to establish intergovernmental co-ordination in specific areas of EU policy. Disputes between British and Spanish fishing vessels, and the United Kingdom's support for Canada in its confrontation with Spain, further damaged bilateral relations. In addition, Spanish and UK policymakers diverged fundamentally in their views of the relative importance of further EU market-opening compared with the need to ensure social and economic cohesion.[46] There was little solid common ground, therefore, upon which to build a viable UK–Spanish approach to European order after the cold war.

Building up the Mediterranean block beyond its *ad hoc* defence of specific sectoral interests was also considered impractical. Greece was too unpredictable. Despite solidarity over the Cohesion Fund, Spanish relations with Portugal were strained. This was due partly to the legacy of historical competition between the two neighbouring countries, within and outside Europe; partly to their different aspirations for European integration, with Portugal, a self-recognized 'small' country, strongly resisting any recalibration of EU voting weights.[47] Despite an affinity of views with Italy towards Europe and the importance of the Mediterranean, internal political upheaval in Italy during the post-cold war period made it impossible to build up a strong bilateral relationship.[48] Spain's relationship with France remained cool.[49] On the one hand, the wounds caused by French obstruction of Spain's EC accession in the early 1980s, and its past indifference to the ETA movement, had largely scarred over. The relationship had been strengthened by regular bilateral summit meetings to discuss areas of common interest such as migration, the Maghreb, anti-terrorism co-operation, French foreign direct investment in Spain, and the Common Agricultural Policy (CAP). Nevertheless, there remained an underlying unease in Madrid about the inherent contradiction between the visionary zeal of French leaders towards the process of European integration and their persistent defence of intergovernmentalism in much EU business.[50] In addition, tensions between French and Spanish farmers and truckers continued to boil over into open hostilities at the border, strengthening for many Spaniards the perception of France as a physical obstacle to Spanish incorporation into Western Europe. Then there was always the competition between the two countries over influence in North Africa.[51]

Germany remained the preferred ally for Spain during the post-cold war period, much as it had been since Helmut Kohl broke the log-jam preventing Spain's accession to the EC. The close ties between the two countries transcended the long-standing personal relationship between Felipe Gonzalez and Helmut Kohl. From the Spanish perspective, these ties were underpinned by the need to put into practice the aphorism that any country should try to remain on good terms with its 'neighbour's neighbour'. The appreciation of Germany as a strategic counter weight to France was reinforced by a shared view between Spain's political élite and the German CDU/CSU coalition of the preferred destination of European integration. Both were prepared to model European construction on their national experience, envisaging more of a federal than confederal end-point to the process of European integration.

Spanish policymakers were conscious, however, that the survival of this privileged bilateral relationship depended upon being sensitive to Germany's own strategic priorities. In other words, the strength of the Spanish–German relationship was linked to consistent Spanish support for the Franco-German axis within the EU. Thus, the Gonzalez government was invariably quick either to join or endorse Franco-German initiatives in the post-cold war period, such as EMU, CFSP, the Eurocorps, and the establishment of a 'rolling',

Franco-German-Spanish EU presidency during 1994–95. By loyally supporting Germany and France's combined role as the 'motor' of the EU, the Spanish government contributed to the momentum for European integration; it reaped material rewards, as seen in Germany's support for the Cohesion Fund and the EU Mediterranean initiative; and it reinforced Spain's claim to have replaced Italy as the third 'big' EU member state and as a strong candidate of any future EU core.[52]

The Spanish government's tight-wire strategy of taking a more belligerent stand in protecting its national interests while trying to raise its profile as a constructive member of the future EU core meant that it had to develop a very measured response to the public debate among EU leaders and commentators during autumn 1994 and early 1995 concerning ways to make the EU more flexible institutionally ahead of its enlargement to the east.[53] Spanish policymakers were alarmed by the fact that the Lamers 'hard core' proposal of September 1994 unconditionally excluded Spain, while Prime Minister Balladur's 'inner circle' dwelt primarily on the need for Franco-German co-operation in all the 'zones de solidarité renforcée'. In Madrid, some politicians and officials questioned whether the 'core' concept would act as the guardian of the flame of integration or whether it foreshadowed new, geostrategic divisions in Europe; the prelude to 'a return to the Congress of Vienna', as one official described it. Others suspected a desire by the CDU to circle the wagons around the original EU founders in an effort to ensure the long-term viability of EMU, to counter growing pressures on national welfare systems, and to prevent further erosion of their global economic competitiveness – all of which would be far harder to achieve with the millstone of poorer EU members.[54] At the very least, they challenged German assertions that a hard core would have a magnetic impact on those left outside, fearing instead the emergence of a dependence–hegemonic relationship between the 'ins' and 'outs'.[55]

Emilio Fernandez Castaño, Spain's Secretary General for European Affairs in 1995, argued that the creation of a European 'hard core' threatened to destroy the new balance of power which had helped sustain European order during the cold war, and which promised to sustain it in the future. Castaño doubted that a 'nuclear fusion' of France, Germany and the Benelux contained an inherent political balance. It was his view that only by incorporating in any European core the United Kingdom, Spain, Italy, Sweden, and Poland, as well as the collection of smaller European powers, could Europe be confident of preserving its internal balance of interests and ensure its long-term stability and prosperity.[56]

Despite these reservations about the two-speed approach, the government had to frame its response without giving the impression of wishing to restrain efforts to deepen European integration and without undermining candidacy for an EU core should it develop. The sensitivity with which the Spanish government and foreign ministry approached the issue was visible in the publication by the foreign ministry on 2 March 1995 of a document, *Bases Para Una Reflexion*, which laid out all of the competing proposals from other member states and from academics about the future course of European integration, and which explained the dangers that these posed to Spanish conceptions and aspirations for European integration.[57] Despite a rigorous analysis of the options, the document made no attempt to challenge the main proposals emanating from France and Germany or to articulate an alternative, distinctively Spanish view of the future of European construction. Spanish policymakers were specific only in their condemnation of the concept of a Europe 'à la carte', and of variable geometry as a way for a few states to get around others' national vetoes. They repeated the familiar refrain that any steps towards a European hard core should be accompanied by a reinforcement of policies supporting intra-EU solidarity, lest a hard core not only drive a wedge into Europe but also threaten the cohesion of the single market. And they constantly evoked the importance of preserving the institutional cohesion of the EU.[58] In fact, the Spanish position could be encapsulated in the observation of one senior official that 'Spain is against the hard core; but if there is a hard core, Spain wants to be part of it.'

Preparing for Europe's transition

Spain's tenure of the EU presidency in the latter half of 1995 gave the Gonzalez government the perfect opportunity to bolster its claim to membership of a future EU core.[59] Supported by an experienced team of diplomats and by a continuing parliamentary consensus on the government's strategy towards Europe, and driven by the determination of Felipe Gonzalez to cap his time in office with a successful EU presidency, the government was able to follow through on two carefully-planned initiatives to raise Spain's political profile and credibility.[60]

First, despite an understandable ambivalence towards the EMU timetable, Pedro Solbes, finance minister, and Luis Angel Rojo, governor of the Spanish Central Bank, brokered a number of important compromises to enable Monetary Union to proceed to its third and final stage within the Maastricht schedule.[61] The Spanish government reinforced its claim to be considered seriously for the first wave of EMU entries, provided it could accelerate its macroeconomic convergence with its EU partners. Second, by giving a high priority during the presidency to solidifying the timetable for the EU's eastern enlargement, the Spanish government gave itself the diplomatic room for manoeuvre to advance the status of EU relations with the two regions of greatest interest to Spain: Latin America and the Maghreb. During the presidency, the EU signed an agreement with Mercosur (Brazil, Argentina, Paraguay and Uruguay) to liberalize trade between the two groups. And on 28–29 November, the Spanish government hosted in Barcelona an EU conference with all of its Mediterranean neighbours, from north Africa to the Near East, at which the EU agreed to create a free trade area with the region by 2010. The Spanish government could rightly claim to have succeeded in its aim to achieve 'a greater sensitivity among all of the member states towards the Union's southern frontier'.[62]

During its 1995 presidency, Spain also had the opportunity to chair the 1996 IGC Reflection Group. Under the leadership of Carlos Westendorp, the Group prepared a Report to the Madrid European Council which tackled some of the difficult issues that were side-stepped at Maastricht.[63] However, it was apparent in the report, which the government submitted to the Parliament in March 1996 in preparation for the launch of the negotiations, that Spanish policymakers were trying to balance two contradictory objectives for the IGC.[64] On the one hand, as Gonzalez frequently repeated, the Spanish government wanted a wide-ranging, 'global', and proactive institutional reform of the EU prior to enlargement. On the other hand, the government, like its EU partners, faced a real dilemma in defining new areas in which it could afford definitively to pool its sovereignty. The persistent theme in the *Bases para Una Reflexion*, therefore, was the need for 'realism' and pragmatism in the 1996 IGC.[65]

For example, Spain continued to put a special emphasis on strengthening the relationship between the citizen and the EU, proposing that the EU incorporate the Social Chapter into the Treaty, sign up to the European Convention on Human Rights, and append to the Treaty a list of fundamental human rights. The Spanish government did not offer, however, to abdicate its own role as the gatekeeper between its citizens and the EU. It rejected a more formal role for the regions within the EU decisionmaking process[66] and the creation of a new 'second chamber' of the national parliaments linked to the European Parliament. It also endorsed the existing executive–legislative division of responsibilities between the Commission and the Council. And it insisted on preserving the centrality of the Council of Ministers (meeting in secret) as the executors of the will of the member states, while continuing to press for a reform of voting weights to reflect better the EU's demographic variety.

Consolidating the third pillar was another policy priority for the Spanish government. Westendorp declared that the fight against terrorism must be one of the essential objectives of political co-operation at the heart of the Union.[67] He had been incensed by the continuing ability of ETA suspects to seek political asylum in other EU member states and the right of the latter to refuse Spanish requests for extradition.[68] The Spanish government strongly supported, therefore, bringing border controls, immigration, visa and asylum policy further under EU competence. It still argued, however, that co-operation between anti-terrorism and police forces should remain intergovernmental. Spanish ministers also supported keeping unanimous voting on key issues that would impinge directly on national sovereignty or that, if transferred to the QMV approach, might carry an unacceptable cost to Spain – such as taxation, structural funds, environmental measures, accession, agreements with third parties and treaty reform. Nor did they accept that the Union should extend its competence to areas such as energy, tourism, or civil protection.

As in 1990–91, the Spanish government welcomed suggestions to strengthen CFSP procedures. But it still did not advocate a radical overhaul of the existing process. While deploring the failures of the EU in handling the break-up of Yugoslavia, Spanish foreign ministry officials expressed little faith that a reinforcement of the institutional mechanisms of CFSP could magically produce the common political will that tended to evaporate when the EU confronted pressing external crises. As *Bases Para una Reflexion* concluded, the unanimity principle could not be blamed for EU inaction. Instead, the Spanish priority was to strengthen co-ordination between the Council Secretariat, the Commission, and the EU presidency, so as to avoid as far as possible the emergence of further restricted membership Contact Group situations.[69]

On the issue of whether to build a more flexible EU, the priority for the Spanish government was to prevent exclusion. It insisted that any flexibility should be temporary and only be approved on a case-by-case basis; that all countries be involved in setting the parameters of new forms of integration and not be excluded from joining if they met the necessary conditions; that assistance be provided to those that wished to join later; and that flexibility take place within the single institutional framework, and without under-mining the *acquis communautaire*.

Spain as a new Atlantic power

The new pragmatism of the Spanish government was most apparent on the issue of constructing a new security order in Europe. During the preparation for the 1996 IGC, Solana reiterated the Spanish position that a genuine European Union would be incomplete so long as it lacked a defence dimension.[70] However, he was far from strenuous in following through on this conviction. In its *Elementos Para Una Posicion Española*, Spain called only for a 'gradual' linkage between the EU and the WEU; stressing instead the principle of national sovereignty over defence matters and the fact that the building of a European Security and Defence Identity must strengthen the Atlantic alliance. There were several reasons for this shift in approach. First, as was the case with other EU governments, Spanish politicians from the left as well as the right came to appreciate the important role that NATO would retain in maintaining peace in the post-cold war European security order.[71] The dominance of US forces and NATO assets in the Gulf war, and the inability of the WEU to play more than a marginal role in Bosnia, confirmed the prediction of Spanish defence ministry officials and diplomats that building a European Defence Identity had to be relegated to a long-term ambition rather than a short-term objective.[72] Second, the disappearance of the Soviet threat fundamentally changed Spanish attitudes to NATO. NATO was no longer an organization that could draw Spain unwillingly into an east–west conflict.[73] Instead, as NATO promised to turn its attention towards its southern flank, Spain had the chance to be a 'core' country within the new European security order.[74] NATO's decision to take on peace-keeping duties on behalf of the UN and OSCE outside the Article V zone overlapped with the Spanish military's increasing involvement in UN peacekeeping operations outside Europe.

These changes in NATO's roles and missions provoked a corresponding search by Spanish officials for a closer working relationship with the integrated military framework of NATO. In June 1992, Spanish forces accepted a specific role within NATO's Rapid Reaction Force and, at the end of September 1995, the socialist government transferred control over Spanish troops serving under the UN in Bosnia to the NATO-led IFOR.[75] At the same time, Spain joined the *ad hoc*, multilateral defence groups, such as Eurofor, Eurocorps and Euromarfor, that were double-hatted for both WEU and NATO operations. Finally, the electoral victory of the Partido Popular, which had always supported Spanish integration into NATO, in the spring of 1996, heralded a more self-conscious Spanish rapprochement with the alliance. From the Spanish perspective, NATO's decision in June 1996 at the Berlin summit to approve the CJTF concept drew NATO closer to the 'Spanish model' for national participation in NATO operations, one in which national politicians could exert greater control alongside NATO's integrated military command.[76] Once in power, Aznar used this argument, along with the decline in public anxiety about NATO, to announce that Spain would rapidly enter into discussions with its NATO partners on NATO's new military structure and how best to incorporate Spanish forces into NATO's integrated military structure.[77] Conscious of Spain's exclusion during the cold war, PP ministers were determined that Spain should be a founder member and co-designer of the new NATO.[78]

The Spanish rapprochement with NATO was, in turn, the culmination of a marked improvement in Spanish relations with the United States. The pivotal moment was the bold decision by the Gonzalez government in autumn 1990 to allow the United States to use Spain as the primary logistics route and staging post for US operations in the war against Saddam Hussein. This included allowing US B-52 bombers to conduct 300 missions from the Moron air base over the war zone.[79] Gonzalez chose to overcome the instinctive antipathy of the Spanish people towards undertaking military operations alongside the United States, to prove to the United States and to his European partners that Spain could serve as a reliable ally in the post-cold war world, even when the crisis had little direct bearing on Spanish national interests. The shrewdness of the government's decision was confirmed by the fact that, at the end of the conflict, 62 per cent of Spaniards supported Gonzalez's handling of the crisis. The Gulf war was the first step in Spain's abandonment of its historical reserve towards involvement in international conflicts. By mid

1992, US–Spanish relations were at their best since Spain had begun the transition to democracy. Spanish support for US forces in the Gulf war played a major part in the US decision to promote Madrid as the venue for the post-Gulf war Middle East Peace Conference of December 1991. In October 1992, Spain sent a sizeable contingent to Bosnia to try to help resolve the conflict there (even though it was excluded from the five-power Contact Group), demonstrating once again that it possessed both the resources and the political will to play a key role in upholding European security.[80]

Having laid the groundwork for improved Spanish–US relations in the Gulf war and Bosnia, Gonzalez, Solana and Westendorp began planning as early as autumn 1994 to use the forthcoming Spanish presidency of the EU to cement Spain's new transatlantic relationship. Their intention was to stake Spain's claim to be an Atlantic power as much as a European power. The culmination of their efforts was the signing of the ambitious New Transatlantic Agenda and related US–EU Action Plan in Madrid by President Clinton, Felipe Gonzalez and Jacques Santer on 3 December 1995. Important factors in this US–Spanish rapprochement were the growing 'hispanization' of the United States, the return of a new generation of Spanish students from graduate courses in the United States,[81] and a willingness within the defence ministry and the PP to treat the United States as a 'European power' that should not be 'extranjerizado'. In contrast to their French colleagues, many Spanish politicians and officials felt comfortable in extolling the political and military value of keeping the United States involved in post-cold war European security structures, without allowing this Atlanticism to clash with their determination to encourage the EU to develop its own security capabilities in the long-term.[82]

The US and Spanish governments had the opportunity to cement their burgeoning relationship when the United States rejected Ruud Lubbers as the candidate to replace Willy Claes as NATO Secretary General. Solana's role in leading a highly-praised EU presidency, including the signing of the New Transatlantic Agenda, helped secure both US and EU support and make him a natural compromise candidate for the post.[83] Subsequently, members of Spain's European policy clique were also selected for two other key international posts: Westendorp taking over as Chief Representative in Bosnia from Carl Bildt and Miguel Angel Moratinos taking up the post of special EU envoy to the Middle East. Within seven years, Spain had not only proved itself to be a reliable western partner in the emerging post-cold war European security order, but, by assiduously improving its relations with the United States, it had carved out an influential place for itself alongside the group of leading powers in Europe.

Economic convergence: the central dilemma

Spain's highly professional management of its European policy stood for many years in stark contrast to the mediocre performance of the Spanish economy. The risk of Spanish relegation to the periphery of the new Europe after 1989 flowed less from the process of EU enlargement to the north and east and more from the persistent structural weaknesses of the Spanish economy. In 1993, the World Economic Forum classified Spain as one of the least competitive economies in the OECD. Spanish as well as foreign commentators have frequently pointed to the structural problems that bedevil the Spanish economy.[84] Spanish unemployment has persisted at a level of between 15–20 per cent of the 'active' population since the mid 1980s. In their efforts to grant Spanish workers levels of social welfare and job protection similar to their EU counterparts, the socialist government priced a large proportion of Spaniards out of the job market.

The high levels of foreign direct investment that followed Spanish accession to the EC were unable to cut these unemployment levels. In fact, FDI masked an underlying low level of domestic saving (falling from 10 per cent of GNP in the 1970s to 6.6 per cent by 1990). It also highlighted the very low levels of FDI by Spanish companies in comparison to other OECD economies that were positioning themselves for global competition. The continuing insularity of Spanish business, even by 1997, was reflected in the small size of most companies, the almost complete absence of Spanish multinationals (Tecnicas Reunidas and certain banks being the rare exceptions to this rule), a worryingly low level of domestic investment in research and development (only 0.7 per cent of GDP compared to roughly 2.5 per cent in the United States and Japan), and an often-noted lack of dynamism among the Spanish managerial class. As Spain trod water economically (its GDP per capita was stuck at roughly 77 per cent of the EC average between 1975 and 1991), it risked being both undercut and overtaken by East Asian and central and east European competitors.

Spain's inability to transfer its economic activity into new, high technology, knowledge-driven manufacturing and service industries was reflected in the persistent imbalance in its current account. In many ways, the collapse of communism at the end of the 1980s exposed the fact that Spain had become one of the most 'dependent' EU member states. It relied upon its EU membership to shield it from the new global economic competitive pressures that proliferated from the late 1970s onwards. Rather than use FDI inflows to restructure the Spanish economy, it became extremely vulnerable to a reverse of these flows as the EU prepared for enlargement, and as Spain's preferential access to EU markets was further eroded under the GATT Uruguay Round.

As Gonzalez realized, and the PP was ready to point out, European redistributive policies such as the EU Cohesion Fund could do little to lift the Spanish economy up to the level of its EU partners.[85] For Gonzalez, the real value of the Cohesion Funds lay in combining them with the EU Structural Funds to try to minimize regional disparities within the Spanish economy, especially as the government sought to reduce its domestic budgetary expenditures in the lead-up to the launch of monetary union. For the PP,

Spain's economic problems required domestic solutions as well as financial transfers. Spain would become strong only by exposing its economy to the rigours of global competition. Both Gonzalez and Aznar, however, looked to the Maastricht convergence criteria to impose a crucial external discipline that would help bring the Spanish economy closer to the standards of its EU partners.

The PP benefited from the fact that its supporters in the Spanish business community, while tempted by the prospect of a weak peseta from an export perspective, were more concerned by the widespread dangers of being outside EMU, such as higher interest rates and rate of inflation, a loss of budgetary discipline and the fear that the EMU 'ins' might seek to exclude the 'outs' from unhindered access to their markets. Reflecting these concerns, Aznar initially suggested that the EU should delay progress to the third phase of EMU if a 'qualified and clear majority' of existing members were unready.[86] As the probability that EMU would go ahead hardened in the latter half of 1996, however, so the PP's initial wavering on the issue evaporated.[87] Spanish officials warned that EMU, far more than the continuing debate over EU institutional deepening, would be the principal catalyst for European political integration.[88] Aznar and the PP made rapid efforts to impose a more disciplined domestic economic policy, despite the constant political horse-trading which accompanied the PP's inability to secure an absolute parliamentary majority in the election. A forceful privatization strategy, tighter control of government spending, and a modest, government-sponsored pact between employers and the unions on reducing the costs of hiring and firing workers all served to create a new sense of fiscal rigour.

The budget for 1997 confirmed the government's view that EMU was not only the trigger for the long needed structural transformation of the Spanish economy, it was also the only way that Spain could secure its position at the core of the new Europe. Symbolic opportunities were also grasped. Aznar very publicly rejected an overture in early 1997 from Romano Prodi, the new Italian Prime Minister, to create a united Spanish–Italian front towards EMU, underlining the fact that Spain should be judged exclusively on objective criteria. These steps, combined with the growing difficulties in 1996 that France and Germany were having in meeting the Maastricht deficit criteria, gave substance to Spain's claim to be eligible for the first wave of EMU. The growing credibility of this claim created a virtuous circle, in which falling interest rates dramatically reduced the cost of servicing Spain's government debt and, in turn, made further budget cuts less painful.[89]

At the close of 1997, Spain's economic outlook, in statistical terms, was the brightest in over two decades. Spaniards enjoyed an unprecedented combination of rapid economic growth (estimated at 3.4 per cent in 1998), low inflation (2 per cent in 1997 rising to a more realistic 2.9 per cent in 1998), and a current account surplus. The holy grail of membership in EMU and in

Europe's new hard core beckoned. Few Spanish policymakers, however, allowed themselves the luxury of believing that life inside EMU would be easy. Only by using the new favourable conditions to undertake far-reaching reforms of Spanish labour laws and its social security, pensions and health systems could Spain hope to overcome its structural weaknesses and integrate itself as a member of the European economic main stream.

Conclusion: a consistent approach to Europe

Spain benefited from a consistent conceptual approach among its leading policymakers towards European integration after the end of the cold war. The Gonzalez government was able to pursue clear policy objectives with negligible interference from other domestic actors, whether at the party political, public, or bureaucratic levels. The PP electoral victory did not herald a change of tack.

PP Parliamentarians repeatedly claimed that they had a clearer understanding of how to defend Spanish national interests in Europe than did the Gonzalez administration. They complained that Gonzalez had supported European integration indiscriminately, as if it constituted a general good – '*a priori*' and '*per se*' – for Spain;[90] that he had placed his ambition to construct a federal Europe ahead of more particular Spanish interests. With their overtly nationalist political heritage, PP deputies were more openly sceptical about Spain's need for a 'federal' Europe. In an article to mark the tenth anniversary of Spain's accession to the Community, Miguel Herrero de Miñon synthesized the right's critique of the Gonzalez years. He chided the socialists for concentrating too hard on the political aspects of European integration, and for hoping that a mere association with the rest of Europe would erase Spain's deeply rooted sense of inferiority in relation to its European partners. He criticized the socialists' mantra of 'mas Europa', blaming this 'beateria Europea' (European cant) for obscuring the fact that Spain should need no *deus ex machina* to reorganize its economy. Reclaiming Ortega's original message, he wrote that, 'Europe is the measure of Spain and not its substitute. Not a guarantee of its competitiveness, just the exigency to be competitive.'[91]

As trenchant as this criticism might have been about the Socialist government's economic strategy, it was marginal in the context of Spanish perspectives about European integration and construction. The PP victory heralded a shift in government tactics towards Europe – from the 'poetic' to the 'prosaic' – but not in Spain's strategic objectives. Aznar inherited intact from Gonzalez the consensus ('acuerdo mayoritario') in the Spanish parliament that the defence of Spain's national political and economic interests depended upon a continued commitment towards European integration. Within the PP, there existed only a small minority that would support either a shift towards a free-market approach to European integration or a Thatcherite disengagement from Europe. Despite sharing some philosophical reservations with the French RPR/UDF coalition about deeper European integration, PP parliamentarians had spent their years in opposition developing their closest personal links with the German CDU and the European Christian Democratic movement. Spanish politicians and their German counterparts were united in perceiving a strong EU as inseparable from the pursuit of their long-term national interests.

Upon coming to power, Aznar and his advisers quickly recognized that Spain risked being a loser in a wider and looser Europe. The need to form part of the emerging European political as well as economic core, if more explicitly as an equal partner rather than as the poor Mediterranean cousin, became as dominant a theme for the PP once in government as it had been for the PSOE. Accordingly, Aznar reinforced the lockhold of the 'European-ists' over the foreign ministry. Abel Matutes, a European Commissioner since 1983, returned to Madrid as Foreign Minister. In addition, the new Secretary of State for Foreign Affairs and his Secretary General, both drawn from the same European clique, were explicitly double-hatted with responsibility for Spain's foreign policy and its European policy; a merging of responsibilities which permitted the conservative government to maintain its highly co-ordinated or 'global' approach to EU policymaking.[92] Under their guidance, the Aznar government adopted within a matter of months precisely the same positions towards the reform of the EU in 1996 as the socialists before them.[93]

Reflecting the pragmatic approach laid out in *Bases Para Una Reflexion*, the Aznar government was not disappointed by the modest outcome of the Amsterdam summit in June 1997. By this time, the government was focused on two priorities: securing admission to EMU in the first round; and ensuring that the EU's imminent enlargement to the east carried the minimum financial and political cost for Spain.[94] The key themes of the Spanish approach to enlargement had been sketched during the Spanish EU presidency in 1995. For example, Spain strongly supported a parallel EU enlargement to Cyprus and Malta as well as the Free Trade Agreement with Turkey, in a continuing effort to balance the eastern and northern slant of the existing enlargement programme.[95] Second, Spanish politicians from the right and the left refused to countenance a situation whereby the CEECs would gain full access to EU markets while Spain's eligibility for structural and cohesion funds was reduced as it 'rose' to become a relatively wealthy EU member. From their perspective, it would be perverse if the 'cohesion' countries, with the least to gain strategically and economically from the eastern enlargement, became the countries who 'paid' the most for that enlargement to take place.[96] Instead, Spanish officials pointed to Spain's own recent experience to argue that new members should be subjected to lengthy derogations and exceptions on common policies such as the CAP and the Structural Funds, as had been the case for Spain before them.[97] Spanish officials were adamant also that enlargement should not serve as an excuse for weakening these common policies.[98]

The PP's combination of a more overtly belligerent attitude towards the EU but continuing underlying support for EU integration reflected the mixed sentiments of the Spanish public towards European integration after 1995. Predictably, there was a decline in the overwhelming level of public approval for the EU that characterized the first five years of Spain's EU membership. By 1995, only 28 per cent of Spaniards believed that EU membership brought positive returns to the country. But the same polling data still revealed overwhelming support (79 per cent) for the transference of greater powers to Brussels and for the construction of a more federal Europe as a means of helping solve Spain's economic problems.[99] In the absence of a detailed public debate on Spain's European policy, the Spanish electorate remained fearful of a return to isolation and sensed that there was no alternative to further European integration if Spain hoped to join the leading rank of European countries in the near future. Andres Ortega commented that, today, the Spanish 'desire for Europe is probably a lot weaker than the need for Europe'.[100]

The mixture of integrationist and nationalist tendencies in the Spanish approach towards European construction also reflected the sensitivity among Spanish policymakers of the left and the right to the constraints facing nation-states in a globalized economy and, at the same time, to the enduring quality of the state as the repository of national aspirations and loyalties. For many Spaniards, European integration remains part of the ongoing process of nation-building. As Fernando Moran wrote in 1995, Europe means not only the end of Spanish isolation, but also 'el fin de la ideologicazión de lo que sea España' (the end to the ideological conflict over what Spain should be) and a stabilization of the political debate within Spain.[101] Given their desire to see Spain grow politically and economically within Europe and globally, there is a widespread consensus among Spanish policymakers on the need to be pragmatic about the end-point of European integration. Gonzalez stated that in order to 'pensar Europa' one must look beyond traditional concepts such as state, federation or confederation.[102] Javier Ruperez, a leading PP parliamentarian, foresees a 'quasi-federal' Europe, with the member states as the 'pivots' of integration. King Juan Carlos quoted Ortega, talking of a Europe comprising 'many bees but one hive'.[103] As the Joint Parliamentary Committee for the EU concluded in 1995, it is sterile to advocate either a federal or intergovernmental future for Europe. Instead, the priority should be more pragmatic: to ensure that the EU can execute its common policies in as effective a manner as possible.[104] For Spain's policymaking élite, the choice lies not between ideal end-points, but between further integration and disintegration, or, correspondingly, between progress and dissipation.[105] Andres Ortega concluded, therefore, that efforts to create a new European 'architecture' are now redundant and a relic of cold-war thinking. The post-cold war world demands a shift in conceptual emphasis from structures to 'process', where the flexibility and adaptability of the structures is more important than their geographic or functional parameters.[106]

The European vision of leading Spanish politicians, and public support for this vision, is predicated on Spain being a core member of the new Europe. If a post-cold war Europe reconfigures its institutional nexus around a new core group of countries that are united monetarily, then Spain, as one of the countries lying towards the bottom of the European economic league, may find that it gradually slips back towards Europe's periphery. The priorities of the Gonzalez government were to lay claim to a position of political leadership for Spain in Europe, while promoting the vision of a socially cohesive Europe that would slowly help Spain rise up the economic ladder. Facing an imminent institutional enlargement of the EU and a concurrent concentration around EMU, the Aznar government could no longer play the role of 'demandeur' and hope for rapid Spanish access to the EMU core. Europe once again forced Spain to reform itself. In the 1970s and 1980s the challenge was political. In the 1990s, Europe demanded not just a democratic Spain, but also an economically dynamic one.

Notes

1. As Carlos Alonso Zaldivar and Manuel Castells observed, 'In the end, Spain's full incorporation into the international order took so long that when it finally happened the old order had disappeared while the new one still did not exist', in *España: Fin de Siglo* (Madrid: Alianza Editorial, 1992) p. 19.
2. King Juan Carlos speech in the Palacio Real on the occasion of the tenth anniversary of Spain's accession to the EC (8 June 1995).
3. Andres Ortega, *La Razón de Europa* (Madrid: El País/Aguilar, 1994) p. 219; 'Hoy, para la identidad nacional es tan importante ser Estado miembro (de la UE) como Estado-nación.' ('Today, as far as national identity is concerned, it is as important to be a member state (of the EU) as a nation state.')
4. Andres Ortega, *La Razón de Europa*, op. cit., pp. 22 and 217.
5. Alfred Tovias, 'Spain in the European Community', in Richard Gillespie, Fernando Rodrigo and Jonathan Story (eds), *Democratic Spain: Reshaping External Relations in a Changing World* (London: Routledge, 1995).
6. Felipe Gonzalez, 'La Europa Que Quiere España', Politica Exterior (VI:30, 1992–93) p. 8. The first Spanish EC presidency (January–June 1989) oversaw the decision to launch the first phase of EMU on 1 July 1990 and to establish an IGC to determine the timetable for its second and third phases. Spain joined the EMS on 16 June 1989.
7. During its 1989 EC presidency, Spain dramatically expanded the range and level of its contacts with third countries, an experience which revolutionized the Spanish ministry of foreign affairs. See, Celestino del Arenal Moyua and Jose Angel Sotillo Lorenzo, 'Relaciones Exteriores de España 1989' in *Anuario de la Politica Exterior de España, 1989* (Barcelona: CIDOB, 1989) p. 15; also see Esther Barbé, 'European Political Cooperation: The Upgrading of Spanish Foreign Policy', in Gillespie *et al.*, *Democratic Spain*, op. cit., pp. 106–22.

8. Felipe Gonzalez, 'La Europa Que Quiere España', op. cit., p. 12. Through the provisions in the Single European Act mandating consistency between EC economic and foreign policies, Spain was able to place the economic weight of the Community behind its initiatives in Central America in 1989 while raising Spain's own international prestige in the region. See Fernando Perpiña-Robert, secretary general for foreign affairs during the 1989 Spanish EC presidency, 'La Cooperación Política Europea', *Politica Exterior* (III:9, Winter 1989) pp. 44–6; del Arenal Moyua and Lorenzo, 'Relaciones Exteriores de España', op. cit., pp. 24–6.

9. Fernando Rodrigo, 'La Opinión Pública en España y Los Problemas de Defensa', *Politica Exterior* (III:9, Winter 1989) pp. 160–1, reports that in 1987 only 23 per cent of Spaniards felt that Spain was threatened externally. Of that 23 per cent, 49 per cent believed that the USA was the greatest threat to Spanish security, 33 per cent the USSR. Similarly, 36 per cent believed that both superpowers represented an equal threat to world peace, as compared to 28 per cent who blamed the USA and 15 per cent the USSR. For a history of the domestic post-Franco debate on Spanish defence policy see Fernando Rodrigo, 'Western Alignment: Spain's Security Policy', in Gillespie et al., *Democratic Spain*, op. cit., pp. 50–66.

10. Fernando Rodrigo, 'La Opinión Pública en España y Los Problemas de la Defensa', op. cit., pp. 162–3.

11. Interview with *El País*, 11 November 1995; and as he also noted, 'for Europe to have a future, we have to share sovereignties'. Quoted in Carlos Alonso Zaldivar, 'El Año Que Nunca Acabó: La Política Exterior de España en 1990', *Anuario de la Politica Exterior de España, 1990* (Barcelona: CIDOB, 1990) p. 21.

12. Zaldivar, 'El Año Que Nunca Acabó', op. cit., p. 20.

13. See, for example, Ramon Armengod, 'Prólogo' in R. Calduch (ed.) *La Politica Exterior Española en el Siglo XX* (Madrid: Ediciones Ciencias Sociales, 1994) p. 15. Reflecting this concern, the Spanish government argued unsuccessfully during the Europe Agreement negotiations in 1991 that financial aid to the CEECs under the Phare programme should be matched by EU assistance to the Mediterranean region; Robin Niblett, *The European Community and the Central European Three, 1989–92: A Study of the Community as an International Actor* (D. Phil. thesis, Oxford, 1995).

14. Carlos Zaldivar, 'El Año en Que Acabó un Mundo: la Política Exterior de España en 1991', *Anuario de la Politica Exterior de España, 1991* (Barcelona: CIDOB, 1991), p. 21.

15. Victor Perez-Diaz, *España Puesta a Prueba, 1976–1996* (Madrid: Alianza Editorial, 1996) p. 14; Celestino del Arenal Moyua, 'Relaciones Exteriores de España', op. cit., p. 15.

16. At its most extreme, it was clear to Gonzalez's advisers that only the creation of a European Central Bank would defuse the persistent calls of the Basque nationalist party for its own central bank.

17. Poll quoted in *El País*, 10 July 1989.

18. In the 1989 Commission, Manuel Marin, who had led Spain's accession negotiating team, gained responsibility for Cooperation & Development and Fisheries policy, and Abel Matutes became the Commissioner for Mediterranean policy, relations with Latin America and Asia and north-south relations. Other members of the negotiating team who played key roles in Spain's relations with the EU in later years included Carlos Westendorp, Javier Elorza and Carlos Bastarreche.

19. Interview with Ramon de Miguel, Secretary of State for European Affairs; also see Ortega, *La Razón de Europa*, op. cit., p. 225. Quoting Pedro Solbes, Spanish finance minister in 1995, Javier Elorza, Spain's permanent representative to the EU, encapsulated the Spanish approach to EU negotiation: 'Tu equilibrio global está en la suma de tus equilibrios parciales. You cannot throw yourself into each battle as if it were a matter of life and death. You have to approach each battle to secure an improvement in your overall position.'

20. The Centro Español de Relaciones Internacionales (CERI) was not established in Madrid until October 1992, with the support of the Fundación Ortega y Gasset – in itself an unlikely source of criticism of Spain's pro-European strategy. Other research institutes, such as the Centre d'Informació y Documentació Internacionals a Barcelona (CIDOB), engaged primarily in academic research, not policy advocacy.

21. Visits to bookstores in Madrid in 1996–97 revealed a significant lack of books on international relations and Spanish foreign policy.

22. Andres Ortega, the international affairs correspondent for *El País*, became an adviser to Fernandez Ordoñez in 1989 and head of the Moncloa's Policy Studies Department in 1990. It is noticeable that Spain's single foreign policy journal, *Politica Exterior*, has primarily served as a vehicle for government ministers and senior foreign ministry officials to put forward their analyses of Spanish policy towards Europe.

23. For a concise review in English of Spanish reactions to the end of the cold war, see Andres Ortega, 'Spain and the End of the Cold War', in Gillespie *et al.*, *Democratic Spain*, op. cit..

24. Carlos Zaldivar, 'El Año Que Nunca Acabó', op. cit., pp. 17–19, in reviewing the Moncloa's immediate reaction to the end of the cold war, chose not to celebrate the defeat of communism, but heralded, instead, the decision of Germans 'with different political cultures and socioeconomic levels deciding to live together in a united state'. In his frequent consultations with the French government in the EC troika in November and December 1989, Fernandez Ordoñez sought to allay French concerns about the impact of German unification on European stability.

25. Felipe Gonzalez speech to the Pleno del Congreso on 4 December 1989 in *Actividades, Textos y Documentos de la Politica Exterior Española, 1989* (Ministerio de Asuntos Exteriores, Oficina de Información Pública) p. 337.

26. Zaldivar, 'El Año que Nunca Acabó', op. cit.; also see Alonso Zaldivar and Castells, *España: Fin de Siglo*, op. cit., pp. 219–25. One of Spain's principal contributions to the Maastricht negotiations, the clauses on the EU and the Citizen, were clearly staked out during the Spanish presidency in the first half of 1989; see the comments by the then foreign minister, Francisco Fernandez Ordoñez, 'El Discurso de la Presidencia Española; Proceso y Objetivos', *Politica Exterior*, (III:9, Winter 1989) p. 35.

27. Gonzalez speech to the Pleno del Congreso, 4 December 1989, op. cit., p. 343; for a review of the Spanish CFSP approach at the Maastricht negotiations, see Esther Barbé, 'EPC: Upgrading Spanish Foreign Policy', op. cit., pp. 111–14. The Spanish government did not foresee the EU moving beyond a common foreign policy to the establishment of 'single' foreign policies, Zaldivar, 'El Año Que Nunca Acabó', op. cit., pp. 21–2.

28. During the Gulf war against Iraq, Spanish troops were forbidden from participating in combat operations and its naval forces had to operate under the WEU flag.

29. Zaldivar, 'El Año Que Nunca Acabó', op. cit., p. 23.

30. See, Esther Barbé, 'Spanish Responses to the Security Institutions of the New Europe', in A. Williams (ed.), *Reorganizing Eastern Europe* (Aldershot: Dartmouth, 1994).

31. Interview with Gonzalez in *El País*, 22 November 1995; and Felipe Gonzalez, 'La Europa Que Quiere España', op. cit., p. 9; Gonzalez's views on EMU are also reported by Zaldivar in, 'El Año en Que Acabó un Mundo', op. cit., p. 23.

32. Zaldivar, 'El Año Que Nunca Acabo', op. cit., p. 20.

33. Gonzalez had apparently taken heed of Margaret Thatcher's comment shortly after he became Prime Minister that, 'entry into the EC consists of two parts. One, agreeing to a whole lot of things to get in and then, once in, trying to undo all of the amazing things that you agreed to in the first place.' Quoted by Simon Serfaty in the Preface to John Van Oudenaren, *Poland's Accession to the European Union: Outlook and Options* (Washington, DC: CSIS, August 1996) p. 6.

34. Gonzalez's view was encapsulated in Zaldivar's comment: 'yes to centralization, but only with solidarity, in other words, sharing sovereignty requires sharing resources' ('centralización sí, pero con solidaridad, es decir, compartir soberanía, pero redistribuir recursos'), in 'El Año en Que Acabó un Mundo', op. cit., p. 23. He went on to argue that 'a European model in which poorer regions might grow more slowly than the rich and at the same time countries such as Spain would be net contributors to the Community is a model without a future, even if Europe takes on CFSP'.

35. Unlike the regionally focused Structural Funds, the Cohesion Fund would pay an annual subsidy directly to the governments of those countries whose overall GDP per capita was under 90 per cent of the EU average.

36. This despite the fact that Gonzalez said he would have preferred greater institutional cohesion than was provided under the three pillar approach. See speech by Gonzalez on 28 November 1991 to the Pleno del Congreso on the progress towards European Political Union, in *Actividades, Textos y Documentos de la Politica Exterior Española, 1991* (Madrid: Ministerio de Asuntos Exteriores, Oficina de Información Pública) p. 385.

37. During the ratification vote on 29 October 1992, only the three members of the Basque party voted against Maastricht ratification, while the eight IU members abstained.

38. These included access for EU boats using drift nets to Spain's tuna fisheries; the slow pace of opening EU fisheries to Spanish boats; and, most dramatically, the fish-war with Canada in March 1995. Antonio Remiro-Brotons, *La Politica Exterior de España, 1995* (Barcelona: CIDOB, 1995) p. 33, described how the fishing issue epitomized 'the difficulty of achieving a real integration within the EU of the localized interests of isolated medium-sized or small EU member states and the lack of willingness on the part of other states to go beyond rhetorical support and actually defend those interests as their own'.

39. Richard Gillespie and Benny Pollack, 'La Política Exterior Española en 1992: Latinoamericana en el corazón, pero Europeo en la mente', in *La Politica Exterior de España, 1992* (Barcelona: CIDOB, 1992), p. 23.

40. Gonzalez had to play a delicate game. Conscious of the limited impact these funds would have on Spain's long-term economic competitiveness and of the need not to be categorized in the same company as Portugal, Greece and Ireland, Gonzalez claimed in his bilateral summit with Helmut Kohl on 13–14 September 1992 that he was fighting for the principle of intra-EU financial solidarity more than for its direct economic benefit to Spain, *ibid.* p. 23.

41. Fearing that the northern enlargement would precipitate Spain's marginalization from the emerging EU core, Spanish negotiators argued (unsuccessfully) that the new entrants' economic performance should not be included in the assessment of the Maastricht criteria to decide which countries would be eligible to proceed towards EMU. The fact that the Nordic countries out performed Spain in most economic indicators would raise the overall standards Spain would have to meet to be eligible to join EMU; *Gaceta de los Negocios*, 23 February 1994, p. 8; see Javier Solana, *Boletín Económico ICE*, No. 2414, 30 May–5 June 1994, pp. 1337–42 for a full report on Spanish thinking behind the negotiations on the 'Nordic enlargement'.
42. The Mediterranean region provides 25 per cent of the EU's energy needs, accounts for six times as many migrants within the EU than do the former communist states, and will have a population approximating 600 million by the year 2025. 'Política exterior y de seguridad de España en 1995', *Anuario de la Politica Exterior de España, 1995* (Barcelona: CIDOB, 1995) pp. 29–30. Javier Solana argued that, 'Europe and the Mediterranean states are not separated by a geological fault – the Mediterranean sea – rather we should see that we find ourselves in a sort of magnetic field which draws together, not separates, the two shores'; statement to the Comisión Mixta para la Unión Europea, Congreso, 2 March 1995, pp. 19–20; also see Solana, 'Hacia Una Nueva Arquitectura Mediterranea', in *El País*, 18 July 1994.
43. See *El País*, 28 September 1994.
44. For a thorough analysis of Spanish activism towards the Mediterranean see Juan Baixeras, 'España y el Mediterraneo 1989–95', *Politica Exterior* (X:51, May–June 1996) pp. 149–62; for a good account of Spanish activism during 1992, see Gillespie and Pollack, 'La Política Exterior Española en 1992', op. cit., pp. 24–7.
45. Esther Barbé, *España y la Construcción Europea: Mirando al Norte*, unpublished paper, Centre d'Estudis sobre la Pau, Universidad Autónoma de Barcelona, March 1994, p. 5. Solana's conclusion was that, 'what is good for Europe is good for Spain'; interview in *El País*, 27 February 1994.
46. Spain insisted on the revision of voting weights in the Council to protect its sectoral interests; the UK wanted to maintain blocking minorities on political issues. Spain saw accession by the EFTA countries as an opportunity to increase the Cohesion Fund, the UK as a chance to make savings on the EU budget.
47. See *El País*, 'España y Portugal discrepan sobre todos los aspectos de la integración europea', 25 October 1993.
48. On Spain's affinity with Italy, see Javier Solana's comments to the Comisión Mixta para la Unión Europea on 1995 March 2, in *Diario de Sesiones de las Cortes Generales* (#66; Sesiones No. 20) p. 22; on Mediterranean co-operation, see Susana Agnelli and Javier Solana, 'Una Estrategia Hispano–Italiana', in *El País*, 10 May 1995.
49. See Paloma Gonzalez del Miño, 'Las Relaciones Bilaterales Hispano–Francesas' in R. Calduch (ed.), *La Politica Exterior Española en el Siglo XX* (Madrid: Ediciones Ciencias Sociales, 1994) pp. 223–7.
50. See, for example, comments by Gonzalez at the Turin European Council about apparent French back-tracking on European integration, in *El País*, 30 March 1996. This was not a uniquely PSOE perspective: see, for example, comments by the PP parliamentary spokesman, Rafael-Arias Salgado during the debate in the Comisión Mixta para la Unión Europea on 2 March 1995, op. cit., p. 14.
51. In Morocco, for example, where the Spanish government believed that it had the more pressing national interests of the two given its geographic proximity,

the extent of its foreign direct investments, and the position of Ceuta and Melilla, French influence continued to be sustained by levels of bilateral aid that dwarfed the Spanish contribution at a rate of roughly seven to one. As a result, the Spanish government sought to encourage a more active EU policy towards the Maghreb, a policy which only appeared to receive clear French support in 1994–95; see Gillespie and Pollack, 'La Política Exterior Española en 1992', op. cit., p. 28, and Gillespie, 'Spain and the Mediterranean', *Mediterranean Politics* (1:2, 1996) pp. 193–211.

52. *The Economist* (25 June 1993) concluded that Spain had more weight in the EU because of its stable government and ideas about Europe.

53. For a review of the Spanish reaction, see Emilio Fernandez Castaño, then a senior Spanish official in the ministry for european affairs, in 'Europa y la Fusión Nuclear', *Politica Exterior* (VIII:42, 1994/95) pp. 8–17; comments by Foreign Minister Solana in *Diario de Sesiones de las Cortes Generales*, 11 October 1994, No. 52; and Antonio Remiro Brotons, Director of CERI, 'Mosqueteros de Europa', *Politica Exterior* (IX:43, February–March, 1995) pp. 52–66.

54. Emilio Fernandez Castaño, 'Europa y la Fusion Nuclear', op. cit., pp. 12–13, observed that 'precisely because American-style economic liberalisation is unacceptable, Europe's industrial leadership could be tempted to opt for a strategy that restricts the physical and human territory dedicated to preserving the European social model around the Franco-German axis ... a mutual support system for the strong, for the equals'.

55. Castaño provided the following analogy: 'It is not convincing to argue that, just as the European locomotive is about to leave the station, one unhooks the carriages containing those 'who are unwilling or unable' and promises that the departing train will draw those carriages along behind it', *ibid.*, p. 14.

56. Ibid. pp. 15–16, Castaño argues that Europe's balance of power 'is no longer based upon on individual states' strategies of co-operation and conflict, but on an institutionalized network of balanced interests and counterweights dedicated to the achievement of shared objectives'. Similarly, Andres Ortega, *La Razón de Europa* (op. cit.) p. 27, insists Europe must avoid a return to a balance of power and entrench the existing balance of interests and benefits.

57. *La Conferencia Intergubernamental de 1996: Bases Para Una Reflexion* (Madrid: Ministry of Foreign Affairs, 2 March 1995).

58. See Javier Solana, 'Prólogo' in *Cuatro Puntos de Vista Sobre la Unión Europea* (Madrid: INCIPE, 1995) p. 10; Emilio Fernandez Castaño, 'El Transfondo Político de la UEM', *Politica Exterior* (X:52, July–August 1996) pp. 112–15; Marcelino Oreja, 'Europa debe hablar con una sola voz', *El País* 24 May 1996; and comments by Pedro Solbes, finance minister in 1995, to the Comisión Mixta para la Unión Europea on 13 February 1995, p. 4, who observed that the multi-speed approach has always been a part of European integration. The priority was to ensure that it did not now become a mechanism to exclude other member states from areas of policy integration.

59. In an interview at the end of the Spanish presidency, Javier Elorza, Spain's ambassador to the EU, was asked what Spain had achieved. He replied that it had demonstrated that it possessed the credibility to be one of the big five EU countries; in that 'it does not just do things well, it has its own initiatives'.

60. As a result of its presidency, an editorial in *Le Monde* noted that Spain had won 'strong international recognition and a place, even if a modest one, in the concert of nations'; see *Le Monde*, 'Une Consecration pour l'Espagne', 17–18 December 1995.

61. These included agreement on a fixed timetable for the introduction of the single currency and resolution of the vexed issue of a name for the currency (the euro) acceptable to Germany; see the article by Javier Gomez-Navarro Navarrete, Spanish minister for commerce, 'La Presidencia Española de la UE', in *Boletín Económico ICE*, #2489, 12–18 February 1996, p. 3; *El País*, 5 December 1995.

62. Javier Solana, statement to the Comisiones Mixtas para la Unión Europea on 2 March 1995, p. 23 and *Comunicacion del Gobierno sobre la Presidencia Española de la UE* (Madrid: Boletín Oficial de las Cortes Generales) 19 June 1995, pp. 7–10.

63. See, Felipe Gonzalez's interview with *El País*, 11 November 1995. Spanish policymakers were sensitive to the fact that, whereas Maastricht was a hang-over from the cold war, the new IGC would lead to the first EU Treaty of the post-cold war era, Emilio Fernandez Castaño, 'La CIG de 1996', *Boletín Económico ICE* #2489, 12–18 February 1996, p. 5.

64. *Elementos para una posición española en la Conferencia Intergubernamental de 1996* (Madrid: Ministry of Foreign Affairs, March 1996).

65. The following analysis of Spain's position in the 1996 IGC is taken from the *Elementos para una Posición Española*, op. cit., *Bases Para una Reflexion*, op. cit.; Javier Conde, 'Conclusiones del Consejo Europeo de Madrid', in *Boletín Económico ICE* #2489, op. cit.; and Fernandez-Castaño, 'La CIG de 1996', op. cit..

66. In 1994, Westendorp became embroiled in a debate with the leaders of Spain's seventeen autonomous communities about the role of their representative offices in Brussels. He insisted that the Spanish Permanent Representation was willing to put their case to the respective ministerial Councils, but that they would not be allowed to have representatives sit in on the meetings. See *El País* 3 June and 15 June 1994.

67. Speech on the Spanish presidency to the Comisión Mixta Congreso/Senado para la Unión Europea, 15 June 1995, p. 9.

68. The Spanish government was infuriated when the Belgian State Council refused to extradite two ETA suspects to Spain in February 1996, *El País* 17 February 1996; backed by the PP, Westendorp went as far as to say that Spain would refuse to ratify the 1996 IGC if the extradition/asylum issue were not resolved; *El País*, 27 February 1996.

69. Carlos Bastarreche talked of Spain 'trying to find a middle way as befits a middle power'.

70. See, Javier Solana, 'España y la UEO; la Otra Presidencia', *El País*, 31 October 1995.

71. Felipe Gonzalez, 'Pilotar Europa Hacia su Rumbo', *Politica Exterior*, Vol. IX, 48, 1995–96) p. 21 talks of NATO 'still being the key component in the European security system'; also see Jorge Dezcallar, 'España Y la Ampliación de la OTAN', *Politica Exterior* (X:51, May–June 1996) p. 130.

72. See Jaime de Ojeda, NATO ambassador 1983–90 and Spain's ambassador to the United States, 'El Futuro de la OTAN, II', *Politica Exterior* (10:52, July–August, 1996) pp. 43–5, who blames the French for the 'ambitious', 'elevated and confused' concept of a European Security Identity. He argues that 'NATO is, in the military dimension, what the EU is in the economic; moreover, it has the advantage of including the United States in a formal way, whereas the EU tries to cover up this gap with formulas for a transatlantic relationship'.

73. A 1995 INCIPE poll reported that, whereas in 1991 31.9 per cent of respondents said that NATO membership had increased Spanish security and 23.4 per cent said membership had reduced it, by 1994–95 the ratio was 34.6 per cent to 16.6 per cent with 30 per cent believing that NATO membership made little difference one way or

the other. Overall, 45 per cent favoured Spain's continued NATO membership; 35 per cent were against.

74. The January 1994 NATO summit in Brussels affirmed that Europe's security was significantly affected by security in the Mediterranean.

75. Gillespie and Pollack, *La Politica Extorior de España, 1992*, op. cit., p. 27.

76. Interview with Carlos Miranda in *El País*, 8 July 1996; Jaime de Ojeda 'El Futuro de la OTAN II', op. cit., p. 50.

77. Aznar said he would present a bill before the Parliament to change the status of Spain's relationship with NATO. Providing that NATO agreed to abolish the GIBmed command, the PSOE, CiU and PNV all expressed their support for the PP policy. Only the IU was vigorously opposed. See *El País*, 15 June and 1 July 1996.

78. Under pressure from the CiU, Aznar quickly decided to begin transferring the Spanish armed forces onto a professional footing. Professionalization would enable Spain to take part fully in future NATO-led operations and strengthen its voice in the debate on the moulding of a new European security order. It also marked a further step in the rehabilitation of the Spanish military, which had gathered pace during the course of its contribution to peacekeeping in the former Yugoslavia.

79. This was such a sensitive decision that it was hidden from the Spanish public until the closing stages of the land war. Of the total US airlift to the Gulf 35 per cent passed through Spain, including 200 000 tons of material and 100 000 troops, 237 US boats put into Spanish harbours. Zaldivar, 'El Año en Que Acabó un Mundo', op. cit., p. 16.

80. Spain pushed to join the Contact Group in its capacity as holder of the EU presidency during 1995, but was rejected, Brotons 1995, p. 36.

81. See Zaldivar and Castells, *España: Fin de Siglo*, op. cit., pp. 237–43; Brotons, 'Mosqueteros de Europa', op. cit., p. 31.

82. One PP parliamentarian characterized this approach as rejecting the 'zero-sum' French approach to West European security.

83. See *El País*, 4 December 1995; Spanish policymakers also boasted the fact that, after their presidency, high-ranking members of the Clinton administration had stated they now knew which number they had to call when they wanted to 'talk to Europe'.

84. See Segura Sanchez, 'Spain: Shaping Factors', in Alexis Jacquemin and David Wright, *The European Challenges post-1992* (Aldershot: Edward Elgar, 1993) pp. 400–8; Zaldivar and Castells, *España: Fin de Siglo*, op. cit., pp. 83–99; Maria Nieves Garcia Santos and Sebastian Ubiria, 'La Competitividad de la Economía Española', *Politica Exterior* (VII:36, 1993–94) pp. 13–21; Keith Salmon, 'Spain in the World Economy' in Gillespie *et al.*, op. cit., pp. 67–87.

85. Rafael Arias-Salgado, PP spokesperson in the Parliamentary Committee for the EU, 'Hacia Otra Política Europea', in *El País*, 8 June 1995.

86. Jose Maria Aznar, 'La Reforma de la Unión Europea', *Politica Exterior* (Vol. IX, 43, February–March 1995) pp. 168–73.

87. See *Financial Times*, 10 May 1996 for report of remarks by Abel Matutes and Rodrigo Rato about stopping the EMU clock for a few months to enable everyone to join at the same time.

88. Emilio Fernandez Castaño describes how EU leaders launched two boats in 1990–91; one bearing the flag 'EMU' the second 'EPU', conscious that the latter would draw the fire of the anti-federalists while the former – the real harbinger of political

integration – sailed safely into port under its 'economic' and 'functionalist' banner; 'El Transfondo Político de la UEM', *Politica Exterior* (X:52, July–August, 1996) p. 109.

89. Spain's interest rate differential with Germany shrank from 350 basis points in June 1996, when the PP came to power, to 035 in October 1997. Spain's budget deficit was forecast at 2.4 per cent for 1998, well inside the Maastricht criteria, *Financial Times*, 2 October 1997.

90. Rafael Arias-Salgado, 'Hacia Otra Política Europea', op. cit.

91. Miguel Herrero de Miñon, 'Europa como nivel de España', *El País*, 9 June 1995, p. 14; Rodrigo Rato, 'Un Nuevo Horizonte para la Economía Española', *Politica Exterior* (IX:48, 1995/96) p. 39.

92. Ramon de Miguel, a former director general at the EC Commission, became the Secretary of State for EU affairs and foreign policy; Carlos Bastarreche, the former No. 2 at the Spanish EU mission in Brussels, became Secretary General with the same remit. This arrangement caused some resentment in the Palacio de la Santa Cruz.

93. See, for example, Abel Matutes, PP foreign minister, 'España en Europa', *Politica Exterior* (X:52, July-August 1996) pp. 95–105.

94. Gonzalez argued that the EU should treat its eastern enlargement as a 'moral, historic, and geopolitical' ambition and not confuse this with its 'economic or financial' ambitions. Felipe Gonzalez, 'Pilotar Europa Hacia su Rumbo', *Politica Exterior* (IX:48, 1995/96) p. 17.

95. Brotons, 'Política Exterior y de Seguridad de España in 1995', op. cit., pp. 27–8.

96. *Bases Para Una Reflexion*, op. cit., pp. 88–91, 'if significant new funds are not obtained and the overall budget is not modified in 1996, the cohesion countries would be the principal funders of enlargement' ('de no obtenerse nuevos fondos adicionales importantes y de no modificarse el acervo en 1996, los actuales países de la cohesión serían los principales financiadores de la ampliación'). This was especially galling for Spanish politicians who noted that Spain had been excluded from the Marshall Plan, but were now expected to carry the principal burden for the EU's Marshall Plan to the east.

97. In an interview with *El País*, 22 November 1995, Felipe Gonzalez envisaged 12 to 14 year transition periods for the CEECs; also see *Bases para Una Reflexion*, op. cit., pp. 86–7; Emilio Fernandez Castaño, Secretary General for European Affairs, 'La Conferencia Intergubernamental de 1996', in *Boletín Económico ICE*, #2489, 12–18 February 1996, p. 8. Against expectations, Spanish exports to eastern Europe had exceeded imports since the signing of the Europe Agreements. However, the threat to specific sectors of the Spanish economy such as coal, steel, and fruit and vegetables had not diminished.

98. See, for example, the interview with Ramon de Miguel in *Financial Times*, 18 November 1997.

99. *Eurobarometer* polls, February–March 1995 and April–May 1995 were analyzed in *ABC*, 28 May 1995 and *El País*, 28 July 1995. Only 18 per cent of those polled actually opposed Spain's membership of the EU.

100. Andres Ortega, *La Razón de Europa*, op. cit., p. 22.

101. *El País*, 8 June 1995.

102. Felipe Gonzalez, 'Pilotar Europa Hacia su Rumbo', op. cit., p. 17.

103. Speech to the College of Europe, Bruges, 15 September 1994.

104. *Dictamen de la Comisión Mixta para la UE en Relación con el Informe Elaborado por la Ponencia Sobre Consecuencias para España de la Ampliación de la UE y Reformas*

Institucionales, Boletín Oficial de las Cortes Generales, 29 December 1995, No. 82, pp. 11–12.
105. Emilio Fernandez Castaño, *Boletín ICE Económico*, No. 96, op. cit., p. 5. See also Fernando Perpiña-Robert, 'La Cooperación Política Europea', op. cit., p. 53, who believes that 'Europe, above all, must be a compromise, a historic pact between diversity and unity. Without stopping being "voluntaristas", those of us who believe in an integrated future for Europe must be realists'.
106. Andres Ortega, *La Razón de Europa*, op. cit., pp. 36–7.

9
Struggling to Change: the Italian State and the New Order

Christopher Hill and Filippo Andreatta

Introduction

Eight years after the cold war had ended, Italy has not yet successfully adapted to the new international system. In this it was not unusual in Europe, where all countries were puzzled by the direction that international politics would take in a more multipolar setting and where most were absorbed by pressing domestic problems. Nonetheless, the difficulties of finding a new consensus on Italian foreign policy could also be attributed to two special factors: the upheaval in domestic politics and the weakness of Italian political culture, which had not yet produced an epistemic community with the critical mass necessary to develop and diffuse new thinking. We argue accordingly that the lack of an intellectual consensus on the meaning of systemic change after the end of the cold war, and on Italy's appropriate international role, hindered the country's ability to adapt successfully to changed circumstances and to advance its own point of view on European order. This despite the fact that the dramatic changes in the international system had influenced Italy, at home and abroad, more than most western countries. The case of Italy demonstrates that even seismic external change is always mediated through the domestic environment.

Italian foreign policy had long been undermined by chronically weak political institutions and a corresponding external scepticism. Moreover after the end of the cold war, despite the relief with which it was initially greeted, Italy came to miss the certainties of bipolarity. It felt uncomfortably exposed in a new environment, which seemed at once more hostile and very difficult to make sense of.

A number of questions crucial to Italy emerged with the transition from the postwar international system. Could Europe produce a fully-fledged common foreign policy? Could European integration and good transatlantic relations be kept in balance? How far had the priorities of European geopolitics changed, with new instabilities coming from east and south? All of Italy's major European partners had either implicit or explicit answers to these questions, even if they differed among themselves.[1] Italian governments, however, as they signed the Amsterdam Treaty and accepted *Agenda 2000's* criteria for eastern enlargement, did not know their own minds, despite the lucid views of some individual decisionmakers. Like Germany, Italy also wanted to reconcile its American and European partnerships, but unlike Germany it had no thorough domestic debates on EU enlargement, or on the recovery of national identity. In Italy, these issues remained the province of specialists. Rather, most public attention and political debate had concentrated on Italy's prospects for membership of European Monetary Union, which was mainly viewed as a way of providing a safe haven from the uncomfortable prospect of exclusion and isolation. It is revealing that Italian press headlines over EMU often referred to the possibility of being excluded 'from Europe', despite Italy's unassailable membership of the EU.

Inclusion in the first group of countries forming EMU would, it seemed, somehow remove the problem of Italy's position in the new international system. Italy would at least be 'in Europe'. That the nature of the policy choice and its ramifications was rarely specified seemed to matter little. In Italy political debate tends either to be highly parochial, about the internal balance of the latest coalition, or to be stratospheric, about the future of the United Nations or the EU. There is very little in between; no Grotian *via media*, one might say, between the well-trodden paths of Machiavelli and Kant (or Marx). This makes pragmatic adaptation a real problem.

Before 1990, Italy had enjoyed a functional equilibrium between international obligations – meaning a solid and almost uncritical commitment to NATO and to European integration – and the domestic imperatives of economic growth and political stability. Italy rose to the status of fifth largest industrial nation while preserving the low international profile necessary to avoid domestic schisms in a politically polarized society. The low profile enabled the country to keep military expenditure well below the NATO and even European averages, while also engaging in fruitful economic exchanges with countries in the Soviet bloc (for example through Fiat and some companies linked to the Partito Communista Italiano [PCI]) and in the Arab world (for example through ENI, the state-controlled energy conglomerate).[2]

The end of the cold war, therefore, posed problems; it is always painful to let go of comfortable certainties. By the same token, however, it acted as a catalyst for some significant changes, especially on the domestic front. The international ideological confrontation had frozen Italian domestic politics by making the possibility of Communist participation in government seem inherently dangerous – not least to the United States. The country had fallen into an increasingly unpopular stagnation. As we shall see below, some have argued that the Italian 'revolution' was inevitable and linked more to developments in the international political economy than to the end of the cold war. By contrast, we take the view that the fall of the Berlin Wall removed the lid on pressures which had been building up for some time without finding a ready outlet, thus generating a series of dramatic changes on the domestic political and social scene, whose conclusion is not yet evident. Moreover these changes have drawn intellectual resources away from the outside world, postponing yet again the consideration of crucial foreign policy problems.

Foreign policy was not, however, immune from the process of change. On the one hand, the influence of new political forces on both left and right challenged the old certainties. On the other, some of the foundations have been laid for a more long-term strategy whereby national and multilateral perspectives might be reconciled more through conscious and assertive choice than through reflex gestures of allegiance to NATO and the EU.

Yet change is slow and gradual. Italy has had a foreign policy over the last few years largely in reaction to the main thrust of multilateral activity and to the initiatives of others. Even imaginative initiatives have failed to gather the momentum to be effective. The initial, rather enthusiastic responses to the end of the cold war in 1991–93 – strong support for the CFSP, a proposal for a common European seat in the UN Security Council, the Pentagonale–Esagonale initiative drawing together Italy with the countries of east-central Europe – foundered due to a combination of further international change and the crisis of the Italian political class. Later initiatives were more pragmatic but also more piecemeal, as domestic reform and financial retrenchment over-shadowed foreign policy. No White Papers were commissioned, no expert committees convened and no parliamentary committee invited to brainstorm on the future of foreign policy.

The failure to adapt was most visible in geopolitical terms. Italy's main concerns to the east and south had not been sufficiently accommodated in either the UN or NATO, and remained at a much lower level of collective priority than the German preoccupation with central Europe or even the Scandinavian interest in the Baltic. Europe's enlargement to the south remained very much in doubt, while the Euro-Mediterranean initiative launched at Barcelona in 1995 was only a watered down version of the original hopes for establishing either a Conference on Security and Cooperation in the Mediterranean (CSCM) or a Mediterranean free trade area.[3] In the Balkans, Italy's exclusion from the Bosnian Contact Group represented a serious blow to its prestige in the area, and did not encourage a more stable and confident national foreign policy – although in 1996–97 joint sponsorship with France of the Slovenian and Romanian candidatures for NATO represented the emergence of something approaching a new regional strategy.

If the Italian polity manages to come through its current transitional phase successfully, there must be a reasonable prospect that the country will be able to develop a more effective foreign policy. The process of domestic reform which had absorbed so many of the country's energies seems a necessary prerequisite for the 'normalization' of Italian foreign policy on the model of its main European partners and for the attainment of a political status commensurate with the country's high economic standing. But an 'epistemic community' of foreign policy expertise will need to develop and to stimulate a broader debate on the options facing Italy in its external environment.[4] In order to explore the prospects for normalization further, this chapter will analyze three issues in more depth: (1) the problems of understanding change given the entanglement of the domestic and the international; (2) the extent to which an adaptation of Italy's international position has been consciously and seriously sought; (3) the character of the epistemic community in Italy which links professional decisionmakers to wider political society.

Two levels of change: the entanglement of domestic and international politics

Contemporary Italy provides a classic case-study for the question: can change in the international system (short of *force majeure*) lead to upheaval inside a particular state? More particularly, was the collapse of the old *partitocrazia* in Italy the direct result of the end of the cold war?

There certainly was an extraordinary domestic flux during the 1990s. Between 1992 and 1997 Italy was governed by six different prime ministers (see Table 9.1). This in itself was nothing new, given the short-lived governments of the whole postwar period, but whereas before 1992 prime ministers changed within an extremely stable political system, these six were supported by completely different majorities, and it was never clear what fundamental change might occur as the result of each taking office.

Whether all this amounted to real change it is not yet possible to judge, but the common talk of a 'Second Republic' replacing that which was established after the Second World War is an indicator of the widespread hope that some political rebirth would be possible, along the lines of de Gaulle's mercy-killing of the French Fourth Republic (if without the military overtones).[5] The *mani pulite* drive by the judges made it possible for the first time to address the

Table 9.1:   Italian governments, 1992–97

	Prime Minister	*Foreign Minister*	*Parties in Government*
1992	G. Andreotti	G. De Michelis	DC, PSI, PRI, PLI, PSDI
1992	G. Amato	E. Colombo	'Government of experts' with support of above five
1993	C.A. Ciampi	B. Andreatta	ditto, plus PDS support
1994	S. Berlusconi	A. Martino	Polo Coalition (Forza Italia, AN, CCD, Lega Nord)
1995	L. Dini	S. Agnelli	'Government of technocrats' (PDS, Lega, PPI)
1996	R. Prodi	L. Dini	Ulivo Coalition of centre and left parties (PDS, Greens, PPI)[6]

question of corruption in Italian political life, while the moves towards electoral reform hastened the subsequent collapse of the Christian Democrat and Socialist parties. The demise of these twin pillars of the old order was little short of sensational. The agenda then soon widened to include constitutional reform, the powers of the executive and even the possible break-up of the Italian state.

Most of this change was concentrated in the years 1992–94, and it seemed too much of a coincidence that it followed hard on the removal of the strategic overlay of the cold war and in parallel to other great changes such as the collapse of apartheid in South Africa. Was indeed the 'first Italian Republic' itself paradoxically being destabilized by the defeat of the very communism against which it had been a bulwark during the cold war? Were previously repressed forces now also bursting forth in Italy, precipitated once again by external forces?

This understandable interpretation has been challenged in a stimulating paper by Stefano Guzzini, who regards the two sets of events as broadly coincidental.[7] Guzzini identifies two main difficulties with the argument, and we might add a third. First, the signs of a coming upheaval in Italy had been present well before the collapse of the Berlin Wall and all that followed. The Mafia had come under pressure in the early 1980s, with hundreds of prosecutions, and the economic crisis of the Italian state had begun to be tackled by such actions as the major privatization programme which began with the key *Mediobanca* bank in 1987. Second, the 'end of the cold war' explanation of Italy's turmoil is essentially strategic and ideological, and ignores the important international political economy dimension. Guzzini argues that Italy is 'a particular case in a more general adaptation and legitimation crisis common to many European countries in the new international political economy of globalized production, communication and finance'.[8] In the Italian case the economic crisis has had three manifestations: in the clientelistic welfare state; in organized crime; and in the networks of family business.[9] The third question mark against the 'new world order' explanation is simply that the mechanisms whereby macro-change were translated into immediate national crisis, were by no means clear. Why, when NATO and the US presence in Europe remained, should the collapse of communism in eastern Europe have suddenly brought down one of the political systems apparently most vindicated by the 'victory of the west', and in the kind of rapid time span normally associated with revolution?

It is possible to reply to this last objection, as Guzzini shows, by arguing that the end of the cold war released forces inside Italy which had previously been 'frozen' for fear of weakening the western alliance – such as the extreme right's sense of national humiliation in 1945. On the left the PCI was also released from its previous role as the threat from within, to be excluded from government at all costs – although by the same token its name and some of its parties also became instant liabilities.

On the other hand, Guzzini's dual argument about change, both predating 1989 and arising primarily from political economic changes, cannot be lightly dismissed. Although this is not the place for a lengthy debate on the matter, it is clearly of critical importance to our understanding of Italian politics and of the Italian debate about the new international order to come to some judgement on the relationship between the external and internal changes which emerged in parallel in the early 1990s. The present authors feel that the coincidence in timing between the two series of events is too great to be ignored, even if it does not tell the whole story. In contrast to Guzzini, we do not think that 'the changes in Italy could have happened in any international context short of heightened east–west conflict or war', even if we allow that some kind of political crisis was becoming ever more likely, by virtue of financial contradictions and the growing dissatisfaction of the new middle class, particularly in the north.[10] Rather, and compatible with the view that the status quo was already under pressure, we argue that a sudden sense of change and opportunity, rather like that in 1848, infected Italy, no less than the states of the Warsaw Pact, and that a suppressed need for change in a deeply flawed political system (*pace* the 'end of history' hypothesis) was given an unexpected opportunity to burst forth. In other words, the lid came off. The same phenomenon was at work in South Africa, another state where the need for change had been denied for too long, and where the timetable for its fulfilment had been anything but clear.

Criticisms which had therefore been searching for an outlet for some time were now legitimized by the evaporation of the ritualized cold war discourse, and by the paradoxically clean hands of the (itself reforming) PCI. Italy was clearly the one state in western Europe where the cold war had prevented a healthy alternation of political tendencies in government, while encouraging subterranean power networks which destroyed any hope of the Italian state acquiring the legitimacy enjoyed by its counterparts in Britain, France and the Federal Republic. In this context, the sense and prospect of great forces in motion made it possible for judges to break taboos and for popular support to be mobilized behind them. Italy seemed on the verge of its own velvet revolution. Who could tell when the chance might recur, if missed in 1992?

There was, then, an inherent entanglement between international change and the Italian crisis, even if it was far more complex a matter than some supposed, of peace dividends and of an end to American pressure. After all, given that the United States had heavily subsidized Italy's foreign and defence policies during the cold war, there were few dividends to be had; and although Washington would henceforth take a more relaxed view of changes in Italian politics and foreign policy, Italy's provision of key bases for the Sixth Fleet and the USAF meant that there could never be much freedom of manoeuvre, even on the 'new security agenda' issues.

Domestic and international forces interacted to destroy parts of the old system – but they did not manage to achieve anything approaching a revolution. There was, as Guzzini says, a 'scissors' effect caused by the huge costs of a clientelist national system and the sharpening competitiveness of global markets, but the cry of 'basta' in relation to corruption was not couched only in financial terms. Many supporters of the Lega Nord and the AN had only turned to such dubious parties out of disillusion with a political class run through with mediocrity and criminality. They wanted to restore pride to their country, and to create a strong, efficient administration. For once an historical opportunity seemed to beckon, less for compromise than for structural change. For the right in particular, regained national pride also meant a return to a less inhibited foreign policy.

In such circumstances the expectations for change tend either to be outrun by events (as in the USSR) or disappointed by their slow pace. In Italy the latter was the case, as the novelty of Forza Italia flattered only to deceive, and the worthy reformist governments which followed struggled painfully to get the slightest movement on a whole range of intractable issues. In our area, of foreign policy, there has been some movement, but few signs of far-reaching debate or of an emerging reconceptualization.

It has to be admitted that the source of such radical foreign policy thinking as there was came mainly from the right, even if the thinking itself was often been muddled or subject to erratic interpretation. The Berlusconi government of 1994–95, with Foreign Minister Antonio Martino in the lead, saw itself as ushering in a new, 'Second Republic' a more assertive, effective foreign policy. It presented itself 'somewhat disingenuously' as untarnished by the mistakes and corruption of the past at home, and not in thrall to allies abroad. Italy, it seemed, was to become 'an ordinary country' again (as Germany seemed to have done), even to the point (unlike Germany) of reclaiming some of the more embarrassing parts of its history, as when Berlusconi's coalition partner Gianfranco Fini asserted that Mussolini had been 'the greatest statesman of the twentieth century' – and refused to retract this remarkable judgement.

But Berlusconi proved an aberration, and his foreign policy excursions did not convince the more technically experienced figures who were to follow him, not least because there was an indelible sense of opportunism about the new right's willingness to subordinate foreign policy to the daily melée of domestic politics. A further proof that Berlusconi remained some way short of founding an Italian Gaullism came in 1997, when the right, now in opposition, asked for the government's resignation on the eve of the Albanian mission in April and then switched its line from endorsement to condemnation of the operation in June – only to return to support in August. Such tactical elasticity sometimes led to unholy alliances with the Rifondazione Communista (RC), the Polo coalition's ideological enemy.

The commitment to European integration, however, remained rock solid among both political élites and the wider public, as shown by the victory in the 1996 elections of the staunchly pro-European Prodi, despite increasing problems with meeting the convergence criteria for Monetary Union. The only reaction to a series of setbacks, even humiliations, over exclusion from the Contact Group over Bosnia, over proposals to reform the UN Security Council to include Germany and Japan but not Italy, over increasingly cap-in-hand status *vis-à-vis* France and Germany, was to call for an ever greater commitment to European solidarity. As in other EU capitals, the dilemmas over enlargement and the effective functioning of the EU were not faced squarely. Instead the familiar mantras over the need for both deepening and widening were endlessly repeated – although in foreign policy, Italian political leaders were trapped by their anxiety that political moves towards variable geometry would mean the exclusion of Rome from an inner core.

The search for adaptation

For medium powers such as Italy, foreign policy during the cold war was defined by bipolarity, given that the risks of being abandoned by one's own superpower or of being attacked by the other were very slim.[11] In consequence Stanley Hoffmann was able to observe in 1977 that Italy had 'largely opted out of active politics in the world arena'.[12] Once the fundamental choice about which camp to choose was set, the main problem was reduced to that of keeping as steady a course as possible. The only serious risk arose from endogenous change within the blocs, as with Hungary in 1956 or France in 1966, which might have upset the strategic balance. Paradoxically Italy itself was perceived in Washington as one of the west's few 'at risk' states, through the strength of the PCI, and the United States was at pains to discourage any move to allow the left access to government. The *immobilismo* which this created, with the Christian Democrat Party (DC) virtually ever present in power, and the communists ritually gnashing their teeth in opposition, did little to encourage healthy discussion of the country's international situation.[13]

In a world bereft of this binary structure, by contrast, the varying dangers – many 'out of area' insofar as that concept still has meaning – were perceived differently according to political and geographical location. In this situation, simple affiliation to an institution became less relevant than during the cold war. Since the possible contingencies were more numerous, and they did not affect all the members in the same way, it was likely that coalitions of the 'willing and able' would be formed (usually with difficulty), which (as in Bosnia) might exclude some members of an organization while not necessarily being limited to members. The weight of each country in any given contingency was coming to be judged, not on its seat at the various tables but on its capacity to make a practical contribution. Compared to the static cold war system, substance was therefore increasing in importance relative to form, because states will choose partners in more volatile arrangements according to the specific advantages they provide. Such a change significantly undermined Italy's comfortable position on the international stage, as a relatively passive member of the main Western multilateral organizations.

In the short period since the collapse of the Soviet Union there have been some eloquent indications of this more dynamic and voluntaristic system, within both NATO and the EU, which have evoked the spectre of an Italian exclusion from the 'top table'. The French move closer to NATO's military structure threatened Italy's privileged position on the alliance's southern flank, while at the same time creating some embarrassing dilemmas as the French government insisted that the AFSOUTH command should be in the hands of the Europeans. Rome had no wish to weaken the US presence in Naples, AFSOUTH's headquarters as well as a main base for the US Sixth Fleet; but a transfer to French command might well weaken the American commitment. In the EU, the very real threat of a hard core breaking away, whether in EMU or in foreign and defence policy, caused serious perturbation in Rome.

As contact groups, hard cores and *ad hoc* partnerships proliferated, with unpredictable new conflicts breaking out in previously 'stabilized' zones, there was a premium on being able to define threats and goals clearly, and on having the resources to be able to count in limited collective actions where they might suddenly be required. On both these counts, Italy remained in a position of weakness. Thinking about foreign policy was still underdeveloped right across the political spectrum, and the means barely existed even at élite level to generate the robust but sophisticated debate which was needed. What is more, the domestic crisis continued to distract all but the most enlightened or *deraciné*; Italians naturally tended to see the international environment now as far less in need of rethinking than their own society and constitution.

Yet Italy had been left on the frontline of the major conflicts in the Euro-Mediterranean region, with Algeria and Bosnia dissolved into civil war, Cyprus, the Aegean, Macedonia and Albania on the brink and the Middle East peace process stalled. And in new crises arising from these issues it could not take allied support for granted. On the contrary, if a problem got out of hand on its geopolitical doorstep, Italy would have no choice but to accept new responsibilities. To use Snyder's terminology again, Italy had passed from a low risk of abandonment to a high risk of entrapment.

Accordingly, decisionmakers have shown some signs of being willing to envisage change – albeit at times hastily and reactively and without much public sense of purpose. The rational response had to be a strategy of adaptation aimed at strengthening those international institutions which had the resources to deal with the actual and potential crises, and at improving Italy's position within them. Passivity and lethargy would have to give way to a more proactive and participatory policy.

To begin with, Rome even seemed capable of anticipating events. Between 1989–92 the dynamic intellectual activity of Andreotti's foreign minister,

Gianni De Michelis, produced a proposal for a single EC seat in the United Nations Security Council, the Pentagonale initiative grouping Italy with the countries of east-central Europe and the notion of a Conference on Security and Cooperation in the Mediterranean. However the failure of the EU–UN mediation in Yugoslavia, and its replacement by a five-member Contact Group excluding Italy was a humiliating setback. At the same time, at the domestic level, the sweeping changes referred to above were gathering full force between 1992 and 1994, virtually obliterating the political class which had hitherto led the country, not least Andreotti and De Michelis themselves.

With these events in mind, the Amato and Ciampi governments began a difficult and painful reassessment of Italian foreign policy; difficult because of the domestic crisis in which the government found itself, and painful because it had to challenge some of the conventional wisdoms governing élite views of Italy's role in the world. The pace of political change was accelerating, however, and in March 1994 Silvio Berlusconi swept to power on the back of his new party, Forza Italia, eventually forming a coalition with the Alleanza Nazionale and the secessionists of the Lega Nord. The new right did at least try to strike out in a new direction. It displayed a new scepticism towards the European Union and other forms of multilateralism, identified itself with the 'British' strand of laissez-faire globalism in foreign economic policy, and introduced a tone of national assertiveness towards the conduct of disputes with Slovenia and the United States. 'The national interest' was rediscovered, as the previously missing link in Italian foreign policy.

The new coalition, which lasted for less than nine months, included the Lega Nord, which had persistently called for secession for 'Padania'. Remarkably, there was very little discussion about the impact secession would have had on 'Italy's' external position, or on wider international relations, not least by the Lega itself. Perhaps even its leader, Umberto Bossi, did not take the prospect seriously, and for his opponents secession simply did not bear thinking about. More relevant has been the push for a federal Italy. Such a development would not have any immediate importance for external relations, but it might in the long run increase the demand for an effective foreign policymaking process in Rome. If domestic functions were to be increasingly devolved to the regions, then foreign and defence policy would be much more visible as central government's major responsibility.

In the event Bossi and Berlusconi proved less than compatible bedfellows, and the collapse of the coalition led to a cabinet of (non-elected) technocrats under Lamberto Dini. Apart from the question of UN Security Council reform (see below) this period, with Susanna Agnelli a quietist foreign minister, did little more than prepare the way for the new left, which emerged victorious from the 1996 elections. The Ulivo coalition attempted in 1996–97 to salvage Italy's traditional allegiance to multilateralism while adapting it to the new international context. To some extent this too was a matter of style, but for the old left at least, it was a real break with the past. Specifically, the Ulivo government, like the technocratic governments of 1993 and 1995, took an unprecedentedly high profile in upholding the (traditional) pro-UN, pro-NATO and pro-EU lines in an attempt to enhance Italy's credibility and reliability.

This pursuit of a new assertiveness within an established multilateral framework was considered the most appropriate response to the increased volatility of the emerging multilateral system. In line with the massive effort in economic policy to meet the Maastricht criteria on Monetary Union, governments in Rome pursued a series of initiatives, ranging from reform of the UN Security Council to EU enlargement, from peacekeeping operations in Somalia to prime responsibility for a 'coalition of the willing' in Albania. Nonetheless, this strategy of adaptation failed to attract a solid consensus, given the complications of domestic politics and the fragility of the RC commitment to support the Coalition (crucial in voting terms in the Assembly, as was demonstrated when Prodi felt it necessary to resign in October 1997, only to return when the RC backed down in a dispute over the 35 hour week). The lack of a proper 'epistemic community' to debate the issues fully and to ensure their wider diffusion to public opinion also limited acceptance or understanding of this adaptive strategy. It has therefore not carried as much weight abroad as it perhaps merited.

The strategy of active multilateralism

Insofar as 'active multilateralism' represented a coherent strategy, it followed two routes: on the one hand, a series of proposals for adapting the existing international organizations to changed circumstances; on the other, a raising of Italy's national profile within them, in contrast with the habitual passivity of the past.[14]

So far as the *adaptation of institutions* is concerned, recent governments have made proposals on both the reform of the United Nations and the pursuit of further European integration. In 1993, the UN Secretary General asked members to submit proposals for the reform of the main bodies of the world organization. At the time the prevailing idea was to enlarge the permanent membership of the Security Council to Germany and Japan, the better to reflect the contemporary configuration of power. Italy was naturally dissatisfied to have been excluded, particularly since De Michelis' earlier proposal for a common EC seat had been sunk by British, French and German objections. The proposed enlargement also seemed too narrow and restricted to western states. Italy therefore proposed at the 1993 General Assembly the establishment of a new category of semi-permanent members, which would include all those countries which contributed most – in terms of economic, political and military capabilities – to UN missions. Apart from Germany and Japan, this category could include other medium powers such as Italy, Spain, Ukraine, India, Brazil, Nigeria and Egypt.[15] The idea was to spread responsibilities, at a time in which demands for UN troops were increasing while states were becoming increasingly reluctant to invest their scarce resources in remote conflicts. This was a genuinely innovative, if self-interested, proposal which held the floor in the debate which followed and is still continuing.

On the European side, Italy finally broke away from its long-standing federalist commitment to a fully sovereign Europe, towards a more pragmatic approach which could realistically be applied in the short term. It was not that the idea of integration was losing favour. Italy continued to be one of the staunchest supporters of the expansion of majority voting within the European Councils (unlike Germany, as demonstrated in the final IGC negotiated at Amsterdam in June 1997). Ciampi proclaimed in his speech on a vote of confidence in the Assembly that the 'European choice' was the beacon of Italian policy. When Romano Prodi was first asked to summarize his foreign policy position, he replied: 'Europe, Europe, Europe', and he made Italy's linkage with Europe one of the main themes in his 1996 electoral campaign.[16] In fact, demonstrating a certain appreciation of changed circumstances, and lowering their expectations of short-term progress, the two prime ministers were merely trying to help integration proceed more easily.

The change of emphasis on Europe had three dimensions. First, Rome was among the first to accept the principle of different speeds and variable geometry, both in terms of the different elements of integration and of the different groups of members which might proceed to further stages. EMU inherently legitimized the idea of different speeds, and Ciampi's foreign minister generalized the idea: 'A nucleus composed by the founding countries … and a larger Union with the functions of the EEC.'[17] Through the concept of 'flexibility', the Treaty of Amsterdam has now legitimized this approach.

Second, the Ciampi government also switched to a preference for a co-operative, as opposed to an explicitly federalist conception of a common foreign policy, which for the first time came to be seen as premature. Italy now perceived some advantages in a more intergovernmental approach, which would allow Rome to pursue its own agenda. Subsequently, there was support for the secretariat for common foreign policy, distinct from the European Commission, which was slowly emerging under the wings of the Secretariat of the Council of Ministers. The Dini government also advocated, in preparatory meetings for the IGC, an EU Secretary-General for Foreign Policy, to be, like the NATO equivalent, very much under the control of the Council.[18]

The idea of a Common Foreign and Security Policy was central to Italy's strategy of multilateralism and adaptation in foreign policy. Without something resembling CFSP Italy would be thrown back entirely on NATO and on a US-dependence which, without the Soviet threat to induce consensus, would rebound at home. The other extreme, of an exposed unilateralism, is something that Italy did not possess the capabilities to underwrite.[19] Moreover Rome was disposed to put great emphasis on the adjective 'common'. One great continuity in Italian foreign policy since 1970, cold war or not, has been the amount of political energy that has been invested in trying to prevent the emergence of a 'directoire' of the three major EU powers, Britain, France and Germany. On general institutional and integrationist questions Italy has not suffered badly from exclusion and, indeed, it has been Britain which has been the odd man out. But in classical foreign policy Italy has carried less clout, and nothing had changed since the end of the cold war and the Maastricht Treaty. Indeed the tendency to extend the concept of subsidiarity or variable geometry to foreign policy made the problem worse, as did Germany's new status as a UN Security Council member-in-waiting, and Italy's cold-shouldering by France and Britain over Bosnia.

The Treaty of Amsterdam merely reinforced the perception of a European foreign policy characterized by flexible intergovernmentalism, with the introduction of 'constructive abstention' and further compromises over defence and finance. For Rome the new fluidity of international relations in Europe meant that the EU was seen even more strongly than before as both shelter and actor.

Given the enormous challenges now facing the EU on all fronts, Italy was not the only country to be taking a 'press on and hope for the best' approach towards the CFSP. No doubt Italian policymakers, bruised by recent experiences in the Balkans and in Somalia, were not naively optimistic about the prospects for effective common policies. Nonetheless, there was little effort in Rome to provide political or intellectual leadership in European foreign policy. Italy did not yet carry the weight to be able to do so, and it may also be that the creative burst of energy in the early 1990s, with initiatives on the UN, central Europe, political dialogues with the Visegrad states, and Mediterranean security, had run its natural course. Italy had devoted its political resources to asserting its own interests rather more than in the past, whether crudely under Berlusconi or more subtly under Dini and Prodi. Despite the inherent merits of the attempt to raise Italy's regional profile, it was soon overshadowed by the tragedies of the Balkan war. For the time being, therefore, the traditional instinct for a more quietist multilateralism, delicately balanced between NATO and the EU, reasserted itself.

Third and last, the more pragmatic approach was complemented by a forward policy on enlargement, with Italy enthusiastically supporting widening despite the apparently damaging consequences for deepening. In 1993, Italy launched an initiative with the United Kingdom to open the Second and Third pillars – relating to CFSP and Justice/Home Affairs respectively – to east European governments. This breached the hitherto unchallenged rule that EPC/CFSP was only open to full members of the EC/EU. Italy's enlargement policy was in fact particularly comprehensive. As the Italian member of the preparatory group for the IGC (the 'Reflection Group') remarked, 'The countries of East and Central Europe have been twice separated from the European democracies, after Munich and after Yalta. The only way not to marginalize them again is to receive them in a strong and functioning Union, extended not only to the East but also to the South.'[20] On NATO enlargement likewise, Italy came to support, with France, the accession of Slovenia and Romania, as part of the attempt to balance Germany's concentration on the Visegrad countries.

In the same vein Italy was active in trying to focus European attention on the Mediterranean, albeit with mixed success. Rome has been one of the major sponsors of EU enlargement to the south and of the Barcelona process which seeks to engage the countries of the southern littoral.[21] In this, as is demonstrated by Robin Niblett's chapter on Spain, Rome was not able to sustain the *entente* with that it began with. Perhaps Dini and Prodi were too idiosyncratic for Spanish tastes: Italy was the first to attempt mediation in the Algerian civil war, while it was also regarded in Ankara as Turkey's ally inside the EU (leading the Greek foreign minister predictably to accuse his Italian colleague of 'turcophilia'). Italy was also active in trying to keep the Middle East peace process in motion, and sought in particular to improve relations with Egypt, seen as a key state in the region. France, however, was not an easy partner in Mediterranean policies, preferring to pursue an independent policy, and capable of dividing and ruling its two southern neighbours.

The second element in the Italian strategy was its *heightened commitment of resources* to multilateral activity, in order to increase the value of Italian participation and the leverage it bestows. On the economic front, the Italian people have undergone painful sacrifices in terms of reduced public spending, in pursuit of the government's aim of qualifying for EMU before the end of the century. The budget deficit would have had to be dealt with in any case, but the Dini/Prodi determination not to be relegated to the slower group of economies was instrumental in sustaining the government's unprecedented austerity programme. A more active internationalism was also evident in Italy's support for the Commission's position in favour of concluding the Uruguay Round which established the WTO, thus breaking the tradition of protectionist alignment with France – in certain sectors at least.[22]

On the military side, despite a certain timidity during the Gulf war, for which Italy sent only naval and air units (and even these were fiercely opposed at home), the Italian contribution to military operations abroad has been substantially strengthened. Under the Amato government Foreign Minister Colombo saw Italy as needing to increase its 'economic or even military' contributions to multilateral operations in international crises.[23] Similarly, the centre-left coalition which won the 1996 elections had called for 'an increased Italian effort in international initiatives', not least because Italy 'lies at the centre of one of the most important areas of crisis'.[24]

This new sense of military commitment had been evident even at the end of the *ancien regime*. The purely national 'Operation Pellicano' was launched in 1991 to bring and distribute supplies to Albania. Italy then sent a sizeable contingent to UN peacekeeping missions in Somalia and Mozambique, and contributed a large logistics base to NATO operations in former Yugoslavia. During its year-long presidency of the WEU from 1 July 1992 Italy pressed for the enforcement of sanctions against Serbia (providing the naval commander for Operation Sharp Guard in the Adriatic) and offered Italian troops for an implementation force in May 1993. When I-FOR was formed in 1995, Rome sent a brigade.[25] Italy was naturally an ardent supporter of the creation of European multinational naval and ground contingents for action in the Mediterranean on the model of Eurocorps (EURMARFOR and EUROFOR), whose headquarters were placed in Tuscany. In autumn 1996, Italy offered troops for a UN operation into eastern Zaire. Finally, in April 1997, Italy finally took the lead in a major peacekeeping operation, Operation Alba – under the auspices of the UN and the OSCE, after the EU and WEU had failed to act – to try to restore order in an Albania sliding rapidly into chaos. By mid August Rome was able to withdraw its forces in some satisfaction with a job well done. Albania remained a vulnerable state, but civil war had been avoided.

Although these contributions seem modest by French and British standards, they still represented a considerable break with the past: particularly in Albania, where Italy found the confidence to overcome history, resource problems and a very real danger of failure to take the lead in a multilateral operation. The previous Italian reluctance to devote significant resources to foreign operations was very deep-rooted, and the change came about only gradually, at the very time in which domestic concerns were paramount, because successive occupants of the Palazzo Chigi (the prime minister's residence) came to realize that a free rider stance was no longer viable. Italy could not risk isolation now that it was facing less intense but more concrete dangers than during the cold war. As variable geometry became a more realistic option in Europe, and European security institutions, so the perceived importance of not being excluded from the hard core grew.

Such change as had occurred by 1997, however, had by no means been smooth and irreversible. The concept of active multilateralism had come under attack from both left and right, while the distractions caused by Italy's long domestic political crisis inhibited a thorough public debate. This resulted in policy which was sometimes erratic and incoherent.

On the right, the strategy of adaptation was criticized for its excessively multilateral character. The end of the cold war was seen as an occasion to renationalize foreign policy. All attempts to anchor Italy deeper within a multilateral framework were condemned as dangerous sell-outs of national sovereignty. This kind of argument was rooted partly in the AN's evolution from the neo-fascist MSI, which from its foundation in 1946 was deeply opposed to what it saw as USA hegemony over Europe, and partly in a delayed form of Euroscepticism, a leading figure in which was Berlusconi's foreign minister Antonio Martino. Forza Italia's public statements were preoccupied with Italy's status and prestige.

The classic example of this approach was the dispute with Slovenia. In the 1994 elections the AN argued – provoking national and international concern – for a revision of the 1975 Treaty of Osimo regulating the Italy's north-eastern border and the status of minorities on either side of it, on the ground that one of the signatories, Yugoslavia, had broken up. Although such openly revisionist ideas were abandoned after the elections, the new government decided to raise the stakes in autumn 1994 (over the issue of the right of Italians to re-acquire their old property in Istria) by vetoing the talks over Slovenia's association agreement with the EU. However, the Slovenian stance predictably soon toughened, and Rome became isolated within the EU. When the subsequent Dini government withdrew the veto, a compromise was soon found which satisfied Italian concerns, and from 1996 Italy became a sponsor of Slovenian membership of both NATO and the EU. The Slovenian red herring served only to accentuate the impression abroad of Italy's fundamental uncertainty over and marginalization from the wider Yugoslav crisis.[26]

At the opposite end of the spectrum, some on the left have criticized the strategy of adaptation because of its pro-Western philosophy and its acceptance of military means. The main party of the left, the PDS, had itself gone through a painful process of change, from ideological opposition to the Gulf war to an enthusiastic assertion of western responsibility for Yugoslavia. However, opposition remained strong in at least two parties which composed Prodi's parliamentary majority: the Greens and the RC. The latter in particular called for the abolition of NATO once the Warsaw Pact had dissolved, and its manifesto still included Italy's withdrawal from the Atlantic alliance. On the eve of the Italian-led operation in Albania the RC voted against, arguing that it could not support Italian soldiers 'going to war' Although these positions were confined to the radical left, other traditional reflexes, such as pacifism, and the preference for an Italian leadership of the Third World within the UN rather than active participation in western institutions were more common. For example, the Chairman of the Foreign Affairs Committee in the Senate praised the Italian vote of condemnation in the UN General Assembly of French nuclear tests in Mururoa in summer 1995 as a model for Italian relations with the non-aligned world – despite the stiff French reaction and the lack of support from the US, Germany, Spain and the United Kingdom.[27]

Such criticism was very popular at home, not least because pacifism remains also a factor among conservative Catholic circles, and a moderate degree of national self-assertion has become more acceptable, beyond the hard right. It was visible in reactions to the management of the peacekeeping mission to Somalia, where Italian troops were seen as having been endangered by *macho* US posturing. In similar vein, the Italian proposal for reform of the Security Council has become for some diplomats and sections of public opinion a meeting place for concerns about both the national loss of face in the event of Germany and Japan acquiring permanent seats, and the currently 'undemocratic' nature of the UN. One of the most striking instances of the new assertiveness, however, occurred during Operation Deliberate Force against the Bosnian Serbs in September 1995. The Dini government denied the use of Italian air bases to American Stealth bombers, in retaliation for its humiliating exclusion from the Contact Group which the USA, Russia, Germany, France and the United Kingdom had formed, in spring 1994, to co-ordinate international policy on former Yugoslavia.

But what has been termed the 'Sigonella syndrome' – after the dramatic and symbolic quarrel between Rome and Washington in 1985, when the American attempt to arrest the Palestinian terrorists responsible for the hijacking of the ship *Achille Lauro* was physically prevented by Italian troops at the US base at Sigonella in Sicily – is arguably even more difficult to emulate in the post-cold war world.[28] Italy has tended to overestimate its leverage and it is revealing that it was unable to obtain more than the most cursory of concessions over the Contact Group.[29] Successive governments have risked falling between two stools, by undermining the credibility required for a multilateralist strategy without having the capabilities to replace it with unilateralism. Not only was the Farnesina unable to lead western policy in the first major crisis on Italian borders since 1948, but it had not even been able to ensure a seat at the main policymaking table.[30]

The epistemic community

Italy has the economic capabilities for a proactive, multilateralist policy and a strong interest in avoiding exclusion. Why then did the opportunity of a new international order not bring forth the kind of debate which might eventually lead to a solid new consensus on the way forward? Part of the answer to this question lies in the lack of an established epistemic community – or critical mass of those with specialized knowledge of international affairs – capable of sustaining an intelligent debate on foreign policy and its objectives. This is not a matter of specific individuals or institutions but of the traditional impermeability of Italian political culture on matters of foreign policy, fostered by the peculiar situation of the cold war.

The problem was the reverse of the familiar problem of 'access'. Instead of being a question of intellectuals having no access to decisionmakers, it has been the other way around. Italian foreign policy in recent years has cried out for inputs from an expert community. But this community is itself only just beginning to develop in Italy. The potential centres for debate outside government – the media, think tanks and universities – have so far been too weak to stimulate a process of public reconsideration. The study of international relations in universities remains underdeveloped (there were in 1997 only five chairs in the whole country) and it is still subordinate to the traditionally strong disciplines of diplomatic history and international law. These disciplines sometimes lead talented individuals to follow contemporary affairs, but they cannot generate a whole élite of such specialists. Appropriately in these circumstances, the entire policy planning staff of the foreign ministry, which is supposed to liaise between policymakers and the intellectual community, consisted throughout these post-cold war years of one official.[31]

It is too early for any of these developments to bear fruit in terms of a mature and articulated debate capable of influencing policy. If they do put down deep roots it will take at least a decade before the benefits can be seen. The key problem is the lack of a critical mass to sustain an intelligible and vigorous debate. Newspapers follow events abroad and hype up crises, but largely ignore the underlying strategic issues. During the 1996 electoral campaign, for example, there were very few articles in major daily journals dealing specifically with the various groupings' proposals on foreign policy. The main external orientation of newspapers is towards cultural and societal issues. This is partly because there is no stimulus coming from expert institutions. IAI, well-known abroad, lacks visibility or prestige in its own country, as was demonstrated by the lack of attention given to its interesting proposal to reorganize the G7, or to its extensive work on the foreign policy aspects of the Ulivo manifesto for the 1996 elections.

In lacking new ideas Italy has not, of course, been alone. In the early 1990s decisionmakers throughout the west were (for once) casting around for help from intellectuals, for ways of making sense of the flux. But the Italian problem has seemed particularly acute, not least to Italians themselves. Italian foreign ministers have been accused of 'not having a foreign policy worthy of the name' and Susanna Agnelli once protested, with a revealingly defensive double negative, 'I still think that it isn't true that Italy doesn't have a foreign policy'.[32]

Yet the ideas which informed decisionmakers, let alone the assumptions behind them, were not widely debated, and there was therefore little chance of successfully adapting the country's image of its national role. Moreover the lengthy internal political crisis also severed such transmission belts between government and public as existed, hindering the formation of a new consensus. Without a legitimate public forum where disputes can be aired, the result was a mere dialogue of the deaf between the many opposing positions.

The only two issues which presented partial exceptions to this rule were the reform of the UN Security Council and the debate on monetary union, both of which aroused traditional concerns over the status of the country in international society. Even here – to the irritation of the handful of officials in the foreign ministry and the Treasury who dealt with these issues – Italian policy was governed more by the perceived need to have a seat at the top table than by any clear idea as to what might be done with any enhanced status. This defensive motivation – the fear of marginalization – was reminiscent of the static days of the cold war, even if the more self-assertive style was certainly not.[33]

Italy's foreign policy community in the 1990s can be divided into four broad groups:

(1) *those for whom foreign policy is inextricably linked to party ideology*. AN on the right and the RC on the left have a highly historical view of international affairs, founded on nationalism and radical pacifism respectively. In particular, both groups are vaguely opposed to the notion of Italy as a member of 'the west' and resent what they consider to be the continuation of American hegemony.

(2) *those*, influential but less unorthodox, *who favour more unilateralism*, seeing the end of the cold war as an opportunity to renationalize foreign policy and to advance a more assertive style, even at the expense of relations with traditional partners. This group is influential in the opposition centre-right coalition, in some policy circles (such as the armed forces' think tanks) and in *LiMes*.

(3) at the opposite end of the spectrum are *those who are primarily motivated by universalist aspirations*. This group holds an idealistic view of the prospects of a new world order based on the internationalist aspiration of the United Nations. This perspective is influential especially in Catholic circles and among some left-leaning intellectuals, including at times the RC. Although connected to an extensive web of NGOs engaged abroad, especially in developing countries, it does not have a coherent view of how to employ the traditional instruments of diplomacy, beyond a vague support for UN action.

(4) the dominant but still frustrated group advocating the strategy of multilateral adaptation. This group was strongly represented in the governing centre-left coalition led by Romano Prodi, and naturally among the civil servants who deal with international institutions as part of their daily environment. It is also influential in IAI and, less intensely, in important daily newspapers such as *La Stampa, La Repubblica* and *Il Sole-24 Ore*.

These four groups have been less distinct in practice than in theory. Nevertheless, they have not interacted, either with each other or with policymakers, to create a fully-fledged national debate on foreign affairs. When discussions did arise, they tended to be more about fundamental principles than the fruitful examination of policy options. Furthermore they did not link up with the wider international debate on trends in international politics, but remained provincially oriented towards domestic political competition. The consequence was that foreign experts, such as Edward Luttwak and Ralph Dahrendorf, occupied the space left, enjoying considerable prominence in the press but still without generating much indigenous reaction.[34] There was no real discussion of the provocative ideas about the future of international order injected by figures such as Paul Kennedy, John

Mearsheimer, Francis Fukuyama and Samuel Huntington. There has been even less discussion of European writers on the new order, which points up the deficiencies of the continental-wide debate and the surrendering of initiative to American intellectual culture. There has not even been much debate about the future shape of the European Union: simply a clinging to the hope that more (integration, enlargement) means better (peace, order, prosperity, culture).

The fragility of the attentive public has hindered the operation of the processes of consensus building described by Karl Deutsch in his cascade model.[35] In this model – optimistic, it is true, in the case of foreign policy – opinion is filtered from government to public by means of opinion-making élites and the media, and then reworked into government policy through the feedback of elections. In the Italian case, the intermediate bodies have remained too insubstantial, which inhibits the circulation of ideas in both directions. Although this might seem at first sight an advantage for decision-makers because they have not had to build a consensus to support their policies, it ultimately creates weakness in a democracy because decisionmakers do not know if and when they can count on public backing in any confrontation with other states. Furthermore, the lack of public debate fosters the pathological tendencies of modern policymaking towards bureaucratic politics and groupthink.[36]

History and national traditions account for some of this weakness. After unification the foreign policy style of the Italian monarchy was secretive and did not stimulate nationwide debate. Crucial decisions such as the entry into the First World War on the Entente side in 1915, despite Rome's membership of the Triple Alliance, were taken by a small circle of advisers around the crown and were presented to the wider public as a *fait accompli*. This initial tendency was naturally accentuated by Fascism and its less than popular alignment with Nazi Germany. After the Second World War, democratic Italy successfully and irrevocably anchored itself to the western camp, despite deep ideological cleavages between the government and the Communist opposition. Debate was actually suppressed on international issues, because a higher profile would inevitably have produced internal turmoil. This mind-set, of avoiding divisive arguments over international politics, then became institutionalized, and after the cold war there were too few civic institutions and intellectually confident leaders to mount an intelligent challenge to it. In this respect, nothing fails like success.

Italy is not incapable of change in this context. Rather, the risk is that change will be sporadic, non-consensual and subject to unpredictable reversals. In any case, the matter goes deeper than a mere shortage of ideas. New thinking can be imported on the international free market of intellects, given Italy's intellectual trade deficit in the area of foreign policy. Moreover if a lack of debate were the problem, then at least a government of sure-footed technocrats would have had the freedom to lead Italy into a new posture, as happened in Spain. The real difficulty has been the relationship between an impoverished epistemic community in the foreign policy sector and Italy's complex, resistant political culture.

In this culture, the collapse of two major parties changed surprisingly little. Small parties still held a disproportionate influence inside governmental coalitions, the impact of historical wounds was still all too evident right across the ideological spectrum, and the combination of fierce articulacy and ingrained parochialism made it difficult to address strategic issues. Both houses of parliament, and the main parties, have their own foreign affairs committees, but they are notoriously incapable of holding decision makers to account or providing a healthily critical environment in which ideas can be tested.

It is true that some things have begun, very slowly, to move in recent years. The more fluid international system, leaving Italy exposed to dangerous developments in the Mediterranean, sparked a series of innovative initiatives, such as the heavyweight magazine *LiMes*, with a circulation of 7000 in 1997, very respectable for a specialist foreign policy journal sold on the newsstands. New think tanks have been created, giving some support to the gallant efforts of IAI and ISPI. There is now CeSPI, set up in 1985 to promote links with academics, plus the defence ministry's CEMISS and CASD, all in Rome.[37] There has also been new interest in external policy from the private Agnelli and Mattei Foundations, and, if not a surge, at least a spurt of interest in International Relations as a separate academic discipline at universities such as Milan, LUISS and Bologna, where the first undergraduate degree course in International Relations is finally underway.[38]

On the domestic front, the *mani pulite* campaign and the new role of the judges did not touch centrally on foreign policy – although both Craxi and De Michelis came under fire for abuse of state office while abroad, and the ministry's Overseas Development Aid office was purged over misdirected funds.[39] Nonetheless the assault on the old morality (sic), the controversy stirred by Berlusconi's attempt to combine the highest political office with hegemonic control of the mass media, and not least the emergence of the loud-mouthed but authentic voice of northern protest in the form of Umberto Bossi together created an atmosphere of iconoclasm in Italy from which even European policy could not be immune. Given the further addition of a more intellectual strand of 'geopolitical' thinking, which seeks principally to re-'concretize' foreign policy, amid a welter of globalist abstraction, we can see that the foundations are being laid for a more substantial public debate on Italy's place in the world.[40]

Domestic change may have been the understandable priority, but foreign policymaking could not remain unaffected by the politics of the attempted transformation. What is more, it may be that the direction of influence was also being reversed, with a more open and effective foreign policy debate starting to chip away at the immobilism of domestic politics. Audience participation television debates about refugees in the wake of the Italian

Navy's accidental sinking of an Albanian boat, for example, opened up issues about the changing nature of Italy's society under the impact of immigration in an unusual and positive manner.[41] The old party habits, let alone their alignments, could not cope with these important new issues and the way in which domestic and foreign affairs were coming to overlap.

Conclusions

Thus the opportunity provided for rethinking and self-examination which occurred with the end of the cold war had not yet been taken in Italy. To be sure, there were longer rhythms at work, such as the gradual development of a Mediterranean policy in concert with France and Spain and the beginnings of a move towards more professionalized armed services, but hopes still far outran achievements. In 1997–98 there was, in truth, neither the élite capability nor mass pressure for anything more.

Theoretically speaking, the relationship between domestic and foreign policies, between internal and external change is always problematical: which is the chicken and which the egg? Furthermore, in systemic terms, whether Waltzian or Wallersteinian, what freedom does the international order allow even a middle-ranking state like Italy to follow its own path, at home or abroad? The parallelism of the end of the cold war and the slow birth of the 'Second Republic' made these particularly important questions for Italy in the late 1990s.

Two broadly opposing interpretations are possible of the general relationship between foreign and domestic politics in contemporary Italy:

(1) that the tumult and change has been largely on the surface; deeper down, nothing has changed. At home, Italy has been governed still by fragile coalitions which lack the power and legitimacy to undertake thorough going reform of the state and the clientelistic networks which have entrapped it. Abroad, Italy has paid the price of domestic weakness by relegation to a second division of west European states, without the ability to exert decisive influence on key issues.

(2) that the upheaval which began in 1989–91 was still continuing several years later, internally and externally, with a dynamic but unstable interaction taking place between the two levels. At home, the end of this period of transformation cannot be predicted, but it is likely to be some distance off, given structural problems like the north–south divide and the chronic *immobilismo* of the public bureaucracy. Abroad, Italy also faces a new set of uncertainties, arising partly out of its new 'front line' vulnerability to economic refugees and regional conflict, and partly out of a new degree of isolation within the EU as Germany moves on from being an analogue state for Italy to its new position as potential hegemon.

Whichever of these two interpretations is preferred – and we tend towards the second – the effects in terms of Italy's participation in the continuing reshaping of European order are conservative. Whether under the old dispensation of 'partitocrazia' or the new one of transformational politics, the stakes are too high and Italy too deficient in stability, cohesion and confidence to assert leadership or provide vision.

Among western European states Italy suffered far more than others from domestic upheaval in the 1990s. Disillusion with the *ancien regime* (the 'First Republic') was not analogous to the casting off of communism among the old CMEA states, but equally it was in sharp contrast to the continuity of assumptions and policies in every other EU state except Germany. It is therefore not surprising that Italy – in the form of its decision makers and intellectuals – was inactive in reconceptualizing the European order. Italy has been preoccupied with a self-liberation which was catalyzed by the wider forces of European change, in the sense that it is difficult to envisage such a rapid movement of events having taken place without the kind of permissive international context which existed in the early 1990s. The contradictions which undoubtedly existed in the Italian system might not have fused together, in the structural crisis of democracy that occurred between 1992–95, without the changes already taking place in relations between capitalism and communism, and between NATO and its principal adversary.

The balance between internal and external priorities has been difficult to strike, not least because Italy is caught in at least two vicious circles. Most Italian observers concede, perhaps too readily, that the country can do little on its own to shape its external environment, leading them to fall back into precisely the kind of introspective defeatism which leads outsiders to dismiss Italian competence. Likewise, while foreign policymakers despair of ever having a stable domestic platform on which to build, they have done little to encourage the kind of open, sometimes painful, debate which might in the long run help to produce such a platform.

In the second half of the 1990s, there were some green shoots emerging. The persistent attempt to lead UN Security Council reform, and the successful leadership of Operation Alba in 1997, were both signs of greater self-confidence in Italy's ability to balance out national and multilateral concerns.[42] The intellectual and political reliance on European integration to provide an umbrella solution for Italy's problems, whether internal or external, was no longer quite so evident. The efforts made to qualify for EMU represented a significant achievement for a state written off as in a financially hopeless position only a few years before. Yet whatever foreign policy initiatives are undertaken, they would have to be accompanied by the reform of the Italian state if they are to carry long-term credibility, and that in turn cannot be isolated from the social context. As it happens Italian civil society has formidable resources.[43] If these could at last be deployed in the previously 'reserved' and underdeveloped area of foreign policy, the benefits would be felt at home and abroad.

Notes

1. See Pierre Hassner, 'Europe Beyond Partition and Unity', *International Affairs*, 66:3 (1990) pp. 461–75 and Robert Art, 'Why Western Europe Needs the United States and NATO', *Political Science Quarterly*, 111:1 (Spring 1996) pp. 1–39, also published as 'Perchè l'Europa Occidentale non può fare a meno degli Stati Uniti e della NATO', *AREL Informazioni*, No. 3, 1996.
2. Filippo Andreatta and Christopher Hill, 'Italy', in Jolyon Howorth and Anand Menon (eds), *The European Union and National Defence Policy* (London: Routledge, 1997). An earlier version of this article was published in *The International Spectator* (Rome), XXX:2 (April–June 1995) pp. 71–89.
3. 'Enlargement to the South' refers, of course, to Malta, Cyprus and Turkey, not to the Maghreb. Italy wishes to have eastern enlargement counterbalanced, but not to call in to question Europe's cultural identity.
4. Peter M. Haas, 'Introduction: Epistemic Communities and International Policy Coordination', *International Organization*, 46 (1992) pp. 1–35. The concept of epistemic community refers to a group of people connected by their shared knowledge and expertise rather than by locale, class or generation. In this case the area of expertise is international relations and foreign policy.
5. In 1997, after the Bicamerale Commission on constitutional reform had reported, it seemed possible that a second postwar Republic might finally emerge. Before then, the term 'second Republic' signified little more than skilful marketing on the part of Silvio Berlusconi – the self-styled new broom.
6. Key to parties: AN: Alleanza Nazionale (sanitized breakaway from fascist Movimento Sociale Italiano [MSI]); CCD: Centro Cristiano Democratico (breakaway Christian Democrats); DC: Democratico Cristiano (old Christian Democrats, before split in 1993; Forza Italia (Berlusconi's new party); Lega Nord [per l'sIndependenza della Padania] (Northern League [for the independence of Padania]); PDS: Partito Democratico della Sinistra (reborn Italian Communist Party [PCI]); PLI: Partito Liberale Italiano (Liberals); PPI: Partito Popolare Italiano (old Christian Democrats); PRI: Partito Republicano Italiano; PSI: Partito Socialista Italiano; PSDI: Partito Social Democratico Italiano; RC: Rifondazione Communista (rump of Communist Party).
7. Stefano Guzzini, *The Implosion of Clientelistic Italy in the 1990s: A Study of 'Peaceful Change' in Comparative Political Economy*, EUI Working paper SPS No. 94/12 (Florence: European University Institute, 1994) pp. 8–11.
8. Ibid., p. 16.
9. Ibid. and *passim*.
10. Ibid., p. 11.
11. Glenn Snyder, 'The Security Dilemma in Alliance Politics', *World Politics*, 36:4 (1984) pp. 461–95.
12. In 'Uneven Allies: An Overview' in Stanley Hoffmann, (ed.), *The European Sisyphus: Essays on Europe 1964–1994* (Boulder, Co.: Westview, 1995) p. 161 [A reprint of an essay written for David S. Landes (ed.), *Western Europe: the Trials of Partnership* (Lexington, Mass.: Lexington Books, 1977).]
13. For the role of the Cold War in Italian domestic politics, see Norman Kogan, *The Politics of Italian Foreign Policy* (London: Pall Mall, 1963) and Sergio Romano, *Guida alla political estera italiana: dal crollodel fascismo al crollo del communismo* (Milan: Rizzoli, 1993).
14. The concept was spelt out by Romano Prodi, in his lecture 'Italy and Europe' at the London School of Economics and Political Science, 26 January 1996.

15. If the Council were to be enlarged to 22 members, besides the five permanent powers and ten members elected by the General Assembly, seven seats could be reserved for semi-permanent members, to rotate among special constituencies.
16. Romano Prodi, 'L'Italia per l'Europa', *AREL Informazioni*, 2 (1995).
17. Nino Andreatta, 'Una nuova architettura europea', *Affari Esteri*, 25:100 (Autum 1993).
18. Silvio Fagiolo (Italian member of the Reflection Group), speech to Chatham House on 'The Italian Presidency of the EU and the Intergovernmental Conference', 7 February 1996. The Treaty of Amsterdam (Articles J.8 and J.16) nominated the Secretary-General of the Council to 'exercise the function of High representative for the common foreign and security policy'.
19. Whether neo-nationalist (i.e. right-wing) unilateralism or neo-neutralist (left-wing), in the terms used by Gianni Bonvicini. See his 'Regional Reassertion: the Dilemmas of Italy' in Christopher Hill (ed.), *The Actors in Europe's Foreign Policy* (London: Routledge, 1996) p. 104.
20. Fagiolo, op. cit. See also note 3.
21. For Italian initiatives of the early 1990s for a 'global' approach to Mediterranean cooperation, which contrasted with the French preference for a more restricted western Mediterranean group, see Esther Barbé and Ferran Izquierdo, 'Present and Future of Joint Actions for the Mediterranean Region' in Martin Holland (ed.), *Common Foreign and Security Policy: the Record and Reforms* (London: Pinter, 1997) pp. 124–5.
22. Incidentally, this opened the way for a successful Italian nominee for the post of secretary-general of the new organization.
23. Emilio Colombo to the Foreign Affairs Committee of the Senate, 9 February 1993.
24. Programma Dell'Ulivo, Paragraphs 26 and 28, Spring 1996.
25. The Italian Garibaldi Brigade consisted of 2100 men. Italy was thus on the same level in I-For as the Netherlands (2000) but well below Germany (4–5000), France (up to 10 000) and Britain (14 000).
26. Richard H. Ullman, (ed.), *The World and Yugoslavia's Wars* (New York: Council on Foreign Relations Press, 1996); Filippo Andreatta, *The Bosnian War and the New World Order: Failure and Success of International Intervention* (Paris: Occasional Paper, WEU Institute for Strategic Studies, 1997).
27. Gian Giacomo Migone, *L'Unità*, 27 April 1996.
28. As John Holmes, at the time minister in the US embassy in Rome has observed, 'we [the Rome embassy] had the impression that Washington might have been unaware of the fact of Italian sovereignty'. Cited in Sergio Romano, 'Rinegoziamo le basi americane' (Let's renegotiate the American bases), *LiMes*, 4 (1996) p. 249 (authors' translation).
29. Italian diplomats argue that in fact Italy was allowed to join the Contact Group for the start of the Italian presidency in January 1996, but there was at least a built-in ambiguity about any Italian access, designed more for face-saving than real influence.
30. 'The Farnesina' refers to the building in which the Italian ministry of foreign affairs is housed and has become the universal shorthand used for the ministry.
31. See Fulvio Attinà, 'The Study of International Relations in Italy', in Hugh C. Dyer and Leon Mangasarian (eds), *The Study of International Relations: the State of the Art* (London: Macmillan in association with *Millennium*, 1989) pp. 344–57.
32. 'La Agnelli Polemica con Bonn', *La Repubblica*, 9 August 1995 (authors' translation).
33. The issue of purpose is addressed in Franco Venturini's 'Vinta la battaglia, serve una strategia' ('the battle may be won, but a strategy would help'), *Corriere della Sera*,

26 November 1997. Venturini argues that foreign surprise at seeing 'an Italy which for once is not bending' creates political capital which poses a challenge to Italian decisionmaking if it is to be made the best use of in other settings.
34. Luttwak is a regular on Italian television and radio. Dahrendorf's books have appeared at the top of the (non-fiction) bestseller list, and in the late 1980s and early 1990s he wrote a regular column in *La Repubblica*, to which he still occasionally contributes.
35. Karl W. Deutsch, *Le Relazioni Internazionali* (Bologna: Il Mulino, 1970) p. 160. For a similar model based on concentric circles see Roger Hilsman, *To Move a Nation* (New York: Doubleday, 1967) pp. 541–4; Eugene R. Wittkopf (ed.), *The Domestic Sources of American Foreign Policy: Insights and Evidence*, 2nd edn (New York: St. Martin's Press, 1994) p. 146.
36. Graham T. Allison, *Essence of Decision: Explaining the Cuban Missile Crisis* (Boston: Little Brown, 1971) chap. 3; Irving Janis, *Groupthink* (Boston: Houghton Mifflin, 1982) pp. 174–97.
37. *LiMes* is a cross between *Foreign Affairs* and *Strategic Survey*, focusing largely on Italy and rehabilitating geopolitical analysis. It provides useful material for research as well as political and philosophical debate. The think tank acronyms are: IAI: Istituto Affari Internazionali (Rome, set up in 1965; it publishes *The International Spectator*); CEMISS: Centro Militare Studi Strategici; CASD: Centro Alti Studi per la Difesa; CeSPI: Centro Studi di Politica Internazionale; ISPI: Istituto Studi Politici Internazionali (Milan, set up 1933 for interdisciplinary training and research; it publishes *Relazioni Internazionali*). The military think tanks exist largely to train officers, and there are few soldier intellectuals.
38. LUISS, in Rome, is the Libera Università Internazionale degli Studi Sociali. International Relations at the University of Bologna is taught on the Forlí campus.
39. On the other hand Giulio Andreotti still retained his high diplomatic reputation inside Italy while on trial for murder and collusion with the Mafia. This might be thought to be taking the Richard Nixon model to extremes. On the Development Aid scandal see, *inter alia*, the announcement of an official investigation reported in *La Repubblica* of 27–28 June 1993, p. 10.
40. *The Economist* (19 April 1997, pp. 41–2) argued that Operation Alba betokens 'a slightly franker perception of Italy's national interest'. On the heterogeneous and to some extent confused nature of the new geopolitical thinking focused on the journal *LiMes*, see Carlo Maria Santoro, 'L'ambiguità de LiMes', *LiMes: Rivista Italiana di Geopolitica*, 4 (1996) pp. 307–14.
41. Gad Lerner's programmes on RAI Uno were probably the most effective and well-publicized, after the loss of 89 Albanians, including many women and children, on 28 March 1997. It was this incident which led to Silvio Berlusconi's now famous dash to Brindisi to show solidarity with the survivors and his lacrimose performance on live television. In consequence the major opposition party of the right for a short time found itself allying with the RC in criticizing the Navy and demanding that more space be found for immigrants.
42. In this context note the view of an experienced outsider: 'the radical improvement ... under Romano Prodi's government belies the stereotypes of Italian politics'. David Calleo, 'An American skeptic in Europe', *Foreign Affairs*, 76:6, p. 149.
43. Robert D. Putnam, with the assistance of Robert Leonardi and Raffaella Nanetti, *Making Democracy Work: Civic Traditions in Modern Italy* (Princeton, N.J.: Princeton University Press, 1993).

10
Conclusions: Strategic Change and Incremental Adjustment

William Wallace

Looking back over eight years since the ice floes of the cold war had begun to break up across central Europe, the radical nature of the shift in the structure and assumptions of European order between 1989 and 1997 is evident. The declarations which accompanied the acceptance of Poland, Hungary and the Czech Republic into NATO, the foreign policy clauses of the Treaty of Amsterdam, the carefully spelled-out conditions contained in the Commission's *Agenda 2000*, together mark out in broad outline the emerging structure of post-cold war Europe. Many details, nevertheless, were still deliberately left unclear. No dates or deadlines were set for further enlargement of NATO or of the EU. The relationship between this evolving structure and the states on Europe's eastern and southern periphery – above all Russia and NATO-member Turkey – was left for later negotiation. The relationship between the two key regional institutions, NATO and the EU, remained a matter which governments on both sides of the Atlantic hesitated to clarify. A certain degree of ambiguity is necessary in diplomacy, as in the domestic and external presentation of the foreign policies of democratic states. This high degree of ambiguity, however, reflected continued disagreement both among and within Western governments on these issues, as well as uncertainty about how the domestic politics of Europe's peripheral states might develop.

West European governments moved, over this eight-year period, from initial brief euphoria, through an American-led discourse on 'European architecture' in 1990–91, on through the confusions and uncertainties which followed the break-up first of Yugoslavia and then of the Soviet Union, to gradual acceptance, from 1994–97, of the incorporation of the lands between Germany and Russia into West European institutions, supplemented by the association of Russia, Ukraine, and the Mediterranean states. The rhetorical language of 1989–91, expressed in leaders' speeches, in NATO communiqués and European Council conclusions, reflected even in the Maastricht Treaty of European Union, ran far ahead of policy formulation and commitments; leaving behind a wide gap between the expectations of hopeful ex-socialist states and the capabilities and intentions of Western governments in responding.[1]

That gap narrowed in the years which followed, as bitter experience in the Bosnian conflict enforced greater modesty in the West European discourse on foreign policy and regional responsibilities, and as EU and NATO governments provided the commitments – and some of the resources – needed to meet the expectations they had aroused. There remained, however, a great many second thoughts within West European capitals in the summer of 1997 (and for some time after) about the desirability of an institutionalized European order which would extend the privileges and mutual obligations which Western states had shared with each other to another 100 million people, in another dozen states, while also shouldering obligations towards the larger peripheral states beyond. There was, moreover, a wide gap between the assumptions on which governments were operating, in multilateral negotiations, and the domestic discourse on foreign policy in different countries; leaving public opinion uninformed about the movement of multilateral policy and unwilling to support either the public expenditure or the economic adjustments needed to carry commitments into effect.

What might the outside observer have expected, other than this sideways shuffle from initial rhetorical gestures to conditional commitments? The academic observer can only suggest some counter factual alternatives – some courses of action which West European governments *might* plausibly have taken in the wake of the events of 1989–91. The rhetoric of a 'second Marshall Plan' suggests one major missed opportunity. American policymakers repeatedly pressed their European counterparts to think in these terms: to offer transitional regimes economic assistance and technical advice on a scale (and a timescale) comparable to that which the postwar USA had offered them, and on similar conditions of regional co-ordination and progressive integration into regional institutions. Economic assistance and technical advice *did* flow, slowly at first but increasing in scale as the EU moved from Europe Agreements to a pre-accession strategy; but without approaching the co-ordinated strategy, or the scale of financial transfers, of the first Marshall Plan. Western Europe's attempted strategy was, moreover, weakened by the repeated successes of domestic lobbies in blocking exports of 'sensitive' products from transitional states to Western markets. Barriers to exports of Polish sausage, Bulgarian jam, Czech apples and other perceived threats to marginal EU interest groups represented the failure of Western governments to articulate a broad conception of political and economic costs and benefits, and to impose that conception on their own national administrations.

Once the immediate shock of systemic change in central and eastern Europe had passed, one might also have expected Western governments to develop a strategic approach to the process of transition: not only giving priority to the political benefits of EU enlargement over the short-term economic costs, but also bringing together the enlargement of the EU with that of NATO, and co-ordinating policy towards Russia (and Ukraine, and Turkey) within an agreed and long-term framework. From 1994–97, however, governments and multilateral institutions shuffled towards dual enlargement without directly or explicitly linking the two processes. Policy towards Russia faltered, with the USA and Germany more active than their partners. Ukraine appeared a higher priority for the USA than for its European allies. West European governments sent confused and contradictory signals to Turkey about its future relationship with the EU, while American officials openly backed Turkey's claim for full EU membership. No European government or political leader in 1996–97 was willing to sketch out the overall design of the European order towards which they were edging – either its intended structure, or its potential boundaries. The rules and conditions for full participation, however, were evident: spelled out by the European Commission in *Agenda 2000*, drawing on the 'conclusions' of successive European Councils.

One might, again, have anticipated clearer political leadership in explaining to domestic audiences, partner governments and ex-socialist regimes what was at stake, which changes were possible within which timescale and which were not. Given the accumulation of experience of co-operation in foreign policy among West European governments over the previous twenty years, and the regular co-ordination of national positions among heads of government through European Councils, one might even have anticipated collective leadership. Alternatively, one or more of the leaders of Western Europe's major states might have provided the language, and the political determination, to redefine the terms of debate, and to shift the agenda of multilateral foreign policy onto a different foundation.

One might also have anticipated a flurry of proposals and publications from those around policymakers: the planning staffs and policy units now established within all West European governments, the policy institutes which existed to promote public debate, the parliamentary committees with an institutionalized role to question the conventional wisdoms of government policy, the academic experts with a longer view of the dynamics of systemic change. Reformulation, reconceptualization, of the structures of European order, of the changing relationship between core Europe and periphery, of the ideas of statehood and sovereignty within a wider more highly-institutionalized regional order, would have helped to reshape debate. The chapters above have shown that some such intellectual efforts were made, within Germany and Britain in particular, but also within Italy and the Netherlands (and Denmark, not covered in this volume). But, as the chapters show, such efforts were scattered, and failed in most cases to attract the attention of a political audience. Political leaders were not searching for new concepts; and neither opposition leaders nor media agenda-setters tried very hard to push alternative conceptions of Europe into the political debate.

Whose Europe, whose transformation?

The most evident distinction between previous redefinitions of European order and that which followed the end of the cold war, as suggested in Chapter 1, was that the events of 1989–91 happened *outside* Western Europe: transforming its external environment, but not impacting directly on the political or social life of West European countries. The sense of crisis, of the necessity of strategic thinking which pervaded Anglo-American planning for the postwar order in 1942–45, was absent.[2] Western Europe had been at peace for over forty years – armed peace, maybe, but at an affordable level of military expenditure. Even within West Germany, where the concentration of allied ground and air forces (both conventional and nuclear) and the closeness of the east–west border made it more difficult to ignore the continued military confrontation, the sense of threat had ebbed away over the 1980s, as evidence of Soviet weakness accumulated and as Mikhail Gorbachev announced cuts in Soviet armed forces. Westphalia, Utrecht, Vienna, Versailles, had each followed wars which had involved all the principal participants and in most cases also seen parts of their territories occupied or devastated. The transformation of European order after 1989, for West Europeans, happened elsewhere: in another Europe, which they had learned to consider only half-European. There was little incentive for imaginative reformulation of national priorities, therefore; national priorities remained, in most respects, unchanged.

What *had* changed was the position of Germany: of far more direct concern to most other West European governments than changes within a Soviet Union which they had already learned to regard as a weak state rather than a military threat, or political and economic transition within a succession of small states between Germany and Russia. The unification of Germany, clearly in prospect within weeks of the Berlin Wall coming down, altered the established balance *within* Western Europe. The reintegration into 'the West' of the three east-central European states, Poland, Czechoslovakia and Hungary (and the likely EU entry of Austria), evident prospects by the summer of 1990, signalled the reemergence of central Europe, focused around Germany, the German economy and the German language. For France, the United Kingdom and the Netherlands this transformation of the balance of the West, far more than the transformation of the east, was the primary concern; for Spain the prospect of German attention, financial transfers and investment shifting away to Europe's north-east threatened what it had gained through its own reintegration into the West.

For these west European states, therefore, it was rational to prefer to focus on the old agenda rather than to accept its subordination to the new. West European integration had, from the outset, been about the containment (and self-containment) of Germany; unification strengthened, rather than weakened, the arguments for institutional containment. Monetary union, as the French government most of all understood, would lock unified Germany into Western Europe's established institutions, thus preventing a return to German hegemony over a wider Europe. Beyond that, however, French imagination failed. The Mitterrand initiative for a European Confederation, as Chapter 4 notes, was too transparent an attempt to block eastern enlargement to attract support, while French refusal to offer the Germans in return the more federal political union which Chancellor Kohl and his advisers thought vital undermined the mutuality of the Franco-German relationship. The British government, like the French, saw German unification as the most immediate and crucial development. Unlike the French, however, its prime minister refused to accept and appear to welcome what it could not prevent. For the Dutch and the Spanish, unification and the prospect of German priorities shifting north and east made strengthening the institutions and policy *acquis* of West European integration more urgent, to entrench their positions and protect their interests before negotiations with the ex-socialist states began.

From this perspective, efforts to promote a 'core Europe', between 1992 and 1996, were an understandable response to the threat that a wider Europe might pull the key members of Western institutions in different directions. The French approach to deepening before widening, as Chapter 4 notes, combined concern to maintain the Franco-German relationship with a deep reluctance to adjust to the changes within the EU needed to accommodate a wider Europe. The German approach, however, as set out in the Schäuble–Lamers paper (discussed in Chapter 3), started from the premise that institutionalized Europe was in the process of expanding east and north-east. It addressed the question of how to prevent the Franco-German partnership – a key relationship for both countries, symbolizing for Germany its commitment to share leadership with its neighbours rather than exert its economic and political weight – from drifting apart, with the Baltic and the Mediterranean providing opposing poles of attraction.

The priority given to Western Europe's old agenda was therefore understandable. The position and role of 80 million Germans, organized into the EU's largest economy, within post-cold war Europe appeared far more important than the position of 100 million poor people within the dozen applicant states. Less understandable is the comparative lack of attention paid by most west European states to Russia (and Ukraine), after forty years during which the perceived Soviet threat had preoccupied their governments. Germany and Sweden (and Finland), for evident geographical reasons, paid more attention than others. One reason why strategy towards Russia remained a second-order issue, perhaps, was that the USA was determined to retain leadership in defining east–west relations. But the contrast between the initiative towards east–west relations demonstrated through *Ostpolitik* and the Helsinki conference twenty years before, and the relative passivity of west European governments towards the states of the former Soviet Union after 1990, is striking; though many within these governments might argue that there was never a clear point at which developments within Russia permitted the launch of a European initiative, as governments rose and fell and the economy faltered.

It would have been easier to take stock and consider strategic options if the situation within the former eastern Europe had stabilized at any point between 1989 and 1997. West European governments began in the spring and summer of 1989 to design a programme to assist transition within Poland and Hungary; extending that after the 'Velvet revolution' in Prague to include Czechoslovakia. Negotiations on Europe Agreements with these three states, in 1990–91, were already overshadowed by the claims presented by transitional regimes in Romania and Bulgaria for similar treatment. The break-up of Yugoslavia and of the Soviet Union in 1991–92 threw a range of additional problems, and demands, onto Western Europe's agenda. Crises in the Caucasus and in Albania, setbacks in political transition in Slovakia and Bulgaria, confusion within Russia, worse confusion within Ukraine and impenetrable autocracy in Belarus, all distracted and discouraged western governments. Kurdish insurgency within Turkey, recurrent tension (even the threat of military conflict) between Greece and Turkey, Greek intransigence over Macedonia, internal conflict within Algeria, progress and setbacks in the Arab–Israeli peace process, crowded the agendas of multilateral meetings and weighed down ministerial intrays. It would have taken determination, and imagination, to impose a strategic framework on this preoccupying succession of unanticipated events. But West European governments applied their reserves of determination and imagination more often to domestic priorities and economic interests.

Economic interests, strategic concerns

The first Marshall Plan was funded by an economically dominant United States, with a structural trade surplus and a self-interest in rebuilding the economies of its potential trade partners. It was launched within the framework of Keynesian economics, in which expenditure to create additional demand (both domestic and international) was an accepted policy option. Proposals for a second Marshall Plan were made within an international monetarist consensus, with governments across Western Europe struggling to contain public expenditure across the board. Perceived pressures on government budgets were increased by the downturn in the West European economy in the early 1990s, compounded from 1991 onwards by rises in interest rates which followed partly from German government borrowing to fund reconstruction of the former East Germany, Chancellor Kohl having won the post-unification election on a promise that the incorporation of the five new Länder would not require substantial rises in taxation. The squeeze on government budgets and economic growth was sharpened by the strict monetarist criteria agreed at Maastricht as pre-conditions for monetary union: criteria which forced the Italian government, above all, into painful reforms of public pensions and benefits, and which contributed further to a slowdown in economic growth across the EU.

A further counter-factual to be considered, therefore, is whether West European governments would have followed a more generous policy towards ex-socialist Europe if the cold war had ended at a time of an economic upswing within the EU; if the strategy adopted for economic transition in eastern Germany had relied more on higher tax revenues than higher borrowing, or if different West German choices on exchange rate for converting Ostmarks into Deutschmarks and in policies towards East German industry had led to a less precipitate collapse in the eastern economy; if negotiations on a single currency had not coincided so closely with the transformation of political and economic relations between east and west. West European integration, after all, has moved ahead most easily during periods of faster economic growth, while governments have bargained harder for immediate national economic interests during recession. Disillusionment with the efficacy of financial transfers in promoting economic development was, however, part of the monetarist consensus; governments which continued to subsidize their own mature industries and agriculture, which accepted the political necessity of financial transfers within the EU, thus found it convenient to recommend market reforms, more than Marshall Plan transfers, to their eastern neighbours.

The German government nevertheless made substantial transfers to eastern Europe after 1989, to assist the Russians to rehouse their returning armed forces and to provide new governments with clear indications of western support. The EU as a collectivity slowly increased its expenditure, as programmes proliferated and the pre-accession strategy got under way; the Commission's proposals in *Agenda 2000* looked for a further expansion within the next budgetary package, though falling far short of the scale of transfers to the four 'cohesion' states already within the EU.[3] Trade concessions however seemed even more difficult than financial transfers. The EU as a whole ran a substantial trade surplus with the transition states of east-central and eastern Europe throughout the early 1990s, including in agricultural trade; its collective ability to resist the pressures of its own domestic lobbies in 'sensitive' sectors nevertheless remained weak. The Keynesian idea that rising prosperity, and thus rising demand, within eastern Europe might also raise demand within western Europe found few proponents.

One common theme to several of the preceding chapters is the priority of perceived economic interests over security concerns. Swedish foreign policy after the cold war, for example, balanced the redefinition of non-alignment against the economic imperatives of closer Western integration. Spanish determination to maintain financial transfers marked its government's approach to both the 1991 and 1996–97 IGCs. Dutch and French perceptions of unavoidable dependence on the German economy reinforced their commitment to consolidation of core Europe through monetary union. All West European governments welcomed the 'peace dividend' of reductions in defence spending as a chance to reduce budgetary deficits without further cuts in welfare. Redirection of expenditure, which had met the perceived Soviet threat, into investment in consolidating democracy and prosperity within the former socialist states, including Russia itself, was scarcely considered as an option.

The first Marshall Plan had been driven by strategic motives as much as by enlightened economic interests; the generosity of postwar America rested on a clear perception of continental Europe as threatened by Communist and Soviet take-over unless economic revival was assured. American policymakers and outside experts worried after 1989 that a remilitarized Russia might again threaten to dominate east-central Europe unless the opportunity was seized to bring the region within the institutionalized West; this was a powerful argument in their domestic debate about NATO enlargement. USA attention to Ukraine reflected the understanding that Ukrainian independence would leave Russia as a second-order power in European terms, while reabsorption into Russia might provide the foundation for military and political resurgence. German policymakers showed in the attention they devoted both to Poland and to Russia that the potential threat of regimes which might turn against the West, or of unstable regimes leading to increased cross border migration and crime, was also of direct concern. Nordic states invested in the consolidation of sovereignty and democracy within the Baltic states, and helped to train their infant armed forces. The rest of Western Europe, however, reacted in civilian power terms. They paid little attention to such longer-term, strategic possibilities. Except for the professionals within defence ministries and the multilateral NATO framework, economic interests in their immediate neighbourhood absorbed ministerial and official attention.

The Western institutional and political *acquis*

The evolution of West European responses to regional transformation provides strong evidence that institutions matter. NATO and the EU provided the multilateral frameworks within which ministers and officials from different governments negotiated their response. To a lesser degree they also provided a focus for expert debate. Europe's third multilateral 'institution', the CSCE, seemed for some optimists in 1989–90 to provide an alternative, pan-European, framework for a post-cold war region. But it lacked a central secretariat, or any extensive transgovernmental network of regularly meeting councils and committees linking its member governments, through which proposals might be floated and moderated, and a multilateral consensus painfully constructed. Most importantly, it lacked any strongly committed member governments, prepared to invest authority and prestige in the organization and to persuade others to lend it their support. If a reforming Soviet Union had managed to persuade two or three other European states to invest with it in converting the CSCE into an effective European institution, as a major foreign policy priority, the reshaped OSCE might perhaps have evolved into a third institutional pillar of post-cold war European international politics. But the USSR was already preoccupied by internal difficulties in 1990; the west European neutrals, like Sweden, were at best only half-committed and preoccupied with post-cold war reorientation towards EU membership; and the transitional regimes not only of east-central Europe but throughout eastern Europe were far more interested in pursuing links with the EU and with NATO.[4] The OSCE's infant conflict prevention centre was unprepared, and unfitted, to manage the conflicts which broke out in disintegrating Yugoslavia in mid 1991, condemning the organization to a secondary role on the fringes of European diplomacy.

NATO, by contrast, possessed a large secretariat, an integrated military structure, an extensive military and civilian transgovernmental network of committees and daily contacts, and – above all – a number of strongly-committed member governments. The Bush administration saw NATO as the institutional vehicle for continued American influence over post-cold war Europe and set out from James Baker's Berlin speech of 11 December 1989 (entitled 'A new Europe, a new Atlanticism: architecture for a new era'), through the negotiations on German unification, to ensure that NATO remained a formative body in the process of transformation.[5] Active support from the German government was a vital factor in this process. The British and Dutch governments were unhappy about the pace of unification, but as strongly committed to the continued integration of Germany into the western alliance, under firm American leadership. The Italian government relied on the Americans to provide security in the Mediterranean, against threats which had not disappeared with the unification of Germany.

With this strong core of support, and an established network which drew in policymakers and advisers from fourteen West European capitals, the role of NATO within a changing European order was an issue to be discussed within the regular cycle of NATO Councils and heads of government meetings. Procedures and precedents were already in place for US-led strategic review. French ministers and officials who wished to interpose a more exclusively European process of consultation found themselves struggling against their partners' memories of previous damaging Franco-American disputes, and hampered by their inability to offer any substantial alternative blueprint of an alternative European security framework. The determination of the new governments of the former socialist states to pursue closer relations with NATO in itself gave the organization a new mission, expressed through Partnership for Peace (PfP) and the North Atlantic Cooperation Council.

Most West European governments did not therefore have to reconsider the underlying assumptions of security policy. Standard operating procedures carried them along, through reviews of the alliance's force and command structures on to the reformulation of the alliance's strategy, agreed (as noted in Chapter 2) in the course of 1991, to the half-opening to the east of PfP and the debate on eastern enlargement, with the crises within former Yugoslavia providing a more difficult – and more divisive – additional focus for alliance activity. Much of this was contained within defence ministries and the political directorates of foreign ministries, without provoking great national debates about new policy departures, as previous chapters have indicated. The paths policies followed were shaped by institutionally-embedded procedures and assumptions. Most governments saw their task as one of adapting Western Europe's security order; they saw no need for a total new design.

The institutional framework of the European Union was much more extensive, and intensive. Its member governments had embarked on the 1992 Programme as Mikhail Gorbachev was developing his rhetoric about a common European home. They were in mid negotiation about moving on from the single market to a single currency as communist regimes gave way to transitional governments in Poland and Hungary. An intergovernmental conference to reform and strengthen the institutional and treaty framework had been agreed before the Berlin Wall came down. Heads of government, foreign and finance ministers, officials from most major national ministries, were meeting regularly, adding discussion of the implications of change within eastern Europe to an already crowded agenda.

The strategy adopted for the unification of Germany, through the incorporation of the former eastern Länder into the existing Federal Republic, also incorporated these 16 million additional Germans into the EU. This was a major achievement in the transformation of Europe, involving the rapid enlargement of the EU, managed as a 'technical' exercise in a skilful partnership between the EC Commission and the German government, without the need for visible political negotiations among EU member governments.[6] Most West European governments were more embarrassed than enthused by the vigour with which the representatives of transitional regimes across east-central and eastern Europe pressed their candidacies for future membership; in 1989 the European Commission was still attempting to negotiate an alternative to full membership for the EFTA states.[7] However reluctant their response, however, the determination of ex-socialist regimes to associate themselves with the EU as the first priority of economic policy reassured Western governments of the continued centrality of the EU's institutional framework and legal and policy *acquis* within a wider Europe. The issues could thus be formulated in terms of adaptation around Western Europe, rather than of major changes within Western Europe: as a choice between a multi-tier (or multiple circle) Europe within which core Western Europe would remain the innermost circle, or of enlargement of the EU to absorb new members, on terms and conditions set by the existing members.

Ministers and officials within west European governments thus felt justified in concentrating first on further development and consolidation of the EU, second on preparations for enlargement. Looking back on the evolution of east–west economic relations between 1989 and 1997, it is clear that much credit in providing momentum towards eastern accession, nevertheless, is due to the Commission – or rather, to the particular Commissioners and services responsible for handling the east European dossier. These pushed forward proposals for distracted and reluctant member governments to consider, following procedures established in previous enlargement negotiations: establishing Commission representations across the region, collecting information, preparing *Opinions*. One can talk of institutional leadership, in the roles played by Leon Brittan and Hans van den Broek, and of standard operating procedures in the way in which Commission officials adapted the methods used in approaching Mediterranean enlargement ten years earlier, and EFTA enlargement then in progress, to the much more difficult challenges presented by the ex-socialist states.[8] Pressures on EU member governments from the governments of the candidate countries themselves strengthened the Commission's hand. There developed, however, in the mid 1990s a wide gap between the progress towards eventual membership implicit in the EU's 'pre-accession strategy' and the level of awareness within national political systems of the implications of enlargement, let alone preparations for enlargement on the scale or the timescale which these pre-negotiations foreshadowed.

Had such Western institutions been less firmly established, their ability to channel the responses of member governments into familiar paths weaker, the gloomy predictions of realists like John Mearsheimer about the disintegration of post-cold war Europe into renewed interstate rivalry might perhaps have been realized.[9] The incremental movement of West European states towards the acceptance of a wider European order based around these parallel multilateral security and economic institutions is, after all, one of the central features of European transition between 1989 and 1997. But this is not to conclude that the parallel decisions on enlargement taken in 1997 represented an easily predictable or unavoidable outcome, let alone that the coincidence of these decisions provides firm evidence of an implicit or co-ordinated strategy. The uncertainty of national political leadership within western Europe, the element of rivalry between NATO and EU, the gap between multilateral commitments and domestic discourses, and the relative weakness of intellectual and conceptual inputs in the European debate, remain to be explained.

Leadership and followership

Re-unification of Germany within the framework of NATO and the EU – the crucial first step towards the reordering of Europe after the collapse of the socialist geopolitical system – was achieved through shared and skilful American and German leadership, matching tactical negotiations to long-term objectives, with Chancellor Kohl and his advisers working closely with the Bush administration. It was more often American officials than German political leaders who spelled out the strategic vision of a 'Europe whole and free'. Kohl and the German government articulated their strategic perspective in more modest terms, focusing on the construction of 'a European Germany rather than a German Europe'.[10] Elsewhere across Western Europe, leadership in terms of reshaping the agenda of policy and the terms of debate to meet new circumstances was much less in evidence: most woefully lacking within Britain, where a prime minister who had courageously identified Mikhail Gorbachev as a strategic partner seven years earlier now refused to adapt to the geopolitical revolution which Gorbachev had unintentionally unleashed.

Chancellor Kohl and President Mitterrand then invested their prestige in the achievement of monetary union, as the key to ensuring that Germany would be irrevocably European. For Kohl, and for other leading Christian Democrats, consolidation of the Franco-German relationship through monetary union was the necessary prerequisite to any opening to the east; only if Germany's western neighbours were entirely confident of the solidarity of Germany's Western commitment would they be confident about Germany pursuing an active eastern policy. But Germany, and Chancellor Kohl, then became enmeshed in the problems of integrating eastern Germany, with a domestic backlash against the costs which it involved. The Chancellor continued to believe in the strategic importance of Poland, and in the need to ensure – as he frequently argued – that 'the eastern frontier of Germany should not remain the eastern frontier of the West'. But he deferred to domestic opposition, to the hesitations of his French partners and other western neighbours, by not spelling out any overall approach to the reshaping of eastern Europe.

German political leaders were self-consciously aware of the limits to German initiative in daring to redefine European priorities. The shadows of the past still hung over the whole idea of a German leadership role, in eastern and in western Europe. The counterfactual question for observers to consider is whether strategic leadership could have been provided by others within Europe, and whether the provision of such redefinitional leadership might have met with a welcoming response. In the 1970s and 1980s the Franco-German relationship had provided collective leadership in promoting initiatives within the EU; the Franco-German letter of April 1990, which set out the agenda for 'political union' for the 1991 IGC, carried this strategic partnership through to the post-cold war era. Yet confusion within Paris over whether and how to adjust conceptions of foreign policy weakened the partnership; and the replacement as French president of François Mitterrand by Jacques Chirac weakened it further. The German government attempted to carry the French with them in east–west policy, experimenting with a 'Weimar triangle' of Franco-German-Polish meetings and with a parallel triangular meeting with Russian leaders, but without succeeding in reshaping the Franco-German relationship into an agenda setting vehicle for east–west relations. Brief hopes that the Major government in Britain might provide an alternative, or supplementary, partner were disappointed by the British retreat to introspection after the 1992 election. Neither French nor British political leaders, for reasons set out in earlier chapters, were able to supply a strategic vision for the pursuit of a wider institutionalized Europe.

Jacques Delors, from his institutional leadership position as President of the Commission, attempted on two occasions to sketch out just such a redefinition, in an hour-long appearance on *L'Heure de Vérité* on French television in January 1990 and in his Alastair Buchan lecture to the International Institute of Strategic Studies in London in March 1991, referring in the former to the long-term requirement for a European federation in order to manage the incorporation of socialist Europe, and in the latter to the long-term objective of a common foreign and defence policy.[11] On both occasions he was attacked, most sharply within France and Britain, for tackling broad issues outside the specific competences of the EC Commission: for assuming a leadership role, in effect, beyond the legitimate limits of his institutional position. The EU Council presidency, rotated from government to government every six months, was far too weak to provide any collective voice on European strategy. In the first six months of 1990 Ireland was in the presidency, followed by Italy. In the first six months of 1991 it was the Luxembourg presidency which spoke for the EU on the emerging Yugoslav conflict and the growing signs of tension within the Soviet Union.

On questions of security policy and of politico-military east–west relations, the cold war and NATO had accustomed West European governments to look to the USA for strategic leadership. The USA was NATO's institutionalized leader. Repeated transatlantic exchanges whenever its West European allies had attempted to develop autonomous approaches to foreign policy and defence had made it clear that American administrations expected to define the alliance's strategic choices. American 'ownership' of NATO, and American preference for managing transatlantic relations within NATO and with the EU along separate tracks, compounded the disjuncture between EU and NATO approaches to enlargement, managed within different institutional networks by different hierarchies within national governments. NATO and the EU lived within the same city, one permanent representative remarked in 1996, but in different worlds.[12]

The whole concept of 'civilian power', discussed in Chapter 1, rested on the implicit assumption that the USA was Europe's defining security provider, underneath whose umbrella the European allies might experiment with the economic instruments of diplomacy. Few European governments thought in grand strategic terms; Henry Kissinger's dismissive assertion in 1973 that Europe was (at best) a regional power, while the USA saw itself as a global power, still described the attitudes of most west European governments twenty years later. US policymakers assumed strategic leadership, and spoke in those terms; European policymakers (with the partial exceptions of Helmut Kohl and François Mitterrand) assumed strategic followership within an American-defined world. Landmark speeches on the redefinition of Europe in this period were almost all American, from Secretary of State Baker in Berlin in December 1989 to President Clinton in Brussels in January 1994, and in Madrid in June 1997. European leaders reserved their rhetoric for the future of the EU, with occasional (and irresponsible) speeches to parliaments and governments of candidate states promising timescales for enlargement which they made no effort to implement.

French *fonctionnaires*, and Gaullist politicians, saw themselves as similarly global and strategic in their approach to the Americans, floating broad proposals for European confederation or autonomous defence. But the lack of detail, or of substance, behind the broad sweep (*grandes lignes*) of successive French proposals deprived them of the capacity to achieve much more than to irritate official Washington. The grand illusion of Common Foreign and Security Policy, as set out in the Maastricht Treaty of European Union at the same time that EU member governments were failing to respond effectively to the break-up of the Soviet Union and the developing conflicts in Croatia and Bosnia, provided a classic example of this wide gap between rhetorical ambitions and practical capabilities.

The intermittent leadership which the United States provided in post-cold war Europe made for confusion, without providing sufficient encouragement for the major West European governments to develop a more autonomous collective strategy. A further counterfactual is thus to consider the likely development of West European approaches to the transformation of Europe if the United States had withdrawn more fully from its European military commitments in 1991–92 (if, for example, there had been no war in the Gulf to reinforce USA commitment to maintaining forces in the Mediterranean, or if progress towards disarmament within the Soviet union had been more orderly). If American political leaders had set out to encourage co-operation in foreign policy and defence among Germany, Britain and France, rather than cautioning repeatedly against any moves which might duplicate the existing structures of NATO, suspicions in Paris and hesitations in London and Bonn might have been far less.

In the Bosnian conflict, American semi-detachment without full disengagement was seen by committed European governments to have undermined the Vance–Owen plan; only for the Americans to impose on their European allies at Dayton, without consultation, a settlement less favourable to the Muslim Bosniacs than the proposals they had undermined 18 months before.[13] On NATO and EU enlargement, a potential strategic bargain was floated within some European capitals in 1996–97, of a first round of NATO enlargement which would include Romania, while EU enlargement would include Estonia within the first group for negotiation, thus signalling to all the states between Germany and Russia that Balkan and Baltic states would in time be brought within the framework of Western institutions.[14] But American negotiators made it clear that no strategic bargain was on offer, even while continuing to press their European allies to press ahead with pledges of EU membership for the Baltic states; Congress, it was bluntly argued, would not stand for more than three NATO entrants.[15] The timing and presentation of NATO enlargement was determined by Washington, with influence and active support for the American position only from Bonn. It, too, was driven partly by domestic politics, without a longer-term perspective as to where it might lead. Those Americans who complained of the domestic orientation of their European allies in managing the transformation of Europe were not innocent of the criticism themselves.

The dominance of domestic politics

The chapters in this volume support the understanding of foreign policy as deeply embedded in domestic politics, in national identity and conventional political assumptions, painfully adjusted only under extreme external pressure. Each political élite, each national political discourse, interpreted the changes of 1989 in distinctive fashion: filtered through the perspective of national self-definition, of perceived national interests and national roles. Geographical diversity also made for different responses. For Sweden the transformation of the Baltic, with its accompanying implications for the 'Nordic balance', was an evident first concern. For Italy and Spain the implications for the Mediterranean (and for Italy also for south-eastern Europe) were more important. The Dutch reorientation from a cold-war Atlantic perspective to an attempt to come to terms with a Germany-centred Europe recognized geographical necessities, but required a different set of mental maps.

Lisbeth Aggestam emphasizes the links between defined national identity and foreign policy traditions, and the difficulties Sweden faced in redefining its foreign policy posture without provoking a debate about the nature of Swedish nationhood. The debate within the United Kingdom, however, was in many ways more agonized, more obsessed with domestic symbols and identity rather than with balancing domestic values against external changes. Except for a brief period after the 1992 election, the UK government almost entirely lacked a German policy. Practical policies to meet the challenges of this new Europe – the KnowHow Fund for eastern Europe, the commitment of troops to Bosnia – coexisted with ideological denial that the agenda of European foreign policy had altered significantly, with a rhetorical commitment to transatlantic solidarity which scarcely coincided with perceptions in Washington. The British government was therefore unable to contribute constructively to the redefinition of European international politics, because even when abroad its ministers were looking over their shoulder at the impact the language they used might have on domestic anxieties.

Italian domestic politics had been deeply penetrated by the cold war. The end of that confrontation thus transformed Italian politics, and almost destroyed its old political élite. Developments across the Adriatic were sufficiently direct in their domestic impact to demand a response – clumsy in the case of the Berlusconi government's dispute with Slovenia, skilful in the case of its successor's brief military intervention in Albania. Beyond this, however, political imagination did not stretch far. German domestic politics was transformed in a different way by the end of the cold war, with unification shifting its internal political and economic balance. Here, however, realization that their country had again become Europe's 'central power', as Hartmut Mayer argues, enforced a more open debate, both on foreign (and defence) policy and on national identity and role. That debate was still under way in 1997, with political leaders reluctant to push the public too far towards a more active military role, and with a wide gap between governmental pursuit of eastern enlargement and popular resistance.

Insiders and outsiders

This incremental process of adjustment to the transformation of Europe was, previous chapters have made clear, largely government-led. We found little evidence of a Europe-wide élite debate on the strategic choices, beyond occasional conferences and contacts among national think tanks.[16] Nor did parliaments or political parties, except for the Christian Democrats within Germany, provide much impetus for broader debate. The evolution of West European thinking on the reshaping of post-cold war Europe was spelled out piecemeal through successive NATO communiqués and documents, and in parallel (but separate) European Commission reports and European Council conclusions. What public debate there was took place within each national context, distinctive and largely self-contained.

Debate within the USA was also largely nationally contained; but it was much more vigorous, and open, with Administration officials spelling out their approach to Congressional committees and interest groups, and with active competition among think tanks, policy journals, and policy-oriented professors. The structure and style of American politics promoted this market in ideas. The core of experts whose careers took them in and out of the policymaking arena served the market. *Foreign Affairs, Foreign Policy, International Security, The Washington Quarterly*, and such weeklies and monthlies as *The New Republic, The National Journal*, and *The Public Interest* were read by insiders and outsiders alike; a piece by Fukuyama or Huntington might supply dinner table conversation at the same time in Washington, New York, Chicago and Cambridge, Mass.. 'Op ed.' columns in the *Washington Post* and *New York Times*, often syndicated widely across the regional American press, spread the ideas and arguments of a shared foreign policy discourse more widely.

Western Europe lacked any comparable structure of shared institutions and means of communicating a shared public debate. The two hierarchies of NATO and the EU provided a focus for separate and limited expert debates, neither of which, however, spilled out to a wider audience, or very often into the quality press. Foreign policy and strategic studies institutes, as previous chapters have indicated, play much less influential roles in European capitals than within Washington, operating within political systems where there is little demand –

from governments or oppositions, parliaments or parties – for the ideas they offer. Foreign policy has remained, in most European democracies, much more a matter for executive leadership than in the USA. There is little in the way of shared foreign policy media across Western Europe, or syndicated articles appearing in different languages. Each national media continues to provide distinctive interpretations of external events, feeding back into self-perceptions of national identity and foreign policy traditions. The *Financial Times* and the *International Herald Tribune* provided in the early 1990s common frames of reference for the small numbers of experts and policymakers who read them; but for most of their politically active readers these served as supplementary reading to national television and the press.[17]

Hartmut Mayer's observation that the most active domestic foreign policy debate, within Germany, looked repeatedly to the USA for intellectual references suggests another dimension to the weakness of intra-European debate. American strategic leadership was underpinned by American intellectual hegemony: the 'soft power' of American ideas, radiating from America's well-staff and well-funded universities and institutes.[18] Western Europe's modest network of foreign policy and strategic studies institutes had depended heavily on American foundation funding to lessen their dependence on government finance.[19] Collaborative studies by international affairs institutes in German, France and Britain in the 1980s on European defence co-operation, for example – a classic issue for cross-national European research – was financially underwritten by the Ford Foundation in New York.[20]

The still small and scattered community of international affairs institutes and international relations scholars in Western Europe, outnumbered and outfunded by their counterparts within the USA, took many of their cues from the American debate. *Foreign Affairs*, rather than any European journal, was the most widely read journal within this community, and very probably the only foreign policy journal widely circulated within different European foreign ministries, the NATO Secretariat, and the European Commission.[21] *Survival*, the journal of the London-based International Institute of Strategic Studies, provided a common frame of intellectual reference in that field; the majority of articles it published on the future of NATO between 1991 and 1997, however, were by American authors. Perhaps the best extended study in this period by a European of the strategic options for European international order, *Europe in the balance: securing the peace won in the cold war*, by Christoph Bertram of *Die Zeit*, was written during a sabbatical in Washington in 1995, funded and published by the Carnegie Endowment for International Peace.[22]

'There arrive certain conjunctures in history when policymakers have to cast around feverishly for the *ideas* which are in principle the academic's stock in trade. The 1990s are one such point …'.[23] For the most part, in Europe, policymakers cast around in vain. This volume records the modest contribution made by expert outsiders to the policy debate on rethinking European order, without venturing to investigate in detail the reasons for this; that would require a further collaborative research effort. One may tentatively suggest that in most European political systems insiders did *not* pursue outside advice very actively; traditions of inside–outside exchanges were weak, points of entry for outside advice – through parliamentary and party committees, or government advisory groups – were few. The greater resort to advisory committees in the Netherlands reflected the particular style of a political system which depended on coalition governments representing different political communities, where, therefore, the construction of consensus as a basis for foreign policy change was a necessarily inside–outside process.[24] Academic self-confidence and prestige was limited in the majority of other West European countries. Many academics resisted engagement with the policy world, fearing that their 'academic virginity' would be compromised by contact with government.[25]

The enclosed and intergovernmental procedures of CFSP, furthermore, did not encourage wider parliamentary attention or public debate. Its structure of ministerial meetings and official committees was classically an insider network, publishing little, reporting little either to national parliaments or to the European Parliament, attracting little attention in the European media. The well established habit of inviting groups of 'wise men' [*sic*] to prepare advisory reports on institutional reform within the EU, presented for publication as well as for government consideration, had not spilled over into the foreign policy field. One of the structural weaknesses of CFSP, indeed, was its lack of any wider constituency within national political systems. Containment within foreign ministries may have made for efficient and confidential communications, but it left a wide gap between the practice of multilateral diplomacy and the focus of each self-oriented national debate.

Nevertheless, eight years after the collapse of socialist regimes across east-central Europe, six years after the collapse of the Soviet Union itself, the outlines of post-cold war European international order were becoming clear. Its outer boundaries remained fuzzy, the relationship between its two central multilateral institutions still loosely defined, the pace of transition in incorporating additional members into the EU and NATO unclear, the pattern of association with those on the periphery at best under negotiation. Too great a degree of clarity of objectives in an uncertain world, it could however be argued, was counterproductive; a sense of strategic direction, combined with tactical flexibility, is the best basis for policy. The analysis of national reformulation of foreign policies described in this volume offers little comfort to those who see foreign policy as a matter of rational calculation. Adjustment in all countries was gradual, marked by reference to deeply rooted domestic traditions and assumptions; objectives were rarely spelled out with any degree of clarity. West European governments shuffled slowly towards a different understanding of European international politics, conveying different messages to their domestic publics from those they agreed on in multilateral meetings. Some will interpret this as a failure of political leadership, or of imagination. Others may see it as a triumph of disjointed incrementalism, shifting the political consensus towards acceptance of a transformation of the European institutional order, without arousing active opposition from hesitant domestic publics.

Notes

1. Christopher Hill, 'The capabilities–expectations gap, or conceptualising Europe's international role', *Journal of Common Market Studies*, 31:3 (September 1993) pp. 305–28.
2. G. John Ikenberry, 'Creating yesterday's new world order: Keynesian "new thinking" and the Anglo-American postwar settlement', chap. 3 in Judith Goldstein and Robert O. Keohane (eds), *Ideas and Foreign Policy: beliefs, institutions and political change* (Ithaca, N.Y.: Cornell University Press, 1993), notes the vigorous debates and the sense of strategic purpose which marked these wartime discussions.
3. Ulrich Sedelmeier and Helen Wallace, 'Eastern enlargement: strategy or second thoughts?', chap. 16 in Helen Wallace and William Wallace (eds), *Policy-making in the European Union* (Oxford: Oxford University Press, 2000). See also Alan Mayhew, *Recreating Europe: the European Union's policy towards central and eastern Europe* (Cambridge: Cambridge University Press, 1998).
4. This generalization holds true even for the states which emerged from the European Soviet Union, with the peculiar exception of Belarus. I attended a seminar in Kiev in December 1991 on foreign policy choices for newly-independent Ukraine, at which the foreign minister announced that the 'two great priorities' for Ukrainian foreign policy 'in the next two years' were to join NATO and the EU. The new Georgian government entertained the same hopes – or illusions.
5. Philip Zelikow and Condoleeza Rice, *Germany unified and Europe transformed: a study in statecraft* (Cambridge, Mass.: Harvard University Press, 1995), p. 142ff.
6. Paul Stares (ed.), *The New Germany and the New Europe* (Washington: Brookings, 1992).
7. Helen Wallace (ed.), *The Wider Western Europe: reshaping the EC/EFTA relationship* (London: Pinter, 1991).
8. Sedelmeier and Wallace, op. cit.; Mayhew, op. cit. (note 3).
9. John Mearsheimer, 'Back to the future: instability in Europe after the cold war', *International Security* 15:2 (Summer 1990) pp. 5–56.
10. Timothy Garton Ash, *In Europe's Name: Germany and the divided continent* (London: Jonathan Cape, 1993).
11. Charles Grant, *Delors: inside the house that Jacques built* (London: Brearley, 1994) pp. 135, 169; see also Chapter 2 of this volume.
12. Personal information. The Transatlantic Policy Network sponsored a joint conference for leading officials and national representatives of the two institutions in autumn 1996, at which (I recall) Javier Solana's speech as NATO Secretary-General on the organization's future role was received with active scepticism by some Commission respondents.
13. Pauline Neville-Jones, 'Dayton. IFOR and Alliance Relations in Bosnia', *Survival*, winter 1996–97, pp. 45–65.
14. William Wallace, *Opening the Door: the enlargement of NATO and the European Union* (London: Centre for European Reform, 1996).

15. Personal information, including meetings in Washington in October 1996 and April 1997. Washington policymakers made their determination to maintain NATO as the vehicle for American strategic leadership across 'Eurasia' entirely clear; the EU, in their perception, should follow NATO.
16. There is a puzzling contrast between the two joint reports on security and economic priorities for Western Europe in 1981 and 1983, published jointly by British, French and German institutes of international affairs in their respective languages (and in the latter case also by Italian, Dutch and Spanish institutes in their home languages) and the much looser exchanges among these institutes when faced with much more radical change in the early 1990s.
17. Personal information from *Financial Times* staff. I have also drawn on a lecture on Europeanization of the media given by Will Hutton to a private conference in Klingendahl, Alsace, in April 1995.
18. The concept of 'soft power' is developed by Joseph P. Nye in his *Bound to Lead: the changing nature of American power*, (New York: Basic Books, 1990), drawing on Antonio Gramsci and others.
19. William Wallace, 'Between two worlds: think-tanks and foreign policy', chap. 8 in Hill and Beshoff, (eds), *Two Worlds of International Relations: Academics, Practitioners, and the trade in ideas* (London: Routledge, 1994).
20. This study, co-ordinated by Pierre Lellouche led to the publication of Karl Kaiser and Pierre Lelleouche, (eds), *Le Couple francot allemand et la defense of Europe* (Paris: Institut Français des Relations Internationales, 1986).
21. Feedback from officials in Brussels and in several diplomatic services to William Wallace and Jan Zielonka, 'Misunderstanding Europe', *Foreign Affairs*, 77:6 (1998) pp. 65–78, was extensive, in contrast to that in articles on a similar theme previously published in British, German and Italian foreign policy journals.
22. Christoph Bertram, *Europe in the balance: securing the peace won in the cold war* (Washington: Carnegie Endowment, 1995). It was not easy, furthermore, to obtain this volume through a London bookshop, and presumably at least as difficult to obtain copies in other European capitals.
23. Christopher Hill, 'Academic International Relations: the siren song of policy relevance', chap. 1 in Hill and Beshoff, op. cit., p. 14.
24. Philip Everts, 'Academic experts as foreign policy advisers: the functions of government advisory councils in the Netherlands', chap. 6 in Girard, Eberwein and Webb, (eds), *Theory and Practice in Foreign Policy-making: national perspective on academic and professionals in international relations* (London: Pinter, 1994).
25. Girard *et al.*, op. cit., p. 107; see also Wallace, 'Truth and power, monks and technocrats: theory and practice in International Relations', *Review of International Relations*, December 1996, pp. 201–23.